EXTENDED CONFISCATION IN CRIMINAL LAW

Series Supranational Criminal Law: Capita Selecta, Volume 23

Recently published in the series:

7. *Individual Criminal Liability for the International Crime of Aggression*, Gerhard Kemp
8. *Collective Violence and International Criminal Justice –An Interdisciplinary Approach*, Alette Smeulers (ed.)
9. *International Criminal Law from a Swedish Perspective*, Iain Cameron, Malin Thunberg Schunke, Karin Påle Bartes, Christoffer Wong and Petter Asp
10. *The Implementation of the European Arrest Warrant in the European Union: Law, Policy and Practice*, Massimo Fichera
11. *The Principle of Mutual Recognition in Cooperation in Criminal Matters*, Annika Suominen
12. *The European Public Prosecutor's Office*, Martijn Willem Zwiers
13. *Victimological Approaches to International Crimes: Africa*, Rianne Letschert, Roelof Haveman, Anne-Marie de Brouwer and Antony Pemberton (eds.)
14. *The United States and International Criminal Tribunals*, Harry M. Rhea
15. *EU Sanctions: Law and Policy Issues Concerning Restrictive Measures*, Iain Cameron (ed.)
16. *Whose Responsibility?* Malin Thunberg Schunke
17. *Genocidal Gender and Sexual Violence*, Usta Kaitesi
18. *Addressing the Intentional Destruction of the Environment during Warfare under the Rome Statute of the International Criminal Court*, Steven Freeland
19. *Individual Criminal Liability for the International Crime of Aggression*, Gerhard Kemp
20. *Selective Enforcement and International Criminal Law: The International Criminal Court and Africa*, James Nyawo
21. *The Governance of Complementary Global Regimes and the Pursuit of Human Security: The Interaction between the United Nations and the International Criminal Court*, Andrea Marrone
22. *The Rationality of Dictators: Towards a More Effective Implementation of the Responsibility to Protect*, Maartje Weerdesteijn

EXTENDED CONFISCATION IN CRIMINAL LAW

National, European and International Perspectives

Malin Thunberg Schunke

intersentia
Cambridge – Antwerp – Portland

Intersentia Ltd
Sheraton House | Castle Park
Cambridge | CB3 0AX | United Kingdom
Tel.: +44 1223 370 170 | Fax: +44 1223 370 169
Email: mail@intersentia.co.uk
www.intersentia.com | www.intersentia.co.uk

Distribution for the UK and Ireland:
NBN International
Airport Business Centre, 10 Thornbury Road
Plymouth, PL6 7 PP
United Kingdom
Tel.: +44 1752 202 301 | Fax: +44 1752 202 331
Email: orders@nbninternational.com

Distribution for Europe and all other countries:
Intersentia Publishing nv
Groenstraat 31
2640 Mortsel
Belgium
Tel.: +32 3 680 15 50 | Fax: +32 3 658 71 21
Email: mail@intersentia.be

Distribution for the USA and Canada:
International Specialized Book Services
920 NE 58th Ave. Suite 300
Portland, OR 97213
USA
Tel.: +1 800 944 6190 (toll free) | Fax: +1 503 280 8832
Email: info@isbs.com

Extended Confiscation in Criminal Law. National, European and International Perspectives

Cover illustration: Francisco DE GOYA (1746–1828), Etching, Plate 42 from 'Los desastres de la guerra'

ISBN 978-1-78068-478-9
D/2017/7849/70
NUR 824

British Library Cataloguing in Publication Data. A catalogue record for this book is available from the British Library.

PREFACE

This book would not have been possible without the generous funding from the Swedish Research Council (*Vetenskapsrådet*), which has financed the research. During the project, I have also received assistance from a number of people. First of all, many thanks to Professor Iain Cameron and Professor Magnus Ulväng who gave valuable commentaries and other support to my application for funding. The research environment of Uppsala University is very inspiring, and special gratitude goes to the participants of the research seminar organised by Magnus Ulväng at the Law Faculty, where I was able to present and discuss my subject. When in Uppsala, I am always spoilt by the generous support of Professor Nils Jareborg.

I would further like to thank the following experts for help in various ways, for example by answering my questions relating to the European Union and confiscation: Hans G. Nilsson, Guy Stessens, Steven Cras and Sebastiano Tiné. At a seminar at the Prosecution Development Centre in Stockholm, I was able to discuss financial investigations and confiscation practice. Many thanks go to the participants and to the Deputy Director of Public Prosecution Ewa Nyhult, who organised the seminar. Words of thanks are also due to Chief Prosecutor Eva Thunegard, who has assisted me with materials relating to the confiscation practice of the prosecuting offices.

And finally, as always, I am proud and grateful to be a part of such a great and loving family: Maximilian, Emma, Nicholas, Alexander and the rest of the big Thunberg-Schunke clan.

Hannover, February 2017

CONTENTS

TABLE OF CASES

ENGLAND

GERMANY

LANDESGERICHT

OBERLANDESGERICHT

OBERVERWALTUNGSGERICHT

BUNDESGERICHTSHOF

BUNDESVERFASSUNGSGERICHT

SWEDEN

JUDGMENTS FROM THE DISTRICT COURTS

JUDGMENTS FROM THE COURTS OF APPEAL

JUDGMENTS FROM THE SUPREME COURT

NORWAYS

ITALY

FRANCE

EUROPEAN COURT OF HUMAN RIGHTS

LIST OF ABBREVIATIONS

AC	Appeals Cases
Act 2011:423	Swedish Act (2011:423) on Recognition and Execution of Confiscation Orders within the European Union
All ER	All England Law Reports
Appl.	Application
ARA	Assets Recovery Agency
ARO	Asset Recovery Office
Art.	Article
AZ	Aktenzeichen
BGH	Bundesgerichtshof
BKA	Bundeskriminalamt
BRÅ	Brottsförebyggande rådet
BT-Dr	Bundestagsdrucksache
BVerfG	Bundesverfassungsgericht
BVR	Bundesverfassungsbeschwerden
CARIN	Camden Assets Recovery Interagency Network
CJEU	Court of Justice of the European Union
Dir.	Utredningsdirektiv
Directive on EIO	Directive 2014/41/EU of the European Parliament and of the Council of 3 April 2014 regarding the European Investigation Order in Criminal Matters
Directive 2014/42/EU	Directive 2014/42/EU of the European Parliament and of the Council on the Freezing and Confiscation of Instrumentalities and Proceeds of Crime in the European Union
Ds.	Departementsserien
EAW	European Arrest Warrant
ECAB	European Criminal Assets Bureau
ECBA	European Criminal Bar Association
ECHR	European Convention for the Protection of Human Rights and Fundamental Freedoms
ECtHR	European Court of Human Rights
ed.	editor
EEW	European Evidence Warrant
EIO	European Investigation Order

ERA Forum	Journal of the Academy of European Law
ETS	European Treaty Series
EU	European Union
eucrim	The European Criminal Law Associations' Forum
EWCA	England and Wales Court of Appeal
EWHC	High Court of England and Wales
FATF	Financial Action Task Force
FD	Framework Decision
FD 2001/500/JHA	Framework Decision 2001/500/JHA of 26 June 2001 on Money Laundering, the Identification, Tracing, Freezing, Seizing and Confiscation of Instrumentalities and the Proceeds of Crime
FD on Freezing Orders	Council Framework Decision 2003/577/JHA on the Execution in the European Union of Orders Freezing Property or Evidence
FD 2005/212/JHA	Framework Decision 2005/212/JHA of 24 February 2005 on Confiscation of Crime-Related Proceeds, Instrumentalities and Property
FD on Confiscation Orders	Council Framework Decision 2006/783/JHA of 6 October 2006 on the Application of the Principle of Mutual Recognition to Confiscation Orders
FD on Asset Recovery Offices	Council Framework Decision 2007/845/JHA concerning Cooperation between Asset Recovery Offices of the Member States in the field of Tracing and Identification of Proceeds from, or other Property related to, Crime
FD on EEW	Council Framework Decision 2008/978/JHA on the European Evidence Warrant for the purpose of Obtaining Objects, Documents and Data for use in Proceedings in Criminal Matters
FIU	Financial Intelligence Unit
FRA	European Union Agency for Fundamental Rights
EESC	European Economic and Social Committee
GDP	Gross Domestic Product
GG	Grundgesetz
HD	Högsta domstolen
ILA Act	Swedish Act 2000:562 on International Legal Assistance in Criminal Matters
JHA	Justice and Home Affairs
JIT	Joint Investigation Team
KLs	Aktenzeichen Landgericht
KriPoZ	Kriminalpolitische Zeitschrift
LA	Lagmannsrett

LG	Landgericht
MLA	Mutual Legal Assistance
NCA	National Crime Agency
NCB	non-conviction-based
NJA	Nytt Juridiskt arkiv, Avd. 1
NJW	Neue Juristische Wochenschrift
No./Nr.	number
NOU	Norges Offentlige Utredninger
NStZ	Neue Zeitschrift für Strafrecht
OJ	Official Journal of the European Union
OLG	Oberlandesgericht
Ot. prp	Odelstingsproposisjon (Norge)
p.	page
para.	paragraph
POCA 2002	Proceeds of Crime Act 2002
prop.	Proposition
Report on Extended Confiscation	Betänkande av Utredningen om utvidgat förverkande, m.m., "*För att brott inte ska löna sig*", SOU 2015:67
Report on Freezing	Report from the Commission based on Article 14 of the Council Framework Decision 2003/577/JHA of 22 July 2003 on the Execution in the EU of Orders Freezing Property or Evidence, COM (2008) 885 final
RIR	Riksrevisionen
RP	Regeringens proposition (Finland)
Rt	Norsk Retstidende
Sec.	section
SFS	Svensk författningssamling
SIENA	Secure Information Exchange Network Application
SOCA	Serious Organised Crime Agency
SOU	Statens offentliga utredningar
SPC	Swedish Penal Code (Brottsbalken SFS 1962:700)
SPOC	Single Point of Contact
StGB	Strafgesetzbuch
StPO	Strafproceßordnung
StR	Revisionen in Strafsachen
Subsec.	Subsection
SvJT	Svensk juristtidning

Swedish Initiative	Council Framework Decision 2006/960/JHA of 18 December 2006 on Simplifying the Exchange of Information and Intelligence between Law Enforcement Authorities of the Member States of the European Union
TEU	Treaty of European Union
TFEU	Treaty of the Functioning of the European Union
The 1959 Convention	European Convention on Mutual Assistance in Criminal Matters
The 2000 EU Convention	Council Act of 29 May 2000 establishing the Convention on Mutual Assistance in Criminal Matters between the Member States of the European Union
The 2001 EU Protocol	Council Act of 16 October 2001 establishing the Protocol to the Convention on Mutual Assistance in Criminal Matters between the Member States of the European Union
UK	United Kingdom
UKHL	United Kingdom House of Lords
UK SC	United Kingdom Supreme Court
UN	United Nations
v.	versus
Vol.	volume
WLR	The Weekly Law Reports
ZIS	Zeitschrift für Internationale Strafrechtsdogmatik
ZJS	Zeitschrift für das Juristische Studium
ZRP	Zeitschrift für Rechtspolitik
ZStW	Zeitschrift für die gesamte Strafrechtswissenschaft

PART I
INTRODUCTION

"We're innocent until proved guilty ... Or until our assets are seized."[1]

---

1 J. Summers, an article in *The Times*, published on 25.11.2003.

CHAPTER 1

BACKGROUND AND SCOPE OF THE STUDY

1.1. *GO FOR THE MONEY!*: THE DEVELOPMENT AND EXPANSION OF A NEW LAW ENFORCEMENT STRATEGY

In the 1980s, law enforcement authorities, especially in the USA, started to focus more intensively on a strategy "*to go for the money*" and to pay increased attention to the financial sides of criminality. This was not a new method; already in the 1930s the prosecution of Al Capone for tax evasion was the result of such focus. However, in the 1980s a criminal justice policy with the purpose of taking away the financial incentive to commit crime was promoted more intensively as an effective strategy against serious crime. The rationale for this development was that the more traditional law enforcement methods, whereby criminal offences are investigated and the offender is punished by a criminal sanction, were not regarded as sufficient to deal with new and more advanced forms of criminality. It was argued that the strategy to take away illicit proceeds would lead to a general deterrence from crime, as the defendants would be prevented from benefitting financially from crime, and from reinvesting illegal assets into new criminality.[2] In addition, society would be compensated as the State would be reimbursed the costs of combating crime. More far-reaching powers within a profit-based law enforcement strategy were furthermore motivated by the necessity to preserve public confidence in the white economy by sending out a signal that crimes should not pay. The following quotation from the English legislative process illustrates the "moral" arguments which were used in many States at this time:

> Acquisitive crime affects everyone in society. Victims whose homes are burgled, whose cars are stolen, who lose their savings to fraudsters or are robbed in the street all have their lives inextricably altered. The rest of the law-abiding community, to a greater

---

2 For an interesting discussion of the credibility of such motives, W. Perron, "Vermögensstrafe und Erweiterter Verfall – im Spannungsfeld zwischen öffentlichen Strafverfolgungsinteressen und privaten Eigentumsrechten" (1993) 19 *Juristen Zeitung*, pp. 918–25.

> or lesser extent, lives in the fear of being victimised and suffers the indirect impact through rising prices, higher taxes and increased insurance premiums. The visible face of acquisitive crime is increasingly the wealth flaunted by criminals at all levels. Whether it is the large house, yacht and Ferrari of the "crime baron" or the Rolex, Armani suit and BMW convertible of the street-level drug dealer, the proceeds of crime are a signal that, for many, currently crime does pay.[3]

A law enforcement strategy "*to go for the money*" has now been practised in many States for decades, and the method has developed rapidly in many different ways.[4] Against the background that serious forms of criminality often take place at an international level, the interest for a profit-based crime control policy has led to several international conventions and recommendations. The tendency has thereby often been to encourage States to develop very far-reaching models. The central tenet of the international policy has been the criminal confiscation regime,[5] and the institute of confiscation has thus expanded dramatically over the years.[6] This study focuses on one of the new and more advanced forms which have been developed: *extended confiscation in criminal matters.*

Traditionally, an order for confiscation has only been possible in criminal proceedings where a link has been established between the asset to be confiscated and the criminal offence for which the defendant is to be sentenced. However, in practice it has often been very difficult – especially within the framework of organised crime – to establish such links and to provide sufficient evidence that assets have a criminal origin. Accordingly, the measure of extended confiscation has been developed to permit confiscation in certain cases *without* such a link being established. If a suspect has committed certain offences for financial gain, it is presumed that there is more property of illegal origin to confiscate. Consequently, as the term "extended confiscation" implies, such a measure may thus *extend* to other assets than can be directly linked to the criminal conviction

---

3 This quotation is taken from a review of the confiscation legislation in the UK, see *Payback Time: Joint Review of Asset Recovery since the Proceeds of Crime Act 2002*, published on 1 November 2004, p. 5.

4 On the evolving series of proceeds of crime models, R.E. Bell, "An Evolving Series of Proceeds of Crime Models" (2000) 8 *Journal of Financial Crime*, pp. 21–31.

5 N. Ryder, "To Confiscate or not to Confiscate? A Comparative Analysis of the Confiscation of the Proceeds of Crime Legislation in the United States and the United Kingdom" (2013) 8 *Journal of Business Law*, p. 767, p. 774.

6 For a general overview of the development and the different types of confiscation, see G. Stessens, *Money Laundering; A New International Law Enforcement Model*, Cambridge University Press, 2000, pp. 29–81, A.M. Maugeri, "The Criminal Sanctions against the Illicit Proceeds of Criminal Organisations" (2012) 3 *New Journal of European Criminal Law*, pp. 257–97 and Ryder, n 5 above, pp. 769–76. For a critical examination of the method in crime control policy, R.T. Naylor, "Wash-out: A Critique of Follow-the Money Methods in Crime Control Policy" (1999) 32 *Crime, Law and Social Change*, pp. 1–57. On the development of confiscation especially from an EU perspective, B. Vettori, *Tough on Criminal Wealth: Exploring the Practice of Proceeds from Crime Confiscation in the EU*, Springer, 2006.

in question. However, one prerequisite for extended confiscation is still that there is a prior criminal conviction of the individual. This measure was first used in the areas of drug offences and organised crime, but then spread to other areas of criminality, for example terrorism (especially after 11 September 2001) and corruption. The instrument has also successively developed in different ways regarding the procedural setting, scope of application and evidentiary standards.

In parallel with the expansion of the criminal confiscation regime, a system of *non-conviction-based confiscation* has emerged. This regime allows for confiscation of assets *without* a prior conviction of the individual in a criminal court. Such a measure is not classified as directed against a person, but against the property itself (so-called "*in rem* proceedings").[7] Action may then take place in separate civil proceedings and the issue of whether property is the proceeds of crime may be decided according to the civil standard of evidence (often a balance of probabilities). A non-conviction-based regime was first used in the USA, but then spread to several other States, for example South Africa and Australia. The UK was one of the first countries in Europe to adopt such legislation.[8] Some other EU Member States have followed, for example Ireland, Slovenia and Italy, but the operating civil confiscation regimes vary greatly in extent. One form of non-conviction-based confiscation is, for example, provided for within criminal law proceedings.[9]

The development of a profit-based strategy within law enforcement has thus led to more far-reaching powers in different areas, and the traditional way of conceiving confiscation has thereby changed. In addition to the emergence of extended confiscation and non-conviction-based confiscation, provisions have also been adopted which, for example, allow for a reversal of the burden of proof or different statutory presumptions regarding the origin of assets.

---

7 See further on such procedures, Stessens, n 6 above, pp. 39–43, N. Nikolov, "General Characteristics of Civil Forfeiture" (2011) 14 *Journal of Money Laundering Control*, pp. 16–31, S. Cassella, "The Case for Civil Forfeiture, Why in Rem Proceedings are an Essential Tool for Recovering the Proceeds of Crime" (2008) 11 *Journal of Money Laundering Control*, pp. 8–14, Maugeri, n 6 above, pp. 272–78, and F. Alagna, "Non-conviction Based Confiscation: Why the EU Directive is a Missed Opportunity" (2015) 21 *European Journal on Criminal Policy and Research*, pp. 447–64.

8 Nikolov, n 7 above, p. 21. Compare also on civil recovery in the UK, Section 3.2 below.

9 See for different systems in the EU States, European Commission, JUST/2011/JPEN/PR/0153/A4, *Comparative Law Study of the Implementation of Mutual Recognition of Orders to Freeze and Confiscate Criminal Assets in the European Union*, Final Finding Report, pp. 240–66 and Nikolov, n 7 above. Compare also *Proposal for a Directive of the European Parliament and the Council on the Freezing and Confiscation of Proceeds of Crime in the European Union*, Compilation of replies to questionnaire, 12219/2/12, REV 2, Brussels 20.7.2012, Center for the Study of Democracy, *Disposal of Confiscated Assets in the EU Member States, Laws and Practices*, 2014, p. 18 and Eurojust, *Report on Non-Conviction-based Confiscation*, General Case 751/NMSK-2012), 2.4.2013. For an interesting discussion of the justifications for civil recovery of criminal proceeds, see A. Kennedy, "Justifying the Civil Recovery of Criminal Proceeds" (2004) 12 *Journal of Financial Crime*, pp. 8–23.

However, the challenge has been to develop such new measures in accordance with human rights law. In principle, confiscation clashes with the right of property in Article 1 of the first Protocol to the ECHR, and may violate for example Article 6 ECHR (presumption of innocence and the right to a fair trial). A fundamental principle of international and national constitutional law requires that guilt must be proven to a criminal law standard and that persons accused of a criminal offence have the right to be *presumed innocent*. Against this background, some legislative initiatives in order "*to go for the money*" may risk violating basic fundamental principles traditionally applied within criminal law. In legal doctrine many of the reforms are thus controversial, and national and international courts have dealt with various human rights issues in this field.

1.2. INTERNATIONAL AND NATIONAL LEGISLATIVE ACTION

The first multilateral international convention which contained provisions on the financial aspects of narcotic offences and contained an obligation to confiscate the criminal proceeds of such offences was the United Nations Convention against Illicit Traffic in Narcotic Drugs and Psychotropic Substances in 1988. In 2000 the United Nations Convention against Transnational Organized Crime followed, which also contain provisions on confiscation applying not only to drug offences, but also to serious forms of organised crime. In 2003, the United Nations Convention against Corruption was adopted, providing for additional obligations in the area of confiscation. Alongside the United Nations the Council of Europe has also been active in this field; in 1990 the European Convention on Laundering, Search, Seizure and Confiscation of the Proceeds of Crime was adopted containing obligations to confiscate the proceeds of crime derived from organised and economic crime. This instrument was later updated by the so-called Warsaw Convention in 2005: European Convention on Laundering, Search, Seizure and Confiscation of Proceeds of Crime and on the Financing of Terrorism.[10] These instruments also contain provisions on different forms on international cooperation in confiscation cases.

Legislative action in order to enhance the strategy of recovering the proceeds from crime has also been held high on the EU agenda.[11] Strong powers of

10 The importance of confiscating the proceeds of crime has also been recognised by FATF, which has made several recommendations for legislation within this area. See for example *Best Practices on Confiscation* (Recommendations 4 and 38) and a *Framework for ongoing work on Asset Recovery*, Financial Action Task Force, October 2012.

11 For a summary of the international legislative developments in the area of freezing and confiscation, see N. Kaye, "Freezing and Confiscation of Criminal Proceeds" (2006) 77 *International Review of Penal Law*, pp. 323–31.

confiscation in national legislation and an efficient system of cooperation between judicial authorities in different States are seen as a necessary counterweight to the free movement of goods and persons within the Union. The need for effective legislation in the Member States was recognised back in 1997 in the EU *Action Plan to combat organized crime.*[12] In the *Millennium Strategy* in 2000, the EU legislator, for example, emphasised the need for exploring the possibilities of mitigating the onus of proof regarding the source of assets held by a person convicted of an offence related to organised crime.[13] The focus on confiscation has since then continued,[14] and several EU instruments have been adopted in this area.[15] Such instruments have been directed both towards the approximation and harmonisation of *substantial* criteria for confiscation, as well as towards the development of *transnational cooperation* in matters regarding asset recovery.

The first instrument, adopted in 1998, was the Joint Action of 3 December 1998 on Money Laundering, the Identification, Tracing, Freezing, Seizing and Confiscation of Instrumentalities and the Proceeds from Crime.[16] This instrument obligated the States not to make or uphold treaty reservations in respect of some of the provisions of the Council of Europe Convention on Laundering, Search, Seizure and Confiscation of the Proceeds from Crime. It further provided for the preparation of user-friendly guides on best practice regarding freezing and confiscation procedures and promoted direct communication between the judicial authorities. The instrument was partly modified by Framework Decision 2001/500/JHA of 26 June 2001 on Money Laundering, the Identification, Tracing, Freezing, Seizing and Confiscation of Instrumentalities and the Proceeds of Crime (hereafter "FD 2001/500/JHA").[17] The Member States were (again) obligated not to make or uphold reservations in respect of some of the provisions of the Council of Europe Convention. The framework decision aimed to harmonise the confiscation legislation within the EU by creating a common minimum approach. It is therefore generally provided that if an offence is punishable by imprisonment for a maximum of more than one year, it *must* be possible under national law to order confiscation

12 See *OJ* C 251, 15.8.1997, pp. 1–16: Political guideline No. 11. See also the *Vienna Action Plan* of December 1998, *OJ* C 19, 23.1.1999, pp. 1–15.

13 See Recommendation 19, *Prevention and Control of Organised Crime: a European Union Strategy for the Beginning of the new Millenium*, *OJ* C 124, 3.5.2000, pp. 1–33.

14 See for example the 2009 Stockholm Programme, *An Open and Secure Europe Serving and Protecting the Citizens*, Council Document 17024/09, 10–11 December 2009.

15 A useful overview of the EU regulation is given in Directorate-General for Internal Policies, Policy Department Citizens' Rights and Constitutional Affairs, *The Need for New EU Legislation allowing the Assets Confiscated from Criminal Organisations to be used for Civil Society and in particular for Social Purposes*, 2012, pp. 21–28.

16 *OJ* L 333, 9.12.1998, pp. 1–3.

17 *OJ* L 182, 5.7.2001, pp. 1–2.

of proceeds generated by that offence (Article 1). In 2005, the Framework Decision 2005/212/JHA of 24 February 2005 on Confiscation of Crime-Related Proceeds, Instrumentalities and Property (hereafter "FD 2005/212/JHA") was adopted.[18] This instrument aimed to further boost the degree of approximation of national legislation. For the first time the measure of extended confiscation was introduced into EU legislation.

In addition to such harmonising measures, legislative initiatives have also been taken in order to increase the effectiveness of cross-border cooperation between the authorities when it comes to identifying, tracing, freezing, seizing and confiscating proceeds from crime. In 2003, the Framework Decision 2003/577/JHA on the Execution in the European Union of Orders Freezing Property or Evidence was adopted.[19] The purpose of this instrument was to obligate judicial authorities to recognise and execute freezing orders issued by authorities in other Member States in the anticipation of a subsequent confiscation order. In 2006, the Council Framework Decision 2006/783/JHA of 6 October 2006 on the Application of the Principle of Mutual Recognition to Confiscation Orders followed, which introduced the system of mutual recognition to final orders of confiscation issued in other Member States.[20] In order to support the practical cooperation between the judicial authorities transnationally, Member States have also been required by Council Framework Decision 2007/845/JHA concerning cooperation between Asset Recovery Offices of the Member States in the field of tracing and identification of proceeds from, or other property related to, crime (hereafter the "FD on Asset Recovery Offices") to establish or designate national Asset Recovery Offices ("AROs"). Their function is to facilitate effective cooperation and exchange of information in the asset recovery area.[21]

In spite of the numerous instruments which have been adopted, the confiscation regimes have generally not been considered to function sufficiently well.[22] In 2014, a new directive on confiscation was therefore adopted: Directive 2014/42/EU of the European Parliament and of the Council on the Freezing and Confiscation of Instrumentalities and Proceeds of Crime in the European Union (hereafter "Directive 2014/42/EU").[23] This directive had to be implemented into national law by 4 October 2016.

Parallel to this international legislative activity, national legislative initiatives in order to allow for a strategy "*to go for the money*" have taken place. Within

---

18 *OJ* L 68, 15.3.2005, pp. 49–51.

19 *OJ* L 196, 2.8.2003, pp. 45–55.

20 *OJ* L 328, 24.11.2006, pp. 59–78 and an Amending Act thereto (Framework Decision 2009/299/JHA), *OJ* L 81, 27.3.2009, pp. 24–36.

21 *OJ* L 332, 18.12.2007, pp. 103–05.

22 The reviews of the EU confiscation powers between 2005 and 2014 are described in Section 2.2 below.

23 *OJ* L 127, 29.4.2014, pp. 39–50 and *Corrigendum* to the Directive published on 29 April 2014.

the EU, the development began in Italy in the 1960s, and then spread to other States in the 1980s and 1990s.[24] The domestic legal action was often triggered by international pressure for States to develop more efficient regimes, and there was thus a significant international impact on the development of national legislation.[25] In some States there were during this period also certain national high-profile cases which led to public outcry and pressure for new legislation. An example of such a case was the *Cuthbertson* case in the UK.[26] In Ireland, new powerful legislation on measures of confiscation was especially triggered by the assassination in 1996 of the journalist Veronica Guerin, who had published articles on organised crime and the illicit profits made by such groups. In Italy, more far-reaching legislation on confiscation took place as a result of several assassinations of public servants and law enforcement officials by the mafia.[27]

1.3. ON THE SUBJECT MATTER

1.3.1. THE OVERRIDING PURPOSE OF THE STUDY

The overarching aim of this book is to study the measure of extended confiscation as an instrument of criminal policy within the EU. As described above, the intention of the EU legislator is to ensure that the confiscation regimes of the Member States are as efficient as possible, and the legal instrument has therefore developed and expanded in the last few years. It is my understanding that a study of the provisions provided at the national as well as the international level including its application in practice may help to give a better understanding of this strategy of confiscating criminal assets. The EU has so far mainly taken action in this area by approximating and harmonising substantial criteria and enhancing cross-border cooperation by providing for rules on mutual recognition of judicial decisions.

In spite of the legislative initiatives being taken at the international and the national level, there is today a common concern that the regimes are not

24 *Study for an Impact Assessment on a Proposal for a New Legal Framework on the Confiscation and Recovery of Criminal Assets*, RAND Europe, 2012, p. 2.

25 Bell, n 4 above, pp. 24–25.

26 This case is described in Section 3.1 below.

27 L. Paoli, "Seizure and Confiscation Measures in Italy: An Evaluation of Their Effectiveness and Constitutionality" (1997) 5 *European Journal of Crime, Criminal Law and Criminal Justice*, p. 256, p. 261. Italy has today in comparison to other Member States in the EU a very far-reaching approach to criminal asset recovery. The existing system is of a mixed character and rather complicated, as it contains forms of both conviction-based and non-conviction-based confiscation. See for a discussion of the Italian system, A. Balsamo, "The Delocalisation of Mafia Organisations and the Construction of a European Law against Organised Crime" (2016) 17 *Global Crime*, pp. 99–121.

functioning sufficiently. The political aim "*to go for the money*" is not believed to have been realised or enforced fully at the law enforcement level. Within the EU such concerns led to the adoption of Directive 2014/42/EU. One method used in this instrument is harmonisation of the substantive requirements, as it is argued that the current national and EU regimes are unsatisfactory.[28] There is much hope that this new directive will boost the regimes on confiscation as well as the international cooperation in this area. At present, there are many similarities in the domestic regimes within the EU, but there are also many different approaches, as it varies from jurisdiction to jurisdiction how far the legislator has been able and willing to go. Furthermore, there are different legislative views on how to create an effective confiscation regime which is not in conflict with human rights law. Some States have, for example, adopted rules for a reversal of the burden of proof on the defendant or have provided a reduced standard of evidence regarding the origin of assets, whereas this has been more difficult within other systems.

Against this background, an important purpose of this study is to examine whether the methods chosen so far will lead to improved opportunities to confiscate illicit proceeds. Do stronger or more harmonised powers for confiscation *per se* lead to greater efficiency, or are there any other reforms or measures which might have similar or even more effect? In addition, there is a significant need to study under which circumstances extended confiscation can, may and should be used, as well as to provide some answers to the question of which changes are reasonable and proportionate to the objectives pursued. Accordingly, the perspective of human rights law will be kept throughout the whole study.

1.3.2. THE DIFFERENT STAGES OF CONFISCATION

The legal discipline of confiscation is complicated, because it concerns issues of a rather technical character and at the same time it is influenced by many fundamental legal principles. The subject lies between criminal and civil law and touches not only substantive criminal law, but also procedural law as well as international law and the human rights *acquis*. Broadly speaking, the confiscation process may in terms of chronology be divided into several steps:

(1) the *investigation stage*, where the proceeds from criminal offences are investigated, identified, traced and seized,
(2) the *judicial stage* involving the legal proceedings dealing with criminal responsibility and the issue of confiscation,

---

28 See further on this directive, Section 2.3 and Chapter 7 below.

(3) the *maintenance stage* during which the seized asset is stored, managed and maintained, and
(4) the *execution stage* where the confiscation order is executed and the asset disposed of.

Generally speaking, the whole process of recovering the proceeds from crime is difficult, time-consuming and expensive.[29] The reason for the significant resources needed is often that complex financial investigations are necessary and may require specialised knowledge. The storage of certain property may further be complicated and lead to significant costs.

Against the background that assets may be transferred very swiftly between different States, the importance of international cooperation in cases regarding confiscation is obvious. Different forms of international cooperation may in principle take place during all of the above stages.

It is obvious that the different stages of the confiscation process cannot be considered separately from each other, as the success of a confiscation regime depends on efficient provisions and administrative routines in all these aspects. If, for example, there are insufficient powers to investigate the financial circumstances of a suspect or to seize the assets found, there may be no pleas for confiscation. If there are no resources or effective administrative structures regarding the execution of confiscation orders, no assets will be confiscated. Even if this may sound self-evident, it is remarkably often forgotten when the regimes of confiscation are discussed and evaluated.

Against this background, the purpose of this book is to analyse the regime on confiscation from a multi-faceted perspective by as far as possible viewing the discipline as a whole instead of restricting it to a particular stage of the process. However, it is here not possible to provide a complete analysis regarding all stages. Considering the overarching aim of the study, it seems reasonable to focus more in depth on stages 1 and 2 above. Accordingly, the legal provisions and reforms regarding the substantive requirements for extended confiscation as well as the procedural framework and the provisions on international cooperation will be examined. The EU legislator has so far been most active within this area, even if issues regarding the maintenance of assets and the final disposal of confiscated assets (stages 3–4) have received more attention in the last few years.[30] Examples are new provisions regarding asset sharing of confiscated proceeds between States at the execution stage or rules which direct the use of confiscated assets to certain social purposes.[31] Some provisions have also been adopted in order

---

29 N. Cribb, "Tracing and Confiscating the Proceeds of Crime" (2003) 11 *Journal of Financial Crime*, p. 168, p. 180.

30 See for example Recital (35) and Art. 10 Directive 2014/42/EU.

31 See in this respect the study from the Center for the Study of Democracy, *Disposal of Confiscated Assets in the EU Member States, Laws and Practices*, 2014, which i.e. analyses

to enable a more efficient execution of final confiscation orders. To some extent such provisions will be described and touched upon in the study.

1.3.3. A NOTE ON TERMINOLOGY

In principle, there is no generally used or accepted terminology in this area. A study of the international conventions and agreements as well as national legislation shows differences and certain inconsistency. It can be noted that the terms "confiscation" and "forfeiture" are often treated interchangeably and synonymously,[32] and both terms refer to the final deprivation of assets by order of a court or other competent authority. However, it may vary from State to State which term is preferred and in what context it is used. In, for example, England and Wales the domestic legislation (POCA 2002) uses both terms "confiscation" and "forfeiture".[33] In German law, there is a classification between the terms "*Verfall*" (forfeiture) and "*Einziehung*" (confiscation). The former term concerns the recovery of that which the defendant has acquired through a criminal offence or for its commission. The term "*Einziehung*" is used for measures regarding objects which were generated by a crime, or used in its commission or preparation.[34] This terminology is sometimes – especially in transnational relations – rather confusing. In Germany it has therefore on different occasions been proposed that the legislator shall adopt a uniform terminology and avoid this distinction.[35] In, for example Swedish law, one term ("*förverkande*") is used regarding all such measures. At the moment a proposal for a significant reform of the German legislation in the area of confiscation (presented in 2016) is being discussed. Within this framework it

---

the need for EU action in order to enhance the social re-use of confiscated criminal assets and Directorate-General for Internal Policies, Policy Department Citizens' Rights and Constitutional Affairs, *The Need for New EU Legislation allowing the Assets Confiscated from Criminal Organisations to be used for Civil Society and in particular for Social Purposes*, 2012. See also on the provisions on social re-use of assets in Directive 2014/42/EU, F. Meyer, "Zivilgesellschaftliche Nutzung konfiszierter Vermögenswerte – ein zukunftsträchtiges Paradigma?" (2015) 8 *ZRP*, pp. 244–47 and S. Montaldo, "Directive 2014/42/EU and Social Reuse of Confiscated Assets in the EU: Advancing a Culture of Legality" (2015) 6 *New Journal of European Criminal Law*, pp. 195–212.

32 Compare for example *Manual on International Cooperation for the Purposes of Confiscation of Proceeds of Crime*, United Nations, New York 2012, p. 2 and Ryder, n 5 above, pp. 768–69.

33 This legislation is described in Chapter 3 below.

34 Compare also Section 4.1 below.

35 See, for example, the formal request directed to the German Parliament in 2013 with proposals to develop an improved and more coherent policy for combatting economic crime, made by the Social Democratic Party of Germany ("SPD"), *Antrag Wirtschaftskriminalität effektiv bekämpfen*, Drucksache 17/13087, 16.4.2013, p. 3. Compare also for critic against the terminology, O. Katholnigg, "Die Neuregelungen beim Verfall" (1994) 9 *Juristische Rundschau*, p. 353, p. 356.

has been suggested that the term "*Verfall*" must be abolished and changed it into "*Einziehung*". The Government argues that the current German terminology is misleading, and the purpose is to adjust the national term to the terminology used within the EU.[36] Such a future amendment is to be welcomed.

Generally, it must be pointed out that it would be preferable if at least the English translations of the national terms in this area were used in a consistent way. In a Swedish unofficial translation of the domestic Criminal Code by the Ministry of Justice the term "forfeiture" is, for example, used.[37] The reason seems unclear, and it is regrettable because the legal text partly implements provisions in international conventions and EU instruments that in the English versions use the term "confiscation" and "extended confiscation". In German legal jurisprudence it varies among different authors whether they use the term of "extended confiscation" or "extended forfeiture" when describing the domestic provisions in English.[38]

It can be noted that the term "confiscation" is more often used in the context of this study, and is referred to in the international conventions and agreements referred to in Section 1.2 above.[39] In Chapter I Article 1 of the European Convention on Laundering, Search, Seizure and Confiscation of the Proceeds of Crime the term "confiscation" is defined as "a penalty or a measure, ordered by a court following proceedings in relation to a criminal offence or criminal offences resulting in the final deprivation of property". This use of terminology has been adopted also by the EU. In FD 2005/212/JHA this definition has been copied.[40] In Directive 2014/42/EU the terms "confiscation" and "extended confiscation" are used (Articles 4 and 5). Article 2(4) defines confiscation as "a final deprivation of property ordered by a court in relation to a criminal offence". In accordance with this use of terminology, I will for the purpose of this study refer to "confiscation". Furthermore, the term "extended confiscation" will be used, as this is the terminology of the official English translation of

---

36 See further Sections 4.1 and 4.4.4 below.

37 This translation was made by and provided at the homepage of the Swedish Ministry of Justice (http://www.government.se/sb/d/3288). This link has now expired. See further on the Swedish Act, Sec. 5.2 below.

38 See for example M. Kilchling, "Tracing, Seizing and Confiscating Proceeds from Corruption (and other Illegal Conduct) within or outside the Criminal Justice System" (2001) 9 *European Journal of Crime, Criminal Law and Criminal Justice*, p. 264, p. 273 who uses the term "extended forfeiture" for Sec. 73d *StGB* and "confiscation" when addressing the provisions in Sec. 74 *StGB*. Compare also *Evaluation Report on the Fifth Round of Mutual Evaluations, Financial Crime and Financial Investigations*, Report on Germany, 16269/2/11, REV 2, Brussels, 19.1.2012, pp. 58 and 73.

39 See Art. 5 of the United Nations Convention against Illicit Traffic in Narcotic Drugs and Psychotropic Substances, Art. 12 of the United Nations Convention against Transnational Organized Crime, Art. 31 of the United Nations Convention against Corruption and Art. 3 of the European Convention on Laundering, Search, Seizure and Confiscation of Proceeds of Crime and on the Financing of Terrorism.

40 See Arts. 1–3 of FD 2005/212/JHA.

FD 2005/212/JHA and Directive 2014/42/EU. Furthermore, "extended confiscation" is an accepted term in legal doctrine dealing with this form of confiscation. The traditional classic form of confiscation which requires that a link is established between a specific criminal offence and certain assets will be referred to as "ordinary confiscation".

Some international conventions cover the whole process of tracing, seizing, confiscating and returning property or proceeds to the rightful owners.[41] Sometimes the term "asset recovery" is used to describe this general procedure of recovering the proceeds from criminal activity. However, this term is also sometimes used in a more limited sense in order to describe the efforts of governments to repatriate to the country of origin proceeds of crime hidden in foreign jurisdictions.[42] In the FD on Asset Recovery Offices the term "asset recovery" is used in the context of cross-border cooperation between the Member States regarding the exchange of information and freezing and confiscating the proceeds of crime. For the purpose of this study I will use the term "asset recovery" or "recovery of the proceeds from crime" to define the whole process of measures to be taken at the investigative, judicial and executive stages in order to confiscate the proceeds from crime. This means that asset recovery will not be limited to transnational relations.

Finally, it can be noted regarding national issues, that I will use the term "extended confiscation" when addressing the present German provision on "*erweiterter Verfall*" in Section 73d *Strafgesetzbuch*. This is in line with the terminology used in the English translation of FD 2005/212/JHA, Directive 2014/42/EU and the official translations of the *Strafgesetzbuch* which have been produced by the German Ministry of Justice.[43] For reasons of a uniform use of terms I will also use this terminology regarding the Swedish provisions, even if, as mentioned earlier, this departs from the unofficial translation of the statute provided for by the Ministry of Justice.

---

41 See for example the United Nations Convention against Transnational Organized Crime (2000), the United Nations Convention against Corruption (2003) and the European Convention on Laundering, Search, Seizure and Confiscation of proceeds of Crime and on the Financing of Terrorism (2005).

42 Compare for example *Manual on International Cooperation for the Purposes of Confiscation of Proceeds of Crime*, United Nations, New York 2012, p. 1 and *Best Practices on Confiscation* (Recommendations 4 and 38) and a *Framework for ongoing work on Asset Recovery*, Financial Action Task Force, October 2012, p. 1.

43 Compare http://www.gesetze-im-internet.de. See also the *Evaluation Report on the Fifth Round of Mutual Evaluations, Financial Crime and Financial Investigations*, Report on Germany, 16269/2/11, REV 2, Brussels, 19.1.2012, pp. 58 and 73 which refer to "extended confiscation" regarding Sec. 73d *StGB*.

1.4. THE PERSPECTIVES OF THE STUDY AND DELIMITATIONS

1.4.1. NATIONAL AND INTERNATIONAL PERSPECTIVES

As the title of the book reveals, the analysis has both national and international perspectives, and the focus is mainly on the legislative framework of the European Union. It is obvious that national and international legislative action and other initiatives interact in different ways. The international influence on provisions of extended confiscation nationally has been very significant, both regarding the introduction of such a measure in the first place as well as when it comes to the scope of application. Further, a regime for international cooperation in confiscation cases is often a prerequisite for the functioning of national regimes, for example when it comes to executing domestic orders on confiscation abroad. This being said, there is also a national influence on the work of the international legislators. It is, for example, in several areas obvious that national approaches to confiscation and other legal traditions or constitutional law influence and limit the scope of the instruments adopted. In this study, the aim is to view and highlight the different issues discussed from various perspectives in order to give a more comprehensive analysis of the subject of extended confiscation. This is mainly done in the following way.[44]

In Part II the regime of extended confiscation is, on the one hand, viewed from the national perspective; here some national legislation and practice is presented and examined. Important emphasis is placed on issues like the motives for domestic provisions on extended confiscation and the specific characteristics or difficulties regarding its application in the jurisdiction in question. On the other hand, this national perspective is contrasted with the international perspective. This is done in several ways. For example, the ways in which legislative action at EU level has influenced the contents of national legislation are examined. National legislation is further evaluated on the basis of comparisons to similar provisions in other jurisdictions. Finally, the comparative survey of national systems is used as a point of reference for an evaluation of the provisions on extended confiscation adopted at the international level. This includes especially the changes to this regime brought by Directive 2014/42/EU. In contrast to this, the starting-point of the study in Part III is the international perspective, which involves an examination of the judicial cooperation between law enforcement agencies in transnational cases regarding confiscation. The overriding purpose is here to assess how the provisions given in the international legal framework influence the functioning of the national regimes of confiscation and vice versa.

---

44 See further Section 1.5 below for an outline of the different parts of the study.

1.4.2. DELIMITATIONS

Turning to delimitations, it must firstly be emphasised that extended confiscation as a legal institution may be questioned on many grounds. In this book there is, however, no space to deal in detail with the fundamental question of whether the instrument of extended confiscation may be considered as fully legitimate from the perspective of legal theory. The same goes for the more dogmatic issue of whether it is to be considered a criminal punishment or not. There may in fact be many doubts as to whether extended confiscation in all parts may be considered as legitimate and fair. However, it is obvious that this form of confiscation is here to stay and that the trend is rather to expand its use than to limit it. Against this background, it seems more fruitful to evaluate how the measure is applied and developed nationally and internationally, and to find ways in which it may be used in a proportionate way with full respect for human rights. The provisions on extended confiscation have been challenged in view of human rights law many times before national and international courts, and some of this case-law will be described and referred to.

It can further be noted that different forms of confiscation and asset recovery strategies in the area of financial crime are closely related to legislation on money laundering, as these two strategies influence and complement one another. The criminalisation of money laundering seeks to prevent proceeds of criminal activity from being concealed and "laundered" into the licit economy. As with the confiscation of proceeds of crime, the criminalisation of money laundering thus seeks to prevent crime.[45] Accordingly, it is a very important part of a profit-oriented crime control model.[46] However, in general there is no space for an analysis of money laundering initiatives within the framework of this study.

---

45 See Stessens, n 6 above, pp. 84–87.

46 The EU has adopted several instruments in the area of money laundering. See for example Directive (EU) 2015/849 of the European Parliament and of the Council of 20 May 2015 on the Prevention of the Use of the Financial System for the Purposes of Money Laundering or Terrorist Financing, amending Regulation (EU) No. 648/2012 of the European Parliament and of the Council, and repealing Directive 2005/60/EC of the European Parliament and of the Council and Commission Directive 2006/70/EC, *OJ* L 141, 5.6.2015, pp. 73–117. A new proposal for legislation in this area has been presented, see *Proposal for a Directive of the European Parliament and of the Council amending Directive (EU) 2015/849 on the Prevention of the use of the Financial System for the Purposes of Money Laundering or Terrorist Financing and amending Directive 2009/101/EC*, COM(2016) 450 final, Strasbourg 5.7.2016. In Sweden a new act regulating money laundering came into force in 2014; see Act (2014:307) on Penalties for Money Laundering Offences (Bill 2013/14:121). See *Money Laundering*, Legal Memorandum 2015:2 from the Prosecution Development Centre, Stockholm and the Swedish Economic Crime Authority.

1.5. AN OUTLINE OF THE DIFFERENT PARTS AND CHAPTERS

The book is divided into three parts. Part I contains an introduction and presentation of the subject. Part II is concentrated on the *substantive requirements* for extended confiscation. In the introductory chapter (Chapter 2) the development and adoption of different legislative instruments by the EU are presented. The FD 2005/212/JHA is described in more detail. Thereafter, the process of adopting Directive 2014/42/EU and its provisions on extended confiscation is described. In what follows, a comparative study presents some different national models. The main study is concentrated on the domestic legislation in the jurisdictions of England and Wales (Chapter 3), Germany (Chapter 4) and Sweden (Chapter 5). Further, a short overview is given of legislation and the most central requirements for extended confiscation in Norway, Denmark and Finland (Chapter 6). The description of the national legislation in Chapter 6 is not intended to be detailed, but serves to be used more as a broad source of comparison, especially in regard to the Swedish legislation.

The reason for the choice of England and Wales is that it represents a *common law* State and possesses one of the world's most comprehensive pieces of criminal assets legislation.[47] It was in fact one of the first Member States in the EU to introduce a confiscation regime.[48] Germany and Sweden on the other hand represent the *civil law* system. These States have a similar approach to extended confiscation, but there are also certain significant differences. Even if this study in principle has an EU perspective, two reservations to this can be made. First, it can be observed that although the UK and Denmark are EU Member States, they are in this respect not participating in Directive 2014/42/EU. In addition, in June 2016 an EU referendum took place in the UK which resulted in a decision to leave the European Union. Until exit negotiations are concluded, though, the UK remains a full member and all the rights and obligations of EU membership remain in force. The full consequences of this decision remain to be seen.[49]

Secondly, the short overview of some national legislation also encompasses Norway, which is not a Member State of the EU. The reason for this is that Norway has interesting legislation on extended confiscation with a reversed burden of proof. The Nordic States have in principle rather similar criminal

---

47 A. Kennedy, "An Evaluation of the Recovery of Criminal Proceeds in the United Kingdom" (2007) 10 *Journal of Money Laundering Control*, p. 33, p. 33.

48 Ryder, n 5 above, p. 784.

49 See for an analysis of the options avaliable to the UK Government regarding the future UK-EU security and police cooperation, House of Lords, European Union Committee, 7th Report of Session 2016–17, *Brexit: Future UK-EU Security and Police Cooperation*, December 2016.

justice systems and traditionally concur closely in the area of criminal policy.[50] Against this background, it is especially interesting to compare the Swedish legislation with the Norwegian, Danish and Finnish, which all have in some areas chosen another approach to extended confiscation or have different legal solutions regarding certain aspects. The analysis of the Swedish legislation in Chapter 5 will thus especially include and refer to similarities or differences in the legislations of these jurisdictions.

The chapters on Sweden, England and Wales and Germany contain a presentation of national legislation and case-law. Some of the areas being studied are the scope of application, evidentiary standards and whether there is a mandatory or discretionary application of the regime. The comparative study ends with some commentaries on the national regime, but this analysis does not focus on all specifics of each system nor is it exhaustive. Rather, some interesting areas are highlighted and discussed, and certain strong and weak features are addressed. Some recommendations for improvement are given. Important overall issues in Part II are: How did national legislation on extended confiscation develop and how is it drafted? How is the provision applied in case-law? Does the national legislation strike the right balance between the public interest of not letting criminals benefit from criminal proceeds and offenders' due process rights? Some proposals are presented in order to restrict and apply the measure in a way in which a reasonable balance between the interest of efficiency and the respect for human rights is struck.

Part II closes with a holistic analysis and discussion of Directive 2014/42/EU (Chapter 7). The process of adopting this instrument is described in order to show how the original proposal from the European Commission was changed during the negotiations. The effects of this new directive on the efficiency of national regimes on extended confiscation are assessed and discussed. Thereby the results from the comparative study are a source of reference. Some fundamental issues in focus in this chapter are the following: Is there any shared approach by the States to extended confiscation? Are the legislative instruments developed by the EU legislator regarding extended confiscation sufficient and in balance with human rights? What changes can be expected to the existing EU regime by the new directive? Is extended confiscation in practice applied in the cases and for the purposes it was originally intended for? Some suggestions for improvement of the EU regulation will be given. Directive 2014/42/EU is an innovative EU instrument, and there is at the moment a significant need for guidance on how to interpret and apply the rules. This concerns practitioners in the EU Member States (police, prosecutors, courts, etc.), as well as the national legislators, which

---

50 Accordingly, the Swedish legislator took some consideration of how the legislation in other Scandinavian States was drafted when the new act on extended confiscation was prepared. See Bill 2007/08:68 pp. 45–48.

are still busy with the implementation and drafting of national legislation in this area.

In Part III of the study international cooperation within the area of confiscation is in focus, and the requirements and practice for the *transnational handling of confiscation cases* is dealt with. As has rightly been pointed out; "an elegant legislative scheme cannot alone deliver effective recovery" of criminal assets.[51] An evaluation of the measure of extended confiscation is thus not complete without analysing whether there are any legislative instruments which provide for efficient judicial cooperation and safeguard that the national asset regimes may be enforced abroad. In the last few years, more powerful provisions on extended confiscation have often been justified with the argument that harmonisation of substantive requirements achieves more efficient international cooperation. One example is Directive 2014/42/EU. In order to assess the effects of such reforms, the national regimes of extended confiscation and Directive 2014/42/EU must thus be placed in a broader context. How is the current EU legal framework for transnational cooperation in confiscation matters functioning? And is it in practice of significant importance in such cases that similar requirements operate regarding extended confiscation?

In Part III an overview of the international legal framework for handling transnational confiscation cases is given in order to clarify the scope and requirements for cooperation. As will further be described, the legal framework for such issues within the EU is built on either mutual legal assistance in criminal matters or on mutual recognition of judicial decisions. There are at present various instruments available, but the regulation is fragmented and very user-unfriendly. A practitioner must in many cases decide between different partly over-lapping international instruments. The first chapter (Chapter 8) aims at providing an overview of the different initiatives which have been taken. Here the most important instruments from the United Nations, the Council of Europe and the EU are presented, and the difference between the model of mutual assistance and mutual recognition is described. Thereby a description is given of Directive 2014/41/EU of the European Parliament and of the Council of 3 April 2014 regarding the European Investigation Order in criminal matters.[52] The central international instruments which are dealt with in Part III are further, for example, the United Nations Convention against Illicit Traffic in Narcotic Drugs and Psychotropic Substances (1988), the European Convention on Laundering, Search, Seizure and Confiscation of the Proceeds from Crime (1990), the European Convention on Laundering, Search, Seizure and Confiscation of the Proceeds from Crime and on the Financing of Terrorism (2005) and the European Convention on Mutual Assistance in Criminal Matters from 1959.

---

51 Kennedy, n 47 above, p. 34.

52 *OJ* L 130, 1.5.2014, pp. 1–36.

The EU instruments on legal assistance referred to are the Council Act of 29 May 2000 establishing the Convention on Mutual Assistance in Criminal Matters between the Member States of the European Union and the Council Act of 16 October 2001 establishing the Protocol to the Convention on Mutual Assistance in Criminal Matters between the Member States of the European Union.

At present, a national practitioner who is in need of assistance abroad must resolve many legal and practical problems. Obviously, an efficient regime of asset recovery requires a system of international cooperation at all stages of the confiscation process. Building upon the different stages referred to in Section 1.3.2 above, the study of the current EU legal framework have been divided into three areas.

Chapter 9 addresses international cooperation regarding the tracing of assets and exchange of information in cross-border confiscation cases. The main EU instruments dealt with are the Council Framework Decision 2006/960/JHA of 18 December 2006 on simplifying the exchange of information and intelligence between law enforcement authorities of the Member States of the European Union and the FD on Asset Recovery Offices.

Chapter 10 discusses international cooperation in order to seize or freeze assets located abroad. Here especially the Framework Decision 2003/577/JHA on the Execution in the European Union of Orders Freezing Property or Evidence is in focus.

Chapter 11 deals with international cooperation in order to execute final confiscation orders. In this area, the EU has adopted the Council Framework Decision 2006/783/JHA of 6 October 2006 on the application of the principle of mutual recognition to confiscation orders.

Chapter 12 presents and discusses the new proposal for a Regulation of the European Parliament and of the Council on the Mutual Recognition of Freezing and Confiscation Orders.[53] This instrument was proposed as late as December 2016 and could be crucial for the future development of the transnational confiscation regime within the EU.

In Chapters 9–11, the applicable legal instruments as well the scope for future improvement are discussed. In addition, certain issues regarding the organisation of the judicial agencies handling cases of cross-border asset recovery will be addressed. Within the analysis of the new Proposal for a Regulation of the European Parliament and of the Council on the Mutual Recognition of Freezing and Confiscation Orders in Chapter 12, it will be especially considered whether any identified difficulties or deficiencies of the current cooperation regime have been corrected. Part III does not contain any complete comparative study of national law when it comes to the regime for international cooperation. However, as further stated in Section 8.5 below, a comparative perspective will

[53] COM(2016) 819 final, Brussels 21.12.2016.

still be adopted regarding some selected issues of national law. Hereby domestic legislation or practice in the three main States which have been studied in Part II (Sweden, Germany and the UK) will be included, in order to highlight some national difficulties, advantages or approaches to confiscation.

The book concludes with some brief final remarks on the regime of extended confiscation from the national and the international perspective (Chapter 13). Here the general findings of the study are summarised in the shape of four overarching guidelines for the future development of the measure.

PART II

SUBSTANTIVE PROVISIONS ON EXTENDED CONFISCATION

CHAPTER 2
LEGISLATIVE ACTION BY THE EU

2.1. FD 2005/212/JHA

2.1.1. INTRODUCTION

As described in Section 1.2 above, the EU has adopted several instruments in the area of confiscation and asset recovery. In the context of this study, FD 2005/212/JHA is especially important as it introduced a system of extended confiscation into the EU regime.[54] The last date for the national implementation of this framework decision was 15 March 2007. At present, all Member States except for Greece, Italy, Luxembourg and the United Kingdom have implemented it. In some of the States which have not implemented the instrument the measure of extended confiscation is provided for anyway (one example is the UK), and in other States the implementation process is ongoing.[55] In the following, the most central provisions of FD 2005/212/JHA are presented. Thereafter the reviews of the European confiscation powers in the years 2005–2014 are described (Section 2.2). The chapter closes with a presentation of the new directive adopted within the EU in 2014 (Section 2.3).

The aim of FD 2005/212/JHA has been to harmonise national confiscation laws, and to ensure that all Member States have effective rules. At its adoption, the EU legislator argued that the existing instruments in the area of confiscation had neither to a sufficient extent achieved powerful confiscation measures nor more effective routines for cross-border cooperation. This was considered to be due to certain differences between the domestic legislation, and also as resulting from the poor implementation rates regarding the existing instruments.[56] Article 2 FD 2005/212/JHA deals with the powers of ordinary confiscation. This form of confiscation requires that a link is proved between a specific criminal offence and the assets to be confiscated. The Member States are obligated by this provision to enable their authorities to confiscate, either wholly or in part, instrumentalities and proceeds from criminal offences punishable by deprivation

---

54 *OJ* L 68, 15.3.2005, pp. 49–51.

55 As of 10 February 2017, see the homepage of the European Judicial Network (www.ejn-crimjust.eu).

56 Compare Recitals (1) and (9) FD 2005/212/JHA.

of liberty for more than one year, or property the value of which corresponds to such proceeds. An exception is made for tax offences, where the Member States are permitted to use procedures other than criminal procedures to deprive the perpetrator of the proceeds of such an offence.[57]

2.1.2. EXTENDED CONFISCATION

Article 3 FD 2005/212/JHA obligates the Member States to introduce the measure of extended confiscation into national legislation. Such far-reaching powers of confiscation were at this time already used in the national legislation of some Member States, for example the UK, Ireland and Germany.[58] Article 3 states that the measure of extended confiscation shall be available against persons who have been convicted of certain serious criminal offences related to organised crime or terrorism. In this respect, it provides that, as *a minimum*, the necessary measures shall be adopted to confiscate, either wholly or in part, property belonging to a person convicted of an offence in two ways:

(a) offences committed within the framework of a criminal organisation as defined in Joint Action 98/733/JHA of 21 December 1998 on making it a criminal offence to participate in a criminal organisation in the Member States of the European Union.[59] According to Article 1 of this instrument a criminal organisation shall mean

> a structured association, established over a period of time, of more than two persons, acting in concert with a view to committing offences which are punishable by deprivation of liberty or a detention order of a maximum of at least four years or a more serious penalty, whether such offences are an end in themselves or a means of obtaining material benefits and, where appropriate, of improperly influencing the operation of public authorities.

Apart from being committed within the framework of such a criminal organisation, it is further provided that the offence must be covered by one of the following instruments:

- Framework Decision 2000/383/JHA of 29 May 2000 on increasing protection by criminal penalties and other sanctions against counterfeiting in connection with the introduction of the euro,[60]

---

57 Compare Art. 1(a) FD 2001/500/JHA.
58 See further Sections 3.1 and 4.1 below.
59 *OJ* L 351, 29.12.1998, p. 1.
60 *OJ* L 140, 14.6.2000, p. 1.

- Framework Decision 2001/500/JHA of 26 June 2001 on money laundering, the identification, tracing, freezing, seizing and confiscation of instrumentalities and the proceeds of crime,[61]
- Framework Decision 2002/629/JHA of 19 July 2002 on combating trafficking in human beings,[62]
- Framework Decision 2002/946/JHA of 28 November 2002 on the strengthening of the penal framework to prevent the facilitation of unauthorised entry, transit and residence,[63]
- Framework Decision 2004/68/JHA of 22 December 2003 on combating the sexual exploitation of children and child pornography,[64] or
- Framework Decision 2004/757/JHA of 25 October 2004 laying down minimum provisions on the constituent elements of criminal acts and penalties in the field of illicit drug trafficking.[65]

(b) or offences which are covered by Framework Decision 2002/475/JHA of 13 June 2002 on combating terrorism.[66]

For all offences covered by alternatives (a) or (b) above, there are two further requirements. Firstly, the offence in question must be *punishable with criminal penalties of a maximum of at least between five and 10 years of imprisonment.* However, an exception to this is the offence of money laundering where it is sufficient to be punishable with a maximum term of at least four years' imprisonment. Second, the offence must be of such a nature that it *can generate financial gain.*

FD 2005/212/JHA establish *three alternative options* for the construction of the national provisions on extended confiscation. Article 3(2) provides that the necessary measures to enable confiscation shall *at least* be taken:

> (a) where a national court based on specific facts is fully convinced that the property in question has been derived from criminal activities of the convicted person during a period prior to conviction for the offence referred to in paragraph 1 which is deemed reasonable by the court in the circumstances of the particular case, or, alternatively,
>
> (b) where a national court based on specific facts is fully convinced that the property in question has been derived from similar criminal activities of the convicted person during a period prior to conviction for the offence referred to in paragraph 1 which is deemed reasonable by the court in the circumstances of the particular case, or, alternatively,

61 *OJ* L 182, 5.7.2001, p. 1.
62 *OJ* L 203, 1.8.2002, p. 1.
63 *OJ* L 328, 5.12.2002, p. 1.
64 *OJ* L 13, 20.1.2004, p. 44.
65 *OJ* L 335, 11.11.2004, p. 8.
66 *OJ* L 164, 22.6.2002, p. 3.

(c) where it is established that the value of the property is disproportionate to the lawful income of the convicted person and a national court based on specific facts is fully convinced that the property in question has been derived from the criminal activity of that convicted person.

Accordingly, the Member States are free to choose any or all of these minimum alternatives as the basis for a provision on extended confiscation. The significant difference between the first two alternatives is that alternative (b) provides that the preceding criminal activities must be *similar* to the offence which triggered the provision on extended confiscation in the first place. This means that this alternative is more restrictive. Alternative (c) is of different design, as it is built upon a financial comparison of the value of certain property in relation to the lawful income of a convicted person.

The evidentiary standard contained in Article 3 is identical for all legislative solutions in (a)–(c); a court is to be "fully convinced" that the property in question has been derived from criminal activities. This standard has been considered to be on a level with the criminal standard of proof (often referred to as "beyond reasonable doubt").[67] Against the background of the significant difficulties in the evidentiary context in the area of confiscation, it was however emphasised in Recital (10) in the framework decision that the aim of the instrument is to ensure effective rules in relation to the onus of proof regarding the sources of assets held by a person convicted of an offence related to organised crime. The Member States were therefore encouraged to consider a reversal of the burden of proof regarding the origin of property.[68] It has further been specifically emphasised that the Member States are allowed to use procedures other than criminal procedures to deprive the perpetrator of the property in question.[69]

2.1.3. THIRD PARTY CONFISCATION AND RULES ON PROCEDURAL RIGHTS

FD 2005/212/JHA contains an *optional* rule on third party confiscation. According to Article 3(3) the Member States are encouraged to consider adopting:

> the necessary measures to enable it to confiscate, in accordance with the conditions set out in paragraphs 1 and 2, either wholly or in part, property acquired by the closest

67 See for example Bill 2007/08:68 p. 66 and J. Boucht, "Extended Confiscation and the Proposed Directive on Freezing and Confiscation of Criminal Proceeds in the EU: On Striking a Balance between Efficiency, Fairness and Legal Certainty" (2013) 21 *European Journal of Crime, Criminal Law and Criminal Justice*, p. 127, p. 133.

68 Recital (6) FD 2005/212/JHA which refers to Art. 12 in the UN Convention of 12 December 2000 against Transnational Organised Crime.

69 Art. 3(4) FD 2005/212/JHA.

> relations of the person concerned and property transferred to a legal person in respect of which the person concerned – acting either alone or in conjunction with his closest relations – has a controlling influence. The same shall apply if the person concerned receives a significant part of the legal person's income.

There are no provisions in FD 2005/212/JHA which in detail specify the procedural safeguards for the persons affected by confiscation orders. Article 4 simply obligates Member States to take the necessary measures to ensure that interested parties affected by a confiscation order "have effective legal remedies in order to preserve their rights". Article 5 contains the well-known standard formulation for safeguards which may be found in many framework decisions on judicial cooperation in criminal matters:

> This Framework Decision shall not have the effect of altering the obligation to respect fundamental rights and fundamental principles, including in particular the presumption of innocence, as enshrined in Article 6 of the Treaty on European Union.[70]

In addition, Recital (11) states that:

> This Framework Decision does not prevent a Member State from applying its fundamental principles relating to due process, in particular the presumption of innocence, property rights, freedom of association, freedom of the press and freedom of expression in other media.[71]

2.2. REVIEWS OF THE EUROPEAN CONFISCATION POWERS

Back in 2005, the European Commission proclaimed the necessity to review the EU legislation on confiscation, especially regarding the possibility to reverse the onus of proof or lighten the standard of proof regarding the lawful origin of

70 Compare for example Art. 1(3) in Framework Decision of 13 June 2002 on the European Arrest Warrant and the Surrender Procedures between Member States, *OJ* L 190, 18.7.2002, pp. 1–18, Art. 1(3) in Framework Decision 2008/978/JHA on the European Evidence Warrant, *OJ* L 350, 30.12.2008, pp. 72–92 or Art. 1 in Framework Decision 2003/577/JHA on the Execution in the European Union of Orders Freezing Property or Evidence, *OJ* L 196, 2.8.2003, pp. 45–55.

71 The question, of which meaning is to be given to such general formulations in the recital of framework decisions and whether they have any binding effect, has been discussed. See for example regarding the Framework Decision of 13 June 2002 on the European Arrest Warrant and the Surrender Procedures between Member States, M. Thunberg Schunke, *Whose Responsibility? A Study of Transnational Defence Rights and Mutual Recognition of Judicial Decisions within the EU*, Intersentia, 2013, pp. 15–19.

assets.[72] In the following years, different reports and action plans highlighted the shortcomings of the various confiscation regimes. In 2008, the European Commission, for example, stated that the overall number of confiscation cases in the EU was relatively limited and that an increased use of confiscation powers was desirable.[73] This conclusion was based on several implementation reports, which had shown significant delays in the transposition of certain EU instruments as well as substantial differences between the national confiscation regimes. According to the European Commission, one reason for such difficulties was the lack of clarity and coherence of the existing EU instruments.[74]

The implementation reports had, for example, shown that the FD 2001/500/JHA and the FD on Asset Recovery Offices had been transposed relatively well, but that there were significant problems regarding the implementation and the execution of warrants regarding Framework Decision 2003/577/JHA on the Execution in the European Union of Orders Freezing Property or Evidence.[75] Despite the intention at the adoption of this instrument to simplify requests for seizing and freezing of property via a system of mutual recognition, the judicial authorities of the Member States had continued to prefer the (old) legal assistance framework.[76] Furthermore, the report regarding FD 2005/212/JHA had concluded that the instrument was unclear, with a slow and incomplete transposition process.[77] Serious drawbacks regarding the application of the provisions of extended confiscation were considered to result from the three alternative criteria for drawing up national legislation. This construction of the framework decision had also resulted in difficulties regarding the implementation and practical application of Framework Decision 2006/783/JHA on the Application of the Principle of Mutual Recognition to Confiscation Orders, as

72 See Secs. 22 and 23, *Communication from the Commission to the Council and the European Parliament, Developing a strategic concept on tackling organised crime*, 2.6.2005, COM(2005) 232 final.

73 *Proceeds of Organised Crime; Ensuring that "Crime does not Pay"*, 20.11.2008, COM(2008) 766 final, p. 4.

74 COM(2008) 766 final, p. 5.

75 See for example *Report from the Commission based on Article 6 of the Council Framework Decision of 26 June 2001 on Money Laundering, the Identification, Tracing, Freezing, Seizing and Confiscation of Instrumentalities and the Proceeds of Crime*, COM(2004) 230 final, *Report from the Commission based on Art. 14 of the Council Framework decision 2003/577/JHA of 22 July 2003 on the Execution in the EU of Orders Freezing Property or Evidence*, COM(2008) 885 final and *Report from the Commission based on Article 8 of the Council Decision 2007/845/JHA of 6 December 2007 concerning Cooperation between Asset Recovery Offices of the Member States in the Field of Tracing and Identification of Proceeds from, or other Property related to, Crime*, COM(2011) 176 final.

76 See further I. Cameron, M. Thunberg Schunke, K. Påle-Bartes, C. Wong and P. Asp, *International Criminal Law from a Swedish Perspective*, Intersentia, 2011, p. 147.

77 *Report from the Commission pursuant to Article 6 of the Council Framework Decision of 24 February 2005 on Confiscation of Crime-related Proceeds, Instrumentalities and Property* (2005/212/JHA), COM(2007) 805.

the national choice of criteria for confiscation was linked to the possibility of refusal of the execution of a request in an executing Member State.[78] Against this background, the strengthening of the legal framework for extended confiscation was given strategic priority at EU level.[79]

In 2011, the European Parliament urged the European Commission to present a draft on a new directive on confiscation.[80] A proposal was submitted a year later.[81] The legislation was based on an impact assessment,[82] and the need for a new directive was motivated in the following way:

> This proposal for a Directive aims to make it easier for Member States' authorities to confiscate and recover the profits that criminals make from cross-border serious and organised crime. It seeks to attack the financial incentive which drives crime, to protect the licit economy against criminal infiltration and corruption, and to return criminal profits to public authorities providing services for citizens. It responds to the current economic context, where a financial crisis and a slowdown in economic growth creates new opportunities for criminals, increased vulnerabilities in our economy and financial system, and new challenges for public authorities to finance growing needs for social services and assistance.[83]

The European Commission emphasised the very large earnings of organised crime groups, referring to UN estimates, according to which the total value of criminal proceeds in 2009 was approximately US$2.1 trillion, or 3.6 per cent of the global GDP.[84] It was acknowledged that there are no reliable figures on the

---

78 This is further described in Chapter 11 below.

79 See the *2009 Stockholm Programme, "An Open and Secure Europe Serving and Protecting the Citizens"*, Council Document 17024/09, 10–11 December 2009, p. 48, *Justice and Home Affairs Council Conclusions on Confiscation and Asset Recovery adopted in June 2010*, Council document 7769/10, Action 3 in Communication from the Commission to the European Parliament and the Council, *"An Internal Security Strategy in Action"*, COM(2010) 673 final, 22.11.2010, European Parliament, *Report on Organised Crime in the European Union*, 25.10.2011 and *Final Report on the Fifth Round of Mutual Evaluations, Financial Crime and Financial Investigations*, 12657/2/12, Brussels 3.10.2012, p. 28.

80 European Parliament Resolution of 25 October 2011 on Organised Crime in the European Union.

81 *Proposal for a Directive of the European Parliament and of the Council on the Freezing and Confiscation of Proceeds of Crime in the European Union*, COM(2012) 85 final. For an analysis of this proposal, see Boucht, n 67 above.

82 Commission Staff Working Paper, *Accompanying Document to the Proposal for a Directive of the European Parliament and the Council on the Freezing and Confiscation of Proceeds of Crime in the European Union*, SWD(2012) 31 final, Brussels 12.3.2012. Compare also *Study for an Impact Assessment on a Proposal for a New Legal Framework on the Confiscation and Recovery of Criminal Assets*, RAND Europe, 2012 and the Matrix Study, *Assessing the Effectiveness of EU Member States' Practices in the Identification, Tracing, Freezing and Confiscation of Criminal Assets*, Final Report 2009.

83 COM(2012) 85 final, p. 2.

84 United Nations Office on Drugs and Crime, *Estimating Illicit Financial Flows Resulting from Drug Trafficking and other Transnational Organised Crime*, October 2011.

size of criminal profits in the EU, but some statistics from two Member States were presented. In Italy, the proceeds of organised crime laundered, were in 2011 estimated at €150 billion and, in the UK, at £15 billion in 2006.[85] The European Commission also claimed that organised crime groups

> increasingly hide and reinvest assets in Member States other than the one where the crime is committed. This weakens our ability to fight cross-border serious and organised crime in the EU as a whole, and affects the functioning of the Internal Market by distorting competition with legitimate businesses and undermining trust in the financial system. Finally, serious and organised crime deprives national governments and the EU budget of tax revenues.[86]

The existing EU confiscation-regime as well as national laws were classified as "underdeveloped and underutilised".[87] This seems to have been based upon the argument that "the overall amount recovered from crime in the EU remains modest" compared to the estimated revenues of organised criminal groups. In this respect, certain figures from 2009 were cited which showed confiscated assets amounting to €185 million in France, £154 million in the UK, €50 million in the Netherlands and €281 million in Germany.[88]

The proposal for a new directive was discussed and negotiated in the Council. In December 2012, the Council presented a *general approach*, which was a compromise package and adjusted the original proposal from the European Commission in some areas.[89] On 3 April 2014, Directive 2014/42/EU was then finally adopted.[90]

The participating Member States were obligated to implement the directive into national law by 4 October 2016. Ireland takes part in the application of

---

85 COM(2012) 85 final, p. 2.

86 COM(2012) 85 final, p. 2.

87 Major problems with the existing legal framework on confiscation and its implementation had been concluded in Commission Staff Working Paper, *Accompanying Document to the Proposal for a Directive of the European Parliament and the Council on the Freezing and Confiscation of Proceeds of Crime in the European Union*, SWD(2012) 31 final, Brussels 12.3.2012. Compare also the Matrix Study, *Assessing the Effectiveness of EU Member States' Practices in the Identification, Tracing, Freezing and Confiscation of Criminal Assets*, Final Report 2009.

88 COM(2012) 85 final, pp. 2–3.

89 Proposal for a Directive of the European Parliament and of the Council on the Freezing and Confiscation of Proceeds of Crime in the European Union, *General Approach*, Council Document 17117/12, 3.12.2012.

90 Directive 2014/42/EU of the European Parliament and of the Council on the Freezing and Confiscation of Instrumentalities and Proceeds of Crime in the European Union, *OJ* L 127, 29.4.2014, pp. 39–50 and *Corrigendum to the Directive* published on 29 April 2014. See for an analysis of the directive, M. Fazekas and E. Nanopoulos, "The Effectiveness of EU Law: Insights from the EU Legal Framework on Asset Confiscation" (2016) 24 *European Journal of Crime, Criminal Law and Criminal Justice*, pp. 39–64.

the new Directive, but not the UK and Denmark.[91] At the moment, Austria, Cyprus, the Czech Republic, Estonia, Finland, France, Hungary, Italy, Latvia, Luxembourg, Malta, the Netherlands, Romania, Spain and Sweden have adopted national legislation in order to implement the directive.[92]

2.3. DIRECTIVE 2014/42/EU

2.3.1. THE GENERAL FRAMEWORK OF THE DIRECTIVE

The new directive has replaced Joint Action 98/699/JHA on Money Laundering, the Identification, Tracing, Freezing, Seizing and Confiscation of Instrumentalities and the Proceeds from Crime and has in part replaced FD 2001/500/JHA and FD 2005/212/JHA.[93] Accordingly, some of the old EU provisions on confiscation remain in force, both in respect of the offences which are not included in the directive and in relation to Member States which are not participating in the application of the new directive.

Article 1 Directive 2014/42/EU clarifies that it is only establishing *minimum rules* on the freezing and confiscation of property in criminal matters, and that this is without prejudice to the procedures that Member States may use to confiscate property under national law. Accordingly, national legislation on confiscation may be more extensive and provide more potent powers.[94] The overall aim of the directive is to "approximate the Member States' freezing and confiscation regimes, thus facilitating mutual trust and effective cross-border cooperation".[95]

There are no explicit provisions in Directive 2014/42/EU on the transnational judicial cooperation in the area of confiscation. The fact that the directive did not incorporate the *acquis* in relation to international cooperation between judicial and investigative authorities has been regretted by many.[96] However, it has been anticipated that the transnational execution of warrants will be improved by the abolishment of the three alternative grounds for drafting the provision on

---

91 Compare Recitals (42)–(44) Directive 2014/42/EU. Denmark has an opt-out right in the area of EU criminal justice and home affairs. On 3 December 2015 a referendum was held regarding the issue of whether Denmark should abandon some opt-outs in order to be able to participate in certain EU initiatives. However, the Danes did not want to change this situation.

92 As of 9 January 2017, see the homepage of the European Judicial Network, www.ejn-crimjust.eu.

93 Recital (9) and Art. 14 Directive 2014/42/EU.

94 Compare Recital (22) Directive 2014/42/EU.

95 Recital (5) Directive 2014/42/EU.

96 See, for example, Section 1.3 in the *Opinion of the European Economic and Social Committee on the proposal for a directive, OJ* C 299, 4.10.2012, pp. 128–32.

extended confiscation (compare Section 2.1.2 above).[97] In 2016, a proposal on a new instrument on mutual recognition in the area of confiscation was presented (compare further Chapter 12 of this volume).

Article 3 Directive 2014/42/EU gives the *general scope* of application listing certain criminal offences to which it applies:

(a) the Convention drawn up on the basis of Article K.3(2)(c) of the Treaty of the European Union on the fight against corruption involving officials of the European Communities or officials of the Member States of the European Union,[98]
(b) Council Framework Decision 2000/383/JHA of 29 May 2000 on increasing protection by criminal penalties and other sanctions against counterfeiting in connection with the introduction of the euro,[99]
(c) Council Framework Decision 2001/413/JHA of 28 May 2001 on combating fraud and counterfeiting of non-cash means of payment,[100]
(d) Council Framework Decision 2001/500/JHA of 26 June 2001 on money laundering, the identification, tracing, freezing, seizing and confiscation of instrumentalities and the proceeds of crime,[101]
(e) Council Framework Decision 2002/475/JHA of 13 June 2002 on combating terrorism,[102]
(f) Council Framework Decision 2003/568/JHA of 22 July 2003 on combating corruption in the private sector,[103]
(g) Council Framework Decision 2004/757/JHA of 25 October 2004 laying down minimum provisions on the constituent elements of criminal acts and penalties in the field of illicit drug trafficking,[104]
(h) Council Framework Decision 2008/841/JHA of 24 October 2008 on the fight against organised crime,[105]
(i) Directive 2011/36/EU of the European Parliament and of the Council of 5 April 2011 on preventing and combating trafficking in human beings and protecting its victims, and replacing Council Framework Decision 2002/629/JHA,[106]
(j) Directive 2011/93/EU of the European Parliament and of the Council of 13 December 2011 on combating the sexual abuse and sexual exploitation of children and child pornography and replacing Council Framework Decision 2004/68/JHA,[107]

---

97 Recital (19) Directive 2014/42/EU.
98 *OJ* C 195, 25.6.1997, p. 1.
99 *OJ* L 140, 14.6.2000, p. 1.
100 *OJ* L 149, 2.6.2001, p.1.
101 *OJ* L 182, 5.7.2001, p. 1.
102 *OJ* L 164, 22.6.2002, p. 3.
103 *OJ* L 192, 31.7.2003, p. 54.
104 *OJ* L 335, 11.11.2004, p. 8.
105 *OJ* L 300, 11.11.2008, p. 42.
106 *OJ* L 101, 15.4.2011, p. 1.
107 *OJ* L 335, 17.12.2011, p. 1.

(k) Directive 2013/40/EU of the European Parliament and of the Council of 12 August 2013 on attacks against information systems and replacing Council Framework Decision 2005/222/JHA.[108]

Additionally, it is specifically stated in the provision that other legal instruments are also included if those instruments provide that this directive applies to the criminal offences harmonised therein.

Further, the directive contains general definitions of legal concepts (Article 2) and a provision stating an obligation of the Member States to take the necessary measures to enable the freezing of property with a view to confiscation and to take urgent action when necessary in order to preserve property (Article 7).[109]

2.3.2. THE PROVISION ON ORDINARY CONFISCATION

Article 4(1) Directive 2014/42/EU states an obligation for the Member States to provide for ordinary confiscation. The directive hereby sets out a single common standard for the confiscation of criminal proceeds following a final conviction for a criminal offence. Accordingly, it regulates so called *conviction-based confiscation*. The original proposal for a directive from the European Commission (Article 5) contained a provision introducing *non-conviction-based confiscation* into the EU scheme for certain limited cases where a criminal conviction could not be obtained.[110] This proposal was, however, highly controversial and much debated in the Council as well as in the Parliament. Even if many EU Member States have not adopted such a system, there are sometimes limited possibilities to confiscate property without a previous conviction in certain cases. However in the end the provision was deleted, as many Member States argued that such a system would be in violation with the presumption of innocence in Article 6

---

108 *OJ* L 218, 14.8.2013, p. 8.

109 The provision on freezing of property is further discussed in Section 10.2.3 below.

110 The provision was inspired by *inter alia* the UN Convention against Corruption, see COM(2012) 85 final, p. 11. For a critical analysis of the proposal on non-conviction-based confiscation, see for example J.P. Rui, "Non-conviction based Confiscation in the European Union – an Assessment of Art. 5 of the Proposal for a Directive of the European Parliament and of the Council on the Freezing and Confiscation of Proceeds of Crime in the European Union" (2012) 13 *ERA Forum*, pp. 349–60 and F. Alagna, "Non-conviction Based Confiscation: Why the EU Directive is a Missed Opportunity" (2015) 21 *European Journal on Criminal Policy and Research*, pp. 447–64. See generally on non-conviction-based confiscation in Europe, P. Rui and U. Sieber (eds.), *Non-Conviction-Based Confiscation in Europe: Possibilities and Limitations on Rules Enabling Confiscation without a Criminal Conviction*, Berlin, 2015. Compare also Section 1.1 above.

of the European Convention on Human Rights (ECHR).[111] Nevertheless, it was agreed that the European Commission should carry out a more extensive study of the necessity and requirements for an EU civil confiscation scheme.[112] In September and November 2016, different expert meetings regarding this issue were organised, and the European Commission has envisaged a feasibility analysis in 2017.[113]

At present only a limited provision on confiscation without a criminal conviction has been agreed upon. According to Article 4(1) of the directive, it covers only confiscation measures following a final conviction for a criminal offence. (This may also result from proceedings in absentia). However, Article 4(2) obligates the Member States to enable confiscation *without a final conviction* at least in cases where a suspect or accused person is ill or has absconded.[114] For such cases it is required that criminal proceedings *have been initiated* regarding a criminal offence and that such proceedings *could have led to a criminal conviction* if the suspected or accused person had been able to stand trial.[115] In legal doctrine, it has been argued that this provision should in fact not be construed as a provision on non-conviction-based confiscation in the traditional sense, but rather as something between this and a conviction-based system.[116]

---

111 For information on the availability of non-conviction-based confiscation in the Member States and their views on EU wide provisions in this respect, see for example Proposal for a Directive of the European Parliament and the Council on the Freezing and Confiscation of Proceeds of Crime in the European Union, *Compilation of replies to questionnaire*, 12219/2/12, REV 2, Brussels 20.7.2012.

112 See for example the *Joint Statement by the European Parliament and the Council* issued upon the adoption of Directive 2014/42/EU, Council of the European Union, Document No. 7329/1/14, COPEN 83, Brussels 31.3.2014, p. 1. Obviously, the Member States with non-conviction-based confiscation systems view the directive as a missed opportunity in this respect. They saw a need to harmonise and introduce such a measure on a European-wide basis, mainly due to difficulties in getting national warrants executed abroad. See on this Alagna, n 110 above and A. Balsamo, "The Delocalisation of Mafia Organisations and the Construction of a European Law against Organised Crime" (2016) 17 *Global Crime*, p. 99, pp. 113–14. Compare further Section 11.2.3 below on international cooperation.

113 See COM(2016) 819 final, Brussels 21.12.2016, p. 3.

114 The death of a suspect or accused was also a criterion for non-conviction-based confiscation during the legislative process, but was deleted in the final version. Compare Art. 5(a), COM(2012) 85 final. Especially Germany opposed such a provision out of consideration for any heirs.

115 See also Recital (15), Directive 2014/42/EU. The requirement that "such proceedings could have led to a criminal conviction" can be considered as rather vague. In many cases it must be very difficult to assess this criterion.

116 See further Rui, n 110 above and Alagna, n 110 above. Compare also on the provisions on non-conviction-based confiscation in Directive 2014/42/EU, M. Simonato, "Directive 2014/42/EU and Non-Conviction based Confiscation: a Step Forward on Asset Recovery?" (2015) 6 *New Journal of European Criminal Law*, pp. 213–28.

2.3.3. THE PROVISION ON EXTENDED CONFISCATION

Directive 2014/42/EU aims at providing more potent powers of extended confiscation. According to the European Commission the old EU provisions are "unclear" and have been transposed "piecemeal".[117] The most important reform in this respect is the change to one single standard for national legislation by *abolishing the three alternative solutions* which are allowed by FD 2005/212/JHA.[118] Article 5(1) therefore provides that:

> Member States shall adopt the necessary measures to enable the confiscation, either in whole or in part, of property belonging to a person convicted of a criminal offence which is liable to give rise, directly or indirectly, to economic benefit, where a court, on the basis of the circumstances of the case, including the specific facts and available evidence, such as that the value of the property is disproportionate to the lawful income of the convicted person, is satisfied that the property in question is derived from criminal conduct.

A first requirement for extended confiscation is thus that a person must be convicted of a criminal offence which is liable to give rise, directly or indirectly, to economic benefit. Article 5(2) specifically lists the criminal offences to which extended confiscation *at least* shall apply:

> (a) active and passive corruption in the private sector, as provided for in Article 2 of Framework Decision 2003/568/JHA, as well as active and passive corruption involving officials of institutions of the Union or of the Member States, as provided for in Articles 2 and 3 respectively of the Convention on the fight against corruption involving officials;
> (b) offences relating to participation in a criminal organisation, as provided for in Article 2 of Framework Decision 2008/841/JHA, at least in cases where the offence has led to economic benefit;
> (c) causing or recruiting a child to participate in pornographic performances, or profiting from or otherwise exploiting a child for such purposes if the child is over the age of sexual consent, as provided for in Article 4(2) of Directive 2011/93/EU; distribution, dissemination or transmission of child pornography, as provided for in Article 5(4) of that Directive; offering, supplying or making available child pornography, as provided for in Article 5(5) of that Directive; production of child pornography, as provided for in Article 5(6) of that Directive;
> (d) illegal system interference and illegal data interference, as provided for in Articles 4 and 5 respectively of Directive 2013/40/EU, where a significant number of information systems have been affected through the use of a tool, as provided

117 COM(2012) 85 final, p. 10.
118 COM(2012) 85 final, pp. 10–11.

for in Article 7 of that Directive, designed or adapted primarily for that purpose; the intentional production, sale, procurement for use, import, distribution or otherwise making available of tools used for committing offences, at least for cases which are not minor, as provided for in Article 7 of that Directive;

(e) a criminal offence that is punishable, in accordance with the relevant instrument in Article 3 or, in the event that the instrument in question does not contain a penalty threshold, in accordance with the relevant national law, by a custodial sentence of a maximum of at least four years.

This means that the general scope of Directive 2014/42/EU given by Article 3 (see Section 2.3.1 above) is limited when it comes to the measure of extended confiscation.

A decision on extended confiscation will be possible in cases where a court – on the basis of the circumstances of the case – "*is satisfied*" that the property in question is derived from criminal conduct. It is unclear how the standard of "satisfied" should be interpreted in the evidentiary context, but Recital (21) explains that:

> Extended confiscation should be possible where a court is satisfied that the property in question is derived from criminal conduct. This does not mean that it must be established that the property in question is derived from criminal conduct. Member States may provide that it could, for example, be sufficient for the court to consider on the balance of probabilities, or to reasonably presume that it is substantially more probable, that the property in question has been obtained from criminal conduct than from other activities. In this context, the court has to consider the specific circumstances of the case, including the facts and available evidence based on which a decision on extended confiscation could be issued. The fact that the property of the person is disproportionate to his lawful income could be among those facts giving rise to a conclusion of the court that the property derives from criminal conduct. Member States could also determine a requirement for a certain period of time during which the property could be deemed to have originated from criminal conduct.

Article 5(1) as well as Recital (21) especially mention the financial circumstances of a defendant as a certain circumstance which may be taken account of. The current standard of evidence provided for by Article 3(2) FD 2005/212/JHA is that a court is to be "*fully convinced*", which seems to indicate a requirement of full proof.[119] The use of "satisfied" in Directive 2014/42/EU thus indicates a lowering of the standard of proof in this respect. However, the formulation is rather vague, and it may be expected that many Member States will continue to apply the evidentiary standard chosen in national law. The interpretation of the

---

119 Compare Section 2.1.2 above.

evidentiary standard and its implications for national legislation will be further discussed (see especially Section 7.4.2 below).

2.3.4. THIRD PARTY CONFISCATION

According to the European Commission, mutual recognition of confiscation orders is sometimes hampered due to differences in legislation regarding third party confiscation in the Member States.[120] The practice of suspects to transfer property to a knowing third party with a view to avoiding confiscation is supposed to be "common and increasingly widespread".[121] As further described in Section 2.1.3 above, FD 2005/212/JHA only contain a rather limited *optional* rule. In order to overcome such shortcomings and to create a binding obligation for the Member States, Article 6 Directive 2014/42/EU provides that the necessary measures shall be taken to enable that property transferred to third parties may be confiscated at least if those third parties knew or ought to have known that the purpose of the transfer was to avoid confiscation.[122] A closer definition of such "bad faith" is not given in the directive, but it is stated that this must be based on concrete circumstances, for example that the transfer or sale was for free or under the market value.[123] Rights of bona fide third parties are not to be prejudiced.

2.3.5. PROCEDURAL SAFEGUARDS

Against the background that confiscation orders may interfere with the right to property or other fundamental human rights, affected parties must be able to challenge such orders in an effective way. Directive 2014/42/EU sets down certain concrete minimum standards for procedural rights at EU level. This has been motivated by the need to fully comply with the EU Charter of Fundamental Rights, especially when it comes to the respect for the presumption of innocence, the right to a fair trial, the existence of effective judicial remedies before a court

---

120 COM(2012) 85 final, 12.3.2012, p. 12.

121 Compare Recital (24) Directive 2014/42/EU.

122 Compare also Recitals (24)–(25) Directive 2014/42/EU.

123 Such circumstances are already commonly used in many national legal systems to define bad faith by third persons. See, for example, the comparative study of acquisition of ownership and bad faith in the legal systems of Germany and the UK, A. Rahmatian, "A Comparison of German Moveable Property Law and English Personal Property Law" (2010) 3 *Journal of Comparative Law*, pp. 197–248.

and the right to be informed on how to exercise such remedies.[124] It is also in line with the general measures within the EU to strengthen the procedural rights of suspected and accused persons in criminal proceedings.[125]

The following important rights have been included in Article 8:

1. Member States shall take the necessary measures to ensure that the persons affected by the measures provided for under this Directive have the right to an effective remedy and a fair trial in order to uphold their rights.
2. Member States shall take the necessary measures to ensure that the freezing order is communicated to the affected person as soon as possible after its execution. Such communication shall indicate, at least briefly, the reason or reasons for the order concerned. When it is necessary to avoid jeopardising a criminal investigation, the competent authorities may postpone communicating the freezing order to the affected person.
3. The freezing order shall remain in force only for as long as it is necessary to preserve the property with a view to possible subsequent confiscation.
4. Member States shall provide for the effective possibility for the person whose property is affected to challenge the freezing order before a court, in accordance with procedures provided for in national law. Such procedures may provide that when the initial freezing order has been taken by a competent authority other than a judicial authority, such order shall first be submitted for validation or review to a judicial authority before it can be challenged before a court.
5. Frozen property which is not subsequently confiscated shall be returned immediately. The conditions or procedural rules under which such property is returned shall be determined by national law.
6. Member States shall take the necessary measures to ensure that reasons are given for any confiscation order and that the order is communicated to the person affected. Member States shall provide for the effective possibility for a person in respect of whom confiscation is ordered to challenge the order before a court.
7. Without prejudice to Directive 2012/13/EU and Directive 2013/48/EU, persons whose property is affected by a confiscation order shall have the right of access to a lawyer throughout the confiscation proceedings relating to the determination of the proceeds and instrumentalities in order to uphold their rights. The persons concerned shall be informed of that right.

124 COM(2012) 85 final, p. 13.

125 See for example *Roadmap on Procedural Rights*, *OJ* C 295, 4.12.2009, pp. 1–3, Directive on the Right to Information in Criminal Proceedings, *OJ* L 142, 1.6.2012, pp. 1–10 and Directive on the Right of Access to a Lawyer in Criminal Proceedings and in European Arrest Warrant Proceedings, and on the Right to have a Third Party Informed upon Deprivation of Liberty and to Communicate with Third Persons and with Consular Authorities while Deprived of Liberty, *OJ* L 294, 6.11.2013, pp. 1–12.

8. In proceedings referred to in Article 5, the affected person shall have an effective possibility to challenge the circumstances of the case, including specific facts and available evidence on the basis of which the property concerned is considered to be property that is derived from criminal conduct.
9. Third parties shall be entitled to claim title of ownership or other property rights, including in the cases referred to in Article 6.
10. Where, as a result of a criminal offence, victims have claims against the person who is subject to a confiscation measure provided for under this Directive, Member States shall take the necessary measures to ensure that the confiscation measure does not prevent those victims from seeking compensation for their claims.

The new directive means a significant improvement in this area, because the provision on procedural rights in FD 2005/212/JHA merely states that Member States are required to have "adequate legal remedies". However, it remains to be seen how the procedural rights in Article 8 will be interpreted and whether they are sufficient to really make a difference. This will be further discussed, especially in Sections 7.7 and 12.10 below.

CHAPTER 3

LEGISLATION IN ENGLAND AND WALES

3.1. THE DEVELOPMENT OF THE LEGISLATION ON EXTENDED CONFISCATION IN ENGLAND AND WALES

The need for powers to confiscate the proceeds of crime in the context of a criminal conviction came into focus in the UK in connection with a police operation named "Julie" during 1978. Over years, several defendants had manufactured and sold large quantities of LSD. The police had seized cash, cars and other property to a value of £750,000, and it was claimed by the prosecution in the criminal proceedings that this represented the proceeds of narcotics offences. However, in the judgments which followed (e.g. the *Cuthbertson* case) the courts came to different conclusions. The first trial judge made an order for confiscation, which was upheld by the Court of Appeal. In the House of Lords this decision was "with considerable regret" overturned with the argument that the legislation in force did not permit the confiscation of the profits or proceeds of crime, but only regarded things "related to the offence".[126] The seized assets were thus returned to the defendants under public outcry. The government established the so-called Hodgson Committee with the task of giving proposals for a new confiscation regime.[127] The report, which was published in 1984, recommended a new power of confiscation.

In 1986, provisions on the confiscation of the proceeds of crime were introduced by the Drug Trafficking Offences Act 1986. This measure was initially only applicable in drug-trafficking cases, but was then extended by the Criminal Justice Act 1988 to also embrace any indictable offence and certain other offences. The purpose for adopting such legislation was to ensure that offenders were deprived of the proceeds from criminal conduct, and thereby also to create a certain deterrent effect, especially regarding serious organised crime. During the following years, the confiscation regime was extended by several new pieces of legislation, for example the Criminal Justice (International Cooperation) Act 1990, the Drug Trafficking Act 1994 and the Proceeds of Crime Act 1995.

---

126 *R v. Cuthbertson*, [1980] 2 All ER 401, [1981] AC 470.

127 See Hodgson Committee, *The Profits of Crime and their Recovery*, 1984.

In 1998, the Performance and Innovation Unit ("PIU") of the Cabinet Office was given the task to evaluate and examine how the existing regime could be further improved in terms of efficiency. The report was published in 2000 and contained several proposals for new legislation.[128] An overall conclusion was that the existing legislation had been developed in a piecemeal fashion, was difficult to apply and that the tool of confiscation was underexploited.[129]

In July 2002 the Proceeds of Crime Act 2002 (hereinafter referred to as "POCA 2002") received Royal Assent.[130] Part 2 of this Act – which came into force on 24 March 2003 – provides powers for the courts in England and Wales to make confiscation orders following a conviction for a criminal offence. Thereby this part of POCA 2002 extended and replaced the schemes set out in Part 1 of the Drug Trafficking Act 1994 and Part 6 of the Criminal Justice Act 1988, creating a single consolidated piece of legislation.[131] In addition to more far-reaching powers for confiscation, POCA 2002 also reformed the offence of money laundering[132] and introduced the Assets Recovery Agency ("ARA"), which was a new authority with special responsibility for restoring the proceeds of crime to the state.[133] Furthermore, new powers were introduced to recover criminal assets through civil proceedings without the need for a conviction in a criminal case.

---

128 *Recovering the Proceeds of Crime*, A Performance and Innovation Unit Report, June 2000.

129 Compare a review of the British experience of confiscation legislation until 1995 performed by Levi, who argues that the strategy of asset recovery had led to only a small proportion of proceeds recovered, with little effect on organised crime. See M. Levi, "Taking the Profit Out of Crime: The UK Experience" (1997) 5 *European Journal of Crime, Criminal Law and Criminal Justice*, pp. 228–39 and M. Levi and L. Osofsky, *Investigating, Seizing and Confiscating the Proceeds of Crime*, Crime Detection and Prevention Series Paper 61, Police Research Group, 1995.

130 For the legal text of POCA 2002, see www.legislation.gov.uk. See also the *Explanatory Notes to the Proceeds of Crime Act 2002* ("*Explanatory Notes to POCA 2002*"). This commentary has been prepared by the Home Office in order to assist in the understanding of the law. However, the notes do not form part of the law and have not been endorsed by Parliament. See also *National Best Practice Guide to Confiscation Order Enforcement*. Both this guide and the Explanatory Notes to POCA 2002 may be found on www.legislation.gov.uk. See also the 2004 study of the operational effectiveness of POCA 2002, *Payback Time: Joint Review of Asset Recovery Since, the Proceeds of Crime Act 2002*, 11 November 2004.

131 For a description of the legal situation before POCA 2002, see R. Alexander, "Do the UK's Provisions for Confiscation Orders breach the European Convention on Human Rights?" (2000) 3 *Journal of Money Laundering Control*, p. 297, pp. 297–99, M. Raphael, "Tracing and Confiscating Illicit Proceeds: the Perspective of the Defence" (2011) 11 *ERA Forum*, p. 545, pp. 545–48, N. Ryder, "To Confiscate or not to Confiscate? A Comparative Analysis of the Confiscation of the Proceeds of Crime Legislation in the United States and the United Kingdom" (2013) 8 *Journal of Business Law*, p. 767, pp. 784–86, D. McClean, *International Cooperation in Civil and Criminal Matters*, Oxford University Press, 2002, pp. 301–17 and A. Kennedy, "An Evaluation of the Recovery of Criminal Proceeds in the United Kingdom" (2007) 10 *Journal of Money Laundering Control*, p. 33, pp. 33–34. A short overview of successive changes in law to English confiscation legislation is further given in a judgment from the House of Lords, *R v. May*, [2008] UKHL 28.

132 Part 7 POCA 2002.

133 Part 1 POCA 2002.

There are currently some provisions allowing for confiscation in connection with crime elsewhere in British legislation, for example in the area of terrorism. However, in this study only the central provisions of POCA 2002 will be described. This Act has been changed on several occasions through new legislation, e.g. by the Serious Organised Crime and Police Act 2005 and the Serious Crime Act 2007. Thereby the ARA was for example merged with the Serious Organised Crime Agency ("SOCA").[134] This agency was then in 2013 replaced by the National Crime Agency ("NCA").[135] On 1 June 2015 changes to the confiscation process in POCA 2002 were also made by Part 1 of the Serious Crime Act 2015. This Act gave effect to a number of legislative proposals set out in the Government's *Serious and Organised Crime Strategy*,[136] for example it created a new offence of participating in activities of organised crime groups.[137] The Serious Crime Act 2015 gave the law-enforcement agencies more far-reaching powers in many areas of confiscation law. Some of these changes will be referred to in the following.

In October 2016, the Criminal Finances Bill 2016–2017 was presented, which consists of new legislation in order to tackle money laundering, corruption, and counter terrorism financing. This piece of law also aims at improving the system of POCA 2002 in some areas. The law enforcement agencies will, for example, be given new powers to seize the proceeds of crime. A new measure of "unexplained wealth orders" has also been proposed, which will require an individual suspected of serious criminality to explain the origins of their wealth or face civil recovery action. The new Bill is at the moment being processed.

3.2. OVERVIEW OF POCA 2002

POCA 2002 is a very comprehensive and complicated piece of legislation consisting of 12 parts (over 450 sections!).[138] The aim of the legislation is to

[134] See Sec. 74 Serious Crime Act 2007 and Serious Organised Crime and Police Act 2005.

[135] Part 1 Crime and Courts Act 2013. See for criticism against the many changes of the UK's confiscation agency, Ryder, n 131 above, pp. 796–98.

[136] HM Government, *Serious and Organised Crime Strategy*, Cm 8715, October 2013.

[137] Part 3 Serious Crime Act 2015.

[138] For a description and analysis of the regime of confiscation in the UK, see for example *Mitchell, Taylor and Talbot on Confiscation and the Proceeds of Crime*, 3rd edn, Sweet and Maxwell, 2016, *Millington, Sutherland and Williams on the Proceeds of Crime*, 4th edn, Oxford University Press, 2013, A. Eissa and R. Barber, *Confiscation Law Handbook*, Bloomsbury Professional, 2011, A. Giles, "The Assessment of Benefit under Part 2 of the Proceeds of Crime Act 2002: a Sledgehammer to Crack a Nut?" (2013) 1 *Plymouth Law and Criminal Justice Review*, p. 85, D. Dickson, "Towards More Effective Asset Recovery in Member States – the UK example" (2009) 10 *ERA Forum*, pp. 435–51, Ryder, n 131 above, B. Vettori, *Tough on Criminal Wealth: Exploring the Practice of Proceeds from Crime Confiscation in the EU*, Springer, 2006, pp. 104–09 and Kennedy, n 131 above. On the Crown Prosecution Service

"prevent the enjoyment of the fruits of criminal activity".[139] In view of the extensive tools for confiscation provided by POCA 2002, it has been suggested that the UK possesses one of the world's most comprehensive pieces of criminal assets legislation.[140] The legislation provides for *four different means* to recover the proceeds of crime:

(1) confiscation orders following a conviction for a criminal offence (Parts 2–4),
(2) civil recovery of the proceeds etc. of unlawful conduct (Part 5),
(3) taxation (Part 6), and
(4) civil recovery of cash (Part 5, Chapter 3).

Whereas a confiscation order requires a criminal conviction (i.e. the identification of a specific crime), there is no such requirement for the measures pursuant to paragraphs 2–4. The power of civil recovery allows for confiscation of property obtained through unlawful conduct.[141] The procedure is known as "*in rem* proceedings", i.e. it is directed towards particular property and not – as for confiscation orders – towards a person ("*in personam* proceedings").[142] In case-law, the difference between such measures has been explained in the way that a confiscation order "focuses on the criminal" whereas civil recovery "concentrates on the fruits of crime themselves".[143]

Part 5 Chapter 3 of POCA 2002 provides for a UK-wide regime for the recovery of cash in summary proceedings.[144] These provisions empower a customs officer or police constable to seize any cash exceeding £1,000 if there are reasonable grounds for suspecting that it is obtained by unlawful conduct or intended for use by any person in unlawful conduct.[145] There must be objective grounds for any suspicions, based on the context and circumstances of each situation. Within 48 hours an application to the Magistrates' Court must be

("CPS") website there is exhaustive guidance and several directions on confiscation matters, see www.cps.uk. See also report from the joint assessment within the EU, Council of the European Union, *Report on the United Kingdom*, 9636/2/10, REV 2, p. 70, *Payback Time: Joint Review of Asset Recovery since the Proceeds of Crime Act 2002*, published on 1 November 2004 and *Study for an Impact Assessment on a Proposal for a New Legal Framework on the Confiscation and Recovery of Criminal Assets*, RAND Europe, 2012, Appendix I.

139 See for example para. 1 *Gale and Another (Appellants) v. Serious Organised Crime Agency (Respondent)*, [2011] UKSC 49.

140 Kennedy, n 131 above.

141 Such conduct is defined in Secs. 240–242 POCA 2002.

142 See further on civil recovery, J.P. Rui, "The Civil Asset Forfeiture Approach to Organised Crime" (2011) 4 *eucrim*, pp. 153–61 and Kennedy, n 131 above, pp. 37–40.

143 See for example paras. 1–2 *Gale and Another (Appellants) v. Serious Organised Crime Agency (Respondent)*, [2011] UKSC 49.

144 Cash is defined as also including, for example, cheques of any kind or bankers' drafts. See Part 5, Ch. 3, Sec. 289(6) POCA 2002.

145 Part 5, Ch. 3, Sec. 294 POCA 2002.

made, which can extend the period of detention for a certain period and this process can be repeated up to a maximum of two years' detention.[146] During this time, the police must investigate the origins of the cash. At any time during detention an application for permanent forfeiture of the cash may be made to the Magistrates' Court.[147] The proceedings in this court are civil proceedings and no conviction is required for the forfeiture of the cash to be ordered. The civil standard of proof applies, i.e. the court need only be satisfied on the balance of probabilities that the cash has been obtained by unlawful conduct or intended for use in such conduct.[148]

Civil recovery according to Part 5 of POCA 2002 may be brought whether or not proceedings have been brought for an offence in connection with the property.[149] Accordingly, it may be used in cases where a suspected person has escaped or has died, but also in cases where there are insufficient grounds for prosecution or even after an acquittal in a criminal case.[150] An example of such a case is *Gale and Another (Appellants) v. Serious Organised Crime Agency* where a Civil Recovery Order of property to the value of some £2 million was brought under Part 5 of POCA 2002 against a married couple for property alleged to have been derived from narcotics crime, money laundering and tax evasion in the UK, Spain, Portugal and other jurisdictions. It was in that case considered irrelevant that neither of them had been prosecuted or convicted for such crimes in the UK. Nor was it of significance that Mr Gale had been *acquitted* of narcotics crime in Portugal, and that a prosecution for drugs crime had been dropped in Spain.[151] Mr Gale argued before the courts that the recovery orders violated the presumption of innocence in Article 6(2) ECHR and that the criminal standard of proof must be applied to the question of whether property derive from crime. The Supreme Court dismissed the appeal, ruling that it was proved on a balance of probabilities that the property had been derived through unlawful conduct. However, the Court held that there was some inconsistency in the Strasbourg case-law regarding the application of Article 6(2) ECHR in civil proceedings following an acquittal in criminal proceedings. At the moment an application before the ECtHR has been lodged, and the applicants complain under Article

[146] Part 5, Ch. 3, Sec. 295 POCA 2002.

[147] Part 5, Ch. 3, Sec. 298 POCA 2002.

[148] See K. Mahmutaj, "Cash forfeiture following Acquittal: 'An Affront to Public Perception' or a Breach of a Fundamental Human Right?" (2009) 11 *Criminal Law Review*, pp. 783–93 for a discussion of the cash forfeiture regime under Part 5 POCA 2002. The author argues *inter alia* that some cases of cash forfeiture following acquittal may violate Art. 6(2) ECHR.

[149] Sec. 240(2) POCA 2002 and *Explanatory Notes to POCA 2002* p. 47.

[150] For a legislative background to the introduction of "civil recovery powers", see for example *Director of Assets Recovery Agency and Others v. Green and Others*, [2005] EWHC 3168 (Admin).

[151] *Gale and Another (Appellants) v. Serious Organised Crime Agency (Respondent)*, [2011] UKSC 49.

6(1) and (2) ECHR that as a result of the acquittal in the Portuguese proceedings, there should be no further proceedings making the same allegations in a civil proceeding, or alternatively that the criminal standard of proof must be applied.[152] It remains to be seen how the European court will decide on the issue.

POCA 2002 contains no provision on whether the criminal route or the civil route has precedence. During the legislative process it was emphasised that civil recovery should not be used *instead* of criminal proceedings. During the debate in the House of Lords, the Attorney General (Lord Goldsmith) stressed that the law enforcement authorities must ensure in every case that the possibilities for bringing a criminal prosecution have been fully considered:

> It is clear from the hierarchy which has been identified that the prosecution of offences will remain the priority in all cases. That is not intended as a soft option. For example, it is made clear in the draft guidance that it would not be a proper exercise of the prosecutorial discretion – there are two tests for prosecution, the evidential and the public interest test – to say that in the public interest there is no need to prosecute because there is the alternative of civil recovery.
>
> However, in what kinds of cases may civil recovery take place? One example would be where the law enforcement authority has carried out a criminal investigation and consulted the prosecuting authority and a decision not to institute criminal proceedings has been taken applying normal evidential and public interest criteria. I acknowledge that that would be such a case, but I emphasise that the decision not to prosecute would be taken without regard to whether civil recovery may be available.[153]

The relationship between criminal confiscation orders and civil recovery is described in the following manner in the guidelines regarding the application of POCA 2002, which have been issued by the Secretary of State and the Attorney General:

> 1. The reduction of crime is in general best secured by means of criminal investigations and criminal proceedings. However, the non-conviction based asset recovery powers available under the Act can also make an important contribution to the reduction of crime where (i) it is not feasible to secure a conviction, (ii) a conviction is obtained but a confiscation order is not made, or (iii) a relevant authority is of the view that the public interest will be better served by using those powers rather than by seeking a criminal disposal.[154]

152 Appl. No. 25092/12, lodged on 16 April 2012.

153 Hansard, 13.5.2002, col. 72.

154 See www.gov.uk/asset-recovery-powers-for-prosecutors-guidance-and-background-note-2009.

In the light of the purpose of this book, the following description of the confiscation regime will only deal with conviction-based confiscation, i.e. confiscation orders. POCA 2002 introduced a UK-wide system of confiscation orders; Part 2 concerns England and Wales, Part 3 governs Scotland and Part 4 provides for legislation for Northern Ireland. The provisions are similar but, as Scotland and Northern Ireland have their own legal systems for example regarding competent authorities, there was a need for separate sections.[155] For purposes of simplification, this study will exclusively consider the provisions in England and Wales.

By way of introduction, it may be mentioned that the UK decided during the negotiations of the new instrument not to take part in the application of Directive 2014/42/EU. Even though this directive was broadly in line with existing UK legislation and practice, it was not considered to offer any direct benefit to the national system and even to undermine and weaken the civil recovery powers.[156] It was therefore argued that there was a risk that its participation in the EU instrument might result in an obligation to assert more stringent criminal law standards and safeguards in this area.

3.3. CONFISCATION ORDERS PURSUANT TO PART 2 OF POCA 2002

3.3.1. INTRODUCTION

As mentioned in the previous section, confiscation orders are only available following a conviction for a criminal offence. A further requirement is that the offence has resulted in financial benefit. The purpose of confiscation proceedings is to recover the financial benefit that the offender has obtained from his criminal conduct.[157] A confiscation order pursuant to POCA 2002 means that an obligation is imposed on a defendant to pay a sum of money to the state, and not to hand over any particular item of property.[158] The order must be paid out of any assets held by a defendant and it is up to him to convert assets in order to pay

155 *Explanatory Notes to POCA 2002*, p. 38.

156 Compare Recitals (42)–(44) in Directive 2014/42/EU. See further on the opt-out arrangement for the UK, D. Brodowski, "Strafrechtsrelevante Entwicklungen in der Europäischen Union – ein Überblick" (2015) 1 *ZIS*, p. 79, pp. 82–83, E. De Busser, "The Lisbon after-burn effect" (2015) 16 *ERA Forum*, pp. 1–13 and E. Baker, "The United Kingdom and its Protocol 36 Opt-Out: Is Police and Judicial Cooperation in Criminal Matters within the EU Losing Momentum?" (2013) 21 *European Journal of Crime, Criminal Law and Criminal Justice*, pp. 237–45.

157 *Explanatory Notes to POCA 2002*, p. 1.

158 Dickson, n 138 above, p. 437.

the amount in question. The regime may thus be defined as value-based,[159] and the term "confiscation order" has been designated a "misnomer", as a decision does not mean that specific assets are to be confiscated:

> Although "confiscation" is the name ordinarily given to this process, it is not confiscation in the sense in which schoolchildren and others understand it. A criminal caught in possession of criminally-acquired assets will, it is true, suffer their seizure by the state. Where, however, a criminal has benefited financially from crime but no longer possesses the specific fruits of his crime, he will be deprived of assets of equivalent value, if he has them. The object is to deprive him, directly or indirectly, of what he has gained. "Confiscation" is, as Lord Hobhouse of Woodborough observed in *In re Norris* [2001] UKHL 34, [2001] 1 WLR 1388, Para 12, a misnomer.[160]

Only Crown Courts are competent to issue a confiscation order. Magistrates' Courts no longer have this competence, but – after conviction in such a court – the matter can be *referred* to the Crown Court for sentencing, which can mean that a confiscation order will be considered.[161] New legislation has, however, been envisaged in order to allow the Magistrates' Courts to hear cases regarding confiscation orders of a lower value (i.e. below £10,000).

Confiscation proceedings are initiated by the prosecutor, but the court has also the power *ex officio* to consider confiscation.[162] The confiscation procedures are mandatory; if there is a plea for confiscation it is *obligatory* for the court to consider the matter.[163] However, there is an exception in cases where a victim of the criminal conduct has started or intends to bring civil proceedings against a defendant and the offender has insufficient means. In such a case, the court has been given discretion to decide whether to make a confiscation order and to set an amount which the court believes as just.[164] In the light of the fact that it is mandatory for the court to hold a confiscation hearing if the prosecutor so requests, it is of great importance that the prosecution authority gives the matter due consideration.[165] In *R v. Paulet* the Court of Appeal stated that it

---

159 See, for example, Council of the European Union, *Report on the United Kingdom*, 9636/2/10, REV 2, p. 67 and P. Alldridge, "The Limits of Confiscation" (2011) 11 *Criminal Law Review*, p. 827, p. 827.

160 Para. 9, *R v. May*, [2008] UKHL 28. Compare para. 2, *R v. Waya*, [2012] UKSC 51.

161 See on the competence of the Crown Court, Sec. 6(1)–(2) POCA 2002.

162 Sec. 6(3) POCA 2002.

163 Compare *Explanatory Notes to POCA 2002*, p. 5 and Sec. 6 POCA 2002, which states that the Crown Court "must proceed under this section". A strict obligation for the court to consider a confiscation order under the conditions stipulated in law had already been introduced by the Proceeds of Crime Act 1995, where the discretion which the courts previously had enjoyed was abolished.

164 Compare Secs. 6(6) and 7(3) POCA 2002.

165 See *Legal Guidance on the Proceeds of Crime*, at www.cps.gov.uk.

may in limited and exceptional cases be considered oppressive to initiate confiscation proceedings, and suggested that the prosecution authorities should be given guidelines as to the policy to be followed in order to establish a uniform approach.[166] In May 2009, the *Guidance for Prosecutors on the discretion to instigate confiscation proceedings* was issued. The prosecutors were thereby encouraged to use their discretion whether or not to initiate confiscation proceedings in accordance with the three established aims of confiscation set out in case-law:

- to punish convicted offenders,
- to deter the commission of further offences, and
- to reduce the profits available to fund further criminal enterprises.[167]

The *Guidance* further emphasises that the prosecutors need to consider in every case whether the statutory provisions on confiscation would operate in a way that would be oppressive.

3.3.2. A TWIN TRACK CONFISCATION SYSTEM

Pursuant to Section 6(4) POCA 2002 the Crown Court must proceed as follows when confiscation proceedings are initiated:

(a) it must decide whether the defendant has a criminal lifestyle;
(b) if it decides that he has a criminal lifestyle, it must decide whether he has benefited from his general criminal conduct;
(c) if it decides that he does not have a criminal lifestyle, it must decide whether he has benefited from his particular criminal conduct.

Accordingly, the first central issue for the court to decide is whether a defendant has a *criminal lifestyle*. The *Explanatory Notes to POCA 2002* explain this mode of approach as follows:

> Section 6 also makes it clear that Part 2 provides for confiscation of the defendant's benefit from either his "general criminal conduct" or his "particular criminal conduct".

---

166 See Secs. 20–22, [2009] EWCA Crim 288.

167 See for example para. 14, *R v. Rezvi*, [2002] UKHL 1. In exceptional cases where the prosecutorial discretion has been misused, the court has a power to stay proceedings as an "abuse of process". This matter was discussed in e.g. *Shabir v. R*, [2008] EWCA Crim 1809, *R v. Morgan and Bygrave*, [2008] EWCA Crim 1323 and *R v. Baden Lowe*, [2009] EWCA Crim 194. Compare also para. 11, *R v. Farquhar*, [2008] EWCA Crim 806. See further Sections 3.6.3. and 3.6.4. below.

> General criminal conduct means any criminal conduct of the defendant's, whenever the conduct occurred (see section 76) and whether or not it has ever formed the subject of any criminal prosecution. Particular criminal conduct means the offences of which the defendant has been convicted in the current proceedings, together with any taken into consideration by the court in passing sentence (again, see section 76). So general criminal conduct includes particular criminal conduct.[168]

The terms "*criminal lifestyle confiscation*" (corresponding to "general criminal conduct") or "*criminal conduct confiscation*" (corresponding to "particular criminal conduct") are sometimes invoked to distinguish between the different forms of confiscation governed by Section 6(4) POCA 2002. A conviction for any offence may result in confiscation proceedings being started under POCA 2002, but certain listed crimes trigger the "classification" of a defendant in a group which has a criminal lifestyle which gives rise to more far-reaching powers of confiscation.[169] The motive for concentrating the entire application of the English legislation on the central decisive issue of establishing a *criminal lifestyle* has been explained in the following way:

> The criminal lifestyle regime is based on the principle that an offender who gives reasonable grounds to believe that he is living off crime should be required to account for his assets, and should have them confiscated to the extent that he is unable to account for their lawful origin. The criminal lifestyle tests, therefore, are designed to identify offenders who may be regarded as normally living off crime.[170]

Criminal lifestyle confiscation in the English confiscation regime is a form of extended confiscation, whilst criminal conduct confiscation can be designated as ordinary confiscation. The Crown Court is not entitled to choose which of these forms of confiscation is to be used, but this is entirely governed by POCA 2002. The more detailed requirements for this decision are governed by Section 75 and Schedule 2, which are described below.

There is much case-law dealing with the POCA 2002 powers. Even if some of it relates to the prior legislation, certain basic principles are in general still valid for the current statute.[171] In 2008, the House of Lords gave three unanimous judgments which give fundamental guidelines on the interpretation and application of the confiscation regime. These cases are *R v. May*,[172] *Crown*

---

168 *Explanatory Notes to POCA 2002*, p. 5.

169 Compare on these powers, Section 3.4 below.

170 *Explanatory Notes to POCA 2002*, p. 23.

171 Compare J. Ulph, "Confiscation Orders, Human Rights and Penal Measures" (2010) 26 *Law Quarterly Review*, p. 251, p. 252.

172 [2008] UKHL 28.

Prosecution Service v. Jennings[173] and *R v. Green*.[174] These will be referred to below.

3.4. CRIMINAL LIFESTYLE CONFISCATION

3.4.1. BASIC REQUIREMENTS

The basic criteria for establishing that a defendant has a criminal lifestyle are given in Section 75 POCA 2002:

> (1) A defendant has a criminal lifestyle if (and only if) the following condition is satisfied.
> (2) The condition is that the offence (or any of the offences) concerned satisfies any of these tests –
> (a) it is specified in Schedule 2;
> (b) it constitutes conduct forming part of a course of criminal activity;
> (c) it is an offence committed over a period of at least six months and the defendant has benefited from the conduct which constitutes the offence.
> (3) Conduct forms part of a course of criminal activity if the defendant has benefited from the conduct and –
> (a) in the proceedings in which he was convicted he was convicted of three or more other offences, each of three or more of them constituting conduct from which he has benefited, or
> (b) in the period of six years ending with the day when those proceedings were started (or, if there is more than one such day, the earliest day) he was convicted on at least two separate occasions of an offence constituting conduct from which he has benefited.
> (4) But an offence does not satisfy the test in subsection (2)(b) or (c) unless the defendant obtains relevant benefit of not less than £5000.[175]

Accordingly, a defendant is considered to have a criminal lifestyle in any of three situations. *Firstly* if he is convicted in the current proceedings of a crime set out in Schedule 2 POCA 2002. This *exhaustive* list of crimes sets out the so-called lifestyle offences.[176] These include e.g. drug-trafficking offences, money laundering,

---

[173] [2008] UKHL 29.
[174] [2008] UKHL 30.
[175] The Secretary of State has authority to vary this amount (Sec. 75(8) POCA 2002). For a definition of criminal conduct, see Sec. 76 POCA 2002.
[176] The Secretary of State may by order amend Schedule 2 (Sec. 75(7) POCA 2002).

people- or arms-trafficking, directing terrorism, blackmail or counterfeiting.[177] The scheme aims at listing serious offences of such nature as to justify an assumption that a defendant has committed also other types of crime. As explained by Ulph, the offences in the scheme are "easily repeated, lucrative and with a low rate of detection" which mean that they are highly appealing to career criminals.[178] A conviction for one of these crimes is sufficient to lead to an assumption that a defendant has a criminal lifestyle.

Secondly, a criminal lifestyle may be determined if the defendant is convicted of a combination of crimes amounting to "a course of criminal activity". As the *Explanatory Notes to POCA 2002* admit, this criterion is relatively complicated.[179] A course of criminal activity may be found where a defendant has been convicted, in the current proceedings, of three or more other offences (the type of crime is irrelevant) all from which he has benefited. A course of criminal activity may further be found when a defendant has been convicted of an offence from which he has benefited *and* he has been convicted on at least two separate occasions in the last six years with benefit on both such occasions. For both alternatives pursuant to (2)(b) it is, moreover, required that the total relevant benefit must not be less than £5,000.

Thirdly, a criminal lifestyle may be determined when the defendant is convicted of any offence which was committed over a period of at least six months and the benefit from that conduct was not less than £5,000. The tests set out for the determination of criminal lifestyle in POCA 2002 were partly based on earlier legislation on confiscation, partly newly drafted. As mentioned earlier, a decision that the defendant has a criminal lifestyle triggers wider powers of confiscation. As will been seen in the following sections, the court is in such a case *required* to rely on certain statutory assumptions for the determination of benefit.

3.4.2. THE DETERMINATION OF BENEFIT IN CRIMINAL LIFESTYLE CASES

3.4.2.1. *The Statutory Assumptions*

According to POCA 2002 a person benefits from criminal conduct if he obtains property as a result of or in connection with the conduct. A person ordinarily *obtains* property if in law he owns it, whether alone or jointly, which connotes a power of disposition or control.[180] The benefit is defined as the value of the

177 For a commentary on various types of crime, see *Explanatory Notes to POCA 2002*, pp. 25–26.
178 Ulph, n 171 above, p. 272.
179 Compare *Explanatory Notes to POCA 2002*, p. 23.
180 See for example para. 48(6), *R v. May*, [2008] UKHL 28.

property obtained.[181] According to case-law, benefit is not equated with "profit", and one cannot deduct costs.[182] This was confirmed in *inter alia* the case of *R v. May*:

> The legislation is intended to deprive defendants of the benefit they have gained from relevant criminal conduct, whether or not they have retained such benefit, within the limits of their available means. It does not provide for confiscation in the sense understood by schoolchildren and others, but nor does it operate by way of fine. The benefit gained is the total value of the property or advantage obtained, not the defendant's net profit after deduction of expenses or any amounts payable to co-conspirators.[183]

English law provides two methods for calculating the value of benefit from criminal conduct. In cases where the court has decided that there is no criminal lifestyle, the benefit is calculated in relation to the value of property obtained from the commission of the offence in respect of which he is to be sentenced (particular criminal conduct). When it comes to criminal lifestyle confiscation, the court is required to examine a defendant's financial history, which both triggers the use of certain statutory assumptions and puts a certain burden of proof on the defendant. According to Section 10 POCA 2002 the court is required in cases of a criminal lifestyle to apply the following four assumptions. These are supposed to help the court to establish whether a defendant has benefited from general criminal conduct and, if so, to what amount:

> (2) The first assumption is that any property transferred to the defendant at any time after the relevant day was obtained by him –
> (a) as a result of his general criminal conduct, and
> (b) at the earliest time he appears to have held it.
>
> (3) The second assumption is that any property held by the defendant at any time after the date of conviction was obtained by him –
> (a) as a result of his general criminal conduct, and
> (b) at the earliest time he appears to have held it.
>
> (4) The third assumption is that any expenditure incurred by the defendant at any time after the relevant day was met from property obtained by him as a result of his general criminal conduct.

---

181 Sec. 76(4) and (7). Compare also Sec. 80 POCA 2002.

182 Compare Sec. 8 POCA 2002 and para. 8, *R. v. Green*, [2007] EWCA Crim 1248. The definition of "benefit" has also been an issue in e.g. *Crown Prosecution Service v. Jennings*, [2008] UKHL 29, para. 18, *R v. Aujla*, [2008] EWCA Crim 637 and *Ahmad and Ahmed v. R*, [2012] EWCA Crim 391. For a critical discussion of the definition of benefit in English legislation and case-law, see Giles, n 138 above, Ulph, n 171 above, Alldridge, n 159 above, pp. 833–41 and P. Alldridge, "Proceeds of Crime Law since 2003 – two key areas" [2014] *Criminal Law Review*, p. 171, pp. 171–83.

183 Para. 48(1), *R v. May*, [2008] UKHL 28. Compare para. 13, *R v. Harvey*, [2015] UKSC 73.

(5) The fourth assumption is that, for the purpose of valuing any property obtained (or assumed to have been obtained) by the defendant, he obtained it free of any other interests in it.

Accordingly, the court presumes that any property transferred to or held by a defendant in the six years prior to confiscation proceedings constitute benefit from criminal conduct. It is further assumed that all expenditure he has incurred during this period have been met from such benefit. The fourth presumption in Section 10(5) means that it is presumed that all property owned by the defendant is free of third party interests. If someone is deemed to have a criminal lifestyle, the court may, in its assessment of the confiscation issue, take into account criminal conduct even before POCA 2002 came into force.[184] It is not required that the criminal conduct be proved by way of a conviction or finding of guilt by a court.

The issue of whether a defendant has benefitted concerns both property which remains in a defendant's possession and that which he has obtained in the past but which he no longer retains. As has been pointed out in case-law, lifestyle confiscation is thus a matter of a historical inquiry into past transactions.[185] As will be further described in Section 3.4.2.2 below these statutory assumptions concern the question of the source of the assets and are only triggered after the prosecution *has shown the existence* of certain property.

The court is *bound* to apply these assumptions, and must state express reasons if this is to be deviated from in an individual case.[186] There are only two exceptions to this:

(1) if the assumption is shown to be incorrect, or
(2) there would be a serious risk of injustice if the assumption were made.[187]

These exceptions may, however, not be interpreted as giving the judge *general discretion* to determine whether or not it is fair to make a confiscation order *at all*.[188] The aim of the provision is instead to provide a means of *moderating the calculation of benefit* in cases where the confiscation sum is unjustified:

> It is only when considering the appropriateness of applying those assumptions that section 10(6) bites. It is there in order to ensure that assumptions made under section 10 are not so unrealistic or so unjust in relation to a particular defendant that they should not be made. It provides a means of moderating the ultimate calculation of benefit.[189]

184 Sec. 76(2) POCA 2002.
185 Para. 48(5), *R v. May*, [2008] UKHL 28.
186 Sec. 10(7) POCA 2002.
187 Sec. 10(6) POCA 2002.
188 Para. 14, *R v. Jones*, [2006] EWCA Crim 2061. Compare Ulph, n 171 above, p. 271.
189 Para. 13, *R v. Jones*, [2006] EWCA Crim 2061.

3.4.2.2. *The Burden and Standard of Proof*

In English law, conviction in criminal cases requires a full criminal standard of proof, i.e. the prosecutor must prove *beyond all reasonable doubt* that the defendant has committed the crime. Regarding the issue of confiscation there is a reduced standard of proof; Section 6(7) POCA 2002 states that the court shall decide such a matter "on a balance of probabilities". This means that a *civil standard of proof* is required.[190] The prosecutor has thus the burden of establishing to the civil standard of proof both that there is benefit and the amount of that benefit.[191] This means that the prosecution must first of all show that a defendant has obtained certain property, which will either be known property he still possesses or which he has possessed.[192] Once the prosecution has proved this, the statutory assumptions in Section 10 POCA 2002 are triggered and assist in proving the *source of that property*. Accordingly, the court *must assume* in such cases that the source is "general criminal conduct".[193] (The only exceptions are if an assumption is shown to be incorrect or there would be a serious risk of injustice if the assumption is made.)[194] In practice, this leads to a considerable easing of the burden of proof, since it is sufficient for the prosecutor to prove that the defendant has or has had certain property or has had certain costs:

> Thus, once a criminal lifestyle has been established, it falls to the prosecution, if it can, to prove, on the balance of probabilities, that the defendant has obtained property. The prosecution, as the first three assumptions in s.10 indicate, may do so by proving that property has been transferred to the defendant (s.10(2)), that he has obtained property (s.10(3)) or that he has incurred expenditure after the relevant day (s.10(4)). Only when the prosecution has established that the defendant has held property in one of those

---

190 There is, however, one exception to the civil standard of proof in cases where the statutory assumptions in Sec. 10 POCA 2002 are not to be deployed. If the prosecution in such a case argues that the defendant has obtained property in the past by proof of criminal offences other than those charged on the indictment, it must prove those offences to a criminal law standard ("beyond reasonable doubt"). See *R v. Briggs Price*, [2009] UKHL 19, 2 WLR 1101. In this case the defendant was convicted of conspiracy to import heroin under the Drug Trafficking Act 1994. No heroin had been imported, but the prosecution alleged at the trial that the defendant had an existing cannabis supply network that he was intending to use to distribute the heroin. However, he had not been charged with any offences relating to cannabis. The figure of benefit was based largely upon these cannabis allegations. The House of Lords ruled that in cases where the prosecution relied on new criminal offending *to prove the existence of benefit*, they had to prove that offending to the proof of the criminal standard. The appeal was anyway dismissed because it was considered, on the facts, that the evidence regarding the cannabis offences was sufficient to satisfy the higher criminal standard. Mr Briggs-Price has taken the case before the ECtHR. See *Briggs-Price v. United Kingdom*, Appl. No. 59494/09. The case has not yet been decided.

191 Para. 33, *R v. Barwick*, [2000] EWCA Crim 3551.

192 Para. 13, *Whittington v. R*, [2009] EWCA Crim 1641.

193 Para. 32, *Whittington v. R*, [2009] EWCA Crim 1641.

194 Compare Sec. 10(6) POCA 2002, described in Section 3.4.2.1 above.

> three ways does any question of the source of that property arise. The prosecution may establish the possession of property or expenditure by any manner of means according to the civil standard of proof.[195]

The English system thus leads to a *reversed burden of proof* as regards the *source* of the assets, i.e. the burden of proof shifts to the defendant, upon whom it is incumbent to prove that the assets have been acquired through legal means. The ECtHR has in this respect ruled that the placing of the burden on the defendant is not in violation of Article 6 ECHR, as it is not unreasonable to expect a defendant to account for assets which are in his possession.[196]

The importance of a rigorous step-by-step approach to the process of considering a confiscation order has been underlined in case-law:

> The purpose of the first three assumptions within s.10 is to assist in the proof of the *source* of property obtained by the defendant. The assumptions have nothing to do with the logically prior question as to whether the defendant has or has had the property in issue.[197]

The question of which assets exist must thus be rigidly separated from the matter of their source, but the same goes for the last step of the proceedings, i.e. the calculation of the recoverable amount. In addition to the defendant's burden of proof regarding the origin of his assets, there is a further obligation on the defence when it comes to showing realisable assets. This will be described in what follows.

3.4.2.3. Benefit and the Available Amount

The aim of the confiscation proceedings is that the court shall establish a *recoverable amount* that relates to the benefit that the defendant has enjoyed from criminal conduct.[198] A defendant may, however, show that such an amount exceeds his available assets. In such a case, the court shall make a confiscation order for the lesser amount, or for a nominal amount if the available amount is nil.[199] The scheme of the Act thus requires the court to perform two distinct tasks, and the calculation of benefit and available amount will take place independently of each other. The expression "available amount" does not, however, correspond

---

195 Paras. 14–15, *Whittington v. R*, [2009] EWCA Crim 1641. This case clearly illustrates how the burden of proof shifts under the confiscation proceedings.

196 See further the case of *Grayson and Barnham v. United Kingdom* described in Section 3.6.6.1. below.

197 Paras. 1 and 24, *Whittington v. R*, [2009] EWCA Crim 1641. Compare also para. 41, *Moss v. R*, [2015] EWCA Crim 713.

198 Secs. 6(5) and 7–8 POCA 2002.

199 Sec. 7(2) POCA 2002.

to what is meant in the everyday sense of assets "being available" for payment, but is rather established through a mathematical calculation of "all free property" owned by a defendant with certain deductions and with the inclusion of so-called "tainted gifts".[200]

The following example illustrates how the amount to be confiscated can be calculated. X is to be convicted of narcotics crime. Pursuant to Section 75(2)(a) POCA 2002 and Schedule 2 the provisions on criminal lifestyle confiscation will be applied. The court has estimated X's benefit from criminal activity at £250,000. The financial investigation shows that X owns £2,500 in a bank account and £5,000 in the form of shares. Three years ago, he gave £2,000 to his daughter. He owns a house worth £400,000 jointly with his wife. This has an outstanding mortgage of £300,000. The available amount is deemed to be £59,500, made up of £2,500 in the bank account, the £5,000 shareholding, £2,000 relating to the gift to a family member (a so-called "tainted gift") and £50,000 for his half of the value of the house (minus the mortgage). A confiscation order will therefore be set at the recoverable amount of £59,500, which in this case is considerably less than the amount the court deemed to be X's benefit. It is to be noted, however, that this available amount is not in practice immediately available to X. In addition to the funds which can be converted via the bank account and sale of shares, the value corresponding to the retrieved gift, for example, is not directly available. In practice funds must thus be "made available", which can, for example, also mean selling the house.

The burden of proof is on the *defendant* to show that the available assets are lower than the benefit from crime.[201] The nature and value of available assets is considered essentially to be within the defendant's personal knowledge. This means, for example, an obligation to show by clear and cogent evidence that he no longer owns or controls certain assets. If a defendant fails to convince the court in such a matter, a confiscation order may be made for the benefit amount. In cases where assets have existed and subsequently disappeared without a satisfactory explanation, the courts sometimes determine that there are grounds for suspecting that there are "hidden assets". There is no obligation for the prosecution to first show a prima facie case that hidden assets exist.[202]

One example of a case concerning "hidden assets" is *R v. Barwick* where the defendant had pleaded guilty to 21 counts of theft and one count of evading liability by deception, and had been sentenced to four years' imprisonment.[203]

---

200 See further e.g. Secs. 9, 77–78 and 82 POCA 2002.

201 Compare the formulation in Sec. 7(2) POCA 2002; "but if the defendant shows ...". See also e.g. para. 33, *R v. Barwick*, [2000] EWCA Crim 3551 and para. 40, *R v. Barnham*, [2005] EWCA Crim 1049.

202 Para. 11, *R v. Summers*, [2008] EWCA Crim 872.

203 [2000] EWCA Crim 3551. The case concerned the application of the Criminal Justice Act 1988, but is of interest, and is quoted regarding issues of evidence in cases concerning POCA 2002.

The benefit from these crimes was set at £502,595. This sum was later adjusted for inflation to £604,657, which was not challenged by the defence. The police had not found any significant assets or been able to trace where the stolen money had gone. Mr Barwick himself maintained that he had lost a considerable part on gambling, but reports from the casinos had recorded only a low volume of gambling by him. The prosecution argued that substantial assets must be hidden from the court. This was based on the following: the defendant had amassed a large amount of cash during the course of the offences of which he was convicted; there was no evidence that he had lived an extravagant lifestyle and there was no documentary evidence produced by the defendant to quantify the spending necessary to dissipate such an amount. The Crown Court set the amount of benefit at £604,657, arguing that this sum equated to the sums listed in the indictment, to which the defendant had pleaded guilty. The Court found that the prosecution had proven that the defendant had obtained this money and that the onus of proof was then on the defendant to establish, on the balance of probability, what he had done with the money. The court underlined that:

> The onus is not upon the police to chase around looking for realisable assets. If the police find realisable assets, all well and good, but the onus here is on the defendant to establish, on the balance of probabilities, that there are no realisable assets.[204]

Mr Barwick had in the case relied solely upon his own oral evidence regarding the financial situation. Mildly speaking, this evidence was found rather unconvincing by the judge:

> I have to say, with regret, that the defendant's evidence before me today, he was about as unconvincing a witness as it would be possible to imagine. The impression that he gave me from the witness box, when he gave evidence, was such that I would have difficulty believing a word that he said ... I am quite satisfied, of course, that he has received – that he benefited – in the sum spoken of. I am quite satisfied that he has not told me the truth about what has happened to it. The affidavits I have already referred to; evasive, hiding the truth, rather than helping. He has not persuaded me that he has no realisable assets, despite his repeated assertions that he has no realisable assets ...[205]

In light of this, the Crown Court rejected the statements from the defendant that there were no realisable assets. However, the amount of the benefit was somewhat reduced, to acknowledge the fact that some of this money had gone. A confiscation order in the sum of £450,000 was made, with a term of imprisonment of two and a half years imposed in default of payment, to be served consecutively to the term for the substantive offences.[206]

---

204 Para. 10, *R v. Barwick*, [2000] EWCA Crim 3551.

205 Para. 11, *R v. Barwick*, [2000] EWCA Crim 3551.

206 See further on default of payment, Section 3.5 below.

Before the Court of Appeal the defendant argued that the burden of proof should not be on a defendant, and that unless the prosecution could prove (on a balance of probabilities) both benefit *and* the existence of realisable property no order could be made. However, the Court of Appeal maintained that the burden of proof is on the defendant to satisfy the court that the amount that might be realised is less, and reasoned as follows:

> Turning to principle, it is likely that an offender may take steps to make the proceeds of crime difficult to trace. Once it is proved that he has received the benefit, it is pragmatic, and entirely fair to the defendant, to place upon him the onus of showing (to the civil standard) that he no longer has the proceeds or that their extent or value has diminished.[207]

The confiscation order was upheld, and it was stressed in the ruling that the scheme of the Act requires the court to perform two distinct and discrete tasks. First, to determine the benefit and secondly, to determine the amount that might be realised:

> In the end, the task of the court at the second stage is to determine the amount "appearing to the court" to be the amount that might be realised. But once the benefit has been proved, it is permissible and ought normally to be the approach of the court, to conclude that the benefit remains available until the defendant proves otherwise.[208]

Another interesting case in this respect is *R v. Barnham*,[209] which concerned an appeal against a confiscation order from the Crown Court. The case concerned the Drug Trafficking Act 1994, but is of interest also for the application of POCA 2002 regarding the burden and standard of proof. Mr Barnham had been sentenced to 11 years' imprisonment for two conspiracy charges involving plans to import large consignments of cannabis into the UK. A confiscation order of over £1.5 million had been made. The importation of the drugs had never materialised, and the whereabouts of the narcotics was not known. The evidence was based largely on testimony from an English undercover agent who had posed as an international money launderer and had had contact with Mr Barnham. He testified about several conversations and meetings with the defendant during which criminal activity had been planned. The defendant had indicated that he was involved in large-scale importation of cannabis into the UK from Morocco, and had told him that his organisation was expected to receive payment of £12 million. He had asked the undercover police agent to help him to "launder" his share of this payment, i.e. £2 million. As the defendant was subsequently arrested in Portugal, none of these transactions took place.

---

207 Para. 35, *R v. Barwick*, [2000] EWCA Crim 3551.
208 Para. 44, *R v. Barwick*, [2000] EWCA Crim 3551.
209 [2005] EWCA Crim 1049.

The Crown Court found proven in the case that the defendant was the lead organiser in an established and internationally based drug-trafficking business. Further, it found that the fact that no cannabis was actually imported was not due to a lack of effort or determination on the part of the defendant. The first hearing on confiscation concerned the determination of benefit, and the prosecution relied to a considerable extent on the conversations between the defendant and the undercover police officer. The defendant did not give evidence, but admitted items of benefit to a total value of £185,615. The judge, however, determined the total benefit to be £1,525,615. This sum included £27,000 that the defendant had given to the undercover agent to establish his trust; various amounts totaling £59,000 which the defendant had referred to during conversations; £11,615 regarding a car; £65,000 regarding renovation costs for the defendant's house; £23,000 which the defendant had told the undercover agent that he had invested in cannabis importation; the amounts of £500,000 and £600,000 regarding the purchase of cannabis (which had been mentioned to the undercover agent) and a further £240,000 which related to another purchase of drugs being discussed. There was no appeal against that finding.

At the second hearing regarding the question of realisable assets, Mr Barnham and his wife gave evidence, and stated that their only asset was their jointly owned house in Spain. Mr Barnham stressed that he had not derived any financial benefit from the sale of narcotics and that he had lived off singing in bars. His wife had a cleaning job. There were no hidden assets and 94.4 per cent of the benefit figure had been expenditure and the remaining 5.6 per cent had been dissipated. The car in question had been confiscated in Portugal. However, the Court found that neither Mr Barnham nor his wife were credible, and stressed that the defendant had not even tried to explain what had happened to the money or the narcotics:

> "He has failed to explain truthfully what he did and what he did with what he earned from what he did. That has been his choice and if it leaves, as it does, this Court with no clear and cogent evidence to persuade it that the benefit sum is not fully realisable, the responsibility for that is Mr. Barnham's and Mr. Barnham's alone".[210]

The confiscation order was thus determined to £1,525,615 with five years and three months' imprisonment if the sum was not paid.

Before the Court of Appeal the issue was whether this confiscation order gave rise to a serious risk of injustice. Therefore the impact of the ECHR on the English confiscation proceedings was also dealt with. Mr Barnham submitted that Article 6(1) ECHR was applicable also to the determination of realisable assets and that if the prosecution claims that a defendant has hidden assets, they

---

210 Para. 17, *R v. Barnham*, [2005] EWCA Crim 1049.

must be required to produce at least prima facie evidence about available assets before the burden of proof is shifted to the defendant. It was submitted that there was a difference between cases where benefit was proven by evidence, and cases where the prosecution had proved benefit by operation of the assumptions. It was claimed that, in the latter case, the assumptions flowed through into the second stage. Further, it was argued that a defendant who faced an allegation of hidden assets was put at a real disadvantage if the prosecution did not first set out the nature of the case which he had to meet.[211]

The Court of Appeal rejected the approach of the defence and confirmed that there is a persuasive burden on a defendant to prove to the civil standard what realisable assets he has:

> In our judgement the correct approach for the court to take when dealing with confiscation proceedings at the second stage is the same whether the benefit has been proved by evidence in addition to the statutory assumptions. Once the prosecution has established the benefit there is no requirement on it to provide a prima facie case. At the second stage the burden of proof shifts to a defendant to establish, if he can, his realisable assets to the satisfaction of the court. By the second stage a defendant will know exactly how the court has determined benefit attributable to him and must prove by evidence what his realisable assets are. It is for him to show why the confiscation order should not be "the value of (*his*) proceeds of drug trafficking". If he proves that he has no, or appreciably less, realisable assets than the amount of the benefit determined by the court the order will be made in the lesser sum. Provided the judge keeps well in mind the principle that the risk of serious injustice to the defendant must be avoided and does not just pay lip service to that principle the order will be in the amount assessed as either the amount of benefit or such other sum as the defendant shows represents his realisable assets.
>
> To hold that the prosecution must, in some way, show a prima facie case that the defendant has hidden assets in our judgement would defeat the object of the legislation. It is designed to enable the court to confiscate a criminal's ill-gotten gains. The expression "hidden assets" is indicative of the fact that the prosecution can have no means of knowing how and where a defendant may have dealt with or disposed of the proceeds of his criminal activities.[212]

The defence had also argued that the decision of the Crown Court was unfair. For example, while the largest elements of the judge's assessment of benefit concerned costs for the obtaining of large amounts of cannabis, these conspiracies had in fact failed, in the sense that no drugs had reached the UK. The determination of realisable assets based on those conspiracies was therefore not fair. Further, the judge had made no allowance for the fact that the defendant must have been only one of a number of conspirators.

---

211 Para. 26, *R v. Barnham*, [2005] EWCA Crim 1049.

212 Paras. 40–41, *R v. Barnham*, [2005] EWCA Crim 1049.

The Court of Appeal did not find this convincing and stressed that the defendant had produced no evidence, documentary or otherwise, of any sort to show that he no longer retained any proceeds of his criminal activities or what had happened to them. His evidence amounted to a bare denial that he had any realisable assets other than his house, and he had not explained what had happened to the drugs in question. Mr Barnham had contacted the undercover agent in order to receive his help to launder significant amounts of money. The Court held that the fact that the drugs did not arrive in the UK did not mean that they were "to be ignored as potential realisable assets", and that the Crown Court was entitled to conclude that they were a valuable asset under the appellant's control.[213] As drugs have a market value it was justifiable to investigate what had become of them. The defendant had, however, given no credible evidence on this issue and it was possible that associates could have sold the drugs on the appellant's behalf. It was held by the Court of Appeal that the defendant had not discharged his burden of proof, and that any risk of injustice to him had not been caused. The confiscation order was reduced to the amount of £1.4 million due to a miscalculation by the Crown Court.

Mr Barnham appealed to the ECtHR, arguing that the burden on him to show the available amount was in violation of the ECHR. The judgment of this court is further described in Section 3.6.6.1 below.

In these cases the courts have thus concluded that there were "hidden assets". The English case-law varies in such cases as to whether a court always issues a confiscation order for the full amount when the defendant is not found to have been given a complete and sufficient disclosure of his financial situation. There are cases where the courts have considered themselves *compelled* to set the confiscated amount at the full amount of the benefit when the defendant is not credible:

> Once we have concluded that the appellant benefited to the amounts revealed in the documents to which we have referred, then in the absence of any evidence as to what has happened to those benefits, or how much profit they represented to him, we are *compelled to conclude* that the available amount is no less than the amount of the benefit. That, after all, is the purpose of shifting the burden of establishing that the available amount is less onto a defendant. If a defendant chooses to give no explanation or no acceptable explanation of benefits identified by the court he has only himself to blame for the failure to discharge the burden of establishing that a lesser amount is available. This is the risk a defendant runs in disputing the amount of benefit, once the prosecution succeeds in establishing a figure which he disputes (emphasis added).[214]

213 Para. 48, *R v. Barnham*, [2005] EWCA Crim 1049.

214 Para. 40, *Whittington v. R*, [2009] EWCA Crim 1641. Compare para. 16, *Attorney General v. McMillan-Smith v. R*, [2009] EWCA Crim 732 and paras. 10–11, *Telli v. Revenue and Customs Prosecution Office*, [2007] EWCA Civ 1385.

On the other hand, there are also examples in case-law of a less strict and rigid approach. In the case of *R v. McIntosh and Marsden* the amount of criminal benefit had been agreed to be £3,668,990. The defendants had argued that they had no realisable assets. The Crown Court found that they were not credible, and concluded that hidden assets must exist. Against this background, the Court argued that it was compelled to order the full benefit amount to be paid. The defendants appealed and argued that even if a court rejects the evidence of a defendant regarding realisable assets, the court is not *bound* to make a confiscation order to the full benefit amount. The Court of Appeal underlined that a court is obligated to make an independent assessment of available assets based on all the facts of a case. At the same time it held that there is no principle that a court is bound to reject a defendant's case that his current realisable assets are less than the full amount of the benefit, merely because it concludes that the defendant has not revealed their true extent or value, or has not participated in any revelation at all. Accordingly, it was reasoned that:

> A defendant who is found not to have told the truth or who has declined to give truthful disclosure will inevitably find it difficult to discharge the burden imposed upon him. But it may not be impossible for him to do so. Other sources of evidence, apart from the defendant himself, and a view of the case as a whole, may persuade a court that the assets available to the defendant are less than the full value of the benefit.[215]

3.5. SOME SPECIAL FEATURES OF THE ENGLISH CONFISCATION PROCEDURE

In cases where there is an application for confiscation, a report is submitted to the court on the estimated benefit, containing information relevant for the decision of a criminal lifestyle.[216] According to Section 17(1) POCA 2002 the defendant can then be required to submit a statement indicating which amounts are accepted and which are contested. If the defendant fails to submit a reply, this may in part be interpreted as meaning that he agrees with the calculations.[217] On the other hand, he is not to be treated as accepting any allegation that he has benefited from general or particular criminal conduct *per se*.[218] The court

---

215 Para. 15, *R v. McIntosh and Marsden*, [2011] EWCA Crim 1501. For other case-law regarding the issue of hidden assets, see *R v. Smith*, [2011] EWCA Crim 2029, *R v. Summers*, [2008] EWCA Crim 872, *Pigott v. R*, [2009] EWCA Crim 2292, *Ahmad and Ahmed v. R*, [2012] EWCA Crim 391, *Attorney General v. McMillan-Smith v. R*, [2009] EWCA Crim 732, *R v. Barnham*, [2005] EWCA Crim 1049 and *Price v. Crown Prosecution Service*, [2016] EWHC 455 Admin.

216 Sec. 16 POCA 2002.

217 A defendant may in principle choose not to give evidence in confiscation proceedings, but such a refusal is unlikely to help his case; compare *R v. Takkar* [2011] EWCA Crim 646.

218 See further s. 17(3) POCA 2002 and *Explanatory Notes to POCA 2002* pp. 8–9.

may also, pursuant to Section 18, *order* the defendant to supply information about his financial situation, for example the extent and location of his assets. If the defendant fails to do so without reasonable excuse, the court may draw such inference as it believes is appropriate.[219] It has also a power to use sanctions against a defendant for contempt of court.[220] In some cases a deal is struck between the prosecution and the defence concerning the amounts that a confiscation order will be based upon, but there is no obligation for the *court* to accept such a deal.[221]

A defendant is not entitled to refuse to supply information in order to avoid revealing other criminality on his part. However, there is a certain protection against self-incrimination. Section 18(9) POCA 2002 states that any information which amounts to an admission by the defendant that he has benefited from criminal conduct is not admissible as evidence in substantive proceedings regarding such an offence. On the other hand, the authorities are not prevented from initiating a preliminary investigation in order to seek other evidence for such an offence.[222]

Confiscation is considered part of the sentencing process, and a confiscation order is in principle made in connection with the criminal conviction. The court has the power to postpone the confiscation proceedings, but such postponement must not exceed two years from the date of conviction unless there are exceptional circumstances.[223] Furthermore there are various opportunities for later reconsideration of confiscation issues.[224] Such a request may be made by the prosecution or the defence. This means that a confiscation order can be made later in cases where none was made in the original proceeding (Section 19), where it was decided that the defendant had no benefit (Section 20) or where the prosecutor believes that the recoverable amount may have increased (Section 21). In such cases, application must be made to the Crown Court within six years of the original conviction. Reconsideration should only be applied for in cases where new evidence comes to light.[225]

Pursuant to Section 22 POCA 2002 the prosecutor is further allowed to initiate a recalculation of the *available amount* in a confiscation order if the defendant has acquired further assets. In contrast to Sections 19–21, there is no time-period mentioned in Section 22.[226] Against this background, this is a

219 Sec. 18(4) POCA 2002.

220 Sec. 18(5) POCA 2002.

221 See on such negotiations, K. Bullock, "Criminal Benefit, the Confiscation Order and the Post-conviction Confiscation Regime" (2014) 62 *Crime, Law and Social Change*, p. 45, pp. 60–61. Compare for an example of such a deal, *R v. Hirani*, [2008] EWCA Crim 1463.

222 *Explanatory Notes to POCA 2002*, p. 9.

223 See further Secs. 14–15 POCA 2002 and *Explanatory Notes to POCA 2002*, pp. 7–8.

224 Compare Secs. 19–26 POCA 2002.

225 *Explanatory Notes to POCA 2002*, p. 9.

226 *Explanatory Notes to POCA 2002*, p. 10.

rather intrusive and far-reaching power leading to significant insecurity for a defendant. In a recent case, *R v. Padda (Gurpreet Singh)*, a confiscation order had been made in 2006 setting the benefit at £156,226 and the available amount at £9,250. The latter sum was paid immediately. After being released from prison, the defendant set up an entirely legitimate business which was profitable. After an application from the Crown in 2013(!) under Section 22 POCA 2002, the court performed a new calculation of the current available amount and he was ordered to pay another £74,652.[227]

The forfeited sum must be paid immediately. On request from a defendant, the court can, however, postpone payment by three months initially, and as a maximum six months' postponement may be allowed.[228] After this time has passed, interest on the sum will begin to accrue (at present a rate of eight per cent) and proceedings for enforcement will begin. The Crown Court is obligated to set a term of imprisonment to be served if the defendant fails to pay the confiscation sum. The Act sets up a scale, and the length of the sentence depends on the size of the confiscation sum. The sentence can vary from six months for an amount of £10,000 or less, and up to 14 years for an amount exceeding £1 million.[229] This sentence will be served after having completed any sentence already imposed for the crime relating to the confiscation order.[230] Section 38(5) POCA 2002 additionally stipulates that the debt does not lapse even if a prison sentence has been served.

3.6. A COMMENTARY ON THE ENGLISH CONFISCATION REGIME ON LIFESTYLE CONFISCATION

3.6.1. A DRACONIAN BUT EFFICIENT CONFISCATION REGIME?

> Enacted ten years ago, the Proceeds of Crime Act was intended to place the recovery of criminally obtained property at the heart of criminal justice policy. It is a laudable ideal, but with its draconian provisions the Act's operation has become the embodiment of Dr Johnson's quip that the road to hell is paved with good intentions.[231]

[227] On appeal the order was upheld. See *R v. Padda (Gurpreet Singh)*, [2013] EWCA Crim 2330.

[228] This was a change to POCA 2002 brought by the Serious Crime Act 2015. Before 1 June 2015 the courts could postpone payment initially for six months and then for up to one year.

[229] This was an increase in default sentences made by the Serious Crime Act 2015. Compare on this, Section 3.6.1 below.

[230] Sec. 38(2) POCA 2002.

[231] J. Fisher, in *The Times*, 23.8.2012, see http://www.thetimes.co.uk/tto/law/article3514554.ece.

The English confiscation regime is very far-reaching and is often described as harsh or "draconian".[232] The defendant is obligated to pay an amount to the state under the threat of further imprisonment in default of payment. The regime thereby involves a rather wide form of extended confiscation as the presumption of the illegal origin of assets extends to all assets of a defendant within a time-period of six years. There is no doubt that this provision allows for very intrusive powers of confiscation, and the classification of defendants as lifestyle offenders sometimes leads to rather peculiar rulings.

The inherent obligation for a defendant to account for all assets (under the risk of a finding of "hidden assets") may indeed be very burdensome. In the concluding sections of this chapter, I will highlight some specific characteristics of the confiscation regime set up by POCA 2002 and discuss why the legislation in certain areas may regarded as having draconian features. In addition, certain difficulties in applying the legislation in practice will be analysed. During the process of enacting POCA 2002, the statute was criticised as not only destroying the essence of the presumption of innocence, but also for having the capacity of leading to arbitrary and irrational results.[233] However, the UK legislator is of the opinion that the reversal of the burden of proof regarding the financial circumstances of a defendant is justified against the significant interest of depriving convicted defendants of any proceeds of crime. In case-law, it has been acknowledged that the provisions are *intentionally* draconian:

> Since the amount of those proceeds and the size of his realisable assets at the time of conviction are likely to be peculiarly within the defendant's knowledge, it is not surprising perhaps if evidential burdens are cast upon him of a kind which are, to say the least, unusual in the area of the criminal law and this, despite the fact that the confiscation order and the penalties for failing to comply with it may be rigorous.[234]

The significant aims of the English confiscation regime are to *deter* offenders from committing crime and to strip the offenders of criminal assets. However, at the same time, the provisions in the Act are very complex and complicated. It has rightly been doubted whether there are any deterrent effects, considering that the scheme of confiscation orders is not very well understood by anyone other than specialists in the field.[235]

In spite of the strong powers, the efficiency of the system has on many occasions been doubted.[236] An early report in 2004 highlighted that the

232 See for example I. Lawrence, "Draconian and Manifestly Unjust: How the Confiscation Regime has Developed" (2008) 76 *Amicus Curiae*, pp. 22–24.

233 See for example Liberty, *Proceeds of Crime: Consultation on Draft Legislation*, May 2001.

234 Para. 11 in *R v. Dickens*, [1990] EWCA Crim 4.

235 Ulph, n 171 above, pp. 267 and 278.

236 See generally J. Harvey, "Asset Recovery: Substantive or Symbolic?" in C. King and C. Walker (eds.), *Dirty Assets: Emerging Issues in the Regulation of Criminal and Terrorist Assets*, Ashgate, 2014, pp. 183–203.

provisions used were patchy and that there was a widespread lack of awareness among practitioners of the powers of the Act.[237] In 2010, a new review concluded that performance had improved considerably, and that the amount of criminal assets recovered had increased from £25 million in 2001–02 to £135 million in 2007–08.[238] However, it was also found that more could be done to optimise the effectiveness and to increase the number and value of the confiscation orders. It was recommended that the issue of asset recovery should be more of a routine consideration in the daily work of the authorities and that the legal tools to identify and freeze recoverable assets must be used in a timely way.[239] In 2014, the House of Commons Committee of Public Accounts concluded that the various bodies involved in the process have "simply not done enough", as in 2012–13 some 673,000 offenders were convicted of a crime, but only 6,392 confiscation orders were made. It was criticised that only 26 pence was collected out of every £100 generated by criminal activity, leading to the conclusion that there is poor implementation of the legislation.[240]

The Crown Prosecution Service ("CPS") responded to some of this criticism and has worked out a strategy in order to achieve a consistent and improved practice for confiscation. According to its figures assets in the amount of £152.2 million were recovered in 2012–13, of which £90 million related to confiscation orders in CPS cases.[241] Figures from the Government provide that for 2013–14 about £190 million was recovered under POCA 2002.[242]

The success of the confiscation regime was also evaluated in the *Serious and Organised Crime Strategy*, which concluded that POCA 2002 is under sustained legal challenge from criminals who are seeking ways to frustrate asset recovery. This report therefore presented certain legislative proposals in order to close the loopholes in the legislation.[243] As a result the Serious Crime Act 2015 brought even greater powers for prosecutors and courts to recover the benefits of criminal offending and to compel criminals to comply with confiscation orders. As described earlier, the time-periods for the postponement of the payment of a confiscation order have thereby been shortened significantly and the prison sentences for default of payment have been increased.[244] This is alarming,

---

237 *Payback Time: Joint Review of Asset Recovery since the Proceeds of Crime Act 2002*, published on 1 November 2004.

238 *Joint Thematic Review of Asset Recovery: Restraint and Confiscation Casework*, Criminal Justice Joint Inspection, March 2010, p. 19.

239 *Joint Thematic Review of Asset Recovery: Restraint and Confiscation Casework*, Criminal Justice Joint Inspection, March 2010, especially, pp. 7–10.

240 House of Commons Committee of Public Accounts, *Confiscation Orders*, Forty-ninth Report of Session 2013–14, HC 942, published on 21 March 2014, p. 2–5.

241 *Crown Prosecution Service Improvement Plan*, March 2014, p. 15. Compare also *CPS Asset Recovery Strategy*, June 2014, p. 4.

242 *Explanatory Notes to the Serious Crime Act 2015*, para. 14.

243 HM Government, *Serious and Organised Crime Strategy*, Cm 8715, October 2013.

244 Compare Section 3.5 above.

particularly against the background of the use of the regime of "hidden assets" in English case-law. The maximum time-limit of six months' postponement of payment is very strict as many defendants may have to sell property (for example real estate) in order to be able to pay a confiscation order. Another rather intrusive change brought by the Serious Crime Act 2015 was the introduction of an obligation for the courts to consider imposing an overseas travel ban or the surrender of a passport for the purpose of ensuring that a confiscation order is effective.[245]

It may generally be concluded that the English confiscation regime seems to have developed in a more oppressive direction. Nevertheless, the practical effects of this approach in terms of efficiency remain to be seen. In any case, it was recently held that the changes introduced by the Serious Crime Act 2015 are not sufficient. In 2016, the National Audit Office published a new progress review evaluating the system of confiscation orders and expressed its disappointment that many of the fundamental weaknesses and systematic problems of the system remain. Once again concerns were expressed about the effectiveness of the way the proceeds of crime provisions are implemented in practice.[246] New proposals for reform are being discussed.

3.6.2. THE CLASSIFICATION OF DEFENDANTS AS LIFESTYLE OFFENDERS

As described in Section 3.4.1 above, the provision on extended confiscation is triggered by the classification of offenders into "lifestyle offenders". Section 75 POCA 2002 provides different alternatives in order to define a criminal lifestyle. First of all, a conviction for one of the so-called lifestyle offences listed in Schedule 2 is sufficient to establish that the defendant has a criminal lifestyle. The legislator argues that the scheme is supposed to address areas of criminal conduct "associated with professional criminals, organised crime and racketeering", and that it is in such cases reasonable to control the finances of an offender.[247] The other ways of establishing criminal lifestyle in Section 75(2)(b) and (c) are rather complicated. As further described above, the prerequisites for a criminal lifestyle finding are here based on certain numbers of convictions during specific time-periods. The aim is to single out multiple or systematic criminal activity, but the qualifying thresholds have been criticised as being too

245 Sec. 13A(4) POCA 2002.

246 See National Audit Office, *Confiscation Orders: Progress Review*, HC 886, March 2016 and House of Commons, Home Affairs Committee, Proceeds of Crime, Fifth Report of Session 2016–2017.

247 *Explanatory Notes to POCA 2002*, p. 26.

low.[248] The provision applies to *any type of offence* committed and can concern only two offences committed in a six-year period regardless of their nature (compare Section 75(3)(b)). This regulation especially was sharply criticised during the legislative process:

> The fact that the system will apply to any type of offence, which a defendant is convicted of twice, represents a new lower threshold for triggering criminal confiscation and can be contrasted to many practices around the world. The scheme appears to be unique in the world in terms of justifying such stringent measures on the basis of such ... minimal qualifying offences.[249]

It was thereby argued that there is a risk that such a legislative construction could lead to the 'net' widening:

> the scheme proposed by the government applies to relatively trivial individual thieves, burglars, fraudsters and robbers who notch up sufficient qualifying offences as well as persons involved in serious, long term organised crime whose activities may indeed threaten the social and economic well-being of a significant section of society.[250]

This being said, one must acknowledge that there is also the further requirement that a defendant must have benefitted from the conduct and that the relevant benefit is not less than £5,000.[251] In this way the provisions are limited to offences of a rather high benefit amount.

A specific feature of the English scheme of extended confiscation is thus that it is triggered by a defendant's criminal record. The aim of targeting defendants who commit offences with high benefit on a systematic basis may be a reasonable starting-point. On the other hand, the lack of a minimum penalty scale for such offences may lead to disproportionate results, as the classification as a lifestyle offender automatically triggers the mandatory assumptions. This sometimes leads to very harsh results, which will be described in the following.

3.6.3. THE ASSESSMENT OF BENEFIT ON THE BASIS OF THE 'CRIMINAL LIFESTYLE' ASSUMPTIONS

The provisions on the assessment of benefit regarding lifestyle offenders in Section 10 POCA 2002 establish a very strict mathematical calculation of the

---

248 See for example Liberty, *Proceeds of Crime: Consultation on Draft Legislation*, May 2001, Section 3.

249 Liberty, *Proceeds of Crime: Consultation on Draft Legislation*, May 2001, Section 3.6.

250 Liberty, *Proceeds of Crime: Consultation on Draft Legislation*, May 2001, Section 4.3.5.

251 Sec. 75(3) and (4) POCA 2002.

amount of a confiscation order. As further described in Section 3.4.2.1 above, the four statutory assumptions are mandatory, and there are only two very limited exceptions. Accordingly, the court is *obligated* to assume that all income and expenditure during the previous six years are the proceeds of crime, unless a defendant – on a balance of probabilities – can show that this is not the case. The burden of proof as well as the evidentiary and procedural difficulties in this respect will be discussed later, but the fact that there is practically no room for judicial discretion sometimes results in rather artificially set confiscation orders. Giles has, for example, called the provision of assessing benefit in POCA 2002 "a sledgehammer to crack a nut".[252]

In some cases very remarkable confiscation orders have been issued. In *Shabir v. R* a defendant who was a pharmacist had submitted false, inflated, prescription claims.[253] As he was convicted on six counts of obtaining a money transfer by deception, he was classified as having a criminal lifestyle. The total amount obtained by deception was approximately £179,000, but the defendant had been entitled to the vast majority of the payments received, except for £464. On the basis of the statutory assumptions the totality of the money transfers was applied as benefit with the result of a confiscation order of about £212,000, notwithstanding the fact that it was based mostly on assets *legitimately obtained by the defendant*. On appeal, the Court of Appeal finally quashed the confiscation order and made a compensation order in the sum of £464. It was argued that the enormous disparity between the excess of the defendant's inflated claims and the confiscation order raised the real likelihood that the order was oppressive. The fact that the prosecution had initiated confiscation proceeds arguing that the defendant had benefited by £179,000 was considered an abuse of process.[254]

Another example of an overestimation of criminal benefit concerns the case of multiple offenders. According to established case-law, benefit from criminal conduct is in principle not apportioned between offenders who are jointly liable for an offence.[255] This means that if several offenders have jointly obtained the proceeds of a crime, a confiscation order may be made in the full amount of these proceeds *against each of them*. An example is four defendants who jointly commit a robbery obtaining £500,000 and put this money in a joint bank account to which each is a signatory. A confiscation order in the whole amount may then be made against each one of them. It does not matter whether some of them have actually withdrawn and spent money from this account, whereas others have yielded nothing. The total confiscation sum for the state is then £2,000,000, which does not reflect the real criminal benefit. According to the House of Lords

252 Giles, n 138 above.

253 [2008] EWCA Crim 1809.

254 Para. 27, [2008] EWCA Crim 1809. Compare on the power of abuse of process, Section 3.3.1 and n 167 above.

255 See for example *R v. May*, [2008] UKHL 28 and *R v. Green*, [2008] UKHL 30.

such a system is in principle not oppressive or disproportionate.[256] However, it is obvious that the same sum would in practice be confiscated from different offenders leading to double counting and an overestimation of criminal benefit.[257]

It is often argued in legal doctrine that the principle of assessing benefit in POCA 2002 is disproportionate in relation to multiple defendants.[258] In 2014, the Supreme Court gave an important ruling in this area. The joined cases of *R v. Ahmad and Another* and *R v. Fields and Others* concerned multiple defendants who had jointly acquired money through different types of fraud. Confiscation-orders in the full benefit amount had been directed towards each one of them. The Supreme Court confirmed that the benefit figure must not be apportioned between the defendants, and that each defendant can be held liable for the whole benefit. However, the Court also found that it would be disproportionate, and in violation of Article 1 of Protocol 1 to the ECHR, if the full benefit amount were recovered several times. It was therefore ruled that each confiscation order regarding multiple defendants shall contain a condition that it must not be enforced if the sum has already been recovered.[259] The *Joint Committee on Human Rights* has recommended that the principle in this judgment ought to be statutorily regulated in POCA 2002.[260] This recommendation has not yet been followed by the Government.[261]

As described in Section 3.4.2.3 above, a confiscation order is set to a lesser amount if a defendant is able to show that the amount of benefit exceeds his available assets. This provision has the aim of moderating the severity of the confiscation regime.[262] However, in case-law, a confiscation order is sometimes set higher than the available amount if it is assumed that an offender has "hidden assets". During the last few years, some confiscation orders regarding very high amounts have been made in such cases, which have in fact also resulted in some overestimation of criminal benefit. This has partly been shown at the enforcement stage, where no or only few identified assets have been found.[263]

---

256 See *R v. May*, [2008] UKHL 28.

257 See further on the problem of multiple defendants, Giles, n 138 above, pp. 93–95 and Ulph, n 171 above, pp. 269–70.

258 See for example Giles, n 138 above, pp. 93–94, who argues that such results follow from the focus on the concept of "obtaining" rather than "retention" of property in assessing the defendants' benefit.

259 [2014] UKSC 36. See for a comment on the case, R. Fortson, "Case Comment, *R v Ahmad and Fields*: Proceeds of Crime – Confiscation Orders – Whether Value of the Benefit Obtained Jointly is to be Shared between Parties to the Joint Criminal Venture" (2014) 10 *Criminal Law Review*, pp. 756–60.

260 House of Lords, Joint Committee on Human Rights, *Second Report of Session 2014–15*, HL Paper 49 HC 746, p. 8.

261 Compare also Section 3.6.6.1 below where the case of *Minhas v. United Kingdom* is described, which also concerns the calculation of criminal benefit regarding several perpetrators.

262 Ulph, n 171 above, p. 266.

263 Compare for such a conclusion, *CPS Asset Recovery Strategy*, June 2014, p. 6.

Furthermore, the assessment of benefit under POCA 2002 may in some cases lead to unjust results.[264] Bullock has, for example, argued on the basis of *inter alia* interviews with financial investigators that the nature of criminal benefit on the basis of the assumptions is highly speculative. When confronted with similar information and sets of circumstances, different financial investigators estimate benefit differently. The benefit figure is thereby worked out more or less cautiously. Some financial investigators count assets which clearly come from legitimate sources or "build in room" in order to be able to negotiate the benefit figure before the confiscation proceedings.[265] The stiff application of the statutory assumptions in Section 10 POCA 2002 and the mandatory nature of the court proceedings are also relevant in this context. This is discussed in what follows.

3.6.4. LACK OF JUDICIAL DISCRETION

Obviously, a prosecutor's decision to apply for a confiscation order is crucial, as the court *must proceed* on the basis of such requests. The absence of judicial discretion within the confiscation regime has been sharply criticised by for example Lawrence:

> [J]udicial discretion has been stripped away so that, apart from where abuse of process can be found, it is practically non-existent. If, for example, a defendant has, before trial, handed back to the loser all of his ill-gotten gains, the judge now has no discretion to take that into consideration before he makes the confiscation order. Unusually, the Proceeds of Crime Act 2002 is quite clear on judicial discretion and the appeal courts have held that it cannot be interpreted away to make room for such an absurd element as common sense![266]

During the legislative process enacting POCA 2002 there was concern from the House of Lords about the absence of judicial discretion and the lack of protection for defendants against the possibility of abuse of power by the prosecutors. However, the Government argued that a mandatory procedure was necessary in order for the prosecution to act against the increasing problem of organised crime.[267] Accordingly, Section 10(6) POCA 2002 only allows the

---

264 Lawrence, n 232 above.

265 K. Bullock, "Criminal Benefit, the Confiscation Order and the Post-conviction Confiscation Regime" (2014) 62 *Crime, Law and Social Change*, pp. 45–64, pp. 50–54. On negotiations on the figures related to the confiscation amount, compare Section 3.5 and n 221 above.

266 Lawrence, n 232 above, pp. 23–24. See further on judicial discretion of judges, Ulph, n 171 above, pp. 274–77 and Giles, n 138 above, pp. 102–07.

267 Giles, n 138 above, p. 102.

courts to set the statutory assumption aside if the assumption is shown to be incorrect or if there is a serious risk of injustice.[268] These exceptions have very limited application, and will only be applied as a means of moderating unjust calculations. It does not take account of any personal hardship on a defendant.[269] Furthermore, as argued by Raphael, it is a heavy burden on the defence to prove a risk of injustice especially after the defendant has been convicted of a criminal offence.[270]

In some case-law, the lifestyle assumptions have been deviated from with reference to the *abuse of process doctrine*. This power has been developed in common law in order, *inter alia*, to protect defendants against a misuse of criminal proceedings. One example of such a case regarding confiscation proceedings was the case of *Shabir v. R*, described in Section 3.6.3 above. In *R v. Morgan and Bygrave*, confiscation proceedings had been started against two defendants in spite of the fact that they had repaid or had intended to repay the victim what had been stolen.[271] The Court of Appeal affirmed that the court has jurisdiction to stay confiscation proceedings for abuse of process in cases where it would be "oppressive" to seek confiscation.[272] The power to quash a confiscation order on the basis of the abuse of process doctrine is, however, exceptional and the cases to which it is applied are very rare. This circumstance has been emphasised by the Court of Appeal in *R v. Baden Low*:

> If it were otherwise the case and the jurisdiction exercised more widely, the court would be defeating the clear decision of Parliament, by enacting the legislation in the terms in which it did, not only to impose a draconian policy but also to remove the discretion of the court to avoid those consequences, save in a case where abuse was established.[273]

Consequently, the abuse of process jurisdiction cannot be interpreted as giving any general judicial discretion, but must be used only in cases of "true oppression".[274] Even if certain guidelines for prosecutors on the discretion to instigate confiscation proceedings have been published, these are not compulsory and it must be doubted whether this may establish sufficient consistency regarding the use of prosecutorial discretion in this area.[275]

---

268 Compare Section 3.4.2.1 above.
269 See further Giles, n 138 above, pp. 100–02.
270 See Raphael, n 131 above, p. 555.
271 [2008] EWCA Crim 1323.
272 Para. 27, *R v. Morgan and Bygrave*, [2008] EWCA Crim 1323.
273 Para. 16 in [2009] EWCA Crim 194.
274 Giles, n 138 above, pp. 105–07 and Ulph, n 171 above, p. 276.
275 See further Giles, n 138 above, pp. 105–06.

3.6.5. THE BURDEN OF PROOF ON A DEFENDANT

English confiscation law has been critically described as "a frontal assault on due process".[276] As described in Section 3.4.2.2 above, the burden of proof is divided between the prosecutor (which must establish to the civil standard of proof that there is benefit from crime and the amount of that benefit) and the defendant (who must establish on the balance of probabilities that he has acquired the assets legally). Critics argue in this respect that the provisions on a lowered standard of proof, on a reversal of the burden of proof and the concept of a criminal lifestyle generate an effect where "guilt becomes *de facto* established" at what would previously have been purely one stage in the preliminary investigation.[277]

A reversal of the burden of proof is indeed a very controversial measure in the area of criminal law, and such provisions have been contested in the area of confiscation law both in national case-law and before the ECtHR.[278] Even if one can argue that an individual is in principle in a better position than the prosecution to account for his financial situation, it is obvious that it may be very difficult in practice – even with a lesser standard of proof – to rebut the criminal lifestyle assumptions in all aspects. It may be difficult to remember different transactions, and to find sufficient supporting documentation or witnesses for expenditure which took place six years earlier.[279] As Nicol has argued, the six-year cut-off may be considered as illusory, because the court may assume that any expenditure during that period was made out of criminal proceeds, meaning:

> In consequence, a defendant who six years prior to his arrest had purchased a house with a down-payment saved over four years would have to demonstrate the lawfulness of his income for the previous 10 years. This would be a daunting task for even the most scrupulous record-keeper and honest citizen.[280]

As rightly pointed out, the system is predicated upon a model of rational economic behaviour, which cannot be safely assumed by society on a case-by-case basis.[281] A complication for the defendant under the system is that any oral evidence given in the confiscation proceedings may have low credibility, because the defendant has just been convicted of an offence and has been classified as a "lifestyle" offender. Furthermore, the burden of proof to show that the available assets are lower than the benefit from crime can be onerous.

---

276 J. Lea, "Hitting Criminals Where it Hurts: Organised Crime and the Erosion of Due Process" (2004) 35 *Cambrian Law Review*, p. 81, p. 83.

277 Lea, n 276 above, p. 94.

278 See further Section 3.6.6 below.

279 See Lawrence, n 232 above, p. 23 and Alldridge, n 159 above, pp. 828–29.

280 A. Nicol, "Confiscation of the Profits of Crime" (1988) 52 *Journal of Criminal Law*, p. 75, p. 77.

281 Liberty, *Proceeds of Crime: Consultation on Draft Legislation*, May 2001, Section 4.3.3.

Especially in cases where there is an allegation of hidden assets, the defendant is compelled to prove "negative circumstances", e.g. that he has no "hidden assets". Also in this area the burden of proof has been challenged under the ECHR.[282]

Under the English confiscation scheme, the defendant is not only put under pressure by the reversed burden of proof. There are also other features of the system that may additionally influence the presumption of innocence. As illustrated by Section 3.5 above, there is no right of silence when it comes to financial circumstances.[283] In principle, this means that there is no right to refuse to make any statements in order not to reveal one's own criminality.[284] This is very unusual in the area of criminal procedural law. The pressure being put on the defendant under POCA 2002 to give statements may therefore be questioned against the presumption of innocence, especially the right of silence and the protection against self-incrimination.

As mentioned before, any information which is provided in writing cannot be used in any subsequent criminal proceedings, but it seems unclear whether the same goes also for oral evidence given at the confiscation proceedings. In the pending case of *Koli v. United Kingdom* the applicant argues before the ECtHR that confiscation proceedings have in this respect violated his right against self-incrimination.[285] The defendant had pleaded guilty to one offence of money laundering, as he had acted as a courier for a package containing £400,000 of cash in return for a payment of £4,000. During the confiscation proceedings, where the criminal lifestyle provisions were applied, the prosecution claimed that Mr Koli had benefited from criminal conduct in the sum of £3.3 million, since he had been involved in further money laundering offences and had been laundering cash from third persons via his bank accounts. Mr Koli denied this and claimed that the assets were legitimate, albeit he had not paid tax on any of this sum. He had been advised before the proceedings by his lawyer that under POCA 2002 the prosecution could use anything he said in oral evidence as evidence against him in future criminal proceedings. The Crown Court disregarded the statements given, concluded that there were "hidden assets" and made a confiscation order in the recoverable sum of £1.6 million. On appeal, Mr Koli admitted that the money going through his accounts had been the proceeds of frauds committed by third parties, but that he had retained none of this money. Out of fear of being prosecuted for further money laundering offences, he had not told the truth in the first proceeding. He argued that Article 6(2) ECHR had been violated, because he had been obligated to incriminate himself

---

282 See for example the case of *Grayson and Barnham v. United Kingdom*, described in Section 3.6.6.1 above.

283 See for criticism against this, Nicol, n 280 above, especially pp. 77–80.

284 There is some protection against self-incrimination provided by POCA 2002, see further Section 3.5 above.

285 Appl. No. 58671/12, lodged on 3 August 2012, communicated on 6 May 2014.

in order to truthfully explain the sources of the assets and the whereabouts of the money. The Court of Appeal dismissed the appeal, but did not specifically answer the question of whether oral evidence given in confiscation proceedings may be used in subsequent criminal proceedings. The court held that the defendant had chosen to give oral evidence and had not argued in the original proceedings that he could not properly defend himself. It remains to be seen how the ECtHR will decide on the matter.

Obviously, it is a significant burden on the defendant to disprove the statutory assumptions of illegal origin. One must agree with Liberty that while it may be easier for a defendant to account for his finances, it does not follow that it is always fair to oblige him to do so.[286] It is not surprising that the confiscation regime in the UK has been challenged on several occasions under the guarantees of the ECHR. The challenges have concerned POCA 2002 as well as previous legislation in the UK.[287] When it comes to issues of the burden of proof and the statutory assumptions, cases under the old confiscation regime are also of importance, because the fundamental principles of the rulings have been decisive in many of the cases regarding POCA 2002. In what follows, some of the most important case-law in this respect from the ECtHR as well as from the national courts will be presented.

3.6.6. CONFISCATION ORDERS AND THE ECHR

3.6.6.1. *Case-law from the ECtHR*

Welch v. United Kingdom[288]

The principal issue in this case was whether a confiscation order under the Drug Trafficking Offences Act 1986 had violated the ban on retroactive legislation under Article 7 ECHR. In determining this question the ECtHR had to rule on whether the order constituted a penalty within the meaning of this article. The UK Government argued that the true purpose of the order was not to impose a penalty or punishment for a criminal offence, but was "essentially a confiscatory and preventive measure".[289] The ECtHR observed that the starting-point for the consideration was whether the measure in question had been imposed following a conviction for a criminal offence. It was concluded that the imposition of a measure according to the Drug Trafficking Offences Act 1986 was in fact

286 Liberty, *Proceeds of Crime: Consultation on Draft Legislation*, May 2001, Section 4.3.3.

287 For a general discussion of the English confiscation regime in relation to human rights and the ECHR, see for example Ulph, n 171 above and Alldridge, n 159 above.

288 Appl. No. 17440/90, Judgment of 9 February 1995.

289 See para. 24, Appl. No. 17440/90, Judgment of 9 February 1995.

dependent on a criminal conviction. The court acknowledged the Government's statements on the preventive purposes of confiscating property, but added:

> However it cannot be excluded that legislation which confers such broad powers of confiscation on the courts also pursues the aim of punishing the offender. Indeed the aims of prevention and reparation are consistent with a punitive purpose and may be seen as constituent elements of the very notion of punishment.[290]

According to the Court the severity of the order is not in itself decisive for the question of classification. In this case the following factors provided a strong indication of a penalty: the sweeping statutory assumptions in the Drug Trafficking Offences Act 1986 that all property acquired over a six-year period was the fruit of drug trafficking; the fact that the order was directed toward the proceeds and not limited to actual enrichment or profit; and the possibility of imprisonment in default of payment. With consideration of these punitive elements it was concluded that the confiscation order amounted to a penalty. The Court stressed, however, that this conclusion concerned only the *retrospective application* of the relevant legislation and did not call into question in any respect the powers of confiscation conferred on the courts as a weapon in the fight against drug trafficking.[291]

Phillips v. United Kingdom[292]

In this case an applicant complained that the statutory assumptions applied by the English courts when calculating benefit under the Drug Trafficking Act 1994 violated the presumption of innocence in Article 6(2) ECHR. Phillips had been sentenced to imprisonment for smuggling cannabis. He had previous convictions, but not regarding narcotics offences. Following from the application of the statutory assumptions in the Act, it was presumed during the confiscation procedure that all assets and expenses Mr Phillips had had during the previous six years constituted benefit from drug trafficking. The financial investigation had showed that he was the registered owner of an estate, five cars and several other assets, although he had no declared taxable income. The applicant had during the confiscation procedures failed to give any credible explanations about the legal source of these assets. The courts found that he had failed to rebut the statutory assumptions, and made a confiscation order of £91,400 with a two-year prison sentence to be served in default of payment. Before the ECtHR the Government argued that the confiscation order was to be regarded as a penalty for the drug-trafficking offence for which the applicant had been tried and

290 Para. 30, Appl. No. 17440/90, Judgment of 9 February 1995.

291 The same conclusion was made regarding the Drug Trafficking Offences Act 1986 in *Elton v. United Kingdom*, Appl. No. 32344/96, Decision of 11 September 1997.

292 Appl. No. 41087/98, Judgment of 5 July 2001.

found guilty, and that the confiscation proceedings did not amount to his being charged with any additional offence.[293] The applicant, on the other hand, argued that the confiscation process must be considered as a judicial process which involved his being "charged with a criminal offence" within Article 6(2) ECHR.

The ECtHR took the view that:

> [I]t is true that the assumption provided for in the 1994 Act, that all property held by the applicant within the preceding six years represented the proceeds of drug trafficking, required the national court to assume that he had been involved in other unlawful drug-related activities prior to the offence of which he was convicted. In contrast to the usual obligation on the prosecution to prove the elements of the allegations against the accused, the burden was on the applicant to prove, on the balance of probabilities, that he acquired the property in question other than through drug trafficking.[294]

However, the Court concluded that the purpose of the confiscation procedure was not to convict or acquit a defendant of a crime, but to enable the national court to determine the amount at which the confiscation order should be fixed.[295] It was added that the confiscation procedure governed by the Drug Trafficking Act 1994 was analogous to the determination by a court of the amount of a fine or the length of a period of imprisonment to be imposed on a defendant who had already been found guilty of a crime. The presumption of innocence was only relevant until a person has been proved guilty of an offence, and not in relation to any allegations made about the accused's bad character and conduct as part of the sentencing process. An exception to this would, however, be made if the allegations were of such nature and degree as to amount to the bringing of a new charge.[296] The ECtHR therefore concluded that Article 6(2) ECHR was not applicable to the confiscation proceedings.

On the other hand, the ECtHR stressed that the presumption of innocence, and the principle that the burden of proof of a crime lays with the prosecution, are components of the right to a fair trial in Article 6(1) ECHR, which is applicable to the sentencing process. It was referred in this regard to *Salabiaku v. France* where the Court had ruled that presumptions of fact or of law operate in every legal system and that the Convention does not prohibit them in principle. However, Article 6(2) does not regard presumptions provided for in the criminal law with indifference, and States are required to confine them within reasonable limits which take into account the importance of what is at stake and maintain the rights of the defence.[297]

---

293 Para. 28, Appl. No. 41087/98, Judgment of 5 July 2001.
294 Para. 33, Appl. No. 41087/98, Judgment of 5 July 2001.
295 Para. 34, Appl. No. 41087/98, Judgment of 5 July 2001.
296 Para. 35, Appl. No. 41087/98, Judgment of 5 July 2001.
297 See para. 28, Appl. No. 10519/83, Judgment of 7 October 1988.

In the *Phillips* case, the ECtHR emphasised that the purpose of the statutory assumptions in question was not to facilitate the burden of proof regarding the matter of responsibility for crime, but rather to make it possible for a court to determine the amount to be confiscated. Even if the confiscation order concerned a considerable amount with two years' imprisonment as a sanction for a failure to pay, it did not amount to a conviction of an additional drug-trafficking offence. Furthermore, the system provided safeguards for a defendant, for example a judicial procedure including a public hearing, advance disclosure of the case and a right for the defendant to submit his own evidence. The ECtHR emphasised that the most important safeguard was the right of the defendant to rebut the assumptions and to show that the assets had been acquired legally. Furthermore, the national court had a discretion not to apply the assumptions in cases of a serious risk of injustice.

The ECtHR ruled that the national courts had in the current case applied the presumptions within reasonable bounds and had respected the defendant's procedural rights. No violation of Article 6(1) ECHR was found. The applicant had also claimed that the confiscation order violated his right to peaceful enjoyment of his possessions under Article 1 of Protocol 1 to the ECHR. The ECtHR also dismissed this appeal, arguing that the interference suffered by the defendant was not disproportionate. The Court thereby took account of the important aim of the English legislation to combat serious problems of drug trafficking, and acknowledged that confiscation orders are to function as a deterrent and deprive offenders of criminal proceeds.

Grayson and Barnham v. United Kingdom[298]

In this case two applicants alleged that the English legislation on confiscation was in breach of Article 6 ECHR, as the burden of proof is on the defendant to show that the available amount is less than the established benefit. The case concerned the Drug Trafficking Act 1994. The first case of *Grayson* concerned a defendant who had been sentenced to 22 years' imprisonment for narcotics crimes relating to 28 kg of heroin which had been seized by the police. A confiscation order for over £1.2 million had been made based on the defendant's assets and his expenses and income for the six years before the relevant crime. Mr Grayson had maintained that his available assets did not amount to this benefit, and the police had only found available assets to a value of £236,000. However, the court of first instance stated that Mr Grayson had, for example, been able to explain neither why monetary transactions for high amounts had passed through his bank accounts, nor how he had obtained £70,000 to pay the costs of legal assistance in the current case. On appeal, the Court of Appeal had found – with reference to *inter alia Phillips v. United Kingdom* – that the burden

298 Appl. Nos. 19955/05 and 15085/06, Judgment of 23 September 2008.

of proof incumbent on the defendant concerning his available assets did not breach Article 6.

The second applicant before the ECtHR was Mr Barnham who had been sentenced to 11 years' imprisonment in the Crown Court for conspiracy to commit narcotics crime, with a confiscation order of over £1.5 million. This case, *R v. Barnham*,[299] has been described in Section 3.4.2.3 above. In the *Phillips* case the ECtHR had noted in a passage in the ruling that an issue relating to the fairness of the procedure might arise in circumstances where the amount of a confiscation order was based on the value of assumed "hidden assets".[300] The applicants therefore argued that the burden on a defendant to prove an available amount, in combination with conclusions of "hidden assets", was in violation of the concept of a fair trial.[301]

The ECtHR stressed by way of introduction that its task was to determine whether the way in which the statutory assumptions had been applied in the particular proceedings offended the principles of a fair trial in Article 6 ECHR. It was underlined that the task of evaluation of evidence lies with national courts.[302] The ECtHR observed that the applicants had been protected by several statutory procedural rights within the confiscation proceedings. In each case a court had considered the plea within the framework of a legal and public procedure, the financial investigation had been presented to the applicant in advance and he had been given the opportunity to present his own evidence. Each applicant had been represented by legal counsel. *Firstly*, the Court pointed out that the prosecutor had had the burden of proving that the applicant had held the assets in question, and added the following on the burden of proof for the defendant:

> Although the court was required by law to assume that the assets derived from drug trafficking, this assumption could have been rebutted if the applicant had shown that he had acquired the property through legitimate means. Furthermore, the judge had a discretion not to apply the assumption if he considered that applying it would give rise to a serious risk of injustice (see *R v. Benjafield*: paragraph 27 above).
>
> Before the Court, neither applicant seriously complained about the fairness of this first stage of the confiscation procedure, whereby the benefit from drug trafficking was calculated. The Court does not consider that in either case, in principle or practice, it was incompatible with the concept of a fair trial under Article 6 to place the onus on the applicant, once he had been convicted of a major offence of drug dealing,

299 [2005] EWCA Crim 1049.

300 See para. 46, Appl. No. 41087/98, Judgment of 5 July 2001.

301 In fact, in the proceedings before the Court of Appeal in the *Barnham* case, the counsel for the defendant referred to the passage in the *Phillips* case and argued that the ECtHR had envisaged that a different approach might be adopted in cases involving an allegation of hidden assets. See paras. 34–35, [2005] EWCA Crim 1049.

302 See para. 42, Appl. Nos. 19955/05 and 15085/06, Judgment of 23 September 2008.

> to establish that the source of money or assets which he had been shown to have possessed in the years preceding the offence was legitimate. Given the existence of the safeguards referred to above, the burden on him did not exceed reasonable limits.[303]

Secondly, when it came to the assessment of available assets during the confiscation proceedings, it was observed that the national courts were not compelled to make any assumptions of past criminality. The Court emphasised that even if the burden of proof lay with the defendants to prove that their available assets were less than the benefit, both defendants had been protected by the above-mentioned procedural rights. They had, however, failed to give any credible explanations as to their finances. The ECtHR underlined that it was not its task to express an opinion on the actual evaluation of the evidence in the cases, and concluded:

> The Court agrees with the judgments of the Court of Appeal in the instant cases (see paragraphs 11 and 18 and see also *R v. Barwick*, paragraphs 25–26 above), that it was not incompatible with the notion of a fair hearing in criminal proceedings to place the onus on each applicant to give a credible account of his current financial situation. In each case, having been proved to have been involved in extensive and lucrative drug dealing over a period of years, it was not unreasonable to expect the applicants to explain what had happened to all the money shown by the prosecution to have been in their possession, any more than it was unreasonable at the first stage of the procedure to expect them to show the legitimacy of the source of such money or assets. Such matters fell within the applicants' particular knowledge and the burden on each of them would not have been difficult to meet if their accounts of their financial affairs had been true.[304]

Minhas v. United Kingdom[305]

The case concerned a robbery of jewellery worth £580,112 committed by three perpetrators. Mr Minhas had pleaded not guilty, but had been convicted as his DNA had been found on clothing recovered together with some items of the stolen jewellery. At the confiscation proceedings, he continued to deny his participation. He was questioned about his assets, and in particular about a house which he had purchased some months after the robbery. His counsel argued that the judge must – by setting the amount of the confiscation order – take into account of the fact that the robbery had been committed by three men and that it was unlikely that the stolen jewellery had been sold for its full value. However, the Crown Court set the confiscation order regarding Mr Minhas at

303 Paras. 45 and 46, Appl. Nos. 19955/05 and 15085/06, Judgment of 23 September 2008.
304 Para. 49, Appl. Nos. 19955/05 and 15085/06, Judgment of 23 September 2008.
305 Appl. No. 7618/07, Decision of 10 November 2009.

£602,812, allowing for an increase in the value of money. It was maintained that there were no grounds not to ascribe the total benefit to one single defendant, and that the defendant had declined to give any information to the court about what happened to the proceeds or any credible explanation about his financial circumstances.

The Court of Appeal refused leave to appeal against the confiscation order. Mr Minhas complained to the ECtHR about a violation of Article 6(1) ECHR. The court first observed that the rules on confiscation orders in POCA 2002 "merely update and consolidate" previous legislation on confiscation, which means that the principles of its own rulings in *Phillips v. United Kingdom* and *Grayson and Barnham v. United Kingdom* were applicable. It was repeated that Article 6(2) is not applicable to such proceedings as they are analogous to a sentencing procedure, but that Article 6(1) – with the inherent notion of the presumption of innocence – must be respected. Further, the Court noted that the burden of proof must generally fall on the prosecution in criminal proceedings, but that, once discharged, it may be transferred to the accused. With reference to the above described cases of *Phillips* and *Salabiaku*, it was added that the presumption of innocence may be limited by different presumptions of fact or of law, but only within reasonable limits.

The ECtHR observed that in the present case it was clear that the defendant had benefited from criminal conduct, because he had been convicted of robbery and it was not disputed that jewellery with a value of £580,112 had been stolen. Under these circumstances the Court did not consider it to be inappropriate that the burden of proof was passed to the defendant to demonstrate, on a balance of probabilities, that his benefit was less than the full value of the jewellery. It was argued that such information fell within the defendant's particular knowledge, and the burden on him would thus not have been difficult to meet. However, the defendant had neither provided any information as to the other perpetrators, nor explained what had happened to the proceeds of the robbery. As to the calculation of the recoverable amount the Court held that it would not have been unduly burdensome on the defendant to give evidence as to how he had disposed of the jewellery and to provide full disclosure as to the assets that he held. However, he had only given unlikely explanations about his financial circumstances. As in the other cases referred to above, an important factor was the safeguards built into the proceedings under POCA 2002.

After an overall assessment, the ECtHR ruled that it was not incompatible with the concept of a fair trial to place the burden of proof on the defendant to provide credible information in order to reduce the value of the benefit under the applicable legislation. Nor was it incompatible with the notion of a fair hearing in criminal proceedings to place the onus on him to account for his current financial situation.

Bagnall v. United Kingdom[306]

This is a pending case before the ECtHR where an applicant argues that the confiscation proceedings have violated Article 6(1) and (2). Mr Bagnall has been convicted on one count of money laundering after being caught with a bag containing £99,200 in banknotes. The confiscation order in the amount of over £1.8 million in the Crown Court was based on money credited to bank accounts held by the defendant during the previous six years. The prosecution was of the opinion that these assets were related to criminal conduct, particularly VAT fraud. The defence argued that the reliance of the prosecution on a specific accusation that the defendant was involved in VAT fraud amounted to the bringing of a criminal charge, and required that such an allegation must be proven to the criminal standard.

The Court of Appeal denied this in its ruling, underlining that this case was different to *R v. Briggs-Price* which had dealt with the question whether the defendant had been in possession of property at all.[307] It was emphasised that there was no dispute in the instant case about the assets possessed by the defendant, but the only question concerning their source. As the defendant had claimed that the assets were legitimate, the prosecution had been entitled to produce evidence in rebuttal of these assertions. The Court of Appeal ruled that there could be nothing unfair in requiring the defendant to demonstrate that his businesses were carried out lawfully or that there had been no VAT fraud. It remains to be seen how the ECtHR will rule on this question.

3.6.6.2. *Confiscation Orders and the Human Rights Act 1998*

The English courts have in several cases confirmed that the confiscation regime is compatible with the Human Rights Act 1998, which is the legislation that has incorporated the ECHR into national law. The House of Lords has, for example in *R v. Benjafield and Others*[308] (regarding the Drug Trafficking Act 1994) and *R v. Rezvi*[309] (regarding the Criminal Justice Act 1988) ruled that the confiscation scheme is not disproportionate to its purpose of responding to the public interest in depriving criminals of their criminal proceeds. In holding that the statutory assumptions are proportionate, the House of Lords has especially relied on the obligation of the courts not to apply the scheme in cases of a serious risk of injustice.

In the case of *R v. Waya*[310] the Supreme Court considered whether the application of the provisions of POCA 2002 for the calculation of benefit may, in

306 Appl. No. 54241/12, lodged on 8 August 2012.
307 This case is described in Section 3.4.2.2 above.
308 [2002] UKHL 2.
309 [2002] UKHL 1.
310 [2012] UKSC 51.

some circumstances, violate the ECHR. Hereby it was recognised by the Court that there may be cases in which orders calculated strictly on the basis of the provisions of POCA 2002 might produce results which are disproportionate to the objective of the legislation and which might infringe Article 1 of the First Protocol to the ECHR. It was held that the courts are in such cases obligated to reduce the amount of the order so that it will not infringe the defendant's human rights. At the same time, the Court underlined that it was not the intention of the ruling to create a wide-ranging general discretion for the courts.[311] The Joint Committee on Human Rights has recommended that the principle of the *Waya* judgment ought to be statutorily regulated in order to "bring greater legal certainty".[312] The Serious Crime Act 2015 has therefore amended Section 6(5)(b) POCA 2002, which now provides that the provision only applies if it would not be disproportionate to require the defendant to pay the recoverable amount.[313] It is important to note that the *Waya* case did not concern an application of the statutory criminal lifestyle assumptions. The Supreme Court indicated that in such a case a confiscation order did not – except in very unusual circumstances – risk being disproportionate as the assumptions are not to be applied if they are shown to be incorrect or if there is a risk of serious injustice.[314]

3.6.6.3. *Remarks on the Compatibility of the Regime with the ECHR*

> [T]he presumption of innocence in Art. 6 (2) is imported by Art. 6 (1), but it may be displaced by the terms of the legislation and the right may still be satisfied by appropriate procedural safeguards.[315]

To sum up, case-law from both the ECtHR and national courts has thus concluded that the confiscation proceedings do not involve the defendant being charged with a new offence. It has been held that Article 6(2) ECHR is not engaged, but that the presumption of innocence and due process rights in the right to a fair trial in Article 6(1) are applicable. The ECtHR has in principle found that neither the statutory presumptions working against a defendant nor a reversal of the burden of proof within confiscation proceedings are *per se* in violation of the concept of a fair trial. If a defendant has been convicted of certain offences, it may be justified to oblige him to show the legitimacy of the source of certain property. It is, however, required that procedural safeguards are provided so that

311 See paras. 24–25, [2012] UKSC 51. See further a commentary to the case, Alldridge, n 182 above, especially pp. 175–78.

312 House of Lords, Joint Committee on Human Rights, *Second Report of Session 2014–15*, HL Paper 49 HC 746, pp. 6–8.

313 Para. 19 of Schedule 4 to the Serious Crime Act 2015.

314 Sec. 10(6) POCA 2002.

315 Alldridge, n 159 above, p. 832.

a defendant may rebut the assumptions and that national courts may disregard the statutory assumptions in cases where there is a risk of serious injustice.

The English confiscation regime seems so far have provided a sufficient balance between the interest of confiscation and human rights protection. With reference to the *Grayson and Barnham* case, Ulph has for example argued that any legal challenge to the statutory assumptions would have little hope of success.[316] This may well be the case. On the other hand, the task of the European Court is to test how the assumptions have been applied in *particular* proceedings, and it may be questioned whether all issues regarding the compatibility of the system have been sufficiently considered. The ECtHR has, for example, placed significant emphasis on provisions on procedural rights of the defence and the possibility to rebut the criminal lifestyle assumptions. However, it may be doubted whether *provisions* on a right to certain procedural rights are *per se* sufficient to rebut such assumptions in practice. As discussed in Section 3.6.5 above, there are in some cases significant evidentiary and practical difficulties in discharging the burden of proof regarding transactions going back six years in time. Even if there is a *right* to present own evidence, this does not necessarily mean that it is practically possible to do so. The principle of equality of arms (i.e. that one party to the proceedings must not be placed at a substantial disadvantage) may require a guarantee of stronger procedural safeguards.[317]

In this respect, it is also interesting to note that the ECtHR as well as the House of Lords have taken special account of Section 10(6) POCA 2002, even though this provision does not give the judge any general discretion to avoid disproportionate orders.[318] Quite the opposite, this rule has in practice a rather limited impact on confiscation proceedings when it comes to the issue of whether a defendant enjoys a fair proceeding in all aspects.

3.6.7. DIFFICULTIES REGARDING THE ENFORCEMENT OF CONFISCATION ORDERS

One special feature of POCA 2002 is the regime of *imprisonment in default of payment*.[319] The motive for such a system is that it is claimed that there are many criminals, particularly those with high confiscation orders, who choose to serve a prison sentence rather than to pay an order.[320] In 2014, about £490 million was

316 Ulph, n 171 above, p. 274.
317 For a further discussion of the asset recovery proceedings in the UK in the perspective of the defence, See Raphael, n 131 above.
318 Giles, n 138 above, p. 101. Compare also Section 3.6.4 above.
319 Compare Section 3.5 above.
320 HM Government, *Serious and Organised Crime Strategy*, Cm 8715, October 2013, p. 35.

outstanding in the UK for offenders who had served or were currently serving default sentences.[321] In order to strengthen the enforcement mechanisms, an *increase in default sentences* was therefore introduced by the Serious Crime Act 2015, which increased the maximum term from 10 years to 14 years (for an amount exceeding £1 million) and the minimum term from seven days (for an amount not exceeding £200) to six months (for an amount not exceeding £10,000).[322] In addition, a new provision was introduced stating that where the confiscation order exceeds £10 million, release half way through a sentence will not be allowed. This means that such defendants will have to serve the full 14 years consecutively to any imprisonment sentence for the substantive offence in question. It must be doubted whether this will actually decrease the outstanding debt regarding confiscation orders. Instead, the risk is high that there will be an enormous rise of the prison population as many defendants cannot or (still) do not want to pay the orders.

In fact, it seems that the whole issue of enforcing confiscation orders is a major problem in the UK.[323] According to a report from the House of Commons Committee of Public Accounts published in 2014 a total of around £1.5 billion of confiscation order debt remain uncollected.[324] The enforcement bodies are therefore obviously more successful in collecting proceeds from low-value orders than high-value ones, with an enforcement rate of nearly 90 per cent for orders under £1,000 compared to 18 per cent for orders over £1 million.[325] At September 2015, the total debt outstanding from confiscation orders had risen

---

321 House of Commons Committee of Public Accounts, *Confiscation Orders*, Forty-ninth Report of Session 2013–14, HC 942, published on 21 March 2014, p. 5.

322 See for the motives, HM Government, *Serious and Organised Crime Strategy*, Cm 8715, October 2013, p. 35.

323 Council of the European Union, *Report on the United Kingdom*, 9636/2/10, REV 2, p. 68. See generally on confiscation order enforcement, D. Gardner, "Closing Loopholes to Take the Cash Out of Crime – Practical Changes in Legislation to Improve Confiscation Order Enforcement" (2009) 2 *Criminal Law Review*, pp. 90–99.

324 House of Commons Committee of Public Accounts, *Confiscation Orders*, Forty-ninth Report of Session 2013–14, HC 942, published on 21 March 2014, p. 11.

325 House of Commons Committee of Public Accounts, *Confiscation Orders*, Forty-ninth Report of Session 2013–14, HC 942, published on 21 March 2014, pp. 3–4 and 7–12. Compare a study by P. Sproat, "To what Extent is the UK's Anti-Money Laundering and Asset Recovery Regime used against Organised Crime?" (2009) 12 *Journal of Money Laundering Control*, p. 134–50 which suggests that the POCA 2002 has only been used in cases of organised crime on a small number of occasions. Compare also on the efficiency of the regime, P. Sproat, "An Evaluation of the UK's Anti-Money Laundering and Asset Recovery Regime" (2007) 47 *Crime, Law and Social Change*, pp. 169–84, P. Sproat, "The New Policing of Assets and the new Assets of Policing, a Tentative Financial Cost-Benefit Analysis of the UK's Anti-Money Laundering and Asset Recovery Regime" (2007) 3 *Journal of Money Laundering Control*, pp. 277–99 and P. Sproat, "A Critique of the Official Discourse on Drug and Sex Trafficking by Organised Crime Using Data on Asset Recovery" (2012) 2 *Journal of Financial Crime*, pp. 149–62.

to £1.61 billion.[326] It is suggested that the reason for the poor enforcement rates is the failure of the prosecutors to make sufficient use of restraint orders early in the investigation, and to recover assets hidden abroad.[327]

The CPS has stated that it intends to improve the enforcement rates of the orders.[328] However, a special feature of the enforcement regime in the UK is that the law enforcement agencies receive a proportion of the assets that they recover to help fund their work. According to the Asset Recovery Incentivisation Scheme (ARIS), the Home Office receives 50 per cent of confiscated assets, the relevant law enforcement agency and the prosecutor will each receive 18.75 per cent and Her Majesty's Courts and Tribunals Service (HMCTS) receive 12.5 per cent.[329] The fact that the law enforcement authorities receive a part of the assets which are recovered, may lead to a certain risk that the police and prosecutors are considered to have a vested financial interest and thus risk being "partial" in the confiscation proceedings.[330] Furthermore, they may be put under pressure as certain targets are set for the number of confiscation orders to be made. The CPS seems to be aware of the problem that the ARIS scheme could be seen as an incentive "to pursue criminals' assets inappropriately, due to the potential benefits that accrue to the Service".[331] In the *Asset Recovery Strategy* the authority therefore highlights the importance of a principle-based approach to confiscation.[332]

---

326 National Audit Office, *Confiscation Orders: Progress Review*, HC 886, March 2016, p. 10.

327 The Serious Crime Act 2015 has accordingly also strengthened the powers for the making of a restraint order, see further Sec. 11 Serious Crime Act 2015 and Secs. 40–41 POCA 2002.

328 *CPS Asset Recovery Strategy*, June 2014, p. 6.

329 Compare on this system, *Center for the Study of Democracy, Disposal of Confiscated Assets in the EU Member States, Laws and Practices*, 2014, pp. 103–05 and Ryder, n 131 above, pp. 793–94.

330 According to *The Times* the lawyers from the CPS are even receiving personal bonuses linked to their success in confiscating criminal assets. See an article by F. Gibb in *The Times*, 31 October 2009. For a critical discussion of confiscation to fund law enforcement agencies, see G. Stessens, *Money Laundering; A New International Law Enforcement Model*, Cambridge University Press, 2000, pp. 56–58.

331 *CPS Asset Recovery Strategy*, June 2014, p. 14.

332 *CPS Asset Recovery Strategy*, June 2014, p. 14. See also the *Legal Guidance on the Proceeds of Crime*, at: www.cps.gov.uk.

CHAPTER 4
LEGISLATION IN GERMANY

4.1. THE DEVELOPMENT OF THE MEASURE OF EXTENDED CONFISCATION IN GERMAN LAW

> Indem der Staat dem Täter deliktisch Erlangtes wegnimmt, führt er ihm, wie auch der Rechtsgemeinschaft, vor Augen, dass strafrechtswidrige Bereicherungen nicht geduldet werden und Straftaten sich nicht lohnen.[333]

The German provisions on confiscation and forfeiture of property and proceeds of crime are found in the Criminal Code ("*Strafgesetzbuch*", hereafter "*StGB*") and the Criminal Procedural Code ("*Strafproceßordnung*", hereafter "*StPO*").[334] As already mentioned in Section 1.3.3 above, the legislation differs in the use of two measures; "*Verfall*" (forfeiture) and "*Einziehung*" (seizure). Generally speaking, "*Verfall*" is used regarding the recovery of something that the defendant has acquired through a criminal offence or for its commission. Such provisions are found in Section 73 et seq. *StGB*. "*Einziehung*", on the other hand, refers to the recovery of any instruments or objects which were generated by a crime, or used in its commission or preparation. Such provisions – which for example relate to certain dangerous items – are found in Section 74 et seq. *StGB*.[335]

---

333 *Bundesverfassungsgericht*, Decision of 14.1.2004, 2 BvR 564/95, NJW 2004, 2073, para. 75.

334 See for commentaries to the *StGB*, T. Fischer, *Strafgesetzbuch mit Nebengesetze*, 60. Auflage, C.H. Beck, 2013, the *Beck'scher Online-Kommentar StGB/Heuchemer*, 29. Auflage 2015, the *Münchener Kommentar zum StGB*, 2. Auflage, 2012, Kindhäuser, Neumann and Paeffgen (eds), *Kommentar zum StGB*, 4. Auflage, 2013 and Schönke, Schröder and Eser (eds), *Strafgesetzbuch, Kommentar*, 29. Auflage, C.H. Beck, 2014. All of them are available at www.beck-online.de. For information on the German system of confiscation in English, see also Evaluation Report on the Fifth Round of Mutual Evaluations, Financial Crime and Financial Investigations, *Report on Germany*, 16269/2/11, REV 2, Brussels, 19.1.2012. Practical guidelines for asset recovery under German law are also given in *Vermögensabschöpfung im deutschen Recht*, Hinweise für Praktiker, Bundesministerium der Justiz und für Verbraucherschutz, October 2015. For a critical and detailed discussion of the German system, F. Meyer, "'Reformiert die Rückgewinnungshilfe!' – Denkanstöße für eine Generalüberholung der Vermögensabschöpfung" (2015) 2 *ZStW*, pp. 241–83.

335 See generally on this classification, M. Kilchling, "Tracing, Seizing and Confiscating Proceeds from Corruption (and other Illegal Conduct) within or outside the Criminal Justice System" (2001) 9 *European Journal of Crime, Criminal Law and Criminal Justice*, p. 264, pp. 273–75, J. Benseler, "Forfeiture Legislation in Germany: Legal Basis and Prosecution Practice" (1997)

In German law extended confiscation is provided for in the provision on "*erweiterter Verfall*" in Section 73d *StGB*.[336] This measure was introduced as early as 1992 by the Act against Organised Crime, as a result of a reform of many different areas of criminal law and procedural law with the German legal system in order to create more effective means to prevent and deal with organised criminality.[337] Many rather far-reaching proposals had been made by the legislator during the legislative process, for example regarding new investigative measures like bugging etc.[338] The importance of a profit-oriented law enforcement approach was also strongly emphasised in the legislative works:

> Die Organisierte Kriminalität ist zu einer Herausforderung für Staat und Gesellschaft geworden ... Triebfeder für die Organisierte Kriminalität ist das Gewinnstreben. Eine wirksame Bekämpfung hat daher bei der Abschöpfung dieser Gewinne anzusetzen. Mit dem Zugriff auf die Tatgewinne soll den Straftätern zugleich auch das Investitionskapital für die Begehung weiterer Straftaten entzogen werden. Zur Schaffung neuer Vorschriften über das Abschöpfen von Geldern sollen dem organisierten Verbrechen seine finanziellen Ressourcen entzogen werden.[339]

In line with this policy, the new measures of extended confiscation as well as a form of property penalty ("*Vermögensstrafe*") were introduced by the Act. The legislator was of the opinion that the confiscation regime had not been applied frequently enough in the past and that more efficient rules were needed. Against the background of significant difficulties in practice in sufficiently proving a link between certain property and a criminal offence, a fundamental aim of

---

5 *European Journal of Crime, Criminal Law and Criminal Justice*, p. 203 and Evaluation Report on the Fifth Round of Mutual Evaluations, Financial Crime and Financial Investigations, *Report on Germany*, 16269/2/11, REV 2, Brussels 19.1.2012, p. 58.

336 On the terminological choices made in this study, compare Section 1.3.3 above.

337 *Gesetz zur Bekämpfung des illegalen Rauschgiftshandels und anderer Erscheinungsformen der Organisierten Kriminalität* ("OrgKG"), 15.7.1992, BGBl. I 1992, p. 1302. See for legislative works, especially BT-Dr 11/6623 and 12/989, and on the background to and scope of the reform, M. Pieth, "Gewinnabschöpfung bei Betäubungsmitteldelikten: Zu den Hintergründen und Risiken der neuen Gesetzgebung" (1990) 12 *Strafverteidiger*, pp. 558–62, P. Rieß, "Neue Gesetze zur Bekämpfung der Organisierten Kriminalität" (1992) 11 *Neue Justiz*, pp. 491–97 and O. Katholnigg, "Die Neuregelungen beim Verfall" (1994) 9 *Juristische Rundschau*, pp. 353–56.

338 For a critical description of the legislative proposals and the provisions adopted, see A. Eser, "Neue Wege der Gewinnabschöpfung im Kampf gegen die organisierte Kriminalität? Kritische Bemerkungen zu aktuellen Reformbemühungen" in W. Küper (ed.), *Beiträge zur Rechtswissenschaft: Festschrift für Walter Stree und Johannes Wessels zum 70. Geburtstag*, C.F. Müller, 1993, pp. 833–53, W. Perron, "Vermögensstrafe und Erweiterter Verfall – im Spannungsfeld zwischen öffentlichen Strafverfolgungsintressen und privaten Eigentumsrechten" (1993) 19 *Juristen Zeitung*, pp. 918–25 and E. Weßlau, "Neue Methoden der Gewinnabschöpfung? – Vermögensstrafe – Beweislastumkehr" (1991) 5 *Strafverteidiger*, pp. 226–35.

339 BT-Dr 12/989, p. 1.

the reform was to simplify the prerequisites for the confiscation of criminal assets:

> Ziel der neuen Vermögenstrafe ebenso wie des "Erweiterten" Verfalls ist es, der – u.a. für die Betäubungsmittelkriminalität typischen – Schwierigkeit entgegenzuwirken, daß bei den Tatbeteiligten Vermögenswerte angetroffen werden, deren kriminelle Herkunft zwar naheliegt, die sich jedoch nicht konkret faßbaren, womöglich gar den im anhängigen Strafverfahren zur Untersuchung gezogenen Straftaten zuordnen lassen.[340]

However, the new measures were already controversial even during the legislative process of adopting the Act against Organised Crime, and the provisions were (and have since then been) strongly criticised in German jurisprudence. The fundamental objection has been that they violate certain defence rights and other recognised human rights.[341] Eser has for example called extended confiscation in Section 73d *StGB* a "*Verdachtsstrafe*" (suspicion penalty) which is clearly in violation of the presumption of innocence.[342] In spite of the criticism during the legislative stage, the legislator chose to stick to the proposals on the profit-oriented methods and maintained that they were drafted within constitutional limits. It was, for example, emphasised regarding the measure of extended confiscation that it did not allow for the confiscation of the entire assets of an offender, but that the provision only applied to certain pieces of property and in cases of a criminal conviction for certain very serious offences. Further, the dangers to society arising from organised criminality were underlined.[343]

The provision on the property penalty ("*Vermögensstrafe*") was set down in Section 43a *StGB* and was applicable in cases where a sentence of imprisonment of more than two years was imposed on a defendant for certain offences. The penalty could relate to a part or all available assets of the defendant. There was no requirement that it was proven in some way that the property in question had an illegal origin.[344] The provision was soon challenged in case-law, whereby the

---

340 BT-Dr 12/989, p. 22. Compare also BT-Dr 12/989 p. 23 as well as BT-Dr 11/6623, p. 1.

341 See for example Weßlau, n 338 above, pp. 233–35, K.-P. Julius, "Einziehung, Verfall und Art. 14GG" (1997) 109 *ZStW*, p. 58, pp. 94–100, M Köhler and W. Beck, "Gerechte Geldstrafe statt konfiskatorischer Vermögenssanktionen" (1991) 17 *Juristen Zeitung*, pp. 797–804, Kindhäuser, Neumann and Paeffgen, n 334 above, §73d StGB, Rn 2–4, *Münchener Kommentar zum StGB*, n 334 above, §73d, Rn 15, N. Nestler, "Zur Reichweite von §73d StGB: Der erweiterte Verfall vor neuen Legitimationsdefiziten?", *HRRS Onlinezeitschrift für Höchstrichterliche Rechtsprechung zum Strafrecht*, http://www.hrr-strafrecht.de, Ausgabe 12/2011, pp. 519–27, Perron, n 338 above and *Beck'scher Online-Kommentar StGB/Heuchemer*, n 334 above, §73d, Rn 2–4. These works contain numerous references to other doctrine.

342 Eser, n 338 above, pp. 845–46.

343 See BT-Dr 12/989 and BT-Dr 11/6623, especially p. 5.

344 K. Waechter, "Präventive Gewinnabschöpfung" (2008) 11 *NordÖR Zeitschrift für Öffentliches Recht in Norddeutschland*, p. 473, p. 475.

courts tried to interpret it in accordance with the Constitution.[345] However, in 2002, the German Constitutional Court (hereafter "*Bundesverfassungsgericht*") revoked Section 43a *StGB* as unconstitutional.[346] The main reasoning of the Court was that the legislator had not adopted clear and definite provisions that regulated under which criteria the application of a property penalty could lead to a reduction of a prison sentence. This had been left to the judiciary to decide on a case-by-case basis. Such a system was found to be in conflict with Article 103 (2) of the Basic Law for the Federal Republic of Germany (*Grundgesetz*, hereafter "*GG*"), which requires that legislation is adopted with regard to the principles of legality and clarity ("*Bestimmtheitsgrundsatz*").[347] The *Bundesverfassungsgericht* concluded that the legislator had an obligation to adequately set the limits of such punitive measures in a statute.

The conformity of the provision on extended confiscation has also been challenged before the highest German Courts under the argument that the provision is in violation of the presumption of innocence and the right to property in the national Constitution. These cases are described in more detail in Sections 4.3.3.2 and 4.3.3.3 below.

The adoption of more efficient powers of confiscation in Germany has partly been influenced by international initiatives.[348] Against the background that the instrument of extended confiscation had been introduced into national legislation in 1992, there was no adoption of an implementing act regarding FD 2005/212/JHA, as it was held that the national legislation already fulfilled the obligations following from this instrument.[349] In recent years, the German Government has on many occasions expressed the political aim of simplifying the regime of asset recovery and of facilitating the preliminary seizure of illegal assets and subsequent orders of asset recovery.[350]

At present a major legislative reform of the German regime of confiscation is under way. In March 2016, a first proposal from the Federal Ministry of

345 See for example *Bundesgerichtshof*, Decision of 8.2.1995, 5 StR 663/94 and *Landgericht Hamburg*, Decision of 11.4.1994, 633 KLs 15/93. See for a critical discussion of the property penalty, Eser, n 338 above, pp. 836–42.

346 Decision of 20.3.2002, 2 BvR 794/95. See generally on the tradition of constitutional review in Germany, D. Kommers and A. Russell, *The Constitutional Jurisprudence of the Federal Republic of Germany*, Duke University Press, 2012.

347 This principle follows from Art. 103 (2) *GG*.

348 One international instrument of importance was for example the *United Nations Convention against Illicit Traffic in Narcotic Drugs and Psychotropic Substances* adopted in 1988. See BT-Dr 12/3346.

349 Evaluation Report on the Fifth Round of Mutual Evaluations, Financial Crime and Financial Investigations, *Report on Germany*, 16269/2/11, REV 2, Brussels 19.1.2012, p. 72.

350 See for example Koalitionsvertrag zwischen CDU, CSU und SPD, "*Deutschlands Zukunft gestalten*", 18. Legislaturperiode, p. 145. Compare for a critical discussion of the present German regime for asset recovery with proposals for some changes, Meyer, n 334 above.

Justice and Consumer Protection was presented.[351] This draft legislation not only contained the provisions necessary in order to implement Directive 2014/42/EU, but also suggested more far-reaching changes in many different areas. Statements from experts and different organisations on these changes were then requested.[352] In September 2016, a Government draft for new legislation regarding a reform of the confiscation regime ("*Gesetz zur Reform der strafrechtlichen Vermögensabschöpfung*") was issued and was sent to the German Parliament.[353] The following motives were given for a comprehensive reform in this area:

> Das geltende Recht wird der hohen kriminalpolitischen Bedeutung der strafrechtlichen Vermögensabschöpfung nicht gerecht. Zwar geben das Strafgesetzbuch (StGB) mit dem Institut des "Verfalls" und die Strafprozessordnung (StPO) mit der Möglichkeit der vorläufigen Sicherstellung von Vermögenswerten ("Beschlagnahme" und "dinglicher Arrest") der Strafjustiz ein – jedenfalls im Prinzip – durchdachtes Abschöpfungsmodell an die Hand. Das Regelungswerk ist jedoch äußerst komplex und unübersichtlich. Zudem ist es mit zahlreichen rechtlichen Zweifelsfragen belastet. Strafgerichtliche Entscheidungen auf dem Gebiet der Vermögensabschöpfung sind in hohem Maße fehleranfällig.[354]

It is asserted that the purpose of the new legislation is to simplify the current regulation by providing for a more structured and coherent system, as well as to enhance the powers of confiscation. The legislator argues that this is a necessary step as the current regime is very complex, complicated and user-unfriendly, which has had the consequence that pleas for confiscation are often refrained from in practice.[355] The last assertion that the instrument of confiscation is not sufficiently utilised in German practice has, though, been criticised by practitioners, on the ground that there is no statistical evidence for such a conclusion.[356]

---

351 Referentenentwurf des Bundesministeriums der Justiz und für Verbraucherschutz, *Entwurf eines Gesetzes zur Reform der strafrechtlichen Vermögensabschöpfung*, March 2016.

352 For these statements and opinions on the new proposals, see the homepage of the *Bundesministeriums der Justiz und für Verbraucherschutz*, www.bmjv.de.

353 Gesetzentwurf der Bundesregierung, *Entwurf eines Gesetzes zur Reform der strafrechtlichen Vermögensabschöpfung*, BT-Dr 18/9525, 5.9.2016. For an analysis of the draft proposal, see F. Bittmann, "Zum Regierungsentwurf der Reform der Vermögensabschöpfung" (2016) 2 *KriPoZ*, pp. 120–32.

354 Gesetzentwurf der Bundesregierung, *Entwurf eines Gesetzes zur Reform der strafrechtlichen Vermögensabschöpfung*, BT-Dr 18/9525, 5.9.2016, p. 1.

355 See Gesetzentwurf der Bundesregierung, *Entwurf eines Gesetzes zur Reform der strafrechtlichen Vermögensabschöpfung*, BT-Dr 18/9525, 5.9.2016, pp. 1–2 and Referentenentwurf des Bundesministeriums der Justiz und für Verbraucherschutz, *Entwurf eines Gesetzes zur Reform der strafrechtlichen Vermögensabschöpfung*, March 2016, p. 1.

356 See for example Stellungnahme der *Strafverteidigervereingungen* zum Entwurf *eines Gesetzes zur strafrechtlichen Vermögensabschöpfung*, May 2016, p. 3.

The Government draft for new legislation contains a complete new systematisation and redraft of the German confiscation regime. It has thereby been proposed that the term "*Verfall*" should be completely substituted by the term "*Einziehung*".[357] Accordingly, the present provision on extended confiscation ("*erweiterter Verfall*" in Section 73d *StGB*) is to be replaced by a provision on "*erweiterte Einziehung von Taterträgen bei Tätern und Teilnehmern*". This provision would be inserted in Section 73a *StGB* and will be further described in Section 4.4.4 below.

A significant part of the new proposal concerns a reform of the current provisions on the relationship between confiscation and any claims of an injured party. The present regulation ("*Rückgewinnungshilfe*") has been strongly criticised and is regarded as inefficient.[358]

The Government draft for new legislation is at present being discussed, but the proposals have already been criticised in different quarters. The Association of the German Judiciary ("*Deutscher Richterbund*") has, for example, expressed general disappointment with the proposals for reform. This organisation has come to the conclusion that a change of the regime in the proposed ways would not lead to improvements, but to a considerable additional workload for the law enforcement agencies.[359]

Furthermore, the *Bundesrat* has expressed the need for major changes in certain areas of the draft Bill. The German Government has rejected some of these proposals, but has in other areas confirmed that the proposed amendments will be considered in the further legislative process.[360] It remains to be seen how the provisions will finally be drafted and adopted.

In the following sections of this chapter, there are brief references to the most important changes that have been proposed. In Section 4.4.4, the legislative proposals regarding the instrument of extended confiscation are described in more detail. Further, in Section 4.4.5 below, there is a description of a provision which would introduce a new form of non-conviction-based confiscation into German law.

---

357 Gesetzentwurf der Bundesregierung, *Entwurf eines Gesetzes zur Reform der strafrechtlichen Vermögensabschöpfung*, BT-Dr 18/9525, 5.9.2016, p. 2. Compare Section 1.3.3 above.

358 See on this, Meyer, n 334 above.

359 Deutscher Richterbund, *Stellungnahme* zum Referentenentwurf eines Gesetzes zur Reform der strafrechtlichen Vermögensabschöpfung, June 2016, p. 1. See also Deutscher Richterbund, *Zweite Stellungnahme* zum Gesetzentwurf zur Reform der strafrechtlichen Vermögensabschöpfung, Nr. 19/16, October 2016.

360 Unterrichtung durch die Bundesregierung, Entwurf eines Gesetzes zur Reform der strafrechtlichen Vermögensabschöpfung – Drucksache 18/9525, *Stellungnahme des Bundesrates und Gegenäußerung der Bundesregierung*, BT-Dr 18/10146, 26.10.2016.

4.2. GENERALLY ON THE CONFISCATION REGIME

Confiscation is not classified as a punishment under German law, but is rather seen as a sanction or a *preventive measure* which aims at withdrawing the economic means of criminals in order to prevent them from investing in new offences. The legislator has described and defined it as "*eine strafrechtliche Maßnahme 'eigener Art' mit kondiktionsähnlichem Character*".[361] The *Bundesverfassungsgericht* has also explicitly ruled that extended confiscation is not to be classified as a punishment.[362]

As already mentioned, there are different forms of confiscation in German law. This study will exclusively deal with the form presently classified as "*Verfall*" given in Sections 73 et seq. *StGB*. If such an order is passed, the title to the property or right passes to the State (Section 73e *StGB*). The provision on ordinary confiscation is found in Section 73 *StGB*,[363] which stipulates that:

(1) Ist eine rechtswidrige Tat begangen worden und hat der Täter oder Teilnehmer für die Tat oder aus ihr etwas erlangt, so ordnet das Gericht dessen Verfall an. Dies gilt nicht, soweit dem Verletzten aus der Tat ein Anspruch erwachsen ist, dessen Erfüllung dem Täter oder Teilnehmer den Wert des aus der Tat Erlangten entziehen würde.	(1) If an unlawful act has been committed and the principal or a secondary participant has acquired proceeds from it or obtained anything in order to commit it, the court shall order the confiscation of what was obtained. This shall not apply to the extent that the act has given rise to a claim of the victim the satisfaction of which would deprive the principal or secondary participant of the value of what has been obtained.
(2) Die Anordnung des Verfalls erstreckt sich auf die gezogenen Nutzungen. Sie kann sich auch auf die Gegenstände erstrecken, die der Täter oder Teilnehmer durch die Veräußerung eines erlangten Gegenstandes oder als Ersatz für dessen Zerstörung, Beschädigung oder Entziehung oder auf Grund eines erlangten Rechts erworben hat.	(2) The order of confiscation shall extend to benefits derived from what was obtained. It may also extend to objects which the principal or secondary participant has acquired by way of sale of the acquired object, as a replacement for its destruction, damage to or seizure of it or on the basis of a surrogate right.
(3) Hat der Täter oder Teilnehmer für einen anderen gehandelt und hat dadurch dieser etwas erlangt, so richtet sich die Anordnung des Verfalls nach den Absätzen 1 und 2 gegen ihn.	(3) If the principal or secondary participant acted for another and that person acquired anything thereby, the order of confiscation under subsections (1) and (2) above shall be made against him.

361 BT-Dr 11/6623, p. 6. This has been overtaken in case-law, compare for example *Bundesgerichtshof*, judgment of 21.8.2002, 1 StR 115/02, para. 21.

362 See on this, Section 4.3.3.3 below.

363 The legal text and translations are found at: http://www.gesetze-im-internet.de or www.dejure.com. For commentaries to the provision, see H. Theile, "Grundprobleme der Strafrechtlichen Verfallsvorschriften nach den §§73 ff. StGB" (2011) 4–5 *ZJS*, pp. 333–44, especially pp. 333–39 and Fischer, n 334 above, §73.

(4) Der Verfall eines Gegenstandes wird auch angeordnet, wenn er einem Dritten gehört oder zusteht, der ihn für die Tat oder sonst in Kenntnis der Tatumstände gewährt hat.	(4) The confiscation of an object shall also be ordered if it is owned or subject to a right of a third party, who furnished it to support the act or with knowledge of the circumstances of the act.

Only a court has the authority to decide on extended confiscation. The issue is initiated by the prosecutor in connection with the prosecution for a criminal offence, but a court may also raise such an issue. If a claim for confiscation is directed towards a third person, this person will either be involved in the criminal proceedings or separate proceedings may be instigated.[364]

At present a measure of confiscation under *StGB* is in principle only possible following a conviction for a criminal offence, as German law does not provide for non-conviction-based confiscation like the systems found in, for example, the UK or Ireland.[365] However, there is a possibility to make an order for confiscation in certain cases where a criminal conviction is not possible. According to Section 76a *StGB* ordinary and extended confiscation can be ordered independently ("*Selbständige Anordnung von Verfall*") if *for reasons of fact* no person can be prosecuted or convicted of the offence and if the conditions under which the measure is prescribed or available are otherwise met.[366] This also applies if the court orders a discharge or if the proceedings are terminated pursuant to a provision allowing this in the discretion of either the public prosecution service or the court or with their mutual agreement. The proposal for new German legislation, which at the moment is being discussed, would increase the scope for such orders. Thereby confiscation could, for example, also be ordered independently in certain cases when there are legal obstacles to a confiscation order.[367]

There is further a possibility for a *subsequent order for confiscation* ("*Nachträgliche Anordnung von Verfall*"). Section 76 *StGB* provides that if an order for confiscation is *unenforceable or inadequate* because after making it one of the conditions indicated in Section 73a and Section 73d, Subsection 2 *StGB* has arisen or come to its attention, the court may subsequently order the confiscation or deprivation of the monetary value. This concerns cases of equivalent value confiscation.[368]

---

364 See also Sec. 431 and 442 Subsec. 2 *StPO*.

365 Compare Section 1.1 above. See further Meyer, n 334 above, for a discussion of the possibility to introduce forms of *in rem* proceedings into the German regime of asset recovery.

366 See further Fischer, n 334 above, §76a and Secs. 440 and 442 *StPO*.

367 Compare further Section 4.4.5 below.

368 See further Fischer, n 334 above, §76 and Sec. 462 Subsec. 1 *StPO*.

4.3. EXTENDED CONFISCATION IN GERMAN LAW

4.3.1. BASIC SUBSTANTIVE RULES AND THE PROCEDURAL FRAMEWORK

Section 73d *StGB* states the following prerequisites for a decision on extended confiscation:

(1) Ist eine rechtswidrige Tat nach einem Gesetz begangen worden, das auf diese Vorschrift verweist, so ordnet das Gericht den Verfall von Gegenständen des Täters oder Teilnehmers auch dann an, wenn die Umstände die Annahme rechtfertigen, dass diese Gegenstände für rechtswidrige Taten oder aus ihnen erlangt worden sind. Satz 1 ist auch anzuwenden, wenn ein Gegenstand dem Täter oder Teilnehmer nur deshalb nicht gehört oder zusteht, weil er den Gegenstand für eine rechtswidrige Tat oder aus ihr erlangt hat. §73 Abs. 1 Satz 2, auch in Verbindung mit §73b, und §73 Abs. 2 gelten entsprechend.	(1) If an unlawful act has been committed pursuant to a law which refers to this provision, the court shall also order the confiscation of objects of the principal or secondary participant if the circumstances justify the assumption that these objects were acquired as a result of unlawful acts, or for the purpose of committing them. The 1st sentence shall also apply if the principal or secondary participant does not own or have a right to the object merely because he acquired the object as a result of an unlawful act or for the purpose of committing it. Section 73(2) shall apply mutatis mutandis.
(2) Ist der Verfall eines bestimmten Gegenstandes nach der Tat ganz oder teilweise unmöglich geworden, so finden insoweit die §§73a und 73b sinngemäß Anwendung.	(2) If the confiscation of a particular object has, after the act, become impossible in whole or in part section 73a and section 73b shall apply mutatis mutandis.
(3) Ist nach Anordnung des Verfalls nach Absatz 1 wegen einer anderen rechtswidrigen Tat, die der Täter oder Teilnehmer vor der Anordnung begangen hat, erneut über den Verfall von Gegenständen des Täters oder Teilnehmers zu entscheiden, so berücksichtigt das Gericht hierbei die bereits ergangene Anordnung.	(3) If after an order of confiscation pursuant to subsection (1) above, due to another unlawful act which the principal or secondary participant committed before that order, a decision must again be taken as to the confiscation of objects of the principal or secondary participant, the court in doing so shall take into account the previous order.
(4) §73c gilt entsprechend.[369]	(4) Section 73c shall apply mutatis mutandis.

A power of confiscation of assets according to Section 73 *StGB* (ordinary confiscation) has priority over Section 73d *StGB*.[370] This means that the Court is obligated to first consider in the trial whether assets which may be confiscated can be *directly* derived from the offence for which the offender is to be convicted.

369 The legal text of the Code may be found at: http://www.gesetze-im-internet.de or www.dejure.com. See for commentaries to the provision, Fischer, n 334 above, §73d, the *Beck'scher Online-Kommentar StGB/Heuchemer*, n 334 above, §73d, the *Münchener Kommentar zum StGB*, 2012, n 334 above, §73d, Kindhäuser, Neumann and Paeffgen, n 334 above, §73d StGB, Nestler, n 341 above and Theile, n 363 above, especially pp. 339–41.

370 Fischer, n 334 above, §73d, Rn 9 and §73, Rn 5 as well as *Beck'scher Online-Kommentar StGB/Heuchemer*, n 334 above, §73d, Rn 6. See also *Bundesgerichtshof*, judgment of 11.12.2008, 4 StR 386/08, *Bundesgerichtshof*, judgment of 20.4.2010, 4 StR 119/10 and *Bundesgerichtshof*, judgment of 8.8.2013, 3 StR 226/13.

Only if this is not possible may Section 73d *StGB* be applied. The Federal Supreme Court (hereafter "*Bundesgerichtshof*") in 2011 ruled that it is also allowed to apply the provision on extended confiscation in cases where it cannot be totally excluded that the property derives from the criminal offence for which the defendant is to be convicted. It can thus also be applied in cases where the Court is convinced that the property has an illegal origin, but it cannot be fully clarified whether it comes from the offence for which the defendant is to be convicted or from other criminality. However, in such cases where *concrete* circumstances indicate that property comes from specific criminality, extended confiscation should not be used. Such criminal offences must instead be further investigated and a plea according to Section 73 Subsection 1 *StGB* must be considered.[371] Case-law indicates that the German courts are sometimes not certain about the relationship between ordinary and extended confiscation.[372]

The provision on extended confiscation is invoked on the basis of a conviction for an underlying criminal offence as a perpetrator, inciter or accessory. According to Section 73d *StGB* it is possible to confiscate "*Gegenstände*", i.e. objects like for example cash, cars or assets in bank accounts.[373] An order for extended confiscation may only be given if the objects or assets still exist at the point of decision.[374] However, if the confiscation of a particular object has, after the act, become impossible in whole or part, an *equivalent monetary value* may in some cases be confiscated.[375] The motive is to avoid the defendant seeking to dispose of the property in question before the confiscation order is made.[376]

According to Section 73d Subsection 1 Paragraph 2 *StGB* the decision of extended confiscation must relate to objects which the perpetrator or a participant owns or is otherwise entitled to. There is no general reference in the provision to the possibility of confiscating objects in the possession of a third party, unlike the provision on ordinary confiscation.[377] However, extended confiscation from a *third party* is possible in the case where the perpetrator or accomplices do not

371 *Bundesgerichtshof*, judgment of 7.7.2011, 3 StR 144/11. Compare *Bundesgerichtshof*, judgment of 8.8.2013, 3 StR 226/13 and the commentary thereto in *NStZ* 2014, p. 82. See also *Beck'scher Online-Kommentar StGB/Heuchemer*, n 334 above, §73d, Rn 25–27, and for a discussion on the relation between Secs. 73 and 73d *StGB*, Nestler, n 341 above.

372 See further Sections 4.3.3.4 and 4.4.1 below.

373 Fischer, n 334 above, §73d, Rn 11 and *Münchener Kommentar zum StGB*, n 334 above, §73d, Rn 25.

374 Evaluation Report on the Fifth Round of Mutual Evaluations, Financial Crime and Financial Investigations, *Report on Germany*, 16269/2/11, REV 2, Brussels, 19.1.2012, p. 59.

375 Section 73d Subsec. 2 *StGB*. See further Fischer, n 334 above, §73d, Rn 11 and 17, *Beck'scher Online-Kommentar StGB/Heuchemer*, n 334 above, §73d, Rn 15 and *Münchener Kommentar zum StGB*, n 334 above, §73d, Rn 37–38. Compare also *Bundesgerichtshof*, Judgment of 1.7.2004, 4 StR 226/04.

376 BT-Dr 11/6623, p. 8.

377 Compare Sec. 73 Subsec. 4 *StGB*.

own or have a right to the object merely because they acquired the object as a result of an unlawful act or for the purpose of committing it.[378]

Confiscation according to Section 73d *StGB* is a *mandatory* sanction and there is no discretion of the court. However, the Court is according to Section 73d Subsection 4 obligated to consider a *hardship clause*.[379] This clause is contained in Section 73c *StGB*, and aims at guaranteeing the principle of proportionality. Confiscation should thereby not be ordered to the extent that it would constitute *an undue hardship* for the person affected. In such a case an order for extended confiscation *must* be waived. There is also a conditional ground for a waiver of confiscation in cases where there is no enrichment. Thereby confiscation may be waived to the extent that the value of what was obtained is no longer part of the affected person's assets at the time of the order or if what was obtained is only of minor value.[380] The interest of social rehabilitation of the defendant may hereby also be considered.[381]

The "gross-payment principle" is applied, which means that a confiscation order extends to the whole proceeds of the offence without allowing for any deduction for costs or expenditure.[382] The change from the application of a "*Nettoprinzip*" to a "*Bruttoprinzip*" for confiscation cases was adopted by the Act against Organised Crime in 1992.[383] In 2004, the *Bundesverfassungsgericht* ruled that this change did not affect the legal classification of the measure of confiscation and did thus not affect the constitutionality of Section 73d *StGB*.[384] In

378 Sec. 73d Subsec. 1 Para. 2 and Sec. 73 Subsec. 2 in *StGB*. See further Fischer, n 334 above, §73d, Rn 15.

379 BT-Dr 11/6623, p. 8.

380 See further on the hardship clause, BT-Dr 11/6623, p. 9, *Beck'scher Online-Kommentar StGB/Heuchemer*, n 334 above, §73d, Rn 17–19, *Münchener Kommentar zum StGB*, n 334 above, §73d, Rn 40–42 and Fischer, n 334 above, §73c. See for a proposal to amend this rule in some aspects in order to allow for confiscation orders in cases where property is discovered after the criminal proceedings, Referentenentwurf des Bundesministeriums der Justiz und für Verbraucherschutz, *Entwurf eines Gesetzes zur Reform der strafrechtlichen Vermögensabschöpfung*, March 2016, pp. 52 and 61.

381 Compare BT-Dr 11/6623, p. 9 and *Beck'scher Online-Kommentar StGB/Heuchemer*, n 334 above, §73d, Rn 18.

382 Sec. 73d Subsec. 1 and Sec. 73 Subsec. 2 *StGB*. See further BT-Dr 12/989 p. 23, Fischer, n 334 above, §73, Rn 8 and for case-law, *Bundesgerichtshof*, Judgment of 16.5.2006, 1 StR 46/06 and *Bundesgerichtshof*, Judgment of 21.8.2002, 1 STR 115/02.

383 *Gesetz zur Bekämpfung des illegalen Rauschgiftshandels und anderer Erscheinungsformen der Organisierten Kriminalität* (OrgKG), 15.7.1992, BGBl. I 1992, p. 1302. See for a critical discussion of this change, Eser, n 338 above, pp. 842–44. Compare also for certain difficulties in German practice regarding this principle and possible amendments, Referentenentwurf des Bundesministeriums der Justiz und für Verbraucherschutz, *Entwurf eines Gesetzes zur Reform der strafrechtlichen Vermögensabschöpfung*, March 2016, pp. 51–52 and 58–59 and Gesetzentwurf der Bundesregierung, *Entwurf eines Gesetzes zur Reform der strafrechtlichen Vermögensabschöpfung*, BT-Dr 18/9525, 5.9.2016, pp. 46–47 and pp. 55–56.

384 Decision of 14.1.2004, 2 BvR 564/95, NJW 2004, 2073, paras. 77–78. The case is described in Section 4.3.3.3 below. Compare *Bundesgerichtshof*, Judgment of 21.8.2002, 1 STR 115/02.

order to avoid undue hardship as a result of the application of the gross-payment principle, the abovementioned *hardship clause* must however be considered.[385]

Another general principle of the German confiscation law is that the claims of an injured party against the offender have *priority* over a decision of extended confiscation by the State.[386] This was the result of a change in the legislation which came into force in 2007.[387] However, there are several difficulties in practice regarding the German regime in this area, and the provisions are considered complex and complicated to deal with. The draft for new confiscation legislation, which was presented in 2016, aims at introducing a new model for handling the claims of the injured party.[388] It remains to be seen how this area of the statute will be reformed.

4.3.2. THE TRIGGERING OFFENCES AND THE SCOPE FOR EXTENDED CONFISCATION

The *first criterion* for extended confiscation is that an unlawful act has been committed, which statutory definition *refers to* Section 73d *StGB*. The legislation is thus constructed as a so-called "*Blankettnorm*". This legislative construction means that there is a possibility to add criminal offences without being obligated to change the original provision. At its adoption, the legislator argued that extended confiscation is a particularly far-reaching measure, and that there must be special reasons justifying its use regarding different types of criminality.[389] In line with this, it was proposed in the original draft for legislation from the German Government that the measure should only be used for criminal offences in the area of drug-trafficking offences.[390] However, at the enactment of the statute, the German Parliament decided against such a restriction and extended the scope of the triggering offences to include also certain criminal offences within other areas.[391] Since 1992, several new law reforms have continued to add triggering offences covered by Section 73d *StGB*.[392] The general principle for classifying a criminal offence as a triggering offence is that it belongs to a type

385 Sec. 73c *StGB*.
386 Sec. 73 Subsec. 1 Para. 2 and Sec. 73d Subsec. 1 Para. 3 *StGB*. See further Fischer, n 334 above, §73d, Rn 16 and *Münchener Kommentar zum StGB*, n 334 above, §73d, Rn 10.
387 *Gesetz zur Stärkung der Rückgewinnungshilfe und der Vermögensabschöpfung bei Straftaten*, 24.10.2006, BGBl. I, 2350. See for a critical discussion of the application of this principle in German law, Meyer, n 334 above.
388 See Gesetzentwurf der Bundesregierung, *Entwurf eines Gesetzes zur Reform der strafrechtlichen Vermögensabschöpfung*, BT-Dr 18/9525, 5.9.2016, p. 46 and pp. 49–55.
389 BT-Dr 11/6623, p. 6.
390 BT-Dr 11/6623, p. 6. Compare also BT-Dr 16/90 p. 10.
391 BT-Dr 12/989 p. 24.
392 *Münchener Kommentar zum StGB*, n 334 above, §73d, Rn 8.

of criminality that primarily is committed on a *commercial basis* or by *criminal organisations*:

> Im deutschen Strafrecht sind diejenigen Straftaten, für die der erweiterte Verfall aufgrund eines Verweises auf §73d StGB eröffnet ist, zumeist durch eine gewerbsmäßige bzw. bandenmäßige Tatbegehung gekennzeichnet. Es handelt sich um Straftaten, die typischerweise im Bereich der organisierten Kriminalität begangen werden.[393]

Examples of such triggering offences (in German called a "*Katalogtat*", "*Anlasstat*" or "*Anknüpfungstat*")[394] are drug offences, aggravated robbery, money laundering, aggravated theft, counterfeiting, extortion and the setting-up a criminal or a terrorist organisation. Within the framework of the current proposals for reform of the present provision of extended confiscation, some changes to national law in this respect have been suggested. This is further discussed in Section 4.4.4 below.

The *second criterion* for extended confiscation according to Section 73d *StGB* is that it must be concluded that certain objects have been "acquired as a result of unlawful acts, or for the purpose of committing them" ("*für rechtswidrige Taten oder aus ihnen erlangt worden sind*"). The term "*Herkunftstat*" is often used to denote the offence from which the assets in question are supposed to originate.[395] In principle, every kind of criminal offence may qualify as such an offence and there are no requirements that they are also classified as a "*Katalogtat/Anlasstat*" or are even similar to the triggering offence for which the defendant was convicted.[396] It is further not required that the "*Herkunftstat*" is individually linked to organised criminality,[397] nor is there any specific time-period under which it must have been committed.[398] However, Section 73d *StGB* is not applicable to such objects that origin from unlawful acts which were committed before the Act against Organised Crime in 1992 came into force. It is further only applicable regarding such offences the statutory definition of which was already covered by Section 73d[399] at the time of the offence.

393 BT-Dr 135/12, 11.5.2012, p. 4. See also Fischer, n 334 above, §73d StGB, Rn 2.

394 See for example Fischer, n 334 above, §73d, Rn 7 and 10 and *Münchener Kommentar zum StGB*, n 334 above, §73d, Rn 1 and 22.

395 Compare for example Fischer, n 334 above, §73d, Rn 11 or *Münchener Kommentar zum StGB*, n 334 above, §73d, Rn 1.

396 Fischer, n 334 above, §73d, Rn 11 and *Münchener Kommentar zum StGB*, n 334 above, §73d, Rn 31.

397 See for example H.-H. Jescheck and T. Weigend, *Lehrbuch des Strafrechts, Allgemeiner Teil*, 5. Auflage, Duncker and Humblot, 1996, p. 794 and Schönke, Schröder and Eser, n 334 above, §73d StGB, Rn 14.

398 Compare Art. 3(2)(b) in FD 2005/212/JHA.

399 See further Fischer, n 334 above, §73d, Rn 2, *Münchener Kommentar zum StGB*, n 334 above, §73d, Rn 23, *Bundesgerichtshof*, Judgment of 20.9.1995, 3 StR 267/95 and *Bundesgerichtshof*, Judgment of 27.4.2001, 3 StR 132/01.

In line with the idea behind the measure of extended confiscation, German law does not require that full proof is presented that the property in question is directly related to any specific offence. Accordingly, the "*Herkunftstat*" need not be the subject of the current prosecution, or be fully proven to a criminal law standard.[400] In contrast to the provision on ordinary confiscation in Section 73 *StGB*, there is thus a significant easing of the evidentiary standard.[401] This lower standard provided under national law for the required link between property and (any) unlawful act will now be explored.

4.3.3. THE EVIDENTIARY STANDARD FOR EXTENDED CONFISCATION

4.3.3.1. Legal Provision and the Legislative Works

The standard of evidence required for a decision of extended confiscation according to Section 73d *StGB* is formulated in the following way:

> wenn die Umstände die Annahme rechtfertigen, dass diese Gegenstände für rechtswidrige Taten oder aus ihnen erlangt worden sind.

Accordingly, the court shall order the confiscation of objects *if the circumstances justify the assumption* that these objects were acquired as a result of unlawful acts or for the purpose of committing them. The German legislator argued in the legislative works that the intention behind such a formulation was to provide a legal possibility to confiscate certain assets without the requirement that the specific details of the criminal origin be fully established. This was considered necessary against the background of evidentiary difficulties in legal practice in certain cases.[402] In this context, the option of providing a *reversal of the burden of proof* was also considered, but was rejected on constitutional grounds. To require a defendant to prove the legal sources of his assets was found to be in conflict with the right of property in Article 14 *GG*:

> Die Einführung des Erweiterten Verfalls, d. h. einer als eigenständige Erscheinungsform des Verfalls ausgestalteten neuen Maßnahme, soll Lücken der strafrechtlichen Gewinnabschöpfung in Fällen schließen, in denen die bei den Tatbeteiligten vorgefundenen Vermögensgegenstände, deren rechtmäßiger Erwerb

400 Fischer, n 334 above, §73d, Rn 11 and *Münchener Kommentar zum StGB*, n 334 above, §73d, Rn 27.

401 *Münchener Kommentar zum StGB*, n 334 above, §73d, Rn 2 and 5 as well as *Beck'scher Online-Kommentar StGB/Heuchemer*, n 334 above, §73d, Rn 2.

402 See BT-Dr 11/6623, p. 1 and 12/989, p. 23.

nicht festgestellt werden kann, mit großer Wahrscheinlichkeit aus der Begehung von Straftaten herrühren, in denen indessen die Verhängung einer Vermögensstrafe vom Schuldmaß der begangenen Taten her nicht zu vertreten wäre. Diese Lücke dadurch zu schließen, daß es dem Beschuldigten auferlegt wird, zur Vermeidung des Verfalls womöglich seines ganzen Vermögens den legalen Erwerb aller in Betracht kommenden Gegenstände vollständig nachzuweisen, scheitert an der vom Grundgesetz gewährleisteten Eigentumsgarantie. Verfassungsrechtlich unbedenklich erscheint es hingegen, eine Regelung in der Art des Erweiterten Verfalls einzuführen, soweit überwiegende Interessen des Gemeinwohls, insbesondere im Hinblick auf die Bekämpfung von schweren, für die Rechtsgüter des einzelnen wie der Allgemeinheit besonders gefährlichen Kriminalitätsformen, dies zwingend erfordern.[403]

However, it was considered necessary to considerably *lower the burden of proof*. The evidentiary standard was thereby set by the legislator at a "high likelihood of criminal origin":

Hierbei ist einzubeziehen, daß die vorgeschlagene Regelung den Eigentumsentzug nicht etwa auf Grund eines bloßen Verdachts ermöglicht. Vielmehr setzt sie sowohl voraus, daß die Herkunft des Verfallgegenstandes mit den Erkenntnismöglichkeiten des Gerichts nicht feststellbar ist, als auch, daß sich eine ganz hohe Wahrscheinlichkeit der Herkunft aus rechtswidrigen Taten in dem Sinne ergibt, daß sich die rechtswidrige Herkunft für einen objektiven Beobachter geradezu aufdrängt. Dabei fordert und ermöglicht das normativ wertende Element "wenn die Umstände die Annahme rechtfertigen" eine Anwendung der Vorschrift, die in jedem Einzelfall der Eigentumsgewährleistung hinreichend gerecht wird.[404]

The legislative works state further that the circumstances which might justify the assumption that objects were acquired as a result of unlawful acts can be the personal circumstances of a defendant, such as previous criminality and legal income. As an example cases were mentioned where a significant amount of cash is found in the possession of a person convicted several times for drug offences and whose only legal income is social welfare:

"Umstände" im Sinne der Vorschrift sind alle hinsichtlich der Einkommens- und Vermögensverhältnisse des Täters relevanten Gegebenheiten, soweit sie das Gericht im Rahmen seiner Amtsermittlungspflicht feststellen kann. Die Annahme der Herkunft eines Gegenstandes aus rechtswidrigen Taten ist dann gerechtfertigt, wenn sich diese Herkunftsmöglichkeit von allen in Betracht zu ziehenden Möglichkeiten als die ganz überwiegend wahrscheinlichste darstellt. Dabei verweist das in dem Begriff "rechtfertigen" enthaltene normative Element das Gericht auf eine auch unter dem Gesichtspunkt der Verfassungskonformität der Maßnahme durchzuführende Gesamtbewertung des Sachverhalts. In diesem Zusammenhang ist nicht etwa auf

403 BT-Dr 12/989, p. 23.
404 BT-Dr 11/6623, p. 5. See also BT-Dr 12/989, p. 23 and Rieß, n 337 above, p. 493.

> bestimmte Einzeltaten abzustellen. Vielmehr genügt es, daß dann, wenn sich rechtmäßige Quellen nicht feststellen lassen, sich die Herkunft aus rechtswidrigen Taten im Hinblick auf die Situation des Täters und sein Vorleben einem objektiven Betrachter geradezu aufdrängt. Dies kann z. B. hinsichtlich eines größeren Geldbetrages der Fall sein, der bei einem bereits mehrfach in Erscheinung getretenen Betäubungsmittelstraftäter vorgefunden wird, der ohne erkennbare sonstige Einkunftsquellen seinen Unterhalt durch Sozialhilfe bestreitet.[405]

As mentioned before, the provision on extended confiscation was from the very beginning critically debated in German legal practice and doctrine, and it was soon asserted that such an evidentiary standard was in conflict with the Constitution.[406] It was not very long until this question came up before the *Bundesgerichtshof* and the *Bundesverfassungsgericht*. The judgments from these courts have had significant effects for the interpretation of Section 73d *StGB* especially regarding the burden of proof. Next, these rulings will be described in more detail. Thereafter, an outline of some case-law regarding the application of the evidentiary standard is presented.

4.3.3.2. *Decision by the Bundesgerichtshof in 1994*

The decision from the *Bundesgerichtshof* considered an appeal against a judgment from the *Landgericht Bochum*, in which a defendant had been sentenced to seven years' imprisonment for drug offences on two occasions.[407] These drug offences had for different reasons not generated any profit. However, the police had found 42,520 DM in a savings account, and this asset had been confiscated on the basis of Section 73d *StGB*. The Court reasoned that the defendant had a very spare monthly income of 850 DM, and rather high monthly expenses regarding rent (600 DM) and the running costs of a car. Against this background, it was held that the defendant could not have saved this amount of money, so that the assets must have come from criminal offences. The convictions for two drug offences in the present case indicated that the defendant had been dealing with narcotics, which led the Court to the conclusion that the funds in the savings account came from other drug offences.

Before the *Bundesgerichtshof*, the defendant argued that Section 73d *StGB* was in conflict with the German Constitution. However, the Court held that the legislation could be interpreted and applied in accordance with the Constitution and in such a way as to avoid conflicts with the presumption of

---

405 BT-Dr 11/6623, p. 7.

406 Compare Sec. 4.1 above.

407 Decision of 22.11.1994, 4 StR 516/94, NJW 1995 (7), p. 470. See for commentaries on the decision, for example Kindhäuser, Neumann and Paeffgen, n 334 above, §73d *StGB*, Rn 2–4 and *Münchener Kommentar zum StGB*, n 334 above, §73d, Rn 17–19.

innocence (Article 2(1) and Article 1(1) *GG* as well as the "*Rechtsstaatsprinzip*") and the right to property (Article 14(1) *GG*). By way of introduction the *Bundesgerichtshof* stated that the legislator had introduced Section 73d in order to provide for a new form of confiscation where merely a high likelihood of criminal origin regarding certain assets would be sufficient for an order. In this respect, the Court quoted the legislative works which stated that a decision on extended confiscation is allowed in cases where the conclusion that an asset has been illegally obtained is "almost imposed on an objective observer" in view of the personal circumstances and the (previous) criminality of a defendant.[408]

However, the *Bundesgerichtshof* rejected the application of such a low evidentiary standard, and held that extended confiscation based on mere suspicion of other offences was in conflict with the German Constitution:

> Die danach vom Gesetzgeber einerseits vorausgesetzte, andererseits aber auch für genügend erachtete "ganz hohe Wahrscheinlichkeit" (BT-Dr 11/6623, S. 5) der deliktischen Herkunft reicht aber nicht aus, die verfassungsrechtlichen Bedenken auszuräumen. Diese leiten sich – zusammengefaßt – daraus her, daß das Institut des erweiterten Verfalls auf einer Unterstellung von Straftaten beruht, weil die Regelung in §73 d I 1 StGB jedenfalls nach den gesetzgeberischen Intentionen für den Zugriff auf Tätervermögen eine – allenfalls gesteigerte – Wahrscheinlichkeit in zweierlei Hinsicht genügen läßt: nämlich daß der Angeklagte weitere Straftaten begangen und daß er Vermögen aus solchen wahrscheinlich begangenen Straftaten erlangt hat. Die Grundrechte des Angeklagten wären aber nach Auffassung des Senats verletzt, wenn aufgrund einer Verdachtslage, und sei der Verdacht noch so dringend, sachlich endgültige (§73 e StGB) strafrechtliche Maßnahmen getroffen würden.[409]

The *Bundesgerichtshof* thus rejected the standard of a "high likelihood of criminal origin" and ruled that Section 73d *StGB* must be applied under more stringent requirements:

> Das normativ wertende Element "wenn die Umstände die Annahme rechtfertigen" in §73 d I 1 StGB – dem nach dem Willen des Gesetzgebers die Aufgabe zukommt, bei der Gesamtbewertung des Sachverhalts auch die Grundrechtsverbürgungen zu berücksichtigen (vgl. BT-Dr 11/6623, S. 5 und 7) – ist deshalb verfassungskonform einengend auszulegen: Die Anordnung des erweiterten Verfalls kommt nur in Betracht, wenn der Tatrichter aufgrund erschöpfender Beweiserhebung und -würdigung (vgl. *Lackner* StGB, 20. Aufl. §73 d Rdn. 8) die uneingeschränkte Überzeugung gewonnen hat, daß der Angeklagte die von der Anordnung erfaßten Gegenstände aus rechtswidrigen Taten erlangt hat, ohne daß diese selbst im einzelnen festgestellt werden müßten ...[410]

---

408 BT-Dr 11/6623, p. 7. For quotations from the legislative works in this respect, compare Section. 4.3.3.1 above.

409 Decision of 22.11.1994, 4 StR 516/94, NJW 1995 (7), p. 470.

410 Decision of 22.11.1994, 4 StR 516/94, NJW 1995 (7), p. 470.

Consequently, a more stringent interpretation of the evidentiary standard was introduced and was set to "*uneingeschränkte Überzeugung*". This means in principle that – after surveying all the evidence – a judge must be *absolutely convinced* that (any sort of) unlawful acts have been committed, and that the asset in question is a result of such offences, or for the purpose of committing them.[411] As emphasised by the *Bundesgerichtshof*, reasonable doubts as to illegal origin prevent confiscation. However, it was at the same time stated that the unlawful acts need not to be individually investigated or ascertained in detail, and that "no exaggerated requirements on the evidentiary standard" must be made.[412] It was thereby specifically acknowledged that the courts may take consideration of and draw conclusions from past convictions of the offender:

> Insbesondere ist das Gericht nicht gehindert, sondern gehalten, auch – wie es das Landgericht getan hat – die festgestellten Anlaßtaten selbst dann in seine Überzeugungsbildung einzubeziehen, wenn aus ihnen kein Gewinn erlangt worden ist.[413]

The Court found in the present case that the *Landgericht* had made reasonable assessments of the evidence and had drawn acceptable conclusions from the economic situation, as well as from the criminal offences the defendant was to be convicted of. Accordingly, the decision for extended confiscation was upheld. This ruling was appealed against, and the case came before the Constitutional Court.

4.3.3.3. Decision by the Bundesverfassungsgericht in 2004

The principal question before the *Bundesverfassungsgericht* was whether Section 73d *StGB* or the interpretation given to it by the *Bundesgerichtshof* was in conformity with the German Constitution.[414] The complainant argued that Section 73d had the character of a punishment, and that confiscation thereby violated the *presumption of innocence* and the *right to property*. He further argued that the interpretation of the provision set up by the *Bundesgerichtshof* was in conflict with the express wording of the *StGB* and that, in any case, the assessment made by the *Landgericht Bochum* in the case did not stand up to such a stringent interpretation.[415]

---

411 Compare *Beck'scher Online-Kommentar StGB/Heuchemer*, n 334 above, §73d, Rn 8.

412 See further *Beck'scher Online-Kommentar StGB/Heuchemer*, n 334 above, §73d, Rn 8–10.

413 Decision of 22.11.1994, 4 StR 516/94, NJW 1995 (7), p. 470.

414 Decision of 14.1.2004, 2 BvR 564/95, NJW 2004, 2073. See for commentaries on the decision, for example *Beck'scher Online-Kommentar StGB/Heuchemer*, n 334 above, §73d, Rn 12–14, *Münchener Kommentar zum StGB*, n 334 above, §73d, Rn 20–21 and Kindhäuser, Neumann and Paeffgen, n 334 above, §73d *StGB*, Rn 2–4.

415 See paras. 31–33, Decision of 14.1.2004, 2 BvR 564/95.

The German Ministry of Justice argued before the *Bundesverfassungsgericht* that the setting up of a stricter evidentiary standard for Section 73d *StGB* by the *Bundesgerichtshof* was in conflict with the express will of the legislator to lower the burden of proof regarding the investigation of the origin of certain assets. The aim had been to create more effective means for confiscation, and it was maintained that both the wording of Section 73d and the interpretation of the evidentiary standard given in the legislative works were in conformity with the Constitution.[416]

On the basis of an analysis of the express wording of Section 73d *StGB*, the legislative works and the systematic structure of the legislation, the *Bundesverfassungsgericht* concluded that the provision was neither in violation of the "*Schuldgrundsatz*", the *presumption of innocence* or the *right to property*. The Court based this upon the reasoning that the measure of extended confiscation is not a punishment, because it has no repressive or retributory character.[417] Rather the measure was to be seen as a *preventive measure*, as it has the aim to correct property regimes and prevent the assets from being used for new criminality:

> Insgesamt betrachtet ist die Gewinnabschöpfung gemäß §73d StGB keine pönale Reaktion auf ein früheres normwidriges Verhalten des Betroffenen. Vielmehr antwortet sie auf eine gegenwärtige Störung der Vermögensordnung mit einem korrigierenden und normbekräftigenden Eingriff. Der erweiterte Verfall verfolgt nicht repressiv-vergeltende, sondern präventiv-ordnende Ziele und ist daher keine dem Schuldgrundsatz unterliegende strafähnliche Maßnahme. Die verschuldensunabhängige Ausgestaltung des erweiterten Verfalls begegnet insoweit keinen verfassungsrechtlichen Bedenken.[418]

The *Bundesverfassungsgericht* acknowledged that the *Bundesgerichtshof* had introduced a more stringent interpretation of Section 73d than the legislator had intended:

> Nach der vom Bundesgerichtshof im Ausgangsverfahren vertretenen Auffassung ist die Annahme der deliktischen Herkunft eines Gegenstands nur dann im Sinne des §73d Abs. 1 Satz 1 StGB gerechtfertigt, wenn sich der Tatrichter durch Ausschöpfung der vorhandenen Beweismittel von ihr überzeugt hat. Für eine solche Überzeugungsbildung verlangt der Bundesgerichtshof keine Feststellungen über konkrete Herkunftstaten. Auch sei der Tatrichter nicht gehindert, sondern gehalten, die nachgewiesenen Anlasstaten in seine Überzeugungsbildung einzubeziehen, selbst

416 Paras. 35–40, Decision of 14.1.2004, 2 BvR 564/95.

417 It can be noted that this was one of the differences to the decision on the constitutionality of the property penalty ("*Vermögensstrafe*"), which the Court classified as a punishment. See on this, Section 4.1 above.

418 Para. 81, Decision of 14.1.2004, 2 BvR 564/95.

> wenn aus ihnen kein Gewinn erzielt worden sei. Insgesamt dürften die Anforderungen an den Herkunftsnachweis nicht überspannt werden (BGHSt 40, 371 ff.).[419]

It was concluded that the higher evidentiary standard set by the *Bundesgerichtshof* was reconcilable with the German Constitution and must be used by the Courts when applying Section 73d *StGB*. It was underlined that this interpretation takes account of the legislative objectives, and is not in conflict with the will of the legislator.[420]

The *Bundesverfassungsgericht* emphasised that the evidentiary standard to be used does mean a lowered burden of proof, as it is still not necessary to provide full proof of certain concrete offences:

> Diesen gesetzgeberischen Zielen trägt die Auslegung des §73d Abs. 1 Satz 1 StGB durch den Bundesgerichtshof Rechnung. Sie erleichtert einerseits den für die strafrechtliche Gewinnabschöpfung erforderlichen Nachweis einer deliktischen Vermögenserlangung, indem sie auf die Feststellung einer konkreten Herkunftstat verzichtet und dem Tatrichter in weitem Umfang eine nur mittelbare Beweisführung erlaubt. Andererseits verlangt sie, dass Eingriffe in das verfassungsrechtlich geschützte Legal Vermögen des Betroffenen vermieden werden, indem sich der Tatrichter zumindest vom "Ob" der deliktischen Vermögensherkunft überzeugt.[421]

The Court ruled that Section 73d *StGB* is constitutional if the provision is applied under this strict interpretation.

4.3.3.4. The Application of the Evidentiary Standard in Case-law

The evidentiary standard in German law may thus be summarised as follows. The prosecutor has the burden of proof that an asset has an illegal origin, but there is an easing of this burden regarding the relationship between an asset and a specific criminal offence. As seen above, the highest German Courts have interpreted the evidentiary standard more strictly than the legislator originally intended and the legislative works would imply.[422] More concrete requirements of the assessment of criminal origin have thereby been set, as the evidentiary standard has to be "*uneingeschränkte Überzeugung*"; that is an absolute conviction on the part of the court. Pure speculations of criminal origin are not sufficient; an unlawful background must rather be established through *concrete circumstances*.

---

419 Para. 93, Decision of 14.1.2004, 2 BvR 564/95.

420 See especially paras. 96–98, Decision of 14.1.2004, 2 BvR 564/95.

421 Para. 96, Decision of 14.1.2004, 2 BvR 564/95.

422 See in general on the evidentiary standard, Kindhäuser, Neumann and Paeffgen, n 334 above, §73d *StGB*, Rn 8–9, *Beck'scher Online-Kommentar StGB*, n 334 above, §73d, Rn 8–10, Fischer, n 334 above, §73d, Rn 12 and *Münchener Kommentar zum StGB*, n 334 above, §73d, Rn 27–30. Compare also *Bundesgerichtshof*, Judgment of 10.2.1998, 4 StR 4/98.

Indicators of importance for the assessment of the origin in German case-law are, for example, the personal circumstances and income of the defendant, the possession of significant amounts of cash, "hidden" placement of assets and the consideration of whether explanations of a legal origin are plausible or not.

The courts are obligated to consider an issue of confiscation when relevant circumstances are present in a case. In spite of this, it happens that the *Bundesgerichtshof* must refer cases back to the lower courts as the issue of extended confiscation has been neglected. The following case may be mentioned as an example. A defendant had been sentenced for drug offences to three years' of imprisonment.[423] During a search of the defendant's apartment in the context of another criminal investigation €70,750 had been seized. The cash had been found - partly hidden - together with narcotics. It was noted in the case that the defendant had been unemployed for a long period, but that he now had a monthly income of €780. A motion for confiscation had been turned down by the *Landgericht Berlin* under the argument that it was not proven that this cash derived from the criminal offence for which the defendant was to be convicted. The *Bundesgerichtshof* referred the case back to the lower court and stated that the issue of extended confiscation must be considered. It was thereby emphasised that there were some important indications in the case which spoke for an illegal origin of the assets:

> Das Landgericht hätte sich im Einzelnen damit auseinandersetzen müssen, ob die bei dem Angeklagten beschlagnahmten 70.750 Euro aus anderen rechtswidrigen Taten herrühren. Hierfür bestehen nach Lage des Falls gewichtige Anhaltspunkte. Das Geld war teilweise versteckt und wurde zusammen mit Betäubungsmitteln aufgefunden. Die persönlichen Verhältnisse des Angeklagten, insbesondere seine Einkommensverhältnisse, sind eher bescheiden. Zwischen seiner Vermögenslage und seiner legalen Einkunftsquelle besteht eine deutliche Diskrepanz.[424]

A similar conclusion was reached in a case regarding two defendants who were sentenced to several years' imprisonment for drug offences.[425] During a search of the defendants' apartments a large amount of narcotics had been found. The financial investigation had shown that both defendants had been unemployed for a long period. At the same time they owned, *inter alia*, expensive cars. The *Landgericht Hamburg* had turned down the motion on confiscation with the reasoning that it had not been established in the case that the assets were derived from the drug offences. On appeal, the *Bundesgerichtshof* referred the case back

423 *Bundesgerichtshof*, Judgment of 4.8.2010, 5 StR 184/10.
424 *Bundesgerichtshof*, Judgment of 4.8.2010, 5 StR 184/10, paras. 7–8.
425 *Bundesgerichtshof*, Judgment of 3.9.2009, 5 StR 207/09.

to the lower court and ruled that confiscation according to Section 73d *StGB* must be properly considered:

> Diese Begründung begegnet durchgreifenden rechtlichen Bedenken. Sie lässt besorgen, dass das Landgericht das Rechtsinstitut des erweiterten Verfalls nach §73d StGB verkannt hat. §73d StGB erweitert die Zugriffsmöglichkeit über das aus verfahrensgegenständlichen Taten Erlangte hinaus auf sonstige Vermögenswerte deliktischer Herkunft. Die betreffenden Taten müssen dabei weder Gegenstand der Anklage noch bewiesen sein; es genügt, wenn das Gericht von der Herkunft des Erlangten aus (irgendwelchen) rechtswidrigen Taten überzeugt ist (BGHSt 40, 371). Liegen – wie hier (§33 Abs. 1 BtMG) – die Voraussetzungen einer Rückverweisungsklausel vor, so ist die Verfallsanordnung grundsätzlich obligatorisch.[426]

The Court further noted that there were certain indicators speaking for an illegal origin of the assets in question, for example the fact that the defendants – in spite of their unemployment – owned expensive cars and kept certain monetary funds.

Uncertainty about the prerequisites for extended confiscation seems to be present in case-law. The *Bundesgerichtshof* has in several cases emphasised that a careful consideration and substantiation of the issue of extended confiscation is necessary. Thereby the courts must first deduct any legal income of an offender from the assets, and then it must be decided whether, in view of the costs for daily expenses, the legal origin of any remaining assets is plausible or not. In the overall assessment, indications of any further criminal activity of a defendant, as well as other circumstances like the specific time-period when an asset was obtained, may be used as circumstantial evidence.[427]

Sometimes cases are overruled and referred back to the lower courts as the basis of confiscation is not sufficiently justified.[428] In a decision from the *Landgericht Darmstadt* cash to the value of €5,437 and US$20 had for example been confiscated in addition to a sentence of imprisonment for drug offences.[429] The confiscation order had only a very general motivation that the defendant had kept this large amount of cash in his taxi although he knew that it derived from drug offences. No further justification had been given. The *Bundesgerichtshof* emphasised that the *tatrichterliche Überzeugung* (i.e. the conviction that objects have a criminal origin) must be sufficiently substantiated. It is not enough to make sweeping arguments about criminal origin. A particularly careful substantiation is required, when a defendant has income from legal sources. In

426 *Bundesgerichtshof*, Judgment of 3.9.2009, 5 StR 207/09, para. 7.

427 See for example *Bundesgerichtshof*, Decision of 9.5.2001, 3 StR 541/00.

428 See for example *Bundesgerichtshof*, Decision of 5.8.2004, 4 StR 186/04, *Bundesgerichtshof*, Decision of 5.7.2012, 3 StR 210/12, *Bundesgerichtshof*, Decision of 2.10.2002, 2 StR 294/02 and *Bundesgerichtshof*, Decision of 16.3.2010, 4 StR 497/09.

429 *Bundesgerichtshof*, Decision of 28.7.2004, 2 StR 209/04.

the specific case, the defendant was a taxi driver with a substantial legal income and it could not be excluded that some of the cash had a legal origin. Against this background, the lower court had been obligated to base its decision on more detailed arguments, for example to state exactly where and how the cash had been found. The case was referred back for new proceedings.

Another example is a decision from the *Landgericht Kleve* which made a decision on confiscation of US$3,000 in a case regarding a sentence for drug offences.[430] The defendant had on the instructions of one "Fred" accepted US$3,000 and a parcel of cocaine from one "John" in Amsterdam. He brought it to Germany and was supposed to be paid US$2,000 for this. However, he was arrested and the cash confiscated. The *Bundesgerichtshof* found that the decision on confiscation was not sufficiently justified, and argued especially regarding Section 73d *StGB* that the application of this provision requires more detailed arguments for a criminal origin. The lower court had only stated that "there were no doubts" that the cash derived from "illegal transactions". The case was referred back for new proceedings.

4.4. A COMMENTARY ON THE GERMAN REGIME OF EXTENDED CONFISCATION

4.4.1. A COMPLEX AND PARTLY CONTROVERSIAL ASSET RECOVERY REGIME

The provision on extended confiscation has been applied in Germany since 1992. The measure is especially used in the area of drug offences.[431] In spite of the fact that the constitutionality of Section 73d *StGB* has been confirmed by the highest German Courts, the measure has remained somewhat controversial in the legal doctrine. It is, for example, often argued that the motives given by the legislator for the provision do not justify such a far-reaching law enforcement method and that the measure violates fundamental human rights. Also the legal nature and the classification of the measure of extended confiscation are contested.[432]

Additionally, the national asset recovery regime is regarded as being a very complex and complicated piece of legislation. It has on several occasions been argued that although confiscation according to the *StGB* is a mandatory sanction, the law enforcement agencies have not completely endorsed the

---

430 *Bundesgerichtshof*, Decision of 29.8.2002, 3 StR 287/02.

431 *Beck'scher Online-Kommentar StGB/Heuchemer*, n 334 above §73d, Rn 24 and Fischer, n 334 above, §73d, Rn 2.

432 See for example F. Herzog, "Gewinnabschöpfung unter der Flagge der positiven Generalprävention" (2004) 12 *Juristische Rundschau*, pp. 494–98, *Münchener Kommentar zum StGB*, n 334 above, §73d, Rn 6 and Rn 15 and Fischer, n 334 above, §73d, Rn 4–7.

instrument in practice.[433] It has further been claimed that the German courts are "rather reluctant" towards the notion of extended confiscation.[434] A study of national case-law confirms that there seem to be certain difficulties in applying the provisions on confiscation in legal practice. Alongside the cases referred to above (Section 4.3.3.4), some rulings from the *Bundesgerichtshof* also show that the courts are sometimes insecure about the general system of the legislation and whether to base a decision of confiscation on Section 73 or 73d *StGB*.[435]

4.4.2. THE INTERPRETATION AND APPLICATION OF THE EVIDENTIARY STANDARD

Much criticism in German legal doctrine relates to the evidentiary standard. The stricter threshold set up by the *Bundesgerichtshof* and the dismissal of the legislator's standard of "high probability" has in this respect not really changed that position.[436] It is still argued that there are constitutional problems in basing a decision of confiscation on criminal offences which have not been proven or made more concrete. The requirement that the Court must be *absolutely convinced* of an illegal origin ("*uneingeschränkte Überzeugung*") has been interpreted by some as meaning that a deciding court must be convinced beyond reasonable doubt that the property stems from criminal conduct.[437] However, this threshold cannot be considered as comparable to the criminal procedural standard for a conviction under German law, as the unlawful acts need not be individually investigated or ascertained in any detail. This has led to the conclusion that:

> §73d ähnelt damit einer Walhfeststellung unter Weglassen der Tatbestandsgarantie: Ausreichend ist die Überzeugung des Gerichts, der Angeklagte habe *irgendeine* (nicht feststellbare) Tat begangen …[438]

---

433 See for example Referentenentwurf des Bundesministeriums der Justiz und für Verbraucherschutz, *Entwurf eines Gesetzes zur Reform der strafrechtlichen Vermögensabschöpfung*, March 2016, p. 49.

434 See for example for such a conclusion, Evaluation Report on the Fifth Round of Mutual Evaluations, Financial Crime and Financial Investigations, *Report on Germany*, 16269/2/11, REV 2, Brussels 19.1.2012, p. 74.

435 See for example *Bundesgerichtshof*, Decision of 23.5.2012, 4 StR 76/12, *Bundesgerichtshof*, Decision of 20.4.2010, 4 StR 119/10, *Bundesgerichtshof*, Decision of 27.4.2011, 4 StR 39/11. Compare also *Oberlandesgericht Hamm*, Decision of 13.12,2004, 2 Ss 482/04, *Bundesgerichtshof*, Decision of 2.10.2002, 2 StR 294/02, *Bundesgerichtshof*, Decision of 21.10.2008, 4 StR 437/08, *Bundesgerichtshof*, Decision of 7.1.2003, 3 StR 421/02 and *Bundesgerichtshof*, Decision of 4.4.2013, 3 StR 529/12.

436 Compare for example Kindhäuser, Neumann and Paeffgen, n 334 above, §73d *StGB*, Rn 2–4, Jescheck and Weigend, n 397 above, pp. 794–95, Schönke, Schröder and Eser, n 334 above, §73d StGB, Rn 2 and 15 and Fischer, n 334 above, §73d, Rn 6–7.

437 Benseler, n 335 above, p. 207.

438 Fischer, n 334 above, §73d, Rn 6.

Furthermore, the standard of "*uneingeschränkte Überzeugung*" is criticised against the background that the conclusion will anyway be based on subjective and speculative circumstances. Even if the interpretation set down by the *Bundesgerichtshof* sounds very rigid and strict, circumstantial evidence is allowed and "no exaggerated requirements" of the evidentiary standard shall be made. Accordingly, it has been pointed out that it is in fact more an issue of how to *substantiate* the rulings in the "right way":

> Diese Einschränkung räumt freilich die grundlegenden verfassungsrechtlichen Bedenken nicht aus, zumal der BGH hervorgehoben hatte, dass an die richterliche Überzeugungsbildung "keine überspannten Anforderungen zu stellen sind". Es dürfte damit jedem versierten Tatgericht gelingen, nicht an der Klippe der Begründungsanforderungen zu zerschellen.[439]

In addition, it has been argued that the process of deciding whether certain assets can be explained by legal sources is in practice often performed in a simplified form:

> Die Gerichte machen es sich an dieser Stelle aber zu leicht, wenn sie lediglich die "offiziellen" Einnahmequellen in den Blick nehmen und sodann aus der Diskrepanz zwischen diesem "Hellfeld" und dem tatsächlichen vorhandenen Vermögen auf das "Dunkelfeld" krimineller Quellen schließen. Dabei wird nämlich übersehen, dass es in unserer Gesellschaft eine nicht unbedeutende Grauzone gibt: als Quelle "nicht-offizieller" Einkünfte kommen nachbarschaftliche Dienstleistungen, die Ausübung eines nicht angemeldeten Gewerbes, Prostitution, aber auch Fälle der Ausnutzung wohlhabender Mitmenschen unterhalb der Schwelle von Betrug und Erpressung in Betracht.[440]

The conclusion drawn is thus that not all income that is not officially registered must be derived from criminal activity, but may come from other sources, for example, minor works being done on behalf of a neighbour or self-prostitution. Such assets should lead to taxation, but not be confiscated. It is claimed that the courts are here often influenced by a subjective assumption that the assets of "such persons" must derive from illegal sources.[441]

According to some legal doctrine there is a risk that the German regime on extended confiscation may violate the right to silence. The protection against self-incrimination is supposed to be weakened if a defendant is forced to give statements as to other criminality which is not the object of the present criminal proceedings.[442]

---

439 Herzog, n 432 above, p. 495.
440 Herzog, n 432 above, p. 497.
441 Herzog, n 432 above, pp. 497–98.
442 See further Weßlau, n 338 above, p. 232 and *Münchener Kommentar zum StGB*, n 334 above, §73d, Rn 28.

Even if the aim of the German legislator was to provide an easing of the evidentiary standard for extended confiscation, some commentators have questioned the real effect of Section 73d *StGB* in practice. Is this not really a reversal of the burden of proof? In the words of Weßlau:

> Jede Beweis "erleichterung", die das Beweismaß herabsetzt und anstelle der Überzeugung von der Wahrheit einer Tatsache die Überzeugung von der Wahrscheinlichkeit genügen läßt, hat denselben Effekt wie eine Verschiebung der Beweislast.[443]

The EU legislator has strived against a lowering of the evidentiary standard regarding extended confiscation, and internationally the Member States have even been encouraged to consider a reversal of the burden of proof in some cases.[444] As mentioned in Section 4.3.3.1 above, the possibility of a provision on extended confiscation with a *reversal of the burden of proof* was considered in the German legislative process in 1992, but was rejected. Some reform proposals have also latterly been presented in order to obligate the defendant to account for his financial circumstances and to prove that assets are of legal origin.[445] However, such proposals have so far been turned down, and a reform in this respect has probably a very small chance of success. This has been explained in the following way:

> [T]his idea does not match the general doctrine of German criminal law. Based on constitutional principles, criminal law follows the rule that the accused is innocent until his guilt is proven by the court.[446]

In the context of the adoption of Directive 2014/42/EU, it was originally proposed within the EU that a court must find it "substantially more probable" that the property in question has been derived from criminal activities than that it has not.[447] Such a low evidentiary standard was successfully opposed in the negotiations by, *inter alia*, Germany, which claimed that the threshold violated the right to property and the presumption of innocence in its Constitution. The German delegation even questioned whether such provision on extended confiscation was in line with the right to property in Article 17 of the EU Charter on Fundamental Rights.[448]

---

443 Weßlau, n 338 above, p. 232. Compare BT-Dr 11/6623, pp. 6–7. See generally on the burden of proof in German criminal procedural law, T. Walter, "Die Beweislast im Strafprozeß" (2006) 7 *JuristenZeitung*, pp. 340–49.

444 See further Section 7.4.2 below.

445 See for example BT-Dr 12/6784, 4.2.1994, pp. 10–12.

446 Benseler, n 335 above, p. 207.

447 COM(2012) 85 final, p. 20.

448 BT-Dr 135/12, p. 5. Compare also *Stellungnahme des Deutschen Anwaltvereins durch den Strafrechtsausschuss zum Vorschlag der Kommission für eine Richtlinie des Europäischen Parlaments und des Rates über die Sicherstellung und Einziehung von Erträgen aus Straftaten in der Europäischen Union*, COM(2012) 85, Nr. 70/2012, August 2012, p. 5.

This being said, the present government has on occasions stated a political aim to reform the regime of asset recovery, and has in this context expressed a certain interest in introducing a reversal of the burden of proof:

> Wir regeln, dass bei Vermögen unklarer Herkunft verfassungskonform eine Beweislastumkehr gilt, so dass der legale Erwerb der Vermögenswerte nachgewiesen werden muss.[449]

Again, in the light of the strict German case-law regarding the evidentiary standard, it seems difficult to achieve within the system of criminal proceedings. Accordingly, in 2016, when the proposals for new confiscation legislation in order to implement Directive 2014/42/EU were presented, the current evidentiary standard in the provision on extended confiscation was kept. This is further described in Section 4.4.4 below. At the same time, a new instrument regarding a form of non-conviction-based confiscation was proposed in order to be able to more extensively confiscate "*Vermögen unklarer Herkunft*". This is dealt with in Section 4.4.5 below. It remains to be seen how far-reaching this new legislation will be. As further described in these sections, the German Bundesrat has expressed the need to further lower the burden of proof.

4.4.3. THE PRESENT SCOPE OF THE LEGISLATION

As described in Section 4.3.2 above, the present scope of the German provision on extended confiscation is limited in the way that the triggering offences are typically committed in the area of organised criminality. The motives for this restriction were that specifically such offences justify the use of such a far-reaching method:

> Damit wird dem Umstand Rechnung getragen, dass die Herkunft entsprechender Deliktsgewinne wegen des konspirativen Vorgehens der erfassten Täterkreise häufig nicht vollständig aufgeklärt werden kann. Außerdem soll eine effektivere Gewinnabschöpfung gerade organisiert handelnden Tätern den Anreiz zur Begehung erneuter gewinnorientierter Straftaten nehmen. Vorwiegend bei banden- oder gewerbsmäßiger Tatbegehung sind zudem überhaupt bei den Tätern Gegenstände zu erwarten, die der erweiterten Einziehung unterliegen sollen.[450]

The German legislator has thus strongly emphasised that the use of extended confiscation is only to be used for especially serious cases.[451] This view led to a

449 Koalitionsvertrag zwischen CDU, CSU und SPD, "Deutschlands Zukunft gestalten", 18. Legislaturperiode, p. 145. See for a discussion on this proposal and for the possibilities to reform the German regime of asset recovery, Meyer, n 334 above, especially pp. 265–72.

450 BT-Dr 135/12, 11.5.2012, p. 4.

451 Compare Waechter, n 344 above, p. 474.

certain clash with the proposal for the new EU directive on confiscation, as this instrument abolished the previous link to organised criminality within the area of extended confiscation.[452] In the negotiations on the new directive, Germany argued that regarding offences with no connection to organised crime,

> typischerweise keine kriminalistische Vermutung dafür begründen, dass im Vermögen des Täters festgestellte Vermögenswerte etwa aus weiteren – nicht aufgeklärten – Straftaten stammen.[453]

It was thus argued that not all offences are of such a character as to justify a criminological assumption that the defendants possess further assets of an illegal origin. Against this background, it was suggested that the original proposal from the European Commission should be changed in this respect and that the triggering offences would be restricted in the way done by German law.[454] However, this suggestion was not followed and the German view must now be reconsidered. The necessary changes to national law in this respect are described in what follows.

4.4.4. THE PROPOSAL FOR A NEW GERMAN PROVISION ON EXTENDED CONFISCATION

The new provision on "*erweiterte Einziehung von Taterträgen bei Tätern und Teilnehmern*" has been inserted in Section 73a *StGB*. In the original draft for legislation from the Federal Ministry of Justice and Consumer Protection the rule was drafted as follows:

> (1) Ist eine rechtswidrige Tat begangen worden und ist das Gericht aufgrund der Gesamtumstände davon überzeugt, dass Gegenstände des Täters oder Teilnehmers durch andere rechtwidrige Taten, aus ihnen oder für sie erlangt worden sind, so ordnet es die Einziehung auch dieser Gegenstände an.
> (2) Hat sich der Täter oder Teilnehmer vor der Anordnung der Einziehung nach Absatz 1 an einer anderen rechtswidrigen Tat beteiligt und ist erneut über die Einziehung seiner Gegenstände zu entscheiden, berücksichtigt das Gericht hierbei die bereits ergangene Anordnung.[455]

The wording of this provision was somewhat changed in the Government draft for new legislation, but this principally involved only linguistic changes and had

---

452 See further Section 7.3 below.
453 Drucksache 135/12, 11.5.2012, p. 4.
454 See BT-Dr 135/12, 11.5.2012, pp. 4–5.
455 Referentenentwurf des Bundesministeriums der Justiz und für Verbraucherschutz, *Entwurf eines Gesetzes zur Reform der strafrechtlichen Vermögensabschöpfung*, March 2016, p. 7.

no consequences for the scope of application.[456] Section 73a *StGB* has now been proposed to the German Parliament as follows:

(1) Ist eine rechtswidrige Tat begangen worden, so ordnet das Gericht die Einziehung von Gegenständen des Täters oder Teilnehmers auch dann an, wenn diese Gegenstände durch andere rechtswidrige Taten oder für sie erlangt worden sind.
(2) Hat sich der Täter oder Teilnehmer vor der Anordnung der Einziehung nach Absatz 1 an einer anderen rechtswidrigen Tat beteiligt und ist erneut über die Einziehung seiner Gegenstände zu entscheiden, berücksichtigt das Gericht hierbei die bereits ergangene Anordnung.[457]

If the provision is enacted according to the governmental draft, there will be a significant increase of the scope for extended confiscation under German law, as in the future *every unlawful act* will qualify as an "*Anknüpfungstat*" (triggering offence). A minimum penalty scale for such an offence is not required by Section 73a *StGB*.[458] The German Government has argued that:

> Die bisherige grundsätzliche Systematik, wonach der "erweiterte Verfall" nur bei den typischerweise im Zusammenhang mit organisierter Kriminalität stehenden Straftaten eröffnet wird, kann durch die Aufnahme der in Umsetzung der Richtlinie 2014/42/EU erforderlichen Verweise nicht mehr aufrechterhalten werden. Vor dem Hintergrund der vermögensordnenden und normstabilisierenden Ziele der erweiterten Einziehung von Taterträgen ist es darüber hinaus folgerichtig, diese Systematik vollständig aufzubrechen und den Anwendungsbereich der erweiterten Einziehung von Taterträgen auf alle Straftatbestände zu erstrecken.[459]

Accordingly, it is regarded as necessary in order to implement Directive 2014/42/EU to abolish the limiting requirement of a "*gewerbsmäßige bzw. bandenmäßige Tatbegehung*" regarding a triggering offence, and to safeguard that the German provision includes the specifically listed criminal offences in Article 5 of the

[456] See for a comparison between those drafts, *Ergänzende Stellungnahme der Strafverteidigervereingungen zum Entwurf eines Gesetzes zur strafrechtlichen Vermögensabschöpfung* (Gesetzentwurf der Bundesregierung), September 2016, especially p. 2.

[457] Gesetzentwurf der Bundesregierung, *Entwurf eines Gesetzes zur Reform der strafrechtlichen Vermögensabschöpfung*, BT-Dr 18/9525, 5.9.2016, p. 9.

[458] See further Gesetzentwurf der Bundesregierung, *Entwurf eines Gesetzes zur Reform der strafrechtlichen Vermögensabschöpfung*, BT-Dr 18/9525, 5.9.2016, pp. 57–58 as well as pp. 62–65 and Referentenentwurf des Bundesministeriums der Justiz und für Verbraucherschutz, *Entwurf eines Gesetzes zur Reform der strafrechtlichen Vermögensabschöpfung*, March 2016, pp. 61–62 and 67–71.

[459] Gesetzentwurf der Bundesregierung, *Entwurf eines Gesetzes zur Reform der strafrechtlichen Vermögensabschöpfung*, BT-Dr 18/9525, 5.9.2016, p. 65.

EU instrument.[460] An increase of the scope for extended confiscation was additionally justified in the following way:

> Die vermögensordnenden und normstabilisierenden Ziele der erweiterten Einziehung von Taterträgen können aber nur dann erreicht werden, wenn in allen Fällen, in denen Vermögensgegenstände aufgefunden werden, die aus rechtswidrigen Taten stammen, diese auch eingezogen werden können. Das Vertrauen der Bevölkerung in die Gerechtigkeit und die Unverbrüchlichkeit der Rechtsordnung kann Schaden nehmen, wenn Straftäter deliktisch erlangte Vermögenswerte dauerhaftbehalten dürfen. Eine Duldung solcher strafrechtswidrigen Vermögenslagen durch den Staat könnte den Eindruck hervorrufen, kriminelles Verhalten zahle sich aus, und damit einen staatlich gesetzten Anreiz zur Begehung gewinnorientierter Delikte geben.[461]

The German Government thus argues that the rationales for the measure of extended confiscation may only be achieved if all assets which derive from unlawful acts may be confiscated under the legislation. Furthermore, public confidence in the legal order can be damaged if criminals are allowed to retain the assets acquired by the offence, as the impression could be given that criminal behaviour is paying off.

During the ongoing legislative process, this change of the scope of application for extended confiscation has been criticised.[462] It has *inter alia* been argued that such an increase is in conflict with the principle of proportionality as well as with German constitutional law. It has, for example, been questioned whether it is proportionate that also trivial offences, for example the theft of a bicycle, may lead to such an intrusive measure.[463] In addition, it has been held that it will lead to an unreasonable additional workload for the judiciary, and increased costs for legal proceedings.[464] In this respect, it has further been highlighted that Article 5 Directive 2014/42/EU does not require that extended confiscation is

---

460 See for the motives in detail, Gesetzentwurf der Bundesregierung, *Entwurf eines Gesetzes zur Reform der strafrechtlichen Vermögensabschöpfung*, BT-Dr 18/9525, 5.9.2016, pp. 62–65.

461 Gesetzentwurf der Bundesregierung, *Entwurf eines Gesetzes zur Reform der strafrechtlichen Vermögensabschöpfung*, BT-Dr 18/9525, 5.9.2016, p. 65.

462 See for example *Stellungnahme des Deutschen Anwalt Vereins zum Referentenentwurf des Bundesministeriums der Justiz und für Verbraucherschutz, Entwurf eines Gesetzes zur Reform der strafrechtlichen Vermögensabschöpfung*, June 2016, pp. 13–14, *Stellungnahme der Strafverteidigervereingungen zum Entwurf eines Gesetzes zur strafrechtlichen Vermögensabschöpfung*, May 2016, pp. 5–10 and *Bundesrechtsanwaltskammer, Stellungnahme Nr. 15/2016, zum Referentenentwurf zur Reform der strafrechtlichen Vermögensabschöpfung*, June 2016, pp. 4–5.

463 *Stellungnahme der Strafverteidigervereingungen zum Entwurf eines Gesetzes zur strafrechtlichen Vermögensabschöpfung* (Gesetzentwurf der Bundesregierung), 31 May 2016, p. 8.

464 *Ergänzende Stellungnahme der Strafverteidigervereingungen zum Entwurf eines Gesetzes zur strafrechtlichen Vermögensabschöpfung* (Gesetzentwurf der Bundesregierung), September 2016, p. 2. Compare also *Stellungnahme der Strafverteidigervereingungen zum Entwurf eines Gesetzes zur strafrechtlichen Vermögensabschöpfung* (Gesetzentwurf der Bundesregierung), 31 May 2016.

made applicable to every unlawful act, and it has therefore been suggested that the legislator ought to limit the triggering offences in some way.[465]

When it comes to the evidentiary standard, the current provision on extended confiscation in Section 73d *StGB* provides that a court shall make such an order

> wenn die Umstände die Annahme rechtfertigen, dass diese Gegenstände für rechtswidrige Taten oder aus ihnen erlangt worden sind.[466]

As seen above, this formulation has been deleted in the Government draft for new legislation and the provision has been redrafted. However, no change in substance was thereby intended. Rather it was considered necessary to remove the criterion "*wenn Umstände die Annahme rechtfertigen*" from the legal text in order to more expressly correspond to the requirements set in these cases by the highest German courts. The present standard of "*uneingeschränkte richterliche Überzeugung*" will thus continue to apply, and a judge must also in the future be *absolutely convinced* that (any sort of) unlawful acts have been committed:

> Mit der Neufassung der Vorschrift über die erweiterte Einziehung in §73a StGB-E soll die vom Bundesgerichtshof (BGH, Urteil vom 7. Juli 2011 - 3 StR 144/11 - NStZ-RR 2012, 312 ff., Rn. 7) vorgenommene und vom Bundesverfassungsgericht (BVerfG, a.a.O.) bestätigte verfassungskonforme Auslegung in den Regelungstext übernommen werden. Dies erfolgt rechtstechnisch, indem die im geltenden Recht (§73d Absatz 1 Satz 1 StGB) abgesenkten Anforderungen an die Überzeugungsbildung ("wenn Umstände die Annahme rechtfertigen …") gestrichen werden. Es ist damit notwendig - aber auch ausreichend - dass das Gericht nach erschöpfender Beweiserhebung und -würdigung von der deliktischen Herkunft der betreffenden Gegenstände überzeugt ist.[467]

As seen above, in the draft provision from the Federal Ministry of Justice and Consumer Protection, the evidentiary standard had been formulated as "*aufgrund der Gesamtumstände davon überzeugt*". The new wording was supposed to clarify that a court must be *absolutely convinced* that (any sort of) unlawful acts have been committed, and that the asset in question is a result of such offences.[468]

---

465 Compare Bundesrechtsanwaltskammer, *Stellungnahme Nr. 39/2016, zum Regierungsentwurf eines Gesetzes zur Reform der strafrechtlichen Vermögensabschöpfung*, November 2016, pp. 2–3 and Bundesrechtsanwaltskammer, *Stellungnahme Nr. 15/2016, zum Referentenentwurf zur Reform der strafrechtlichen Vermögensabschöpfung*, June 2016, pp. 4–5.

466 See on the evidentiary standard, Sections 4.3.3 and 4.4.2 above.

467 Gesetzentwurf der Bundesregierung, *Entwurf eines Gesetzes zur Reform der strafrechtlichen Vermögensabschöpfung*, BT-Dr 18/9525, 5.9.2016, pp. 65–66.

468 Referentenentwurf des Bundesministeriums der Justiz und für Verbraucherschutz, *Entwurf eines Gesetzes zur Reform der strafrechtlichen Vermögensabschöpfung*, March 2016, p. 71.

This formulation of the standard was criticised in the legislative process and was not used in the Government draft for new legislation.[469]

During the legislative process, the *Bundesrat* has required that the possibilities to further lower the evidentiary standard for extended confiscation in Section 73a *StGB* must be considered. It has thereby been argued that there must be constitutional room to create more effective criteria for orders of extended confiscation. Accordingly, the existing constitutional limits must be exhausted:

> Das Bundesverfassungsgericht dürfte mit seiner Entscheidung aus dem Jahr 2004 (BVerfGE 110, 1) die Grenzen einer verfassungsrechtlichen Regelung noch nicht abschließend markiert haben, nachdem es die Auslegung der Vorschrift durch den Bundesgerichtshof (BGHSt 40, 371 – mit verfassungsrechtlich gesehen überholter Begründung) zugrunde gelegt und seine Prüfung allein und explizit an diesem Maßstab ausgerichtet hat.[470]

This position from the *Bundesrat* has been criticised, as it has been argued that such proposed amendments would go beyond the bounds of the Constitution.[471] However, the German Government has confirmed that the issue will be reconsidered in the further legislative process.[472]

4.4.5. THE PROPOSAL FOR A NEW FORM OF NON-CONVICTION-BASED CONFISCATION

At present ordinary and extended confiscation can be ordered independently ("*Selbständige Anordnung von Verfall*") if *for reasons of fact* no person can be prosecuted or convicted of the offence and the conditions under which the measure is prescribed or available are otherwise met (Section 76a *StGB*). One purpose of the present reform of the German regime has been to increase the

---

469 See for example *Stellungnahme des Deutschen Anwalt Vereins zum Referentenentwurf des Bundesministeriums der Justiz und für Verbraucherschutz, Entwurf eines Gesetzes zur Reform der strafrechtlichen Vermögensabschöpfung*, June 2016, pp. 13–14. Compare Bittmann, n 353 above, pp. 123–24.

470 Unterrichtung durch die Bundesregierung, *Entwurf eines Gesetzes zur Reform der strafrechtlichen Vermögensabschöpfung* – Drucksache 18/9525, *Stellungnahme des Bundesrates und Gegenäußerung der Bundesregierung*, BT-Dr 18/10146, 26.10.2016, p. 2.

471 See for example *Stellungnahme des Deutschen Anwalt Vereins durch den Ausschuss Strafrecht zum Entwurf eines Gesetzes zur Reform der strafrechtlichen Vermögensabschöpfung* – Empfehlungen der Ausschüsse des Bundesrates (BT-Dr 418/1/16 vom 12.9.2016), Nr. 59/2016, September 2016, pp. 3–5.

472 Unterrichtung durch die Bundesregierung, *Entwurf eines Gesetzes zur Reform der strafrechtlichen Vermögensabschöpfung* – Drucksache 18/9525, *Stellungnahme des Bundesrates und Gegenäußerung der Bundesregierung*, BT-Dr 18/10146, 26.10.2016, pp. 1–2 and 11.

scope for confiscation orders in such cases and to allow the measure to be used also where there are *legal* obstacles to a criminal conviction.[473]

In the Government draft for new legislation Section 76a *StGB* has been redrafted with the new title "*Selbständige Einziehung*". Subsection 4 of the new section introduces a new form of confiscation into German law:

> Die Regelung ermöglicht es, Vermögen unklarer Herkunft unabhängig vom Nachweis einer konkreten rechtswidrigen Tat (selbständig) einzuziehen, wenn das Gericht davon überzeugt ist (vgl. dazu §437 StPO-E), dass der sichergestellte Gegenstand aus (irgend-)einer rechtswidrigen Tat herrührt. Es ist mithin nicht erforderlich, dass die Tat im Einzelnen festgestellt wird; an die Überzeugung dürfen keine überspannten Anforderungen gestellt werden ...[474]

The new provision has been motivated particularly against the background of certain difficulties that have occurred in practice when police officers at airports or during controls of vehicles have found significant amounts of cash. It has been argued that in such cases – which often have an international character – it is very difficult to prove the existence of any specific criminal offence, which means that the property must under the current regime be handed back to the individuals.[475]

Section 76a Subsection 4 *StGB* is drafted as follows:

> Ein aus einer rechtswidrigen Tat herrührender Gegenstand, der in einem Verfahren wegen des Verdachts einer in Satz 3 genannten Straftat sichergestellt worden ist, soll auch dann selbständig eingezogen werden, wenn der von der Sicherstellung Betroffene nicht wegen der Straftat verfolgt oder verurteilt werden kann. Wird die Einziehung eines Gegenstandes angeordnet, so geht das Eigentum an der Sache oder das Recht mit der Rechtskraft der Entscheidung auf den Staat über; §75 Absatz 3 gilt entsprechend.[476]

Accordingly, in a case where certain property has been secured during an investigation, a court may order the confiscation of this property independently if the individual in question cannot be prosecuted or convicted for this offence. The measure may only be used regarding particular forms of serious criminality,

---

473 Gesetzentwurf der Bundesregierung, *Entwurf eines Gesetzes zur Reform der strafrechtlichen Vermögensabschöpfung*, BT-Dr 18/9525, 5.9.2016, pp. 57 and 72–74.

474 Gesetzentwurf der Bundesregierung, *Entwurf eines Gesetzes zur Reform der strafrechtlichen Vermögensabschöpfung*, BT-Dr 18/9525, 5.9.2016, p. 73.

475 Gesetzentwurf der Bundesregierung, *Entwurf eines Gesetzes zur Reform der strafrechtlichen Vermögensabschöpfung*, BT-Dr 18/9525, 5.9.2016, p. 48.

476 Gesetzentwurf der Bundesregierung, *Entwurf eines Gesetzes zur Reform der strafrechtlichen Vermögensabschöpfung*, BT-Dr 18/9525, 5.9.2016, p. 14. Compare Referentenentwurf des Bundesministeriums der Justiz und für Verbraucherschutz, *Entwurf eines Gesetzes zur Reform der strafrechtlichen Vermögensabschöpfung*, March 2016, p. 14.

and the provision contains a list of such criminal offences in the area of organised crime and terrorism.

A further requirement for such confiscation is that the court - on the basis of the overall circumstances of a case – is convinced that the property derives from an unlawful act. In this respect, Section 437 of the Government draft for new legislation provides guidelines for the decision:

> Bei der Entscheidung über die selbständige Einziehung nach §76 a Absatz 4 des Strafgesetzbuches kann das Gericht seine Überzeugung davon, dass der Gegenstand aus einer rechtswidrigen Tat herrührt, insbesondere auf ein grobes Missverhältnis zwischen dem Wert des Gegenstandes und den rechtmäßigen Einkünften des Betroffenen stützen. Darüber hinaus kann es bei seiner Entscheidung insbesondere auch berücksichtigen
> 1. das Ergebnis der Ermittlungen zu der Tat, die Anlass für das Verfahren war,
> 2. die Umstände, unter denen der Gegenstand aufgefunden und sichergestellt worden ist, sowie
> 3. die sonstigen persönlichen und wirtschaftlichen Verhältnisse des Betroffenen.[477]

According to this provision a court may thus base its decision in such cases in particular on a gross disproportionality between the value of the property and the legal income of the person concerned. It may also take account of the results from the investigation into the act which gave rise to the seizure, as well as the circumstances under which the property was found and the personal and economic circumstances of the person concerned.

"*Selbständige Einziehung*" according to Section 76a Subsection 4 *StGB* is supposed to be *subsidiary* to ordinary and extended confiscation.[478] As to the character of the measure, the legislator has provided that:

> Das Verfahren der selbständigen Einziehung nach §76a Absatz 4 StGB-E ist ein Verfahren gegen die Sache (ad rem); es richtet sich nicht gegen eine Person. Es hat damit keinen Strafcharakter.[479]

The German legislator has further underlined that this measure has been drafted in accordance with human rights instruments and case-law from the ECtHR.[480]

---

477 Gesetzentwurf der Bundesregierung, *Entwurf eines Gesetzes zur Reform der strafrechtlichen Vermögensabschöpfung*, BT-Dr 18/9525, 5.9.2016, p. 30.

478 Compare Gesetzentwurf der Bundesregierung, *Entwurf eines Gesetzes zur Reform der strafrechtlichen Vermögensabschöpfung*, BT-Dr 18/9525, 5.9.2016, p. 73.

479 Gesetzentwurf der Bundesregierung, *Entwurf eines Gesetzes zur Reform der strafrechtlichen Vermögensabschöpfung*, BT-Dr 18/9525, 5.9.2016, p. 92.

480 Gesetzentwurf der Bundesregierung, *Entwurf eines Gesetzes zur Reform der strafrechtlichen Vermögensabschöpfung*, BT-Dr 18/9525, 5.9.2016, p. 58.

According to the legislative works, Section 76a Subsection 4 *StGB* is supposed to correspond to the measures of *non-conviction-based confiscation* found in certain common law States and Italy (compare Section 1.1 above).[481] Nevertheless, the introduction of such a power for the law enforcement agencies may not be uncontroversial in Germany, especially considering the criticism which has been directed against the instrument of extended confiscation in legal doctrine.[482] The proposals have also been questioned by many.[483] It has, for example, been pointed out that the construction of Section 76a Subsection 4 in the Government draft for new legislation significantly differs from non-conviction-based confiscation in many other States, because the matter is to be decided by a criminal court on the basis of criminal procedural rules. It is thus not a matter of independent administrative "in rem" proceedings.[484] Furthermore, a common position is that the change would be in conflict with constitutional law, for example the principle of proportionality and Article 14 *GG*. Some commentators have additionally suggested that the provision will in practice lead to a reversal of the burden of proof, as the individual must at a certain stage present his own evidence for a legal origin of property. This would also be in conflict with German Constitutional law.[485]

In contrast, the *Bundesrat* has recommended that the existing constitutional limits should be further expanded, and that the evidentiary standard should be lowered in order to create more effective criteria for confiscation. It has thereby been specifically referred to the "*Koalitionsvertrag zwischen CDU, CSU und SPD*" where the Government has expressed a political will to introduce a reversal of the burden of proof in asset recovery cases.[486] In this respect, recommendations

---

481 Gesetzentwurf der Bundesregierung, *Entwurf eines Gesetzes zur Reform der strafrechtlichen Vermögensabschöpfung*, BT-Dr 18/9525, 5.9.2016, pp. 58 and 73. Compare in this respect Referentenentwurf des Bundesministeriums der Justiz und für Verbraucherschutz, *Entwurf eines Gesetzes zur Reform der strafrechtlichen Vermögensabschöpfung*, March 2016, pp. 62 and 78.

482 Compare for example Section 4.4.2 above.

483 See for example *Stellungnahme* des Deutschen Anwalt Vereins zum Referentenentwurf des Bundesministeriums der Justiz und für Verbraucherschutz, Entwurf eines Gesetzes zur Reform der strafrechtlichen Vermögensabschöpfung, June 2016, pp. 15–18, Deutscher Richterbund, *Stellungnahme* zum Referentenentwurf eines Gesetzes zur Reform der strafrechtlichen Vermögensabschöpfung, June 2016, p. 4 and *Stellungnahme* der Strafverteidigervereingungen zum Entwurf eines Gesetzes zur strafrechtlichen Vermögensabschöpfung, May 2016, pp. 10–20.

484 See for example *Ergänzende Stellungnahme* der Strafverteidigervereingungen zum Entwurf eines Gesetzes zur strafrechtlichen Vermögensabschöpfung (Gesetzentwurf der Bundesregierung), September 2016, pp. 3–4.

485 Bundesrechtsanwaltskammer, *Stellungnahme* Nr. 39/2016, zum Regierungsentwurf eines Gesetzes zur Reform der strafrechtlichen Vermögensabschöpfung, November 2016, pp. 4–5. Compare Gesetzentwurf der Bundesregierung, *Entwurf eines Gesetzes zur Reform der strafrechtlichen Vermögensabschöpfung*, BT-Dr 18/9525, 5.9.2016, p. 92.

486 See on this Section 4.4.2 above.

from the Financial Action Task Force for a reversal of the burden of proof regarding confiscation have also been highlighted.[487] The German Government has confirmed that the issue will be considered in the further legislative process.[488] Against this background, it remains to be seen how Section 76a Subsection 4 *StGB* will be finally drafted.

This being said, a certain form of non-conviction-based "confiscation" of assets has in recent years developed in legal practice in some cases where confiscation in the context of *StGB* is not possible. This method is not based on any federal law, but is practised on an administrative basis in some *Bundesländer* where property is seized on the basis of police laws in order *to prevent future criminal offences*. This practice of administrative seizure of property is rather remarkable, and will be briefly described in the concluding section.

4.4.6. THE PRACTICE OF ADMINISTRATIVE "*PRÄVENTIVE GEWINNABSCHÖPFUNG*"

The measure – called "*präventive Gewinnabschöpfung*" – was first developed by the police and prosecuting authorities in the city of Osnabrück (Lower Saxony) in 2003,[489] but then spread to some other *Bundesländer*.[490] In Lower Saxony, a special circular directive has been issued by the *Ministerium für Inneres und Sport* expressly allowing for the measure.[491] The circular provides that if confiscation according to *StGB* is not possible in relation to property which has been seized within a criminal investigation, the possibility of seizure (so-called "*Sicherstellung*") on the basis of administrative legislation on public security and

---

487 See further Unterrichtung durch die Bundesregierung, *Entwurf eines Gesetzes zur Reform der strafrechtlichen Vermögensabschöpfung* – Drucksache 18/9525, *Stellungnahme des Bundesrates und Gegenäußerung der Bundesregierung*, BT-Dr 18/10146, 26.10.2016, pp. 1–2.

488 Unterrichtung durch die Bundesregierung, *Entwurf eines Gesetzes zur Reform der strafrechtlichen Vermögensabschöpfung* – Drucksache 18/9525, *Stellungnahme des Bundesrates und Gegenäußerung der Bundesregierung*, BT-Dr 18/10146, 26.10.2016, pp. 1–2 and 11.

489 Initiator was apparently the former Kriminaldirektor of the police in Osnabrück Ernst Hunsicker, who has a private website (www.ernsthunsicker.de) with several references to case-law and publications within this area.

490 On this method, see for example Waechter, n 344 above, P. Thiée, "'Präventive Gewinnabschöpfung': Wenn Polizeibeamte Winkeladvokaten spielen" (2009) 2 *Strafverteidiger*, pp. 102–04 and E. Hunsicker, *Die Präventive Gewinnabschöpfung (PräGe) im Überblick*, GRIN Verlag, 2014.

491 Runderlass 15.2.2015, *Präventive Gewinnabschöpfung; Hinweise zum Verfahren der Sicherstellung nach §26 Nds. SOG vor strafprozessualer Herausgabe offensichtlich nicht rechtmäßig erlangter Sachen*, Niedersächsiges Minestrial Blatt Nr. 10, 2015, pp. 258–60. This circular has updated a former circular from 2007.

order can, under certain conditions, be possible.[492] It is provided that there must be sufficient reason to believe that the goods have not been derived legally, and as a general guideline it is stated that the measure should not be used for cash under €500.[493]

The legality of "*präventive Gewinnabschöpfung*" has been confirmed in some cases before the administrative courts. As an example may be mentioned a case before the Higher Administrative Court in Lower Saxony.[494] The customs police had seized €27,000 which had been found in cash during a search of a car registered in Poland. There were positive tests which indicated drug use regarding the two persons in the car, but no narcotics were found. The police confiscated the cash on the grounds of suspected money laundering. As the prosecuting authority did not raise prosecution and revoked the seizure decision, an order of "*Sicherstellung*" was issued by the police on the basis of administrative legislation regarding public security and order.[495] It was argued that the cash was of illegal origin and that there was an immediate danger that it would be used for future dealings in narcotic offences. The decision was challenged without any success, as the Higher Administrative Court ruled that such a preventive measure is allowed under the legislation in question even in cases where a criminal investigation has been discontinued.[496] It was held that a measure must be necessary in order to prevent that cash is used to prepare or commit new criminal offences, and that the estimation of an immediate danger must be performed with care.

The practice of "*präventive Gewinnabschöpfung*" is controversial, and the question of the general constitutionality of the practice has so far not been tested by the *Bundesverfassungsgericht*.[497] Critics have argued that if such practice is used by the police authorities in cases where the confiscation of assets is not possible according to *StGB*, then the strict criteria and procedural safeguards for the measure are circumvented.[498] It has also been pointed out that the aim to

---

492 A reference is made to Sec. 26 *Niedersächsisches Gesetz über die öffentliche Sicherheit und Ordnung* (Nds. SOG).

493 See further on the procedure, Waechter, n 344 above.

494 *Oberverwaltungsgericht Lüneburg*, Judgment of 2.7.2009, Az. 11 LC 4/08.

495 The basis was Sec. 26(1) *Niedersächsisches Gesetz über die öffentliche Sicherheit und Ordnung* (Nds. SOG), which permits "Sicherstellung um eine gegenwärtige Gefahr abzuwenden".

496 See also *Oberverwaltungsgericht Lüneburg*, Judgment of 7.3. 2013, Az. 11 LB 438/10.

497 See for one case regarding this practice, *Bundesverfassungsgericht*, Decision of 24.10.2011, 1 BVR 732/11. However, the constitutionality of the measure was not decided.

498 For critical discussions of several problematic issues regarding this method, see for example Waechter, n 344 above as well as Thiée, n 490 above and P. Thiée, "Polizeirechtliche Sicherstellung nach Freigabe gem. §98 StPO – Erwiderung auf die Erwiderung" (2010) 4 *Strafverteidiger*, pp. 215–18. See for a response to such objections, E. Hunsicker, "Präventive Gewinnabschöpfung (PräGe), Entgegnung auf Philipp Thiée in StV 2/2009, S. 102 ff." (2010) 4 *Strafverteidiger*, pp. 212–15.

prevent assets of an illegal origin being reinvested in new criminality is also an aim of the provision on extended confiscation, but the legislator has only allowed this measure in the context of a *conviction* for certain triggering offences.[499]

The existence of administrative "*präventive Gewinnabschöpfung*" in some regions in Germany is interesting, as the practice seems to allow for a form of non-conviction-based confiscation far above the prerequisites of the Criminal Code. Space unfortunately does not allow for a more detailed description of this administrative case-law, which in many respects seems remarkable.[500] In spite of the fact that the prosecutor has "failed" within the criminal proceedings to show an illegal origin – the property may still in the end be "confiscated" by *administrative* authorities. It seems to make no difference whether the defendant has been acquitted or if the criminal proceedings have been cancelled. In the cases where the administrative courts have approved of the measure it has been argued that there was an immediate danger that future criminal offences would be committed with the use of the cash in question. However, the estimation of the dangers of such future criminal offences seems in many cases rather speculative. It can also be doubted whether this administrative legislation on "*Sicherstellung*" is intended to be used in a way which lead to a *final* deprivation of property.

---

499 Waechter, n 344 above, p. 477.

500 See for example E. Hunsicker, *Präventive Gewinnabschöpfung (PräGe). Entscheidungssammlung in Volltexten und mit Leitsätzen*, 3. überarbeitete and erweiterte Auflage, GRIN Verlag, 2014 and Waechter, n 344 above for numerous references to case-law.

CHAPTER 5
LEGISLATION IN SWEDEN

5.1. THE DEVELOPMENT OF THE MEASURE OF EXTENDED CONFISCATION IN SWEDISH LAW

The regime on confiscation has been continually amended and extended in Swedish law. Space does not allow an exhaustive description of this general development, but in what follows a short outline of the reasons for the introduction of the measure of extended confiscation will be given.[501] Of significant importance for the development of the Swedish system of confiscation as a whole was the *Ministry of Justice Report* on more efficient legislation on confiscation, which was published in 1999.[502] The motive for setting up this inquiry was to elaborate proposals for improved rules in order to counteract large-scale organised and financial crime. The report concluded in general that the measure of confiscation had had limited use in Swedish practice, and that the legal provisions were unclear and ineffective. The significant evidentiary difficulties in showing a link between the crime in question and the property to be confiscated were especially highlighted.[503] Several proposals were made in order to strengthen the measure of confiscation and overcome the investigatory shortcomings. Among these was also a proposal for a form of extended confiscation, which had largely been inspired by the Norwegian legislation.[504] The report resulted in several changes in national legislation regarding ordinary confiscation, but the measure of extended confiscation was not finalised at this legislative stage.

Instead, the development towards the introduction of such a measure was triggered by a number of international undertakings.[505] Of most importance became the adoption in 2005 of FD 2005/212/JHA.[506] The main part of this

501 For a general overview of the development of the regime of confiscation in Swedish law, see G. Almkvist, *Förverkande av egendom*, Iustus förlag, 2014, pp. 30–42.

502 SOU 1999:147, *Effektivare Förverkandelagstiftning*.

503 See SOU 1999:147, pp. 118–21.

504 SOU 1999:147, pp. 216–22. See on the Norwegian law, Section 6.1 below.

505 Compare on different international initiatives, Section 1.2 above.

506 This instrument is described in Section 2.1 above.

instrument was implemented in Swedish law through legal provisions that came into force in 2005.[507] However, the adoption of provisions on extended confiscation, in accordance with Article 3 of the instrument, was left pending on this occasion because the matter was deemed to require more thorough investigation.[508]

After a lengthy legislative process, a provision on extended confiscation finally came into force on 1 July 2008.[509] From an international perspective, Sweden was thus rather late with the introduction of such legislation. The legislator gave the following reasons for the new measure: international obligations; the development and internationalisation of crime; and the general interest in depriving offenders of the proceeds of their criminal activity.[510] In order to create a powerful and effective tool to be used in the fight against serious financial criminality, the implementing legislation was drafted in a more far-reaching way than was required by FD 2005/212/JHA.[511]

The Swedish legislator made clear that extended confiscation, like other forms of confiscation, is intended to be a *reaction to a committed crime*. By committing a serious crime for the purpose of gain, the perpetrator is deemed to be indicating that profits may exist also from other criminality. According to the legislative works it is both reasonable and acceptable from the viewpoint of legal safety that such an assumption should be directed towards someone who for the purpose of gain had committed serious crimes. However, it is also emphasised that the validity of such assumptions is to be properly investigated and tested by a court.[512]

In 2013, the government appointed an inquiry with the task of studying how the provision on extended confiscation had been applied in practice, to analyse if the regulation gave rise to any special difficulties and to consider the need for legislative changes in the national legislation as a result from the adoption of Directive 2014/42/EU.[513] The inquiry finalised a report in 2015, which contained many interesting conclusions regarding the use of extended confiscation in Sweden. The proposals for the necessary changes to domestic

---

507 Bill 2004/05:135.

508 For a general description of the legislative process in Sweden, see I. Cameron, M. Thunberg Schunke, K. Påle-Bartes, C. Wong and P. Asp, *International Criminal Law from a Swedish Perspective*, Intersentia, 2011, pp. 10–12.

509 For the legislative works, see Bill 2007/08:68. Compare also Ds 2006:17, Utvidgat Förverkande m.m. See on the application of the provision in general, for example Almkvist, n 501 above, especially pp. 105–13, M. Ulväng, "Utvidgat förverkande och skattebrott" (2010) 4:10 *Ny Juridik*, pp. 85–97 and Handbook on confiscation etc. from the Prosecuting Office, Utvecklingscentrum Stockholm, 2010.

510 Bill 2007/08:68 pp. 48 and 52.

511 Bill 2007/08:68 especially pp. 52–53.

512 Bill 2007/08:68 p. 50.

513 Justitiedepartementet, *Kommittédirektiv* 2013:14 and *Tilläggsdirektiv till Utredningen om utvidgat förverkande*, 2014:22.

legislation following from the new directive were also presented.[514] This report (hereafter "*Report on Extended Confiscation*") suggested some general changes to confiscation practice.

In March 2016, the Swedish Government presented its proposals for legislation in order to implement Directive 2014/42/EU.[515] The new legislation took force on 1 July 2016, and the changes were basically in line with the conclusions made in the *Report on Extended Confiscation*. The scope for extended confiscation was thereby further increased in national law.

5.2. GENERALLY ON THE REGIME FOR CONFISCATION IN SWEDEN

The legal provisions on confiscation in criminal matters are found in Chapter 36 of the Swedish Penal Code (*Brottsbalken SFS 1962:700*), hereafter referred to as the "SPC".[516] These rules are complemented or partly replaced by provisions contained in certain special criminal law statutes which may contain other prerequisites for confiscation. This means that the regime has a somewhat complicated construction. The Council on legislation ("*Lagrådet*") has on several occasions proposed a general legislative reform of the provisions on confiscation in order to provide for a better systematisation and more overview of the regime. The Swedish Government has confirmed that this must be undertaken.[517] This study will exclusively deal with the provisions on confiscation in Chapter 36 SPC.

In Swedish law, confiscation is not seen as a criminal sanction, but is defined as a so-called "*särskild rättsverkan av brott*", which may be described as a special legal consequence of a crime.[518] Extended confiscation is thus a legal consequence of the *triggering offence* which has been committed. Property which has been declared confiscated accrues to the State unless prescribed otherwise.[519] Confiscation of property according to Chapter 36 SPC may only be imposed following a conviction for a criminal offence. There is no regime for civil confiscation of property like the systems to be found in, for example, the

---

514 Betänkande av Utredningen om utvidgat förverkande, m.m., "*För att brott inte ska löna sig*", SOU 2015:67.

515 Bill 2015/16:155.

516 The SPC contains provisions on most of the criminal offences, as well as rules regarding sanctions and the applicability of Swedish law. For an overview of Swedish criminal law and criminal procedure in English, see Cameron, Thunberg Schunke, Påle-Bartes, Wong and Asp, n 508 above, pp. 12–52. A further source of information on the Swedish system in English is the *Mutual Evaluation Report on Sweden* regarding "Financial Crime and Financial Investigations", Council Document 8639/1/12, Brussels 20.11.2012.

517 Compare Bill 2015/16:155 pp. 23 and 72–73.

518 Ch. 1 Secs. 3 and 8 SPC.

519 Ch. 36 Sec. 17 Subsec. 1 SPC.

United Kingdom or Ireland.[520] However, under certain limited circumstances the proceeds of a crime may be confiscated without a criminal conviction. Such procedures are governed by the procedural rules applying to criminal cases.

As a result of the Swedish implementation of Directive 2014/42/EU the national legislation was changed in order to provide for more scope for confiscation without a criminal conviction in these cases.[521] According to Chapter 36 Section 14 SPC it is now possible to confiscate property if a sanction can no longer be imposed because of the death of the offender or for other cause and a summons has been served within five years from the time when the crime was committed. The formulation "other cause" means cases of limitation of legal proceedings (prescription).[522] However, a plea for confiscation of the proceeds of a crime or confiscation of certain items that are regarded as "typical tools" may always be considered, provided that a summons has been served within one year from the time when the circumstance occurred that resulted in the consequence that a penalty can no longer be imposed. A prosecutor may only initiate such proceedings if it is called for in the public interest.

There are different forms of confiscation in the SPC; Chapter 36 Section 2 deals with confiscation of property used as auxiliary means in the commission of a crime, Chapter 36 Section 3 SPC concerns confiscation of certain items that are regarded as "typical tools" used for criminal purposes, and Chapter 36 Section 4 SPC contains the confiscation powers for crimes committed in the course of business. The rule on ordinary confiscation in criminal matters is found in the first section of Chapter 36 which stipulates as follows:

1 § Utbyte av ett brott enligt denna balk ska förklaras förverkat, om det inte är uppenbart oskäligt. Detsamma gäller vad någon har tagit emot som ersättning för kostnader i samband med ett brott, om mottagandet utgör brott enligt denna balk. Istället för det mottagna får dess värde förklaras förverkat.	1. The proceeds of a crime as defined in this Code shall be declared confiscated unless this is manifestly unreasonable. The same shall apply to anything a person has received as payment for costs incurred in conjunction with a crime, provided that such receipt constitutes a crime under this Code. The value of the article received may be declared confiscated instead of the article itself.
Om inte annat är särskilt föreskrivet, ska bestämmelserna i första stycket också tillämpas i fråga om utbyte av ett brott och ersättning för kostnader i samband med ett brott enligt annan lag eller författning, om det för brottet är föreskrivet fängelse i mer än ett år. Lag (2008:370).	Unless otherwise stated, the provisions in the first paragraph also apply to proceeds of crime and payment for costs incurred in conjunction with a crime under another law or statute, if imprisonment for more than one year is prescribed for that crime.[523]

520 Compare for the system in the UK, Section 3.2 above.

521 See further Bill 2015/16:155 pp. 23–27. Compare SOU 2015:67 pp. 121–29.

522 Bill 2015/16:155 pp. 41–42.

523 This translation is taken from an unofficial translation made by and provided for at the homepage of the *Swedish Ministry of Justice* (http://www.government.se/sb/d/3288). This link has now expired, and only a small selection of some Swedish statutes is now provided for.

The term "proceeds of crime" ("*utbyte av brott*") means on the one hand specific property acquired by someone through crime, and on the other hand a notional amount of money estimated as the value of what has been acquired.[524] Confiscation can take place firstly through object confiscation ("*sakförverkande*"), which means that a specific item of property is declared confiscated and the individual loses the right to the object to the State. Secondly, value confiscation ("*värdeförverkande*") can be used, which means that the value of property or certain profits is confiscated. Value confiscation is in principle seen as an alternative to object confiscation, and means in practice that the individual is obligated to pay a given amount to the State.[525]

An important principle in Swedish confiscation law is that a claim for compensation from any victim of a crime shall be taken into account before a plea for confiscation is considered. Chapter 36 Section 17 Subsection 2 SPC states that if confiscated proceeds correspond to the damage occasioned to an individual, the state shall in the offender's stead pay compensation to the injured party of an amount corresponding to the value that has accrued to the state as a consequence of the decision on confiscation.[526] Upon request from a victim, there is a principal obligation for the prosecutor to prepare and present a compensation claim.[527]

As a general principle, the "net principle" is applied, which means that expenses and costs of the criminal activity must be deducted.[528] The reason is that the aim is to confiscate the benefit of a crime, but not create a financial loss. However, in the area of the confiscation of proceeds connected to narcotics or the illegal sale of alcohol, there has been a development in case-law towards the application of a gross principle regarding certain expenses.[529] It was proposed in the *Ministry of Justice Report* on more efficient legislation on confiscation in 1999, that an express rule on the gross principle should be adopted.[530] At the time of the implementation of FD 2005/212/JHA, the legislator, though, held that this proposal was not suitable, and it was further left to case-law to decide in which cases costs can be deducted.[531] In 2016, the Supreme Court gave some guidance on how costs and expenses might be deducted in the area of narcotic

---

524 Bill 1968:79 pp. 76 and 79.

525 Bill 2007/08:68 p. 36.

526 See also Ch. 36 Sec. 1a SPC, which states that by applying the hardship rule regarding ordinary confiscation, consideration to any obligation to pay damages must be made. Ch. 22 Sec. 2 of the Criminal Procedural Code ("*Rättegångsbalken*").

527 Ch. 22 Sec. 2 of the Criminal Procedural Code ("*Rättegångsbalken*").

528 See for example *Handbook on confiscation etc from the Prosecuting Office*, Utvecklingscentrum Stockholm, 2010, pp. 16–18, SOU 1999:147 pp. 162–69 and Bill 2004/05:135 pp. 90–92.

529 *NJA 1977 p. 735*, *NJA 1991 p. 387*, *NJA 2001 p. 129* and *NJA 2004 p. 204*. For a discussion on the net – and gross principle in Swedish law, see Almkvist, n 501 above, pp. 92–103.

530 *Effektivare Förverkandelagstiftning*, SOU 1999:147, pp. 169–74.

531 Bill 2004/05:135 pp. 90–92.

offences, and confirmed that the "net principle" is to be applied as the general rule.[532]

In what follows, the Swedish provision on extended confiscation will be described. The chapter concludes with some comments on the regime, and some specific features are highlighted which are especially interesting from a comparative law perspective or which sometimes lead to practical difficulties in application. Particular references to similarities and differences to the legislation of some other Scandinavian countries will be included. A short overview of such provisions is given in Chapter 6.

It can be generally noted that according to Swedish established legal traditions, the statements and explanations relating to an Act in the legislative works are regarded as an important source of law. This is the reason for the numerous quotations of the preparatory works in question.[533]

5.3. THE PROVISION ON EXTENDED CONFISCATION IN SWEDISH LAW

5.3.1. BASIC SUBSTANTIVE RULES AND THE PROCEDURAL FRAMEWORK

The rule on extended confiscation is found in Chapter 36 Section 1b SPC

Döms någon för ett brott för vilket det är föreskrivet fängelse i fyra år eller mer och har brottet varit av beskaffenhet att kunna ge utbyte, ska även i annat fall än som avses i 1 § egendom förklaras förverkad, om det framstår som klart mera sannolikt att den utgör utbyte av brottslig verksamhet än att så inte är fallet. I stället för egendomen får dess värde förklaras förverkat.	If a person is convicted of a crime for which is prescribed imprisonment for four years or more and if the crime is of such nature to lead to proceeds, in addition to what is referred to in §1, property may also be declared confiscated if it is substantially more probable that it constitutes the proceeds of a crime than not. The value of the property may be declared confiscated instead of the property itself.
Har brottet varit av beskaffenhet att kunna ge utbyte, gäller första stycket också om någon döms för	If the crime is of a nature to give proceeds, the first paragraph shall also apply if someone is convicted of
1. dataintrång, utnyttjande av barn för sexuell posering, tagande av muta, givande av muta eller barnpornografibrott enligt 16 kap. 10 a § första stycket 1–4,	1. illegal system – and data interference, causing or recruiting a child to participate in pornographic performances, active and passive corruption or offences related to child pornography according to Chapter 16 §10a Subsection 1 paras. 1–4,

532 *NJA 2016 p. 202.*

533 On the importance of the legislative works and travaux préparatoires in Swedish law, see further Cameron, Thunberg Schunke, Påle-Bartes, Wong and Asp, n 508 above, pp. 11–12.

2. narkotikabrott enligt 1 § narkotikastrafflagen (1968:64) eller olovlig befattning med narkotikaprekursorer enligt 3 b § första stycket samma lag,	2. narcotics crime according to §1 of the narcotics law (1968:64) or illegal handling of narcotics precursors according to §3b Subsection 1 of the same law,
3. dopningsbrott enligt 3 § första stycket lagen (1991:1969) om förbud mot vissa dopningsmedel,	3. doping crime according to §3 Subsection 1 of the law (1991:1969) concerning prohibition of certain doping substances,
4. narkotikasmuggling enligt 6 § första stycket lagen (2000:1225) om straff för smuggling,	4. narcotics smuggling according to §6 Subsection 1 of the law (2000:1225) concerning punishment for smuggling,
5. människosmuggling enligt 20 kap. 8 § första stycket utlänningslagen (2005:716) eller organiserande av människosmuggling enligt 20 kap. 9 § första stycket samma lag, eller	5. people smuggling according to Chapter 20 §8 Subsection 1 of the aliens' act (2005:716) or the organising of people smuggling according to Chapter 20 §9 Subsection 1 of the same law, or
6. något annat brott för vilket det är föreskrivet fängelse i två år eller mer och som har utgjort led i en brottslighet som utövats i organiserad form.	6. any other offence for which is prescribed imprisonment for two years or more in cases where the offence has been part of criminality that has been conducted in an organised form.
Vad som sägs om förverkande i första och andra styckena gäller också om någon döms för försök, förberedelse eller stämpling till ett brott som avses där.	What is stated about confiscation in the first and second paragraph shall also apply if someone is convicted of attempt, preparation or conspiracy to commit such a crime.
Förverkande enligt denna paragraf får inte beslutas om det är oskäligt.[534]	Confiscation as described in this Section shall not be decided if this is unreasonable.[535]

Only a court may decide on extended confiscation. The issue is initiated by the prosecutor in the context of a criminal prosecution. A court may also on its own initiative decide on confiscation, but in practice, such cases are rare because the issue of extended confiscation will need the support of an investigation regarding e.g. the financial situation of the defendant. Formally, the court has in such cases the ability to direct the prosecutor to complete or conduct such an investigation.[536] The case for extended confiscation against a person must be brought in connection with the prosecution for the offence triggering the provision, and cannot be brought as a separate issue. A decision of extended confiscation is not possible if the criminal offence triggering confiscation was committed before the law came into force (i.e. 1 July 2008). On the other hand, it

534 SFS 2016:486.

535 This translation is partly built on an old unofficial translation made by and provided for at the homepage of the *Swedish Ministry of Justice* (http://www.government.se/sb/d/3288). This link has now expired, and only a small selection of some Swedish statutes is now provided for.

536 See Ch. 45 Sec. 11 of the Criminal Procedural Code ("*Rättegångsbalken*") and Bill 2007/08:68 p. 72.

is not an obstacle that the proceeds originate from criminal activity which took place before the law came into force.[537]

As is the case with other forms of confiscation, extended confiscation can concern both confiscation of concrete property (object confiscation) and confiscation of a property's value (value confiscation).[538] Chapter 36 Section 1c SPC states that property that has replaced the proceeds of crime, the yield of such proceeds and yield of such property that has replaced the proceeds of crime shall also be regarded as proceeds of crime. Obviously, this provision clarifies that anything that has replaced the proceeds shall be taken into account.

Chapter 36 Section 1b SPC is *subsidiary* to the other rules on confiscation and can therefore only come into play if the relevant property cannot be the object of confiscation according to such rules.[539] Property must, for example, be confiscated according to Chapter 36 Section 1 SPC if it can be proven that it comes from the criminal offence of which the defendant is convicted. However, a study of Swedish case-law shows that the subsidiarity of extended confiscation is not always observed, and that this form of confiscation is sometimes used instead of ordinary confiscation even where the former would have been possible.[540]

A decision on extended confiscation is *not obligatory*. This follows from Chapter 36 Section 1b Subsection 4 SPC, which states that confiscation shall not be ordered if it is *unreasonable*.[541] With the support of this provision, the court may decide either completely or in part against confiscation even if the formal conditions would have been fulfilled. The paragraph is intended to ensure that there is room for considerations of proportionality. It has been left to case-law to develop under what circumstances the provision may be applied. The legislative works mention some circumstances which can be relevant, for example when the penalty scale of the triggering offence is low,[542] when another duty of payment has been imposed on the defendant or when the property has been in the defendant's ownership for a long time. Another circumstance can be that a person who acquired the property has done so in good faith.[543]

---

537 Bill 2007/08:68 pp. 90–92.

538 Ch. 36 Sec. 1b Subsec. 1 SPC, and Bill 2007/08:68 p. 96. See Section 5.2 above for these concepts in Swedish law. Compare also *NJA 2010 p. 374*, described in Section 5.4.4 below.

539 Bill 2007/08:68 p. 95.

540 See for the same conclusion, *Tillsynsrapport, Tillsyn – brottsutbytesfrågor*, Utvecklingscentrum Stockholm, December 2011, p. 3 and *Inspektion av polismyndigheternas handläggning av förverkande av utbyte av brott och brottslig verksamhet*, Inspektionsrapport 2012:7, Rikspolisstyrelsen, August 2012, p. 15.

541 Bill 2007/08:68 p. 95.

542 In a recent case (*NJA 2016 p. 641*) the Supreme Court considered the issue of whether an order of extended confiscation would be unreasonable as the penalty scale of the triggering offence was low. See on this case, Section 5.4.2 below.

543 Bill 2007/08:68 pp. 76–77 and 96–97.

5.3.2. THE TRIGGERING OFFENCES AND THE SCOPE FOR EXTENDED CONFISCATION

The fundamental prerequisite for extended confiscation is that someone is to be convicted of a crime. Criminal offences which may trigger such a decision are established in *different ways*. First, the provision applies generally to such a crime for which *imprisonment for four years or more* is prescribed (Chapter 36 Section 1b Subsection 1 SPC). It is sufficient that the *maximum* punishment for the crimes reaches this level and the actual penalty imposed on the individual is irrelevant.[544] Secondly, the provision on extended confiscation may be applied when a person is convicted of *certain specifically listed* offences with a lower punishment scale (Chapter 36 Section 1b Subsection 2 Paragraphs 1–5 SPC). The list of such offences is exhaustive. Among the offences listed are *inter alia* illegal system - and data interference, certain child pornography offences, narcotics crime and doping - and smuggling offences. Thirdly, the provision applies generally for such offences for which is prescribed *imprisonment for two years or more* and the offence has been part of criminality that has been conducted in an organised form (Chapter 36 Section 1b Subsection 2 Paragraph 6 SPC).

A conviction for such a criminal offence is, however, not in itself sufficient for a decision on extended confiscation. The second fundamental prerequisite is that the crime in question is of *such nature as to lead to proceeds*. This requirement was deemed necessary in order to single out a special group of offences, and prevent confiscation being invoked for serious offences which have not been committed for the purpose of financial gain (for example certain sexual offences or crimes of violence).[545] According to the legislative works, offences of *such nature as to lead to proceeds* can be defined as:

(1) offences which have a *prerequisite of profit*. Examples of such offences are aggravated fraud or embezzlement;

(2) offences without a prerequisite of profit but which *in the individual case have generated or would have been able to generate profit*. In principle any type of offence may thus be considered. The prosecutor has the burden of proof to show to the full evidentiary standard that the offence in question has generated or would have been able to generate profit; and

544 Bill 2007/08:68 pp. 55–56 and 94. Compare Bill 2015/16:155 p. 39.

545 In case-law it has been ruled that, for example, accounting fraud ("*bokföringsbrott*") is not *per se* an offence of *such nature as to lead to proceeds*, which means that it cannot trigger a decision on extended confiscation. See Court of Appeal (*Svea Hovrätt*) Judgment on 25 November 2010, Case B 5119-09 and Stockholm District Court Judgment on 2 June 2009, Case B 4685-09. The Supreme Court did not rule on the question of extended confiscation (Judgment on 3 December 2012, Case 5960-10).

(3) offences without a profit prerequisite but which are of *such nature as to generate profit*. Examples of the last group of offences are smuggling, drug offences and tax offences.[546]

There is no requirement that profit has occurred in the individual case.[547]

Chapter 36 Section 1b SPC was at its adoption based principally on alternative a) of Article 3(2) FD 2005/212/JHA.[548] As discussed further in Section 5.5.2 below, the Swedish legislation was at the outset drafted in a more far-reaching manner on several points than the EU legislation demanded, which means that the scope for extended confiscation is more extensive, as more criminal offences may trigger the measure. Further, the Swedish legislation is also applied in cases of attempt, preparation and conspiracy to commit the triggering offences (Chapter 36 Section 1b Subsection 3 SPC), as well as in cases of perpetration, instigation or complicity.[549] The Swedish legislator has in this respect argued that if the purpose of the confiscation regime is to *initiate investigations* regarding the extent to which an offender has benefited from other criminal activity, it is illogical to exclude cases where the criminal activities have been broken off. Furthermore, the measure of extended confiscation may be justified in cases of preparation or conspiracy in order to target such persons who participate in the planning of organised criminality.[550] As a comparison it may be mentioned that FD 2005/212/JHA includes only attempt, but not preparation or conspiracy to commit crime. (Although, such forms of criminality might anyway in some Member States be targeted by the offence of belonging to a criminal organisation.)

According to the legislative works, the focus in the Swedish legislation is supposed to be on serious criminality which is typically intended to generate large profits, crimes which are committed in more or less organised forms and on crimes which by their nature are particularly dangerous or injurious to society.[551]

5.3.3. SPECIAL CRITERIA FOR EXTENDED CONFISCATION

The introduction of the measure of extended confiscation into Swedish law meant an abandonment of the earlier strict view that confiscation of the

546 See further Bill 2007/08:68 pp. 59–60 and 94–95.

547 Bill 2007/08:68 pp. 59–60 and 94–95.

548 On the three alternative models to draft the legislation on extended confiscation given in FD 2005/212/JHA, see Section 2.1.2 above.

549 Bill 2007/08:68 p. 60. However, the measure has so far seldom been used in such cases, see the *Report on Extended Confiscation*, SOU 2015:67 p. 81.

550 Bill 2007/08:68 pp. 60–61.

551 Bill 2007/08:68 pp. 53–58.

proceeds of crime requires a *direct link* between a particular crime and the benefit from precisely that crime. Unlike the case of confiscation pursuant to Chapter 36 Section 1 SPC, it is thus not a requirement under Chapter 36 Section 1b SPC that what is confiscated can be linked to a particular concrete crime. Accordingly, the prosecutor does not have to give a detailed concretisation of specific crimes, or prove or otherwise define exactly wherein the criminal activity ("*brottslig verksamhet*") consisted.[552] Such a requirement would obviously be difficult to fulfil without investigating the actual offence in question. Instead, the prosecutor often seeks to prove the requirement that the property derives from criminal activity on the basis of circumstances regarding the triggering offence or regarding how certain property has been found. A strong indication is thus also the financial circumstances of the defendant. This is further described in Section 5.4 below dealing with Swedish case-law.

The provision on extended confiscation does not contain any requirement that the property to be confiscated must derive from "similar criminal activities" to the offence of which the defendant was convicted, in the way which was possible according to alternative (b) in Article 3(2) FD 2005/212/JHA. This option was decided against in the legislative process, because it was considered to limit the scope of the measure.[553] There is also neither any limitation in time nor any requirement of a minimum nominal amount regarding the property to be confiscated. Such forms of limitation were, *inter alia*, considered to lead to practical and evidentiary difficulties. However, there is a possibility in exceptional cases to avoid confiscation for reasons of equity on the basis of Chapter 36 Section 1b Subsection 4 SPC.[554]

The necessary starting-point for a motion of extended confiscation is that a suspect *keeps certain property* which may be the object of an "object confiscation" or a "value confiscation".[555] Such property can be owned openly by the defendant, but also property which may be owned by others "on behalf" of such a person can be included if the prosecutor can prove that a defendant is the real owner. The calculation of a plea for extended confiscation relates exclusively to the value of assets *being found*, in contrast to the power of ordinary confiscation according to Chapter 36 Section 1 SPC where there is no need for existing property to have been found but where the plea is calculated in relation to the benefit of a *concrete crime*. Obviously, this means that any available assets must be investigated and secured at an early stage of the preliminary investigation, as this will in practice be decisive for whether and for which amount a motion for extended

552 Bill 2007/08:68 p. 95.
553 Bill 2007/08:68 p. 51.
554 See on this paragraph, Section 5.3.1 above. Compare Bill 2007/08:68 pp. 64–65 and pp. 96–97.
555 *Handbook on confiscation etc from the Prosecuting Office*, Utvecklingscentrum Stockholm, 2010, pp. 20 and 43.

confiscation may be made. The Swedish Supreme Court ("*Högsta domstolen*") has in the case *NJA 2010 p. 374* held that the requirement for extended confiscation is that property "derives" from criminal activity, and that this relates not only to material assets directly generated by criminal activity but also to other assets that the defendant *has been able to acquire* as a consequence of the benefit from his criminal activity.[556] This means that both particular property and substitutes for such property, as well as money and abstract gain may be confiscated.[557] An object confiscation may not be used for such property, like for example a real estate or assets in a bank account; instead a motion for value confiscation regarding the value must be used.[558]

During the Swedish legislative process it was emphasised that an order of extended confiscation does not require that the person convicted of a triggering offence *has himself participated in or has even been aware of* the criminal activity which led to the proceeds.[559] It is in fact an intended aim of the legislation that the measure may be used also against offenders who have no knowledge of the illegal origin of the property.[560] The legislator argued that it is an advantage that property deriving from *any* criminal activity may be confiscated, because it makes clear that the purpose is not to investigate and establish anyone's guilt, but only to confiscate assets with an illegal origin. It was, for example, mentioned that it would be offensive not to confiscate a significant amount of cash found at the search of a brothel or an illegal gambling club or in situations where several defendants have acted together, but assets cannot be specifically linked to certain defendants.[561] Another reason for this construction of the legislation was also that Swedish prosecutors are in principle obligated to initiate a preliminary investigation into an offence, and this was to be avoided in such cases.[562] On the other hand, the legislative works emphasise that if extended confiscation in such cases is unreasonable, a plea should be turned down on the basis of Chapter 36 Section 1b Subsection 4 SPC.[563]

5.3.4. THE BURDEN AND STANDARD OF PROOF

The burden of proof rests with the prosecutor to prove that the property involved in a plea for extended confiscation really does constitute the proceeds from

---

556 See further on this case, Section 5.4.4 below.

557 Ch. 36 Sec. 1c SPC.

558 Compare Section 5.2 above for these different forms of confiscation under Swedish law.

559 Bill 2007/08:68 p. 95.

560 Bill 2007/08:68 pp. 62–63.

561 Bill 2007/08:68 p. 63.

562 Such a duty applies already when there is cause to believe that a crime has been committed (see Ch. 23 Sec. 1 of the Criminal Code (*Rättegångsbalken*)). See further on the prosecutorial principle of legality in Swedish law, Cameron, Thunberg Schunke, Påle-Bartes, Wong and Asp, n 508 above, pp. 34–35.

563 See on this paragraph, Section 5.3.1 above.

criminal activity.[564] The standard of proof set for the link between property and criminal activity is, however, lower than what normally applies in Swedish law in criminal cases (i.e. "*ställt utom rimligt tvivel*", which corresponds to "proved beyond reasonable doubt").[565] According to Chapter 36 Section 1b SPC, it is sufficient that it appears substantially more probable ("*klart mera sannolikt*") that the property constitutes the proceeds of crime than not. The introduction of this new standard into Swedish confiscation law meant that the prosecutor was given a considerable *easing of the burden of proof*.

It comes as no surprise that criticism against a lowered standard of evidence was voiced during the legislative process. The *Swedish Bar Association* was, for example, against an approval of FD 2005/212/JHA in this respect, and argued that investigatory or evidentiary difficulties for law enforcement agencies cannot justify a lowered burden of proof.[566] However, the Swedish legislator argued that in order to adopt a powerful instrument, it was necessary to release the prosecutor from the full burden of proving beyond reasonable doubt that property is the proceeds from a criminal offence. At the same time, it was admitted that there was a challenge to draft the Swedish provision in such a way that the measure would be an effective measure in the fight against serious lucrative crime, but at the same time respect requirements of fundamental rights and legal safety.[567]

The starting-point during the legislative process was that the standard of "fully convinced" in Article 3(2) FD 2005/212/JHA was too strict, because it could be assessed as lying near the evidentiary level of "beyond reasonable doubt". Such a standard was regarded as unsuitable, because extended confiscation can concern unspecified criminality which need not be spelled out in greater detail.[568] The legislator further noted that the possibility to reverse the burden of proof and place it on the defendant had already been rejected on earlier legislative occasions on the grounds of legal safety. Such a solution was therefore not suitable.[569] Instead, a standard of "probable" ("*sannolikt*") was first considered.[570] This standard had, however, been criticised on the ground that it could in practice have the same effect as a reversed burden of proof.[571] Accordingly, the Swedish legislator concluded that such a standard was far too low.[572]

564 Bill 2007/08:68 p. 95.
565 See for this standard of evidence, for example *NJA 1980 p. 725*, *NJA 1991 p. 83* and *NJA 1996 p. 176*.
566 See *Yttrande over Departementspromemorian Utvidgat förverkande m.m.* (DS 2006:17), R-2006/0939, pp. 2–4.
567 Bill 2007/08:68 p. 66.
568 Bill 2007/08:68 p. 66.
569 See for example Bill 1990/91:127 p. 28, SOU 1999:147 p. 125 and Ds 2006:17 pp. 76 and 111.
570 This was in line with a proposal made by the *Ministry of Justice Report* on a more efficient legislation on confiscation in 1999, see SOU 1999:147 p. 219.
571 See Ds 2006:17 pp. 51–52.
572 Bill 2007/08:68 p. 66.

Eventually, the standard was set to "substantially more probable". Some administrative agencies and interest groups which were consulted on the new legislation argued that this standard was too high, but the majority argued that it was too low.[573] The new standard had not before been used in Swedish criminal law, but was found in civil law regarding insurance and tort law.[574] The standard is supposed to be especially useful in cases where a court must assess several circumstances and weigh various more or less probable explanations against each other.[575] The legislative works declare that this level of proof demands on the one hand that what the prosecutor maintains must be probable *per se*, and on the other hand that the probability of the assertion must substantially exceed the probability that the opposite situation pertains.[576] To put it in another way, it is not sufficient that the version of the prosecutor is more probable than anything else, but it is necessary that it is found in an all-round assessment that the version is probable in itself *and* that it is substantially more probable than the explanations of the defendant. The standard of proof is thus described as lying between the standard of "probable" ("*sannolikt*") and "beyond reasonable doubt" ("*ställt utom rimligt tvivel*").[577]

In applying the Swedish standard the courts are supposed to pay particular attention to the nature of the property, the circumstances under which it was encountered as well as circumstances related to the offender's personal and financial situation.[578] During the legislative proceedings, the Council of Legislation ("*Lagrådet*") criticised the chosen level of proof by arguing that it was unclear and did not fully define the level of proof required.[579] Against this background, the legislative works give certain guidelines in order to assist the courts. The following circumstances are set up which may generally indicate that certain property constitutes the proceeds of criminal activity:

- if assets seem unreasonable with regard to the offender's legal means;
- if expensive capital goods or luxury items are found in the possession of someone who lacks a legal source of income;
- if an unreasonably large sum of money is being kept in a dwelling or premises; or

573 See Bill 2007/08:68 pp. 65–67.

574 See for example the following case-law: *NJA 1977 p. 176*, *NJA 1981 p. 622*, *NJA 1982 p. 421* and *NJA 1992 p. 113*.

575 Bill 2007/08:68 pp. 67 and 95.

576 Bill 2007/08:68 pp. 66–67 and 95.

577 Bill 2007/08:68 p. 67. The standard of "high probability" ("*stor sannolikhet*") had been proposed in Ds 2006:17, which was supposed to lie between "probable" and "beyond reasonable doubt". See Ds 2006:17 pp. 10 and 102–18.

578 Bill 2007/08:68 p. 95.

579 Bill 2007/08:68 p. 67 and pp. 165–66. On the role of the Council of Legislation in the legislative process, see Cameron, Thunberg Schunke, Påle-Bartes, Wong and Asp, n 508 above, pp. 10–11.

- if expensive property has been acquired through cash payment and without receipts.[580]

Also some circumstances which in general may indicate that property has a legal origin are indicated:

- legal income in parity with the value of the property;
- reasonable explanations for ownership;
- full documentation of various financial transactions; or
- the use of normal modes of payment.[581]

Obviously, the financial circumstances of an offender play an important role in the considerations. However, the Swedish legislator decided at the outset against an *explicit starting-point* in the financial means of an offender (in the way made in Article 3(2)(c) FD 2005/212/JHA).[582] In Section 5.4 below, a description of some Swedish case-law on extended confiscation illustrates how the courts so far have interpreted and dealt with the new evidentiary standard.[583]

The prosecutor has the full evidentiary burden to prove that the defendant *owns* certain property. In many cases the defendant claims that another person is the real owner of the assets.[584] In such circumstances the prosecutor must decide whether to direct a claim for confiscation against the defendant or against a third person.[585] There is in this respect a possibility for third persons to intervene in the criminal trial in order to claim their rights to the property.[586] A rather "typical" example of a case which involved a consideration of real ownership is a case from 2010 regarding aggravated narcotic offences and a motion for extended confiscation of, *inter alia*, a car valued at SEK 315,000.[587] The defendant challenged the plea, arguing that he was not the owner of the car, but was just using it on occasions. A friend of his – who was registered as the

580 Bill 2007/08:68 pp. 95–96.

581 Bill 2007/08:68 p. 96.

582 See further Bill 2007/08:68 pp. 50–51.

583 A comment on the interpretation of the evidentiary standard in case-law is also given in SOU 2015:67 pp. 70–72.

584 Often family members of the defendant claim to be the rightful owners of certain assets. Under the Swedish criminal procedural system, such persons are not heard under oath, which in some cases may limit the evidentiary value of their statements. See for example Court of Appeal (*Svea Hovrätt*), Judgment on 30 May 2012, Case B 3756-12 and Stockholm District Court, Judgment on 3 April 2012, Case B 1622-12.

585 Compare the rules on third party confiscation described in Section 5.3.5 below.

586 See for example Court of Appeal (*Hovrätten över Skåne och Blekinge*), Judgment on 6 April 2011, Case B 467-11 and Malmö District Court, Judgment on 27 January 2011, Case B 9056-09, described in Section 5.4.2 below.

587 Court of Appeal (*Hovrätten över Skåne och Blekinge*), Judgment on 14 September 2010, Case B 2121-10 and Malmö District Court, Judgment on 16 July 2010, Case B 4581-10.

owner in the official motor vehicle register – was heard in the case. This person confirmed the ownership, but admitted that he had no driver's licence. He gave only vague and partly contradictory statements as to the purchase of the car and the insurances necessary for its keeping. Both the District Court and the Court of Appeal concluded that these statements were not credible and considered that the defendant was the real owner.[588]

5.3.5. THIRD PARTY CONFISCATION

The Swedish rule on extended confiscation regarding third parties is found in Chapter 36 Section 5a Subsection 1 SPC:

Förverkande av utbyte av brottslig verksamhet enligt 1 b § får ske hos	Confiscation of proceeds of crime as provided in Section 1b may be exacted of:
1. gärningsmannen eller annan som medverkat till det brott som förverkandet grundas på,	1) the offender or an accomplice in the crime,
2. den som förvärvat egendomen genom bodelning eller på grund av arv eller testamente eller genom gåva,	2) any person who after the crime acquired the property through the division of jointly held marital property, or through inheritance, will or gift,
3. den som förvärvat egendomen på annat sätt och därvid haft vetskap om eller skälig anledning att anta att egendomen har samband med brottslig verksamhet.	3) any person who after the crime acquired the property in some other manner and, in so doing, knew or had reasonable grounds to suspect that the property was connected with the crime.
Bestämmelser om förfarandet vid en talan om förverkande hos den som avses i första stycket 2 eller 3 finns i lagen (2008:369) om förfarandet vid förverkande av utbyte av brottslig verksamhet i vissa fall.	Provisions on the procedure on a motion for confiscation exacted of a person referred to in the first paragraph 2 or 3 are found in the Act (2008:369) on the Procedure on Confiscation of Proceeds of Crime in certain cases.

As FD 2005/212/JHA only contained an optional rule on third party confiscation, there was much consideration at the adoption of the provision, whether or not extended confiscation should be directed against such persons.[589] In the end, the Swedish legislator took the position that in order to adopt an efficient instrument, it was necessary to prevent criminal proceeds from being

---

[588] See for other case-law regarding ownership: Court of Appeal (*Hovrätten för Västra Sverige*), Judgment on 16 December 2011, Case B 3912-11 and B 4332-11 and Göteborg District Court, Judgment on 2 September 2011 and on 14 October 2011, Case B 6403-11. Compare also Supreme Court, Judgment on 6 December 2011, Case B 2521-11 (only ruling regarded the sentences), Court of Appeal, Judgment on 11 May 2011, Case B 152-11 and Södertörn District Court, Judgment on 22 December 2010, Case B 4751-10. See also the cases of *NJA 2010 p. 374* and *NJA 2016 p. 641* where there was an issue of ownership.

[589] Bill 2007/08:68 pp. 67–71. Compare Art. 3(3) FD 2005/212/JHA and Section 2.1.3 above.

kept elsewhere in order to avoid an order for confiscation.[590] Under the current provision a measure may thus be directed toward someone who has acquired the property in bad faith, or, if it concerns acquisitions under family law (inheritance or gifts), independently of bad faith.[591] Accordingly, for the first situation it is necessary to prove that someone intentionally has acquired property with the knowledge that it derived from criminal activities, or that a person has had reasonable grounds to suspect this.

Special provisions on a separate procedure for third party confiscation regarding extended confiscation are found in the Act (2008:369) on the Procedure on Confiscation of Proceeds of Crime in certain cases. A basic requirement for such confiscation is that the prosecutor proves to the full evidentiary standard that the property in question has been acquired from a defendant who has been convicted of a triggering offence.[592] A plea may only be made after such a conviction has taken legal force, and within one year from this date.[593]

5.4. SWEDISH CASE-LAW ON EXTENDED CONFISCATION

5.4.1. INTRODUCTION

In this section, some Swedish case-law on extended confiscation is presented in order to give some examples of how the courts apply the provision in practice and to illustrate the reasoning of the judges, especially when it comes to the interpretation of the evidentiary standard.[594] The pleas for confiscation which are presented mainly concern the currency of Swedish kronor (SEK). Hereby it might be interesting to know that SEK 100 amounts to €10.51.[595]

The starting-point for a motion for extended confiscation is when a defendant (or in certain circumstances a third party) owns certain assets which may originate from criminal activity. A study of case-law shows that certain factors and circumstantial evidence are of specific importance for the courts in the overall assessment of whether certain assets have an illegal origin or not. A common situation in practice is when an unreasonably large amount of cash or other valuable property is kept under circumstances that are found to be

590 Bill 2007/08:68 p. 68.
591 Bill 2007/08:68 p. 98.
592 Bill 2007/08:68 p. 68.
593 Sec. 3 in the Act (2008:369) on the Procedure on Confiscation of Proceeds of Crime in certain cases. The *Report on Extended Confiscation* in 2015 did not find any cases in the judgments being studied which concerned such a case, see SOU 2015:67 p. 81.
594 Some further case-law is also discussed in Section 5.5 below.
595 This was the stand of 23 January 2017.

"suspicious". Accordingly, the *physical placement* of assets may be decisive as an indication. Thereby the pattern of behaviour for an "average citizen" is often taken as a standard, as it is argued that if the asset was legally acquired it would have been kept in another way, for example in a bank account. The reasoning of the courts in such cases is primarily illustrated in Section 5.4.2 below.

In other cases, the issue of extended confiscation may be initiated more actively by the law enforcement authorities, i.e. valuable assets are *searched for* in the framework of a special financial investigation of a suspect.[596] During the preliminary investigation regarding a triggering offence a parallel inquiry is thereby started into the financial situation of the suspect. Information and results from such financial investigations are collected in the *asset investigation report*, in order to provide the basis for conclusions on whether a defendant has had any legal income to finance certain assets found. In the more advanced form of an asset investigation report also the finances of family members of the defendant may be investigated, and in some cases annual cash calculations are performed in order to assess the expenses of a household's income in relation to the assets available.[597] Asset investigation reports are also used in cases where property has been found under "suspicious circumstances" in order to collect evidence to support a conclusion that it is substantially more probable that the asset in question derives from criminal activity than not.[598] The importance of the asset investigation is particularly illustrated by Section 5.4.3 below.[599]

Since the provision on extended confiscation came into force in 2008 it has mostly been used in the area of narcotics offences and aggravated narcotic offences.[600] There are so far only two cases decided by the Supreme Court. In *NJA 2010 p. 374* certain general guidelines for the interpretation of the Swedish provision in relation to FD 2005/212/JHA were given. The ruling is described in Section 5.4.4 below. *NJA 2016 p. 641* dealt with the general prerequisites for an order of extended confiscation in a case regarding narcotic crime. The case is referred to in Section 5.4.2 below.

---

596 It has been the aim of the Swedish Prosecutor General to increase the cases where the prosecutors more actively start financial investigations in order to test the requirements for property to be confiscated. Compare Section 5.5.6 below.

597 See further on the routines for a more limited respective a more extensive asset investigation report, bilagor 7 and 8, *Handbook on confiscation etc from the Prosecuting Office*, Utvecklingscentrum Stockholm, 2010.

598 The *Report on Extended Confiscation* in 2015 found that this was the most common motive of an asset investigation report in practice, see SOU 2015:67 p. 74.

599 On the routines for initiating an asset investigation, see generally SOU 2015:67 pp. 77–80.

600 Pressmeddelande, Justitiedepartementet, 2 September 2014, *Utökade möjligheter att beslagta brottsvinster* and SOU 2015:67 pp. 69–70.

5.4.2. ASSETS FOUND UNDER "SUSPICIOUS" CIRCUMSTANCES

A common feature in case-law concerns pleas for extended confiscation when a significant amount of *cash has been found together with narcotics*. In one such case there was a motion for extended confiscation of SEK 110,000 and DKK 1,000 which had been found together with cannabis in a guest room in the apartment of a defendant's sister.[601] The defendant had pleaded guilty to drug offences with the intent to supply, and had admitted that he usually used to deposit drugs and the proceeds of his sales at this place. However, he argued that this particular money did not belong to him. The prosecutor anyway directed the motion for confiscation against him, and the defendant's sister and mother intervened in the process claiming that the money was their savings. They claimed that monthly earnings had been put aside and kept in the daughter's flat as they were afraid that the police would find it. The District Court convicted the defendant for narcotics offences and concluded that he had possessed cannabis mainly for the purpose of dealing. This was supported by the fact that the drugs were found in 11 separate packages. Regarding the assertion that the cash did not belong to the defendant, it was held that only the sister could have been able to save such an amount of money. However, she had not been able to give detailed statements as to where the money was kept, and it was held that it would anyway have been more natural to use a bank account if there was a risk that the cash could be mistaken for the proceeds of crime. The circumstances under which the cash was found spoke for a criminal origin, and the statements from the relatives were considered vague and contradictory. The court concluded that it was substantially more probable that the cash constituted the proceeds of crime than not. The decision was upheld by the Court of Appeal with similar reasoning. Two lay assessors, however, disagreed, arguing that the standard of evidence was not fulfilled.

In a similar case, a defendant was convicted of narcotics offences and sentenced to nine months' imprisonment.[602] There was a plea for extended confiscation of SEK 131,500 which had been found during a house search in his home. The defendant denied that it had any illegal origin and stated that it derived from the sales of musical instruments and various paintings. The District Court noted that it was proven that the narcotics found at the home of the defendant had been obtained with the intent of being supplied. The statements of the defendant that he had been selling certain art objects were not

---

601 The Court of Appeal (*Hovrätten över Skåne och Blekinge*), Judgment on 6 April 2011, Case B 467-11 and Malmö District Court, Judgment on 27 January 2011, Case B 9056-09.

602 Court of Appeal (*Svea Hovrätt*), Judgment on 12 April 2012, Case B 2328-12 and Stockholm District Court, Judgment on 17 February 2012, Case B 15263-11.

per se questioned, but it was emphasised that he had only given very imprecise information on which transactions he was supposed to have made. The District Court further held that the amount of cash found was significant in comparison to the yearly income of the defendant. As other factors speaking for an illegal origin were the location of the money next to narcotics and the fact that the defendant had kept the cash in his apartment instead of in his bank account. Against this background, the District Court concluded that it was substantially more probable that the money was the proceeds of criminal activity than not. The Court of Appeal confirmed the confiscation order.

Another example concerned a conviction for aggravated narcotic offences where the District Court first dismissed the motion for extended confiscation, ruling that the circumstance that a significant amount of cash is found together with narcotics is in itself not sufficient to fulfill the evidentiary standard.[603] The motion concerned approximately SEK 215,000 in various currency that had been found in the wardrobe of an apartment. Before the Court of Appeal the defendant admitted that he had placed this cash together with narcotics in the apartment of his ex-girlfriend. However, he claimed that the money did not come from criminal activity, and that a large part of it belonged to his brother. The Court of Appeal found that the financial situation of the defendant, and the fact that equipment for the handling of drugs had been found, were indications that the defendant financed his misuse through criminal activity. It was further held that the statements of the defendant and his brother were vague and contradictory. Taken as a whole, the court found it substantially more probable that the money derived from criminal activity than not.

In *NJA 2016 p. 641* also the Supreme Court ruled on the criteria and the evidentiary standard in such cases. The suspect "W.E." had been stopped in a car and was searched. Thereby the following items were found: a bag with narcotics (Kat) in the car and a small amount of narcotics and SEK 7,900 in cash in his pockets. The money consisted of 54 notes of SEK 100 and five notes of SEK 500. A small amount of narcotics was further found in the fridge at his home. W.E. was convicted of *inter alia* narcotics crime, and the cash was confiscated according to Chapter 36 Section 1b SPC by both the District Court and the Court of Appeal. Two members of the Court of Appeal, though, disagreed. They argued that the evidentiary standard was not fulfilled and that the penal value of the triggering offence (one month imprisonment) was so low that a confiscation order would be unreasonable.

Before the courts, W.E. had argued that the cash did not belong to him, but that he had kept the money on behalf of his son in order to buy him a car.

---

603 Court of Appeal (*Hovrätten över Skåne och Blekinge*), Judgment on 8 July 2009, Case B 1163-09 and Malmö District Court, Judgment on 5 May 2009, Case B 2122-09.

The son had been heard before the Court of Appeal, and had confirmed these statements. He had further stated that he had withdrawn the cash from a cash machine, but he could not give evidence as to which banknotes he had received. The Supreme Court concluded first of all that the cash belonged to W.E. This was mainly justified by the fact that he had given other explanations for the origin of the money at the time of his arrest. The Court then noted the large number of different banknotes and the circumstance that W.E. did not have any legal income. The amount of money was in this respect considered to be significant in relation to the financial circumstances of W.E. The Court emphasised that the cash was found alongside narcotics, and came to the overall conclusion that it was substantially more probable that "most" of the money derived from criminal activity than not. The Supreme Court continued to acknowledge that in some cases of confiscation it may be probable that at least a part of the cash in question derives from something else than criminal activity. Nevertheless, it was ruled out that any of the money in the present case could have a legal origin with reference to the financial circumstances of W.E. and the fact that it involved a large number of different banknotes. The Supreme Court finally considered the issue of whether extended confiscation in this case would be unreasonable according to Chapter 36 Section 1b Subsection 4 SPC, but came to the conclusion that the fact that the triggering offence had a low "penal value" was of no importance in this case. As there were no other factors in favour of such a direction, the property was confiscated.

It can be concluded that the Swedish courts often find that the circumstance that a significant amount of cash is found together with narcotics or equipment for the supply of narcotics is a strong indication that the property derives from criminal activity.[604] On the other hand, as is seen from the cases described above, such circumstances are mostly not *per se* sufficient to fulfil the evidentiary standard, and the financial situation of the defendant is also of interest. This is evident in a case regarding aggravated narcotics offence where the amount of €3,400 was found in the same place as narcotics. The court stated that these circumstances spoke strongly for an illegal origin, but concluded that the amount of cash was not unreasonably high in comparison to the financial information which had been presented by the defendant.[605] Accordingly, as will be described in what follows, the financial circumstances of a defendant may be of significant importance for both the prosecutor and the defence when preparing arguments in support of the origin of assets.

---

604 Compare also Court of Appeal (*Hovrätten över Skåne och Blekinge*), Judgment on 17 March 2011, Case B 2221-10 and Malmö District Court, Judgment on 13 July 2010, Case B 2818-10.

605 Court of Appeal (*Hovrätten för Västra Sverige*), Judgment on 14 January 2013, Case 5069-12 and Göteborg District Court, Judgment on 15 November 2012, Case B 12953-12.

5.4.3. THE FINANCIAL SITUATION OF THE DEFENDANT

An important aim of an asset investigation report is to provide the basis for a decision on a motion on extended confiscation. In many cases, the prosecutor may use such information to provide the courts with evidence that a defendant could not have acquired certain property through the accounted legal sources of income. Especially in cases where the plea for extended confiscation involves significant values, such a report may be crucial for securing a confiscation order. This is shown by a case regarding *inter alia* aggravated narcotics offences in 2011, where the motion for extended confiscation concerned the following items: €31,040 and SEK 547,500 in cash, a car (valued at SEK 600,000), a "Breitling" watch (valued at SEK 15,000–20,000), a "Scott" cycle (valued at SEK 32,000) and a further SEK 28,730 in cash.[606] During a house search a large consignment of, *inter alia*, amphetamines had been found, together with €31,040 and SEK 547,500 in cash. The rest of the money and other assets were found in other rooms of the apartment. The assets investigation report showed that the defendant had had considerably more expenses than income. Although there had been significant capital deficits, the defendant had acquired the various property by paying in cash. Several deposits into his bank account had been made from private persons. The defendant pleaded not guilty to the charges and claimed that the large amount of narcotics and cash to a value of nearly SEK 1 million found at his place was given to him by unknown persons. Accordingly, there was no objection to confiscation in this part. However, he contested the plea for extended confiscation in the remainder and argued that the amount of SEK 28,730 was his savings. During the court proceedings he further claimed that the deposits in his bank account were repayment for disbursements and that he had borrowed some of the money. There were no receipts or agreements regarding such transactions.

The District Court sentenced the defendant for aggravated narcotics offences to three years and six months' imprisonment. It was concluded that it was substantially more probable that the cash which was found together with the drugs was the proceeds of criminal activity than not. As to the other property, the court found that the defendant had inexplicably large amounts of money in relation to his income. His explanations hereto could only explain some of the deposits into his account, especially as he had been a drug misuser for 10 years, had sold drugs to finance his habit and had spent several years in prison. Against this background, his assets appeared unreasonable as regards his ability to build up such capital through legal means. The circumstance that an unjustifiably large amount of cash was stored in a dwelling was also taken into account.

606 Court of Appeal (*Svea Hovrätt*), Judgment on 17 January 2012, Case B 9933-11 and Södertörn District Court, Judgment on 22 November 2011, Case B 10297-11.

The court concluded that it was substantially more probable that his assets derived from criminal activity. The Court of Appeal confirmed the order, adding that the statements regarding any loans were imprecise and partly contradictory. Furthermore, any such transactions were undocumented in all cases, and the defendant lacked legal income which could finance his consumption of drugs.

In another case which concerned *inter alia* aggravated smuggling of cigarettes, there was a motion for extended confiscation of SEK 600,000, which had been found in a bank deposit box.[607] The defendant was unemployed, but claimed that the cash related to a loan from a family member. The District Court held that the fact that the money had been found in a bank deposit box, where another person was named as the holder, spoke strongly for an intention to conceal one's own connection to the money. It was not considered as likely that someone would have chosen to keep a large sum of money for such a long time without wanting to earn interest, and an explanation about mistrust of the banking system was not credible. These circumstances spoke strongly in favour of property deriving from criminal activity. Further, the asset investigation report presented in the case had shown that the defendant could not have earned these sums through the accounted legal sources of income. The defendant was linked to serious smuggling attempts regarding a large consignment of cigarettes, and the purpose had obviously been to make illegal profits through selling illegally imported cigarettes. The court concluded that these circumstances indicated that the assets in question derived at least partly from criminal activity. In addition, the defendant had provided varying information about the origin of the money which undermined the credibility of his statements. A significant indicator of illegal origin was also the high amount of cash (SEK 600,000) in notes. The District Court decided on extended confiscation. The Court of Appeal confirmed this decision.

In the Swedish system, the burden of proof lies exclusively on the prosecutor, who must present evidence for an illegal origin of assets. However, in practice it is obvious that a *certain burden of explanation* also falls on the defendant and in some cases it will be necessary for the defence to be more active and account for, or give details of the financial situation. A rather common argument from defendants is that the asset in question relates to loans from family members or friends. Often is also claimed that certain assets come from gambling or sales of items which have not been reported to the tax authorities.[608] It is in most cases not sufficient to give vague or imprecise information, and in principle it is required that transactions like loans etc. are supported by agreements or receipts. In case-law, written documentation (or a normal mode of payment) is of major

607 Court of Appeal (*Svea Hovrätt*), Judgment on 12 March 2010, Case B 3952-09 and Södertörn District Court, Judgment on 21 April 2009, Case B 82-09.

608 See especially on extended confiscation and tax evasion, Section 5.4.4 below.

importance.[609] In the case of oral evidence the court must proceed by ruling on the reliability of such statements. The courts are here often cautious regarding statements from family members, and the value of such evidence may be affected by the circumstance that they do not give their testimonies under oath.[610]

Even if it thus may be difficult in general to succeed with claims that certain assets are legally obtained without being able to present any written documentation, there are also exceptions in case-law. One example is a case where a paper bag containing one kilo of cannabis and about SEK 3,200,000 were found in a wardrobe in an apartment during a house search.[611] The defendant had some legal income, but stated that the cash found was the profits from many years of gambling. The narcotic in question had been placed at his home by another gambler as a deposit for a loan. The District Court sentenced the defendant for, *inter alia*, narcotics offences to imprisonment for one year. The court emphasised that the cash in question was found together with narcotics, and that the defendant had not given any details about dates or places for the gambling. In an overall assessment – but especially with consideration of how the money was found – the court found it substantially more probable that the money originated from criminal activity. On appeal, the defendant invoked the testimony of some friends in order to confirm his statements on the profits from gambling. The Court of Appeal held that the factors speaking for a criminal origin of the assets were the exceptionally high amount of cash found together with narcotics (kept with the intention of supply) and the fact that no documentation existed regarding the transactions which were referred to. It was especially noted in the ruling that the prosecutor had not claimed that any profits from poker could be perceived as deriving from criminal activity in the form of tax evasion.[612] The Court of Appeal found that in principle high evidentiary value should not be given to any undocumented statements on profits from gambling, but added that in this case certain witnesses of the defence had been heard. Although the court noted that these statements should be handled with care as they were all close friends of the defendant, it was emphasised that they had given their statements under oath. In an all-round assessment it was found proven that the defendant had had profits from poker. The Court of Appeal

---

609 For a case where the statements from a defendant that certain assets originated from a loan were weighed against an asset investigation report, see Court of Appeal (*Hovrätten för Västra Sverige*), Judgment on 1 September 2009, Case B 3095-09 and Göteborg District Court, Judgment on 18 June 2009, Case B 1441-09.

610 See for example Court of Appeal (*Hovrätten över Skåne och Blekinge*), Judgment on 8 July 2009, Case B 1163-09 and Malmö District Court, Judgment on 5 May 2009, Case B 2122-09 (described above) as well as Solna District Court, Judgment on 13 December 2012, Case B 3541-12 (described in the following).

611 Court of Appeal (*Hovrätten över Skåne och Blekinge*), Judgment on 26 October 2010, Case B 1361-10 and Malmö District Court, Judgment on 21 April 2010, Case B 1350-10.

612 A referral was here made by the court to *NJA 2010 p. 374*, see Section 5.4.4 below.

added that neither the narcotics offence itself nor any previous convictions of the defendant supported a conclusion that he had any connections to criminal organisations or any other criminal activity which could generate such high profits. Against this background, the decision on extended confiscation was overruled.[613]

As mentioned before, in cases where the prosecutor presents a detailed asset investigation report, it might become necessary for the defence to present its own calculations. The following case shows how an asset investigation report was successfully contested in such a way. The plea for extended confiscation concerned SEK 2,317,535 relating to a case regarding responsibility for aggravated narcotics offences in the form of dealing in amphetamine.[614] The amount corresponded to assets which had been investigated and referred to in an extensive asset investigation report. The assets consisted of sums in bank accounts and a number of cars and premises. The prosecutors argued on the basis of this report that the financial situation of the defendant indicated that his assets were unreasonable with regard to his legal income. The defendant contested the plea, and submitted written documentation as well as invoking hearings with witnesses. The District Court sentenced the defendant for aggravated narcotic offences to four years' imprisonment. However, the plea for extended confiscation was denied. The court argued that the defendant had very convincingly been able to account for the different amounts and explain the origin of the money.

Before the Court of Appeal the plea for extended confiscation was reduced to SEK 2,200,000 and a new asset investigation report was submitted. This report covered the defendant as well as his girlfriend and brother. It established that the defendant and his girlfriend had only modest income, but that they owned several properties and cars. Yearly cash calculations showed deficits in the household's income, but at the same time a significant increase in assets. The defendant claimed that he had received large amounts from insurance payouts and around SEK 600,000 from his parents. He had also won a large sum from gambling, received SEK 370,000 from the sale of a dwelling and had during a 10-year period made a profit of SEK 200,000 from the sale of cars. He also pointed out a number of omissions and errors in the asset investigation report. The Court of Appeal firstly noted that the available assets appeared significant in relation to the fact that the defendant had been off sick for many years and his girlfriend had studied or had been on maternity leave. However, it was pointed out that considerable documentation had been presented regarding various financial transactions. In addition, the testimony from his father proved that

---

613 See also Court of Appeal (*Hovrätten för Nedre Norrland*), Judgment on 26 April 2012, Case B 1103-11 and Sundsvall District Court, Judgment on 8 November 2011, Case B 1756-11(described in the following).

614 Court of Appeal (*Hovrätten för Nedre Norrland*), Judgment on 26 April 2012, Case B 1103-11 and Sundsvall District Court, Judgment on 8 November 2011, Case B 1756-11.

he had received gifts and other financial assistance from him. The circumstance that normal modes of payment had been used further spoke against the assets having been acquired through illegal means. In sum, the court found that the defendant had been able to show that his income had been higher than established in the asset investigation report. The Court additionally added that the prosecutor had not presented any report which lent support to the conclusion that the defendant was guilty of any form of tax evasion or financial crime of significance. The plea for extended confiscation was denied.

To sum up, Swedish case-law on extended confiscation shows there are certain factors which are especially important for the interpretation of the evidentiary standard. The financial circumstances of a defendant are of central importance, as the asset investigation report may often be decisive in order to show a link between assets and criminal activity. In this respect, the presentation of cash calculations may be a strong piece of evidence. Even if the prosecutor has the full burden of proof, there is in practice also a certain *burden of explanation* on a defendant. If written documentation or reliable information on financial transactions is presented, the prosecution's case may be disproved.

5.4.4. *NJA 2010 p. 374*

This was the first case on extended confiscation which was decided by the Supreme Court.[615] The ruling concerned a motion for extended confiscation of a BMW valued at around SEK 150,000.[616] The prosecutor argued that it was substantially more probable that this asset derived from the proceeds of criminal activity than not. The defendant denied that the car belonged to him, and claimed that he was only using it. A friend of his was registered as the owner in the official motor vehicle register. The District Court sentenced the defendant for *inter alia* aggravated narcotics offences to 12 years and six months' imprisonment and made an order for extended confiscation. The court found it proven in the case that the defendant was the rightful owner of the car. In the light of the circumstances surrounding his involvement in various drug dealings, it also found it substantially more probable than not that he had been able to acquire this relatively expensive car as a consequence of criminal activity.[617]

The Court of Appeal confirmed the conviction regarding aggravated narcotic offences.[618] The defendant argued in the proceedings that he had earned his

615 See for an analysis of the case, Ulväng, n 509 above. The case is also commented upon in SOU 2015:67 pp. 65–68.

616 The plea was based on Ch. 36 Secs. 1b and 1c SPC.

617 Gothenburg District Court, Judgment on 16 June 2009, Case B 12483-08.

618 The Court of Appeal (*Hovrätten för Västra Sverige*), Judgment on 14 September 2009, Case B 2927-09.

living by the sales of cars illicitly, i.e. without declaring this activity for tax. The prosecution referred to excerpts of tax returns for 2007 and 2008, which showed that the defendant had not declared income and that the income of his girlfriend had been relatively modest. In light of this, it was argued that the defendant had had no legal assets which would have allowed him to maintain a car with such a high value. The prosecutor also argued that even if it were not considered substantially more probable that the car *per se* constituted the benefit from crime, then the defendant's illicit trading in cars – which constituted tax evasion – had allowed him to acquire the car. By way of introduction, the Court of Appeal found it established that the defendant was the real owner of the car, and that he had devoted himself to buying and selling cars without reporting this income to the tax authorities. It was further noted that it was unclear when the car (whose value was not seen as unreasonably high) had been acquired. Even if the court found that some evidence spoke for the fact that the car had been acquired with the proceeds of criminal activity, it came to the conclusion that the standard of proof had not been fully met. It also concluded that the application of the provision on extended confiscation in a case where property was obtained as a result of the failure to pay tax would be to take the intention behind the current provisions too far. The motion for confiscation was thereby dismissed. The two lay assessors dissented and wished to confiscate the car.

The Supreme Court gave a detailed ruling on the interpretation of Chapter 36 Section 1b SPC, whereby different criteria in the provision were in focus.[619] The prosecution maintained that income from sales to the extent that this amounted to tax evasion constitutes benefit from criminal activity in the sense of Chapter 36 Section 1b SBC. The Supreme Court noted that Section 13a of Act (1971:69) on Tax Offences stipulates that the provisions for the confiscation of proceeds of crime in Chapter 36 Section 1 SPC (ordinary confiscation) are not to be applied to crimes under this legislation, but rather such proceeds should be impounded by the State in the form of tax.[620] It was further emphasised that during the domestic implementation of FD 2005/212/JHA the provision of extended confiscation had not been limited to property deriving from "similar criminal activities".[621] Nor had the Swedish legislator chosen to apply other procedures than those of the criminal law to deprive the perpetrator of the proceeds of tax evasion.[622] Against this background, the Supreme Court drew the conclusion that tax evasion *can* constitute such criminal activity as envisaged in Chapter 36 Section 1b SPC.[623]

---

619 Judgment of 18 June 2010, Case B 4411-09.
620 Compare Bill 2004/05:135 p. 100.
621 Compare Section 5.3.2.
622 Compare Art. 3(4) FD 2005/212/JHA.
623 See comments on this conclusion, Ulväng, n 509 above, pp. 88–92.

The Supreme Court then turned to the financial circumstances of the defendant, and concluded that any legal income from such sales of cars must first of all have gone to the family's continual maintenance and could not explain the ownership of the car. Accordingly, it was substantially more probable than not that the defendant had been able to acquire the car due to the benefit from criminal activity, in the form of tax evasion and/or other criminality. The Supreme Court then considered the interpretation of the term property which "constitutes" the proceeds of a crime (*"utgör" utbyte av brottslig verksamhet*) in Chapter 36 Section 1b SPC. The court found that this formulation implies that confiscation of *certain* property is the main rule. The court stated that this rather gives the impression, similarly to certain statements in the legislative works, that the possibility of property confiscation would be limited to the *concrete* benefit from crime and property *replacing* such property. This would mean that property confiscation could never take place when the benefit of the criminal activity, as in the case of tax evasion, does not consist of any concrete property. In practice, however, with such an interpretation, in the light of the difficulties of linking certain property to fairly unspecified criminal activity, property confiscation would scarcely be possible. The alternative would be value confiscation calculated according to the benefit that the unspecified criminal activity is supposed to have generated. The Court added that it is quite obvious, however, that it is not possible to make any meaningful calculations as to what benefit a non-specified criminal activity has generated.[624]

In the light of this, it was held that it must be questioned whether the intention of the legislator was really for property confiscation to have such a limited area of application and whether this can be viewed as compatible with the provisions of FD 2005/212/JHA. The Supreme Court drew the conclusion that the framework decision, as regards extended confiscation, in contrast to ordinary confiscation, was only aiming at confiscation of certain property. What is required for property to be confiscated is that it "derives" from criminal activity. This clearly relates not only to material assets directly generated by criminal activity, but also to other assets that the defendant *has been able to acquire* as a consequence of the benefit from his criminal activity. It was further found that the EU provisions in practice mean that confiscation will relate to certain property, which is of such value and which has been acquired under such conditions, that it is clear that the defendant could not have acquired the property if he had not had income from criminal activity.

The Supreme Court observed that during the legislative proceedings the term "derives from" had been used in order to describe such property which has been acquired with the aid of profits from unidentified crime.[625] Furthermore,

---

624 Bill 2007/08:68 p. 65.

625 Compare Ds 2006:17 p. 117.

the legislator had stated that legislative measures had been necessary since the framework decision requires that it shall be possible to confiscate property "deriving" from the defendant's criminal activity. However, in Chapter 36 Section 1b SPC the word "derive" had not been used.[626] The Supreme Court concluded, however, that the expressions "derive from" and "constitute" benefit from crime shall be interpreted as synonymous. It was thus established that Chapter 36 Section 1b SPC shall be interpreted so as to allow room for confiscation of both certain property and substitutes for such property, as well as for money and abstract gain. An order for extended confiscation was issued.[627] This ruling is important, because it confirms that property deriving from tax offences may be the object of extended confiscation.[628]

5.5. AN ANALYSIS OF THE SWEDISH CONFISCATION REGIME

5.5.1. THE ISSUE OF CONFISCATION OF RELATIVELY LOW AMOUNTS OF CASH

As already mentioned, there is no minimum limit in the Swedish legislation as to the monetary amount which may be confiscated. The legislator decided against such a rule and argued that, as there was no limit in this respect in FD 2005/212/JHA, it could lead to practical difficulties. However, it was explicitly stated in the legislative works that the measure of extended confiscation should not be used for the purpose of confiscating insignificant sums.[629] Unfortunately, it was not defined what should be understood by "insignificant". There are many cases in Swedish case-law which concern relatively low amounts of cash. The *Report on Extended Confiscation* in 2015 concluded in this respect that the motions very often relate to the confiscation of cash which has been seized by the apprehension of an offender or during a house search. A plea is seldom directed towards other property kept by a defendant.[630] On the basis of the judgments

626 Compare further Bill 2007/08:68 pp. 48, 62 and 95.

627 As the *Enforcement Service* had seized the car for various debts, the decision on extended confiscation related to the car's value, which was deemed to correspond to the amount which flowed in following the executive sale of the car. The defendant was thus obliged to pay this sum to the State.

628 For another case of extended confiscation, where certain assets were confiscated as they derived from tax offences, see Supreme Court, Judgment on 6 December 2011, Case B 2521-11 (only ruling regarded the sentences), Court of Appeal, Judgment on 11 May 2011, Case B 152-11 and Södertörn District Court, Judgment on 22 December 2010, Case B 4751-10.

629 Bill 2007/08:68 p. 65.

630 SOU 2015:67 p. 68.

on extended confiscation being studied in this report, the value of the assets confiscated within the Swedish regime was divided as follows:

- 32 judgments with a confiscated value under SEK 10,000,
- 66 judgments with a confiscated value higher than SEK 10,000 but lower than SEK 100,000,
- 30 judgments with a confiscated value of between SEK 100,000 and SEK 500,000,
- six judgments with a confiscated value between SEK 500,000 and SEK 1 million, and
- seven judgments with a confiscated value of over SEK 1 million.[631]

Orders of extended confiscation in the Swedish system may thus concern relatively low amounts of cash. As an example of a typical case in practice may be mentioned a defendant who was sentenced by Stockholm District Court for narcotic offences regarding the supply of a couple of grams of cannabis to three months' imprisonment.[632] The motion for extended confiscation concerned SEK 7,600 which had been found on the defendant during a search. He denied that it had an illegal origin and submitted that he worked and lived in Portugal and that he had brought €600 to Sweden. The District Court noted that the defendant had been a month in Sweden before being arrested, and that he had given no explanation of on what money he had lived during this time. Another circumstance, which spoke for illegal origin, was the fact that the cash (which consisted of several different banknotes) had a higher monetary value than what he claimed to have brought to Sweden. As the defendant had been convicted of supplying narcotics, the Court found it substantially more probable that the money was the proceeds of criminal activity than not.

Another defendant was sentenced to six months' imprisonment for *inter alia* one count of a narcotic offence regarding the supply of about six grams of amphetamine. In this case there was a plea for extended confiscation regarding SEK 26,000 which had been found in the apartment of the defendant.[633] The defendant claimed that the cash had been saved in order to finance a baptism that never took place. A financial investigation showed that the defendant and his girlfriend earned SEK 9,000 a month together, and that they were allowed to live in their apartment for free. The District Court held that the defendant had sold narcotics and that the cash in question (52 banknotes of SEK 500) was found in an armchair in the living room. Against this background, the court concluded

631 SOU 2015:67 pp. 68–69. The extent of this study is described in Section 5.5.6 below.

632 Stockholm District Court, Judgment on 12 December 2012, Case B 15461-12.

633 Court of Appeal (*Hovrätten över Skåne och Blekinge*), Judgment on 5 November 2012, Case B 3477-11 and Malmö District Court, Judgment 15 November 2011, Case B 7342-11.

that it was substantially more probable that the cash constituted the proceeds of criminal activity than not. The Court of Appeal confirmed the judgment without giving further reasons.

In a case from 2012, a defendant was sentenced to one year and four months' imprisonment regarding narcotics offences, and the plea for extended confiscation concerned the amount of SEK 28,500 in banknotes found at the defendant's residence.[634] The defendant argued that the money came from job earnings in Spain, which he had changed into Swedish currency shortly before he was apprehended. This information was confirmed by his brother who was heard in the case. The District Court found that the fact that the defendant had dealt in drugs for the purpose of gain indicated with some force that the money kept in a plastic bag in a kitchen cupboard derived from narcotics crime. The fact that he had previous convictions for narcotics offences also pointed in this direction. The court concluded that it was unlikely that the defendant, who had bank accounts in Sweden, would have withdrawn the money in Spain instead of transferring it. No documentation of such a withdrawal or other information regarding the Spanish bank had been presented. The court emphasised that the brother had not given evidence under oath, which affected the value of his statements. It was found substantially more probable than not that the cash constituted the proceeds of criminal activity.

Similarly to this, the Court of Appeal overruled a decision from a lower court in a case of 2014, and made a confiscation order regarding SEK 19,000 which had been found in cash in the pocket of a defendant.[635] The conviction concerned *inter alia* aggravated narcotic offences, and the defendant had argued that he had borrowed the cash from a friend in order to pay a debt. The Court recognised on the one hand that the money was not disproportionate to the financial situation of the defendant, but stated that the argument that he had borrowed the money could not be verified and anyway did not explain why he kept the cash in his pocket. On an overall assessment – and especially with regard to the fact that the cash was found together with narcotics "outside" and "during the night" – it was considered substantially more probable that the cash constituted the proceeds of criminal activity.

There is, however, also some case-law where the courts have turned down motions for extended confiscation reasoning that they concern modest amounts or comparatively low sums. One example concerned criminal responsibility for several cases of narcotics offences, where the prosecution applied for extended confiscation of SEK 5,500 which had been found in the defendant's dwelling.[636]

---

634 Solna District Court, Judgment on 13 December 2012, Case B 3541-12.

635 The Court of Appeal (*Hovrätten för Västra Sverige*), Judgment on 19 August 2014, Case B 3110-14 and Halmstad District Court, Judgment of 30 April 2014, Case B 297-14.

636 The Court of Appeal (*Skåne and Blekinge*), Judgment on 7 June 2012, Case B 1339-12 and B 694-12 as well as Helsingborg District Court, Judgment on 10 April 2012, Case B 530-12.

The defendant claimed that the money came from his unemployment benefit. The District Court approved the plea, giving relatively sparsely worded reasons. In the Court of Appeal the confiscation order was overturned. This Court found that the following circumstances spoke for an illegal origin; that the cash was found in a sofa together with the sort of equipment which is typically used for handling narcotics and that the defendant was now to be convicted of trafficking in drugs. Against this were the statements from the defendant that he had had certain earned income. The Court ruled that even if such an income had not been very high, it was on a par with the found amount. On a collective assessment, the standard of proof was not fulfilled.

A similar conclusion was reached regarding a plea for extended confiscation of SEK 6,500 in a case regarding narcotics offences.[637] The defendant claimed that this money came from his pension, which he just had received, and that he had very low expenses as he always got his food from different wastebins. The District Court convicted the defendant for a narcotic offence with intent to supply and stated that it was probable that the cash found originated from such drug dealings. On the other hand, it was held that the defendant had given explanations for the origin which spoke against such a conclusion, and that there was no information as to whether he was more regularly selling narcotics. Against this background, the evidentiary standard had not been fulfilled.

The same reasoning is seen in a case regarding criminal responsibility for aggravated smuggling of cigarettes, where a plea for extended confiscation concerned cash which was found in the pockets of the defendants at the time of arrest.[638] The first defendant had SEK 23,520 in his pockets, and he argued that this originated from the return of money from another seizure as well as from a loan from his brother. Another defendant had SEK 56,840 in his pockets, which he claimed came from rich relatives in the Iraq. The District Court ruled that the case concerned modest amounts of cash and that even if the explanations of the origin of this money from the defendants were not fully convincing, it couldn't be ruled out that the cash had this origin. The judgment was upheld by the Court of Appeal.

A study of case-law thus shows that the courts often come to different conclusions both regarding the assessment of an "insignificant sum", and on the issue whether a low monetary value of an asset has any importance for the overall assessment of the origin. In cases where the plea for extended confiscation has been rejected, there have been certain indicators of illegal origin for example that cash was found in "peculiar places" or alongside of narcotics. However, the courts have sometimes held that in the case of modest sums it may *generally* be more difficult to rule out that the property comes from something else than

637 Stockholm District Court, Judgment on 5 December 2012, Case B 14525-11.

638 Court of Appeal (*Svea Hovrätt*), Judgment on 26 May 2011, Case B 7018-10 and B 1977-10 and Södertörn District Court, Judgment on 23 July 2010, Case B 3201-10.

criminal activity.[639] As mentioned in Section 5.4.1 above, the courts often take the pattern of behaviour for an "average citizen" as a standard, which means that it is, for example, regarded as unusual to keep certain amounts of cash in one's pockets or hidden away in premises. Even if this may be a reasonable argument within a profit-based law enforcement model, certain caution must be observed, especially when the amounts of cash are not significantly large. It must be acknowledged that some defendants may have a lifestyle where assets are simply not handled in a "normal way". Accordingly, legal and illegal income is not separated or assets may originate from activities which are not illegal *per se* e.g. self-prostitution or gambling.

In the following case, the Court of Appeal adopted a balanced view of the facts . The case concerned responsibility for, *inter alia*, narcotics offences.[640] The District Court had made an order for extended confiscation regarding SEK 4,490 in cash which had been found during a house search together with narcotics under the mattress in the defendant's bedroom. The defendant admitted that the amount of 1,500 derived from drug dealings, whereas 2,990 originated from his social benefit payment. He had kept all the money together because it "seemed like a safe place". The District Court found that the explanations of the defendant did not appear credible, and pointed to the fact that all money had been found together with narcotics. However, the Court of Appeal came to a different conclusion. The Court argued that the fact that the defendant had been dealing with drugs in his apartment together with the circumstances under which the money was found spoke for an illegal origin regarding the amount as a whole. On the other hand, the court found that it concerned a comparatively low sum of money and that the financial situation of the defendant did not exclude that the money derived from something else than criminal activity. It was thereby maintained that a person who carries on criminal activity in the form of drugs dealing may handle his funds, whatever their origin, in ways that appear peculiar as compared to what people in general do. Despite the circumstances under which the money was found, it therefore did not appear substantially more probable than not that the cash constituted the proceeds of criminal activity. The decision of extended confiscation regarding SEK 2,990 was therefore overruled.

Against the background of Swedish case-law, it is interesting to note that in, for example, Denmark, it has been stated that the provision on extended

---

639 This is, for example, seen in the judgments of Court of Appeal (*Hovrätten över Skåne och Blekinge*), Judgment on 3 January 2013, Case B 3223-12 and Helsingborg District Court, Judgment on 16 November 2012, Case B 5064-12 where the courts found that the amounts (SEK 4,000 and 1,500) were not significant and that the defendants had given reasonable explanations regarding the origin. Compare also Jönköping District Court, Judgment on 27 May 2013, Case B 1110-13 and Court of Appeal (*Göta Hovrätt*), Judgment on 24 July 2013, Case B 1673-13, and *NJA 2016 p. 641* which is described in Section 5.4.2 above.

640 Court of Appeal (*Hovrätten för Övre Norrland*), Judgment on 17 December 2010, Case B 709-10 and Umeå District Court, Judgment on 23 July 2010, Case B 1081-10.

confiscation is to be applied in cases regarding higher amounts of cash or property of a *luxury nature*.[641] Obviously, it can be argued that it would be oppressive to avoid confiscation of assets of an illegal origin only for the reason that it concerns a low value. A common case in practice is where a defendant is caught with relatively small amounts of narcotics intended for supply, and where cash found can be strongly presumed to derive from such sales. Nevertheless, it may be questioned whether all such cases were intended to be targeted by such an intrusive measure as extended confiscation. The Swedish legislator argued at the adoption of the provision that the focus had been set on serious criminality, which is typically intended to generate large profits, crimes which are committed in more or less organised forms, and on crimes which by their nature are particularly dangerous or injurious to society.[642] The more far-reaching scope of extended confiscation in comparison to FD 2005/212/JHA was further especially justified by the need to fight *serious financial criminality* ("*allvarlig vinningsbrottslighet*").[643]

Even if one may in principle agree that even assets of a low value should be confiscated if they are of illegal origin, there is a strong argument speaking for the adoption of a more reasonable practice. As seen from the *Report on Extended Confiscation* mentioned in the beginning of this section, the majority of the Swedish cases being studied in this inquiry concerned values under SEK 100,000. Especially when it comes to relatively low amounts of cash kept by defendants (under SEK 10,000), the use of a lowered burden of proof can in some cases result in legal uncertainty. This is particularly the case where the main ground for confiscation is the circumstance that there is no parity with legal income. The evaluation of evidence must therefore be performed with more care and the standard of proof must be applied in a more nuanced way. The Swedish regime is in this respect partly different from other systems within the EU, where the legislation is *more expressly directed* towards defendants with significant proceeds from criminal activities or against offenders who have been classified as having a criminal lifestyle. Against this background, the scope and the targets of the Swedish legislation will now be studied in more detail.

5.5.2. THE SCOPE OF CONFISCATION AND THE TRIGGERING OFFENCES

To begin with, the Swedish practice of restricting extended confiscation to cases where the defendant owns certain property or where certain assets have been found should be continued. This avoids situations like that under the

641 See further on the Danish legislation, Section 6.2.1 below.

642 Bill 2007/08:68 pp. 53–58.

643 See Bill 2007/08:68 pp. 52–53.

English regime where a confiscation order in some cases is made even where no assets have been found. In principle, this is to be avoided according to POCA 2002, as the confiscation order should be set to the "available amount" if this sum is lower than the benefit. However, this has been weakened in practice by the decisions on "hidden assets".[644] The case of *Geerings v. The Netherlands* is an example which shows the dangers of an extensive use of extended confiscation powers.[645] In this case, the Dutch courts had ordered confiscation although it was never shown that Mr Geering had been in possession of any assets whose origin he could not explain. In fact, no assets had been found and there was no property analysis indicating that the defendant was in possession of assets of unexplained origin. The benefit had been calculated on an assessment (estimates in a police report) of the likely proceeds of certain offences (partly regarding offences of which he had been acquitted). The ECtHR took the position that "confiscation" following from a conviction was an inappropriate measure for assets which were not known to have been in the possession of the person concerned. It was further found that such conclusions by the courts amounted to a presumption of guilt which violated Article 6(2) ECHR.[646]

Turning to the scope of legislation and the general prerequisites for extended confiscation, the Swedish regime has from the outset provided for more triggering offences than the EU instruments in force. FD 2005/212/JHA was, for example, limited to certain serious crimes relating to terrorism or to the framework of a criminal organisation.[647] One reason for the Swedish legislator to choose another construction and to identify triggering offences on a more general basis was that an offence of belonging to a criminal organisation was considered alien to Swedish law.[648]

As new Swedish legislation implementing Directive 2014/42/EU came into force in July 2016, the old threshold for the triggering offences (imprisonment for six years or more) was significantly lowered to the current threshold of imprisonment for four years or more. In addition, an adjustment of the catalogue of specifically listed offences in Chapter 36 Section 1b SPC was made, adding the offences of active and passive corruption, child pornography and illegal system – and data interference. The *Report on Extended Confiscation* had concluded that the obligation to implement Article 5(2)(b) of Directive 2014/42/EU (i.e. offences relating to participation in a criminal organisation), only concerned criminal offences with a maximum penalty of at least four years' imprisonment. In spite

---

644 For criticism regarding the risk of artificially built up confiscation orders in the English system, see Sec. 3.6.3.

645 Appl. No. 30810/03, Judgment of 1 March 2007.

646 See especially paras. 46–48, Appl. No. 30810/03, Judgment of 1 March 2007. Compare on this case also Section 7.5 below.

647 Compare Section 2.1.2 above.

648 Instead, provisions on *inter alia* complicity are used in order to target such criminality. Cameron, Thunberg Schunke, Påle-Bartes, Wong and Asp, n 508 above, p. 45.

of this, the report proposed that the Swedish provision should be drafted more extensively.[649] The current legislation was drafted in line with these proposals. Accordingly, extended confiscation is possible if a defendant is convicted of a triggering offence with a penalty scale of two years or more when the offence is part of criminality that has been conducted in an organised form. In that way, theft, fraud and extortion in the area of organised crime qualify as triggering offences.[650]

Sweden has thus in the area of extended confiscation chosen to go further than the EU instruments would have demanded. In this respect, it should be mentioned that it was even considered within the framework of implementation whether the general penalty scale for the triggering offences could be further lowered (i.e. under four years), but this suggestion was abandoned.[651] The EU instruments in this area intended to introduce exclusive investigative powers for certain serious offences. Nevertheless, the Swedish legislative process clearly shows that there is always a risk that this more severe regime will "spread" to less serious offences.[652] This often follows when the national legislator decides to extend such rules to additional offences in order to avoid a complicated and fragmented domestic legislation with difficulties for the law enforcement agencies. In the long run, the EU provisions on harmonisation may in this way lead to increased repression as a whole in the national systems.[653]

Another aspect of the Swedish legislative policy regarding the classification of the triggering offences is that it is considered sufficient that the *maximum punishment* for the crimes in question reaches this level; extended confiscation may thus be ordered in cases where the "penal value" (i.e. the actual penalty imposed on the individual) is much lower than this. During the original legislative process there was a proposal that at least the triggering offences specifically listed should be further limited so that extended confiscation should not be used in a case where the penal value was lower than one year's imprisonment.[654]

---

649 SOU 2015:67 pp. 135–44.

650 Bill 2015/16:155 pp. 27–32.

651 See further SOU 2015:67 pp. 135–38.

652 The *European Criminal Bar Association* (ECBA) has raised concerns that there has been an increase of security legislation within the EU and has pointed to the fact that domestic legislators increasingly provide measures in reliance of such instruments which greatly exceed what is required. See pp. 2–3, *Statement of ECBA*, at http:77www.ecba.org/extdocserv/201210assetseizureECBAstatement.pdf. Compare also the national initiatives in Germany and England and Wales, where the legislation on extended confiscation was initially intended or drafted for the area of drug offences, but then spread to other types of criminality. See Sections 3.1, 4.1 and 4.3.2 above.

653 For a general discussion on the making of EU legislation in the area of criminal law, A. Wetter, *Making EU Legislation in the Area of Criminal Law: A Swedish Perspective*, Uppsala, 2013 and, especially on the risk of increased repression, see T. Elholm, "Does EU Criminal Cooperation Necessarily Mean Increased Repression?" (2009) 17 *European Journal of Crime, Criminal Law and Criminal Justice*, pp. 191–226.

654 Ds 2006:17, p. 184.

However, the legislator did not stipulate any such general guideline in the legislative works, but simply remarked that a low penal value of a triggering offence may be considered in the context of the hardship rule.[655]

The scope of the Swedish legislation in the context of the penalty scale of the triggering offences can be compared with some other national legislation. In, for example, Denmark, extended confiscation may be applied regarding offences punishable by imprisonment *for six years or more*, and the only exception is acts in violation of the controlled drugs legislation. The scope of triggering offences is thus much more limited than in Sweden.[656] In Finland, the scope for the triggering offences is "acts punishable by imprisonment for at least four years" and certain specifically listed offences with a lower penalty scale.[657] The Norwegian legislation first defines a triggering offence as one or more criminal acts that may collectively be punishable by *imprisonment for a term of six years or more*. Secondly, extended confiscation may be triggered by criminal offences punishable by *imprisonment for a term of two years or more*, but this is restricted to recidivist offenders.[658] The present German legislation uses another legislative construction, and there is no general minimum penalty scale given. Instead, there are certain criminal offences – classified by particular criteria – which may trigger the measure. However, there is at present a proposal for new legislation in Germany that would abolish this limiting requirement and allow for extended confiscation regarding every unlawful act.[659]

This being said, the scope of national legislation is not only limited by the setting up of penalty scales or lists of criminal offences. There may also be other qualifying legislative definitions or additional classifications of the triggering offences. The measure of extended confiscation builds upon the idea that a conviction for certain triggering offences *may justify a presumption* that a defendant has been involved also in other criminality which has generated criminal proceeds. Against this background, the measure was originally both internationally and nationally *motivated* by the need to fight serious forms of organised crime. An express link to such offences was, however, abolished by Directive 2014/42/EU,[660] and, in recent years, there has been a development also nationally towards a more general application of extended confiscation to other areas of crime. At the same time, some domestic legislation sets up other forms of requirements or classifications regarding the triggering offences in order to limit the use of the measure to more serious or systematic cases of criminality.

655 Compare Bill 2007/08:68 pp. 76–77 and 96–97.

656 See further on this legislation, Section 6.2.1 below.

657 See further Section 6.3.1 below.

658 See further on this, Section 6.1.1 below. For criticism against the construction of triggering offences in Norway, J. Boucht, "Utvidgat förverkande enligt strl. §34a – ny modell för ökad funktionalitet eller obefogat avsteg från hävdvunna rättssäkerhetskrav?" (2012) 4 *Tidsskrift for Strafferett*, p. 382, pp. 411–12.

659 See further Sections 4.4.3 and 4.4.4 above.

660 This is further discussed in Section 7.3 below.

In the analysis of the scope of the Swedish legislation, it is therefore necessary to comment upon the extent to which there are any additional classifications or limitations of the triggering offences.

At the introduction of the measure of extended confiscation in Sweden, some limiting requirements for the scope of the measure were considered. One of them was a condition that the property to be confiscated must derive from "similar criminal activities", but this was decided against.[661] As seen in Section 5.4.4 above, it is therefore, for example, possible to make an order for extended confiscation of assets which have been acquired as a consequence of tax offences, even though the triggering offence concerns aggravated narcotics offences. This might on first view seem peculiar. It can be argued that a requirement that the other criminal activities of a defendant have to be of a similar nature to the triggering offence may further substantiate an assumption that an offender has had financial gain from his offending. On the other hand, the primary aim of extended confiscation is to permit confiscation without a proven link to a particular crime, and to target assets resulting from unidentified criminal activity. Accordingly, it can be difficult to set up a requirement of "similarity" as the prosecutor is not obliged to prove or even state wherein the other criminal activity consists.

In some cases, the lifestyle of a defendant could, especially in the area of narcotics offences, give indications regarding "similar" criminality. However, such assertions often have a speculative nature, meaning that such a limiting requirement would in the end not necessarily restrict the area of application. The above mentioned case *NJA 2010 p. 374* was in this respect particular, because the defendant actually admitted that the assets in question derived from tax offences. The more usual situation is that the defendant denies any illegal origin or other criminal activities. If the aim of the measure is to confiscate assets deriving from criminal activities, one can further argue that it is of no importance whether the offences are similar or not. A criterion of "*similar* criminal activities" was initially stated in the draft for the new EU directive on confiscation from the European Commission, but was removed during the negotiations.[662] From a comparative perspective it can be noted that such a requirement is also absent from the domestic legislation in England and Wales, Germany, Norway, Denmark and Finland.

Another limiting criterion, which was discussed during the Swedish legislative process in the interest of legal safety, was a specific time-period to limit the scope for extended confiscation.[663] However, this was also decided against.[664]

---

661 Compare alternative (b) in Art. 3(2) FD 2005/212/JHA.

662 See further Section 7.3 below.

663 See for example *Yttrande från Svea hovrätt, Utvidgat förverkande m.m.* (Ds 2006:17), Dnr 561/06 p. 5.

664 Compare Bill 2007/08:68 pp. 64–65 and pp. 96–97.

The lack of a specific time requirement seems reasonable with regard to how the provision is constructed. In a system where the financial circumstances of a defendant are a fundamental starting-point (like for example in the English provision) it may be more suitable to limit the scope to a specific time-period in order to respect the proportionality principle. In the application of the Swedish provision, where a more all-round assessment is used, a specific time limit could require that the prosecutor must prove when an unidentified criminal activity was committed, which seems quite difficult.

The Swedish provision on extended confiscation contains a classification of the triggering offences in the form of a requirement that the offence in question must be of *such nature as to lead to proceeds*. This is also a criterion in Article 5 Directive 2014/42/EU. In this way, offences which have not been committed for the purpose of financial gain are excluded, and it is especially emphasised in the Swedish legislative works that it should not be taken for granted that every triggering offence has been committed with such an aim.[665] This type of limitation of the triggering offences is found in many other States. However, one difference becomes obvious. The Norwegian legislation provides that a triggering offence must have been of a nature to lead to *considerable* criminal proceeds which in practice has been set at 100,000 NOK.[666] In Denmark, it is required that the triggering offence is of a nature which may entail *significant gain*.[667] In the English regime on extended confiscation, there is a requirement of relevant benefit of not less than £5,000 regarding such triggering offences which are not classified as "lifestyle offences" in Schedule 2 POCA 2002.[668] The requirement that a triggering offence must have been of a nature to lead to considerable or significant criminal proceeds does not refer to the actual offence being committed, but concerns more generally the *category* of offences, which leads to a limitation to the most serious cases.

During the original Swedish legislative process, there was a proposal that only triggering offences which have been committed on a *systematic basis* would trigger an order of extended confiscation.[669] However, the legislator decided against such a general limitation, as it was argued that the measure *would anyway often be concentrated on such criminality*.[670] This assertion, which was not further substantiated, must be questioned particularly in view of case-law on extended confiscation so far. Furthermore, general guidelines for the prosecuting offices recommend that the measure is to be used regarding *all* triggering offences of

665 Bill 2007/08:68 p. 59.

666 Compare further Section 6.1.1 below.

667 See Section 6.2.1 below.

668 See further Section 3.4.1 above.

669 *Yttrande från Svea hovrätt, Utvidgat förverkande m.m.* (Ds 2006:17), Dnr 561/06 p. 4 and Bill 2007/08 p. 53.

670 Bill 2007/08:68 p. 55.

such nature as to lead to proceeds. This indicates that the legislation is applied without such consideration.[671]

Obviously, in many States, the national regimes on extended confiscation are explicitly directed to target defendants who commit crimes on a *multiple or systematic basis* or are classified as living a *criminal lifestyle*. In this way, a further qualification of the triggering offences may be obtained. An example of such legislation is the English legislation, where POCA 2002 provides for a very severe regime for extended confiscation when an offender is classified as a "criminal lifestyle offender". As further described in Section 3.4.1 above, this is established in two ways; either the triggering offence concerns a conviction for one of the so-called lifestyle offences especially listed, or the case concerns a course of criminal activity (under certain criteria regarding numbers or time-period of crimes). The Norwegian and Danish legislators have also explicitly stated in their legislative works that the primary aim of the legislation is to target offenders with a criminal lifestyle.[672]

An overriding question is whether the legislation on extended confiscation should target all defendants who commit a triggering offence or if the measure should be reserved for defendants who commit crimes "for a living" or on a systematic or multiple basis? If the main aim is to target only the "lifestyle criminals", the legislative method of establishing this group is apparently of decisive importance. In the English regime, *one* conviction for an offence in Schedule 2 is sufficient to lead to a *mandatory* assumption of a criminal lifestyle. The offences in this schedule are typically supposed to be committed by criminals to acquire wealth. In the Norwegian legislation *one* or more criminal acts that may collectively be punishable by imprisonment for a term of six years or more is in this respect sufficient. There is thus neither in the English nor in the Norwegian legislation in this part of the provisions any other requirements of further criminal offences or past convictions.

Even if the spoken aim is to target criminal lifestyle offenders under these regimes, there is in this respect little difference from the Swedish legislative solution in respect of the general requirement of *one* criminal offence punishable with *imprisonment for four years or more*. A common argument seems to be that, regarding criminal offences with such a high penalty scale, the *offences per se* indicate that the offender may have committed crimes before. However, a significant difference in the Swedish legislation on extended confiscation is that the specifically listed triggering offences with a lower penalty scale have not – unlike for example in England or Norway – been restricted to recidivist offenders.

---

671 See for example *Ett nytt arbetssätt – utredning av förverkande m.m.*, Handledning, RättsPM 2012:10, Utvecklingscentrum Stockholm, December 2012. Compare further on this, Section 5.5.6 below.

672 See Sections 6.1.1 and 6.2.1 below.

Interesting in this context is the change of legislation in July 2016, which allows for extended confiscation regarding a triggering offence with a penalty scale of *two years or more*. For the first time in Swedish law a further classification was set up, so that a triggering offence is expressly linked to a requirement that "the offence has been *part of criminality that has been conducted in an organised form*". The proposal as such was nevertheless criticised during the legislative process, because it was considered that it was too far-reaching to allow this intrusive measure to be triggered by offences with such a low penalty scale. In addition, it was argued that the criterion that the offence has been "*part of criminality that has been conducted in an organised form*" is not sufficiently stringent in terms of legal safety.[673] Such opinions were, however, disregarded by the Swedish Government, which emphasised the need to provide for efficient measures of confiscation in the area of organised criminality.[674] It remains to be seen how such a criterion will be applied in case-law.

There is one peculiarity of the Swedish regime of extended confiscation which also must be addressed, as it influences the scope of the legislation. The fundamental aim of the national legislator at the introduction of the measure was to make sure that assets deriving from any criminal activity can be confiscated in the most effective way. Therefore a link between the property and (any unidentified) criminal activity must be proven, but this does not mean that a particular person need be linked to this criminality. Accordingly, it has not been required for an order on extended confiscation that the person convicted of a triggering offence has any knowledge of the criminal activity which led to the proceeds or even of the illegal origin of the property.[675] This legislative choice was criticised during the legislative process.[676] It was, for example, argued that if extended confiscation is a special legal consequence of a crime under Swedish law, it seems peculiar that the defendant in such a case does not have to have any knowledge of the criminal activity leading to the confiscation of property. However, the legislator argued that such a legislative construction clarifies that extended confiscation is not an investigation into a criminal offence (with a lowered standard of proof), but only a measure to confiscate proceeds from criminal activity. It was further argued that this construction was necessary in order to issue confiscation orders also in cases where it is obvious that property derives from criminal activity, but it cannot be linked to any specific person.[677]

This specific characteristic of the Swedish legislation is interesting, because it shows a feature of an *in rem proceeding*.[678] There is a requirement of a criminal

673 Bill 2015/16:155 p. 27.

674 Bill 2015/16:155 pp. 31–32.

675 See also Section 5.3.3.

676 See for example *Yttrande från Svea hovrätt, Utvidgat förverkande m.m.* (Ds 2006:17), Dnr 561/06 pp. 5–6.

677 See further Bill 2007/08:68 pp. 62–63.

678 Compare on such proceedings, Section 3.2 above.

conviction regarding the triggering offence, and then there is a link between the asset and criminal activity but not necessarily to the person convicted. This construction differs from FD 2005/212/JHA, which only concerns confiscation of property deriving "from criminal activities of the convicted person".[679] It also differs from the regimes in many other States. On the other hand, Article 5 Directive 2014/42/EU states that the property in question shall derive "from criminal conduct". This has been interpreted as meaning that there is no longer any explicit requirement that the person convicted of a triggering offence has also committed or participated in this criminal conduct.[680] In any case, one might argue that if the intention is to target and recover assets derived illegally, it is reasonable to use extended confiscation also in such cases. At the same time, an overriding issue is obviously whether it is in all cases *fair* to do so. The availability of a hardship rule seems necessary in order to avoid confiscation in exceptional cases.

The development of the instrument of extended confiscation in Swedish law gives rise to some concern. The scope of the national legislation is repeatedly drafted in a more far-reaching way than any international obligations would demand. It is thereby not sufficiently considered whether any qualifying thresholds must be added in order to avoid the power of extended confiscation expanding too much. Obviously, Sweden has a rather generously defined scope of application following simply from more triggering offences, and an absence of some requirements used in other States. On the other hand, according to the Swedish system, the courts have a rather wide discretionary power. The question is whether this might lead to a better balance in the system. This is discussed in what follows.

5.5.3. THE SWEDISH HARDSHIP RULE

The Swedish courts have discretion to *partly* or *fully* avoid confiscation. Chapter 36 Section 1b Subsection 4 SPC states that confiscation *shall not* be ordered if it is *unreasonable*. In comparison to the provision applicable to ordinary confiscation, it may thus be applied more generously.[681] From an international perspective, the discretion given to the Swedish courts is rather extensive, but seems reasonable against the background that some limiting requirements for extended confiscation found in other States or in the EU instruments are absent from the domestic legislation.[682] This was also the motive given for the provision

679 Art. 3(2)(a)–(c) FD 2005/212/JHA.

680 Compare for example the conclusions of the *Report on Extended Confiscation*, SOU 2015:67 p. 134 and pp. 148–49.

681 Compare Sections 5.2 and 5.3 above.

682 See for a discussion of (the lack of) discretion of the courts, Section 3.6.4 above and Section 7.6 below.

in the legislative works; the legislator argued that there is a risk that the measure may lead to "offensive results" as there is, *inter alia*, no requirement of a link to a specified criminal offence, no time-limits, no minimum nominal amount and a lowered burden of proof.[683] Accordingly, more room for considerations of proportionality was needed.

Obviously, the hardship rule is important as a "safety rule" in order to avoid that the provision on extended confiscation is applied too harshly. In this respect, it is quite surprising that there seem to be very few cases in Swedish practice where the provision is actually applied by the courts. This is a general observation in respect of both ordinary and extended confiscation, and it does not seem as if the hardship rule is applied more generously in the area of extended confiscation. This conclusion is confirmed by the *Report on Extended Confiscation* in 2015, but this report also pointed out – on the basis of a study of the judgments – that there were few cases where the provision had been neglected.[684]

In spite of this, it must principally be doubtful whether the legislative method of *refraining* from setting up certain limiting requirements in a legal provision by referring to a hardship rule may be justified. Even if a wide discretion of the courts may function as a safeguard against unreasonable results, the regime must in the first place be drafted by the legislator in accordance with proportionality. During the legislative process leading up to the reform of the provision in 2016, criticism regarding the proposals was (again) refuted by the Swedish government by reference to the hardship rule.[685] Against the background of the further increase of the scope for orders of extended confiscation in legislation, the Swedish hardship rule may become even more important in the future.

5.5.4. A LOWERED STANDARD OR A REVERSED BURDEN OF PROOF?

Sweden belongs to a group of States which have opted for a lowered burden of proof. Thereby the prosecutor has the burden of proof regarding the circumstance that certain assets have an illegal origin. The system of a reversed burden of proof has been rejected on several legislative occasions. This position of the legislator is different to the view in some other Scandinavian States, for example, Norway and Denmark where a reversed burden of proof is applied.[686] In Finland, a reversed burden of proof similar to these systems was adopted in 2016.[687]

683 Bill 2007/08:68 pp. 76–77. It can be questioned to what extent a hardship rule may prevent "offensive results" following from a lowered burden of proof?

684 SOU 2015:67 pp. 73 and 84.

685 See Bill 2015/16:155 p. 32.

686 See further Sections 6.1.2 and 6.2.2 below.

687 See further Section 6.3.2 below.

At the adoption of the Swedish provision on extended confiscation, the prosecutor was given a better position than before in two ways: first as a result of the abolishment of the requirement of a link between the asset in question and a specific crime; and secondly in respect of the lowered burden of proof. During the legislative process when the new provision was discussed, the Swedish Bar Association argued that the evidentiary standard of "substantially more probable" was rather a reversed burden of proof than an easing of the burden.[688] Even if such an assertion may go too far, one can agree that to some extent there is not a sharp distinction between a reversed burden of proof and a lowered burden of proof.[689] When the burden of proof for a prosecutor eases, the burden of proof or explanation for a defendant may increase.

A study of Swedish case-law shows that the evidentiary standard of "substantially more probable" is often reached when assets are found under "suspicious" circumstances and the prosecutor presents an asset investigation report which shows that a defendant has not had the legal financial means to acquire such property.[690] At that stage it falls on the defendant to provide plausible explanations or documentation in order to prove a legal origin. The Supreme Court has held regarding the evidentiary standard in *NJA 2010 p. 374* that when it comes to such serious narcotics offences as in this case (aggravated narcotics offence for which a sentence of 12 years and six months' imprisonment was passed), the prerequisites for extended confiscation are normally present if the defendant has particularly valuable property which cannot be explained by legal income or in any other acceptable way.[691]

In the *Report on Extended Confiscation* in 2015 it was concluded on the basis of a study of case-law that the Swedish courts had dealt with the new standard of evidence in a reasonable way and that no difficulties regarding its application could be observed. It was generally recommended that this standard should be kept, and it was specifically emphasised that there was no reason to lower this standard or to consider a reversed burden of proof.[692]

One can generally conclude that the reduced burden of proof for the prosecutor under the Swedish system leads to more pressure on a defendant to account for his financial circumstances. A significant difference to a reversed burden of proof is though that it lies on the prosecutor in the first place to investigate, gather and present evidence to a certain standard on the presence of assets and its criminal origin. Another aspect of legal safety is that the prosecutor is under

688 See *Yttrande över Departementspromemorian Utvidgat förverkande m.m.* (DS 2006:17), R-2006/0939, pp. 2–4.

689 The evidentiary standard regarding extended confiscation is also discussed in Section 7.4.2 below.

690 Swedish case-law is described in Section 5.4 above.

691 See on this case, Section 5.4.4 above.

692 SOU 2015:67 pp. 82–83.

Swedish law obliged to perform the asset investigation in an objective way and also consider factors in favour of a legal origin. In domestic systems where there is a reversed burden of proof, there is often a presumption that assets are illegally obtained and it lies completely on the defendant to rebut this assumption. One example is the English regime of "criminal lifestyle confiscation" where the burden on the offender is particularly significant because there are rather far-reaching obligations on the defendant to account for and to supply information on his financial circumstances. Such obligations have even been supported with certain sanctions in case of failure.[693]

A system of a reversed burden of proof demands from a defendant that he can account for all finances and transactions. This might in practice be difficult for many defendants as special resources (for example legal assistance) may be needed in order to prepare sufficient documentation. Furthermore, there are defendants with a careless (but not illegal) approach to property or others who due to personal reasons, for example illness or psychological problems, cannot account for financial transactions.

This being said, some national legislation provides for a reversed burden of proof, but sets a rather low evidentiary threshold. As an example may be mentioned that the Norwegian provision on extended confiscation provides that a defendant shall render it "probable" that the assets are of legal origin.[694] Also the English system operates with the civil standard of proof.[695] This might mean that even if the burden of proof is on the defendant, this burden may in some cases not be significantly heavier than a system providing for a lowered burden of proof for the prosecutor. As is further argued in Section 7.4.2 below, it may in practice be difficult to render sharp distinctions between different models when it comes to a reversed burden of proof and lowered standards of proof. This is also the case when one tries to compare different national evidentiary standards for extended confiscation.

5.5.5. THE PROCEDURAL FRAMEWORK FOR A MOTION ON EXTENDED CONFISCATION

In Swedish law, a motion for extended confiscation must be made within the criminal proceedings regarding the triggering offence. Such an issue cannot be postponed or handled separately. An exception is a plea for extended confiscation which is directed against a third person.[696] The question whether

---

693 This is further described in Sections 3.5 and 3.6.5 above.

694 See further Section 6.1.2 below.

695 See further Section 3.4.2.2 above.

696 See the special provisions on the procedure for third party confiscation in the *Act (2008:369) on the Procedure on Confiscation of Proceeds of Crime in certain cases.*

there should be an opportunity to handle a plea against a defendant in separate proceedings has been considered. Such rules had, for example, been proposed in the *Ministry of Justice Report* on more efficient legislation on confiscation in 1999 under the argument that necessary financial investigations could otherwise delay the criminal proceedings.[697] During the legislative process regarding the implementation of FD 2005/212/JHA, some law enforcement agencies were recommending such a solution, because in cases where an offender is in pre-trial detention, there are very strict time-limits for the prosecution. This sometimes means that there can be significant difficulties in conducting the financial investigations necessary within such a short time. It is also not allowed under Swedish law to expand the pre-trial detention period in order to conduct an asset recovery investigation. However, the legislator did not find such practical problems decisive, and emphasised the importance of the principle that all criminal sanctions and legal consequences of a crime are to be considered on one occasion.[698] The legislator then considered the possibility of certain provisions allowing for a reconsideration of the confiscation issue, but decided against such rules.[699]

This legal construction differs from some other States. In, for example, the English system the courts have very broad possibilities to postpone an issue of confiscation, and there are even various opportunities for later reconsideration of confiscation issues.[700] Also the Norwegian legislation is rather far-reaching in this respect, as it is in certain cases possible to deal with a motion for extended confiscation separately from the criminal proceedings.[701]

Obviously, it can be a significant drawback if the law enforcement authorities must rush any financial investigations due to the strict time limits of the criminal proceedings. This being said, the reasons given in the Swedish legislative process for not allowing the issue of confiscation to be handled separately from the criminal proceedings regarding the triggering offence also seem reasonable. From the perspective of a defendant it is of significant importance that all legal consequences of a crime are handled on the same occasion. In addition, the practical difficulties for the law enforcement agencies can partly be avoided with more effective routines for investigating the possibilities for a plea for confiscation at an early stage.[702] It is, for example, important to focus on the issue of

---

697 SOU 1999:147 pp. 139–42.

698 Bill 2007/08:68 pp. 73–74. A separation of the issue of extended confiscation had also been found unsuitable in an inquiry in 2006, see Ds 2006:17 pp. 131–36.

699 Bill 2007/08:68 pp. 77–78.

700 See further Section 3.5 above.

701 Compare Section 6.1.3 below. Also the German system allows that such motions are separated from the issue of guilt in some cases, compare in this context further the Referentenentwurf des Bundesministeriums der Justiz und für Verbraucherschutz, *Entwurf eines Gesetzes zur Reform der strafrechtlichen Vermögensabschöpfung*, March 2016, pp. 58 and 93–94.

702 See for a similar conclusion, the *Report on Extended Confiscation*, SOU 2015:67 pp. 85–89.

confiscation early in the preliminary investigation and to use asset investigations as a measure to more actively *search* for assets. Furthermore, an increase of legal costs can be anticipated if the criminal proceedings for a triggering offence are handled separately from the confiscation issue, as practically the same evidence will be presented on two different occasions.[703]

Within the EU legislative process, it has been claimed that suspects often hide property throughout the entire duration of criminal proceedings, and that there is therefore a need to establish a possibility to determine *the precise extent of the property* to be confiscated even after a final conviction for a criminal offence. Thereby the execution of confiscation orders should be possible in cases where no property or insufficient property was initially identified and the confiscation order remains unexecuted.[704] Article 9 Directive 2014/42/EU obliges the Member States to:

> take the necessary measures to enable the detection and tracing of property to be frozen and confiscated even after a final conviction for a criminal offence or following proceedings in application of Article 4(2) and to ensure the effective execution of a confiscation order, if such an order has already been issued.

The precise extent of this obligation is somewhat unclear. Some of the wording could imply the need for rules permitting reconsideration of the confiscation issue even after a final conviction for a criminal offence. On the other hand, it can also be interpreted as meaning an obligation to provide for an opportunity only to *detect* and *trace* property after the final conviction in order to provide for an effective execution of an existing confiscation order. The latter interpretation was endorsed by the *Report on Extended Confiscation* which concluded that there was no need for changes to Swedish law following from this provision, as there are already effective forms for execution in place.[705]

5.5.6. THE EFFICIENCY OF THE REGULATION

The coming into force of the legislation on extended confiscation in 2008 brought fundamental changes into the traditional roles of the law enforcement agencies. Alongside the task of investigating and collecting evidence for a criminal offence, an obligation was added to consider issues of confiscation. It seems as if it has

---

703 For a discussion of the use of separate confiscation proceedings including some arguments for the advantages of such rules, see G. Stessens, *Money Laundering; A New International Law Enforcement Model*, Cambridge University Press, 2000, pp. 42–43.

704 Compare Recital (30), Directive 2014/42/EU.

705 SOU 2015:67 pp. 170–71. Compare also Bill 2015/16:155 pp. 21–23.

taken some time for the Swedish authorities to live up to these new roles, and the need for educational and administrative support has been evident.

This is, for example, illustrated by looking at the experiences of a special joint cooperation between several authorities which was set up in 2009. The agencies include, *inter alia*, the police, and prosecuting and tax authorities as well as the enforcement service and the social insurance office. The aim has been to especially target organised crime, for example with the use of asset recovery. An evaluation of this approach has been presented in a report by the *Swedish National Council for Crime Prevention* ("BRÅ"), which has concluded that the amounts so far recovered have been relatively limited. It has thereby been highlighted that the reason may be a lack of sufficient competence regarding the legal provisions, as well as an attitude among the law officials that asset recovery is of subsidiary importance. This means that there are often only "passive" asset recovery measures in cases where the law officials practically "bump into" property.[706] The report has nevertheless underlined that one cannot measure the efficiency of the method of asset recovery merely by analysing the figures regarding confiscated amounts. It has been highlighted that the strategy of going for the money may have effects which are not necessarily shown by this statistics, for example by forcing criminals to undertake (expensive or complicated) measures to hide money abroad or to face difficulties investing in certain property.[707] In 2015, an *action plan* for the handling of asset recovery measures was presented by the authorities participating in this joint cooperation. Several proposals for a new strategy in order to improve the handling of confiscation issues were thereby presented.[708]

In 2010, *Riksrevisionen* (the National Audit Office) concluded generally that the asset recovery measurers taken by the Swedish law enforcement authorities were not efficient and that improvements must be made.[709] The year after, the Prosecutor General (*Riksåklagaren*) published a review of the use of the measure of confiscation by the Swedish prosecuting authorities.[710] In this review,

---

706 Rapport 2011:20, *Bekämpning av Organiserad Brottslighet, Utvärdering av den myndighetsgemensamma satsningen mot grov organiserad brottslighet*, pp. 124–28.

707 Rapport 2011:20, *Bekämpning av Organiserad Brottslighet, Utvärdering av den myndighetsgemensamma satsningen mot grov organiserad brottslighet*, p. 128. See for similar conclusions, BRÅ Rapport 2014:10, *Gå på pengarna, Antologi om tillgångsinriktad brottsbekämpning*, pp. 146–50.

708 *En myndighetsöverskridande handlingsplan för brottsutbytesarbete i samverkan*, January 2015 and *Myndighetssamverkan på brottsutbytesområdet*, November 2014. Compare also *Redovisning av resultatet av den särskilda satsningen mot den grova organiserade brottsligheten*, Myndigheter i samverkan mot den organiserade brottsligheten 2014, Stockholm 2015.

709 Report from Riksrevisionen, *Statens Insatser för att komma åt vinster från brottslig verksamhet*, RIR 2010:26. See also Report from BRÅ 2008:10, *Tillgångsinriktad brottsbekämpning, Myndigheternas arbete med att spåra och återföra utbyte av brott*. Compare *Riksrevisionens uppföljningsrapport*, 2015.

710 See Tillsynsrapport, *Tillsyn – brottsutbytesfrågor*, Utvecklingscentrum Stockholm, December 2011.

the motions for extended confiscation for the year 2010 had been studied. The report concluded that the instrument was only used to a limited extent and that the prosecutors (with the exception of the prosecutors handling international cases) had not sufficient knowledge of the legal provisions in force. In practice, the preliminary investigations were only concerned with the question of criminal responsibility and it was rather unusual that any financial investigation was started in order to search for assets. Similar conclusions were drawn by the *Rikspolisstyrelsen* (Swedish National Police Agency), which conducted a review regarding five police authorities in the year 2012.[711] A follow up report in 2014 by the same authority confirmed this result.[712]

Against the background of these reviews, certain initiatives regarding information and education have been initiated, and guidelines to the police and prosecuting offices on the handling of motions of confiscation have been issued. Instructions for new methods and routines for handling cases have been given and the prosecuting agencies have been instructed to consider a plea for confiscation regarding *all triggering offences* which are of such nature as to lead to proceeds.[713] The aim is to increase the use of confiscation generally and to promote a more uniform application of cases.[714]

In 2015, some important conclusions regarding the application in practice were made in the *Report on Extended Confiscation*. During this inquiry interviews with law enforcement officers had been conducted, and 174 judgments with *motions* for extended confiscation had been studied. 140 of these judgments had been given from February 2011 until August 2013, and the rest concerned judgments before this date and until spring 2015.[715] It was noted that the court had ordered extended confiscation in 141 of these judgments.[716] The measure had in practice mostly been used in the area of narcotic offences and had mainly concerned cash found during a search. A general conclusion of the report was that the instrument of extended confiscation had not been used effectively or to its full potential by the law enforcement authorities. This was not considered due to any deficiencies regarding the legal prerequisites or the procedural framework.[717] Instead, it was underlined that the initiatives taken by the law

---

711 *Inspektion av polismyndigheternas handläggning av förverkande av utbyte av brott och brottslig verksamhet*, Inspektionsrapport 2012:7, Rikspolisstyrelsen, August 2012.

712 *Polismyndigheternas handläggning av förverkande av utbyte av brott och brottslig verksamhet*, En uppföljande rapport, Tillsynsrapport 2014:8, Rikspolisstyrelsen, 2014.

713 See for example *Ett nytt arbetssätt - utredning av förverkande m.m.*, Handledning, RättsPM 2012:10, Utvecklingscentrum Stockholm, December 2012.

714 See for example *Businessplan* ("*Verksamhetsplan*") 2013 from the Prosecutor General, *Åklagarmyndigheten*, 2013. Some of the initiatives taken by different authorities are further described in *Riksrevisionens uppföljningsrapport*, 2015.

715 SOU 2015:67 p. 55.

716 See further SOU 2015:67 pp. 64–65.

717 SOU 2015:67 pp. 80–90.

enforcement authorities (for example the new routines mentioned above) had not been sufficient in order to raise the efficiency. The recommendation of the report was that an asset investigation report should be made in *every* preliminary investigation of a triggering offence, and that it should be used to a greater extent in order to *trace* assets. It was suggested that a statistical basis for the evaluation of the use of extended confiscation must be built up.[718]

In principle, any measures to improve the working approach of the law enforcement agencies in this area are to be welcomed. It is of significant importance that the financial circumstances of a defendant and the possibilities for a confiscation order are investigated as soon as possible within a preliminary investigation. The setting up of an asset investigation report at an early stage is in this respect crucial. Obviously, far-reaching legislation has little effect if it is not applied in an effective way (or at all).

However, there is one risk with the increased pressure on the prosecution agencies to make more use of confiscation in criminal cases. As described above, the Swedish regime on extended confiscation has a rather wide scope of application and has so far been used also in cases of relatively low monetary amounts. With an increased practice of targeting every triggering offence, there may be an unreasonable expansion of the instrument. It is naturally easier to make a motion for confiscation of cash being found by the arrest of a person being caught supplying drugs, then to more actively start a financial asset investigation into more complicated cases. Even if this might have been an intended aim, a more fundamental discussion ought to be initiated in Sweden concerning which forms of criminality to be targeted. At the end of the day, extended confiscation is a very intrusive measure with significant consequences for an individual. Furthermore, as the resources of the law enforcement agencies are not unlimited, it might be more reasonable to direct the action towards certain types of more serious criminality.[719]

In any case, it does not due in this respect to issue such general guidelines which have been made by the Prosecutor General and simply ignore any upcoming problems with referral to the fact that the courts "anyway have a general task" to decide in which cases a decision on extended confiscation may be *unreasonable*.[720] As concluded above, this hardship rule is not often used in practice.[721]

---

718 SOU 2015:67 pp. 90–99.

719 Compare in this respect the conclusions of the Finnish legislator, who specifically states in the legislative works that the law enforcement agencies should in this respect concentrate on more serious criminaliy, *Regeringens proposition till Riksdagen med förslag till lagar om ändring av 10 kap. i strafflagen och av 6 och 7 kap. i tvångsmedelslagen*, RP 4/2016 rd, p. 39.

720 Tillsynsrapport, *Tillsyn – brottsutbytesfrågor*, Utvecklingscentrum Stockholm, December 2011, p. 15.

721 See Sec. 5.5.3.

CHAPTER 6

BRIEF OVERVIEW OF THE LEGISLATION IN NORWAY, DENMARK AND FINLAND

6.1. NORWAY

6.1.1. THE PROVISION ON EXTENDED CONFISCATION

Norway has a rather broad range of legal powers regarding asset recovery, and the regime on extended confiscation was adopted in 1999. The legal provisions on confiscation are found in the Norwegian Penal Code.[722] This new Penal Code took force on 1 October 2015 (Act of 19 June 2015 No. 65), even though this piece of legislation had already been enacted in 2005. It replaced the Act of 22 May 1902 No. 10 ("*Almindelig borgerlig Straffelov*"). In substance, the former provision on extended confiscation in this Act (Chapter 2 Section 34a) was thereby kept unchanged.[723]

The Norwegian Penal Code (Chapter 13 Section 68) provides for extended confiscation ("*utvidet inndragning*") if the offender is found guilty of a criminal act of such a nature that the proceeds thereof can be considerable, and he has committed:

(a) one or more criminal acts that may collectively be punishable by imprisonment for a term of six years or more, or an attempt at such an act, or

---

722 *Straffeloven*, Act of 20 May 2005 No. 28. See J. Jacobsen and V. Hallgren Sandvik, "An outline of the New Norwegian Criminal Code" (2015) 3 *Bergen Journal of Criminal Law and Criminal Justice*, pp. 162–83 for an overview of this Act.

723 See for motives and guidelines to the provision, Ot. prp. Nr. 8 (1998–99), NOU 1996:21, *Mer effektiv indragning av vinning*, Ot. prp. Nr. 90 (2003–2004) and NOU 2002:4 *Ny straffelov*. See on the Norwegian provision on extended confiscation, for example J. Boucht, "Utvidgat förverkande enligt strl. §34a – ny modell för ökad funktionalitet eller obefogat avsteg från hävdvunna rättssäkerhetskrav?" (2012) 4 *Tidsskrift for Strafferett*, pp. 382–423 and J. Boucht "Extended Confiscation and the Proposed Directive on Freezing and Confiscation of Criminal Proceeds in the EU: On Striking a Balance between Efficiency, Fairness and Legal Certainty" (2013) 21 *European Journal of Crime, Criminal Law and Criminal Justice*, pp. 127–62 as well as M. Matningsdal, *Straffeloven, lagkommentar till §34a*, Oslo, 2015.

(b) at least one criminal act punishable by imprisonment for a term of two years or more, or an attempt at such an act, and the offender during the five years immediately preceding the commission of the said act has been punished for an act of such a nature that the proceeds thereof can be considerable.

Accordingly, several requirements are set up. It is first required that an offender is found guilty of a criminal act. The triggering offences are identified by a link to certain penalty scales. Decisive here are the penalty scales in question and not the actual penalty imposed in the individual case. An interesting provision in this respect is Chapter 14 Section 79 of the Norwegian Penal Code, which provides that under certain conditions it is allowed to increase the maximum penalty laid down in the penal provision (i.e. double its prescribed limit), if a criminal offence has been committed as part of the activity of an organised criminal group. (The limits hereto and the definition of the term "organised criminal group" is given in the provision.) This means that in such cases the scope for extended confiscation may be somewhat increased.

A second requirement is that the triggering offence *could have* generated considerable proceeds. From this formulation it is obvious that it is not required that any proceeds have occurred in the individual case.[724] According to the legislative works "considerable" proceeds means criminal proceeds of at least 75,000 NOK,[725] but in case-law the limit has been successively increased.[726] The limit for considerable proceeds is now approximately 100,000 NOK.[727] Against this background, it is evident that the scope of the Norwegian provision is limited to such offences where more significant proceeds *could* have been expected. However, this limit is not to be understood as referring to which amount can be confiscated, but aims at limiting the offences which trigger the use of the provision on extended confiscation.

An order of extended confiscation is discretionary.[728] According to the legislative works the *primary aim* of the regime is to *target offenders with a criminal lifestyle*, and the provision should therefore be interpreted in this light.[729] In case-law, the Norwegian courts have dealt with the question of whether, and in which cases, the provision may be used on groups of defendants which cannot be considered as the primary target. In one case in 2003, it was for example ruled that, even if the provision is not exclusively reserved for defendants with a

724 See Sec. 10.2.1 in Ot. prp. Nr. 8 (1998–99).

725 100 NOK correspond to €11.16 (on 24.1.2017).

726 Compare Section 22.2 in Ot. prp. Nr. 8 (1998–99) and Judgment of the *Agder Lagmannsrett* 30.8.2005, No. LA 2005-40909, which ruled that the limit must be more than 80,000 NOK.

727 Matningsdal, n 723 above, fn 230.

728 Sec. 10.2.3 in Ot. prp. Nr. 8 (1998–99).

729 Secs. 22.2 and 10.1.2 in Ot. prp. Nr. 8 (1998–99). Compare Ot. prp. Nr. 90 (2003–04) p. 345. See further on the motives for the legislation, NOU 1996:21 and NOU 2002:4.

criminal lifestyle, the rule must, with regard to the reversed burden of proof, be applied with care when it comes to other groups of defendants.[730]

6.1.2. THE BURDEN OF PROOF

There is no requirement in the Norwegian system that the prosecutor can show any link between the asset in question and any concrete criminal offence. The prosecutor has, though, the burden of proof to establish that certain assets belong to the defendant. Thereafter a reversed burden of proof is operated. This means that if the requirements for extended confiscation are met *all assets* belonging to the offender may be confiscated unless he proves on a balance of probabilities that the assets have been lawfully acquired.[731] In order to avoid confiscation, the defendant must prove that it is *probable* that the assets were legally acquired ("*sannsynliggjør*").[732] Despite this relatively low standard of proof, the burden on the offender may be significant. In principle, it is presumed that *all* his property is of illegal origin which means that it may be confiscated unless the defendant can account for the assets in a credible way.

In case-law it has been concluded that in order to prevent extended confiscation the offender must prove that the concrete asset was paid for with legal income and render it probable that his total legal income exceeds what may be assumed to have been spent on ordinary consumption.[733] In addition, an order of extended confiscation may cover the value of all assets belonging to the *offender's present or previous spouse or partner*, unless the offender proves on a balance of probabilities that the assets have been acquired otherwise than by the criminal activity. Exceptions to such confiscation are if the assets were acquired before the marriage was entered into, after the marriage was dissolved or if they were acquired at least five years before the criminal act that provides the basis for extended confiscation.[734]

The legislative works state as motives for the reversal of the burden of proof that it is easier for the defendant than for the law enforcement agencies to account for the financial circumstances.[735] Furthermore, it is claimed that a

---

730 *Høyesterett* Judgment, Rt. 2003 p. 897. See also *Høyesterett* Judgment, Rt. 2004 p. 1126.

731 Ch. 13 Sec. 68 Subsec. 3 of the Norwegian Penal Code.

732 Sec. 10.1.4.3 in Ot. prp. Nr. 8 (1998–99). The interpretation of the burden of proof is considered in for example *Høyesterett* Judgment, Rt. 2004 p. 1126. See also for a critical discussion of the provision, Boucht, n 723 above.

733 See for example Judgment from the *Høyesterett*, on 27.8.2012, HR-2012-01689-A, Case no. 2012/617.

734 Ch. 13 Sec. 68 Subsecs. 4–5 of the Norwegian Penal Code.

735 Sec. 10.1.4.1 in Ot. prp. Nr. 8 (1998–99). See further on the motives for a reversed burden of proof, NOU 1996:21 pp. 97 and 134 and Ot. prp. Nr. 90 (2003–04), pp. 344–46.

defendant will normally have no problems in fulfilling the evidentiary burden, and that the risk must be very small that an offender will have all his legally acquired assets confiscated.[736]

6.1.3. THE PROCEDURAL FRAMEWORK

A special feature of the Norwegian legislation is that a motion for extended confiscation can be handled separately from the criminal proceedings for the triggering offence. According to Chapter 5 Section 51 Subsection 2 of the Norwegian Criminal Procedure Act,[737] a motion for confiscation can be made even after a penalty has been imposed if such a claim was not dealt with at the time. Furthermore, if in the criminal case a claim for confiscation has already been adjudicated, a claim for further confiscation may subsequently be brought if the adjudicated claim was limited to objects that can be directly related to the criminal act.

The Norwegian provision on extended confiscation seems to have been applied only in a limited number of cases.[738] One study of how the rules were applied in practice from their adoption in 1999 until 2004 has shown that there was not a significant increase of confiscation orders.[739] These conclusions were confirmed in a report by the Financial Action Task Force ("FATF") in 2014, where it was generally concluded that the results achieved regarding the confiscation of criminal proceeds in Norway are not satisfactory and need to be improved.[740]

As evident from the *Government's Action Plan against economic criminality*, confiscation remains an area of high priority for the Ministry of Justice in Norway, and the law enforcement agencies have been instructed to give priority to such issues. In this respect, the possibility of adopting provisions on non-conviction-based confiscation similar to the systems in the UK and Ireland has been suggested.[741] At the moment a new legal proposal on non-conviction-based confiscation is being discussed in Norway.[742]

---

736 Sec. 10.1.4.1 in Ot. prp. Nr. 8 (1998–99).

737 *Straffeprosessloven*, Act of 22 May 1981 No. 25.

738 See Boucht (2013), n 723 above, p. 162 and Boucht (2012), n 723 above, pp. 422–23.

739 See A.-M. Dyrnes, *Inndragning – Hva må gøras?*, Oslo, 2004, pp. 17–18.

740 *Mutual Evaluation Report regarding Norway on Anti-money laundering and Counter-terrorist Financing Measures*, FATF, December 2014, especially pp. 61–65.

741 See further *Regjeringens handlingsplan mot økonomisk kriminalitet*, Justis- og Politidepartementet og Finansdepartementet, 2011, p. 13.

742 Professor Jon Petter Rui, Bergen University has been appointed by the Norwegian Government to draft such a proposal. See J.P. Rui, *Betenkning: Sivilrettslig inndragning rettet direkte mot formuesgoder*.

6.2. DENMARK

6.2.1. THE PROVISION ON EXTENDED CONFISCATION

Denmark adopted legislation on extended confiscation in 1997, against the particular background of organised crime and biker-related criminality.[743] The legislator thereby found some inspiration from the *Norwegian legislative inquiry on extended confiscation.*[744] A provision on extended confiscation ("*udvidet konfiskation*") is regulated by Chapter 9 Section 76a Subsection 1 of the Danish Criminal Code.[745] It is here stated that total or partial confiscation of property belonging to a person convicted of an offence may take place:

(1) when the act committed is of a nature which may entail a *significant gain* ("*betydeligt udbytte*") and,
(2) is *punishable by imprisonment for six years or more* or it is a violation of controlled drugs legislation.

There is no requirement that a link between the property in question and a particular criminal offence is established. The provision is not mandatory and, according to the legislator, it has the aim of targeting persons who are making a living from crime or have significant revenues from criminality. There is, however, no need for any proceeds to have resulted in the individual case.[746]

The legislative works state that Chapter 9 Section 76a of the Danish Criminal Code should in particular be applied in relation to higher amounts of cash or other liquid assets which cannot be reasonably explained by a defendant. No minimum limit is given, but it has been stated that amounts lower that DKK 50,000 shall not be confiscated.[747] Regarding property like real estate and

---

743 Law No. 411 of 10 June 1997. For the legislative works, see *Forslag til Lov om ændring af straffeloven, retsplejeloven og våbenloven*, Folketinget 1996–97, Lovforslag nr. L 98. On the background to the legislation, see also *Reversal of the Burden of Proof in Confiscation of the Proceeds of Crime: a Council of Europe Best Practice Survey*, Best Practice Survey No. 2, *European Committee of Crime Problems*, Strasbourg 25.5.2000, pp. 6 and 13–18. See on the confiscation system in Denmark, Council of the European Union, Evaluation Report on the Fifth Round of Mutual Evaluations, Financial Crime and Financial Investigations, *Report on Denmark*, 12659/2/12, REV 2, Brussels 14.11.2012 and B. Vettori, *Tough on Criminal Wealth: Exploring the Practice of Proceeds from Crime Confiscation in the EU*, Springer, 2006, pp. 51–54.

744 See *Forslag til Lov om ændring af straffeloven, retsplejeloven og våbenloven*, Folketinget 1996–97, Lovforslag nr. L 98, p. 29 and NOU 1996:21.

745 *Danmarks borgerliga Straffelov* (1930).

746 *Forslag til Lov om ændring af straffeloven, retsplejeloven og våbenloven*, Folketinget 1996–97, Lovforslag nr. L 98, pp. 29–30.

747 DKK 100 correspond to €13.45 (on 24.1.2017). See further *Forslag til Lov om ændring af straffeloven, retsplejeloven og våbenloven*, Folketinget 1996–97, Lovforslag nr. L 98, p. 30.

motor vehicles, this limit is to be even higher and it is specifically pointed out that the legislation is primarily intended to target property of a *luxury nature* ("*luksuspraæget karakter*").[748]

6.2.2. THE BURDEN OF PROOF

If the general requirements for extended confiscation are present, there is a presumption of an illegal origin of the assets owned by the offender and a reversed burden of proof is applied. According to Section 76a Subsection 4 of the Danish Criminal Code confiscation may not take place if the offender renders *probable* ("*sandsynliggøre*") that the property has been acquired in a legal way or with legally acquired means. The Danish legislative works state that this evidentiary standard must not be too strict.[749]

The property acquired by the spouse or cohabitant of the offender may also under certain conditions be fully or partly confiscated. The exceptions are if the property has been acquired more than five years prior to the punishable act upon which the confiscation is based, or if the marriage or cohabitation had not commenced at the time of acquisition.[750]

6.2.3. DANISH LEGISLATION AND DIRECTIVE 2014/42/EU

Denmark is not participating in Directive 2014/42/EU. The effects of an opt-in regarding this EU instrument have, however, been considered.[751] In this context, it has been concluded that the Danish legislation would have to be changed in order to implement Article 5 on extended confiscation. It would thereby be necessary to increase the scope of this measure, as the current legislation only allows for extended confiscation to be applied regarding criminal offences which are *punishable by imprisonment for six years or more* or are in violation of controlled drugs legislation. It would further be necessary to add several triggering offences, which are covered by Directive 2014/42/EU, but have a penalty scale of under six years imprisonment under present Danish law. Furthermore, it has been concluded that the present requirement of the Danish law that the triggering offence must be of a nature to entail *significant gain*

---

748 *Forslag til Lov om ændring af straffeloven, retsplejeloven og våbenloven*, Folketinget 1996–97, Lovforslag nr. L 98, p. 30. Compare also Bill 2007/08:68 p. 45.

749 *Forslag til Lov om ændring af straffeloven, retsplejeloven og våbenloven*, Folketinget 1996–97, Lovforslag nr. L 98, p. 30.

750 See further Ch. 9 Sec. 76a Subsec. 2 of the Danish Criminal Code.

751 See for example *Samarbejdet om retlige og indre anliggender, En analyse af EU-lovgivning omfattet af retsforbeholdet*, Regeringen Marts 2015.

must be changed, as the EU provision in this respect only requires "economic benefit". Such an amendment is considered to be difficult because this limiting requirement in Section 76a of the Danish Criminal Code has been set up with regard to, *inter alia*, legal safety.[752]

6.3. FINLAND

6.3.1. THE PROVISION ON EXTENDED CONFISCATION

A provision on extended confiscation was adopted in Finland in 2002.[753] At the beginning of 2015, a report was presented with proposals for some legislative changes of this regime following from Directive 2014/42/EU.[754] According to the report, the national legislation in principle fulfilled the requirements of the directive, but some reform in order to broaden the scope of extended confiscation was suggested. With reference to this report, the Finnish Government proposed new legislation.[755]

On 1 September 2016, new legislation on extended confiscation took force.[756] Chapter 10 Section 3 of the Finnish Criminal Code[757] now states as a first requirement for extended confiscation that a person is found guilty of one of the following triggering offences:

(1) an offence which is *punishable by imprisonment for at least four years* (Subsection 1 Paragraph 1),
(2) one of the specifically listed criminal offences (Subsection 1 Paragraphs 2–8), or
(3) a punishable attempt of an offence in Subsection 1 Paragraphs 1–8.[758]

---

752 See further on this, *Notat om tilvalg af konfiskationsdirektivet*, 2015, see www.justitsministeriet.dk.

753 See Act 875 of 26.10.2001 and the legislative works, *Regeringens proposition till Riksdagen med förslag till revidering av lagstiftningen om förverkandepåföljder*, RP 80/2000. Compare also Vettori, n 743 above, pp. 54–57.

754 *Revidering av strafflagens allmänna bestämmelser om förverkandepåföljder*, Betänkande 3/2015 från konfiskationsarbetsgruppen. Compare also Pressmeddelande från Justitieministeriet, *Arbetsgrupp vill öka möjligheterna att döma vinning av brott förverkad till staten*, 20.1.2015.

755 *Regeringens proposition till Riksdagen med förslag till lagar om ändring av 10 kap. i strafflagen och av 6 och 7 kap. i tvångsmedelslagen*, RP 4/2016 rd.

756 See Act 20.5.2016/356 and *Regeringens proposition till Riksdagen med förslag till lagar om ändring av 10 kap. i strafflagen och av 6 och 7 kap. i tvångsmedelslagen*, RP 4/2016 rd.

757 *Strafflag*, Act 39, 19.12.1889. This Act may be found at www.finlex.fi.

758 An order of extended confiscation may also be issued against a participant or person on whose behalf or to whose advantage the offence was committed (Ch. 10 Sec. 3 Subsec. 2 of the Finnish Criminal Code).

The new legislation in 2016 made some changes to Finnish law. The penalty scale for the triggering offences of at least four years' imprisonment was taken over from the old legislation, but it was necessary to broaden the scope for extended confiscation by adding some offences to the specifically listed triggering offences with a lower penalty scale (see point (2) above). Examples of the criminal offences on this list are money laundering, child pornography offences, narcotics crime and smuggling offences.

A second requirement of extended confiscation according to Chapter 10 Section 3 of the Finnish Criminal Code is that the nature of the offence is such that it may result in *financial proceeds*. Also in this respect, the law has been changed as the old provision contained a more limiting requirement of "*considerable financial proceeds*". (According to the legislative works this had meant proceeds to the amount of at least some 10,000 Finnish Marks.)[759] This limiting criterion was abolished by the 2016 law as the Finnish Government argued that Article 5 Directive 2014/42/EU does not allow for such a limitation. Nevertheless, it was underlined in the legislative works that the Finnish hardship rule will still be applicable (Chapter 10 Section 10 of the Finnish Criminal Code).[760]

There is no requirement under Finnish law that a link is established between the property to be confiscated and a particular criminal offence, but it is sufficient that the property is derived from *criminal activity*. The old provision on extended confiscation required that the property should have been fully or partially derived from criminal activity "that was not to be considered insignificant". The legislative works to this legislation provided that the provision should be applied with care and that it was supposed to be used for more serious forms of criminality. As a consequence, a plea for extended confiscation should not be made for property of insignificant value, but be directed toward more valuable assets.[761]

This limiting criterion that the criminal activity must not be considered insignificant was removed from the current legislation in 2016. However, at the same time, some new criteria were added to Chapter 10 Section 3 in the Finnish Criminal Code by the national legislator. A court shall thus, alongside other circumstances, in particular consider whether the property originates from other criminal activities than the criminal activity which can be considered insignificant. Furthermore, it shall be considered whether it is necessary to impose a confiscation order in order to prevent new criminal offences or if a

---

759 *Regeringens proposition till Riksdagen med förslag till revidering av lagstiftningen om förverkandepåföljder*, RP 80/2000, p. 18. 100 Finnish marks correspond to €16.81 (on 24.1.2017).

760 *Regeringens proposition till Riksdagen med förslag till lagar om ändring av 10 kap. i strafflagen och av 6 och 7 kap. i tvångsmedelslagen*, RP 4/2016 rd, p. 15.

761 See further Section 3, *Regeringens proposition till Riksdagen med förslag till revidering av lagstiftningen om förverkandepåföljder*, RP 80/2000.

significant part of the person's income has been repeatedly obtained through criminal activity. The legislative works state as a guiding principle that property valued at under €1,000 is not necessarily to be regarded as property which derives from criminal activities which cannot be considered insignificant.[762] It remains to be seen how the Finnish courts will apply the provision on extended confiscation in light of these new restrictions. The discretion left to the courts is in this respect rather wide.

6.3.2. THE BURDEN OF PROOF

Under the Finnish system the prosecutor must prove that the requirements for extended confiscation are fulfilled and shall present the circumstances which indicate that certain property has an illegal origin. Thereafter a reversal of the burden of proof operates. In order to prevent confiscation *the defendant must render probable* that the assets have a legal origin. This is provided for by Chapter 10 Section 9 Subsection 4 of the Finnish Criminal Code.[763]

Under the legal provision that was in force before the change of legislation in 2016, the prosecutor had the burden of proof to show that there was reason to believe ("*skäl att anta*") that the property in question was fully or partially derived from criminal activity. There was thus a lowered burden of proof for the prosecution. Earlier proposals for the adoption of a reversed burden of proof, obligating a defendant to show probable that the assets in question did not derive from criminal activity, were not accepted by the Finnish Parliament.[764] The Finnish Government has, though, not given up on this issue, and in its national action plan for the years of 2012–2015 against financial criminality the need for a reconsideration of the issue was emphasised.[765] In 2016, a reform thus succeeded and a reversal of the burden of proof on the defendant was finally introduced.

---

762 See further *Regeringens proposition till Riksdagen med förslag till lagar om ändring av 10 kap. i strafflagen och av 6 och 7 kap. i tvångsmedelslagen*, RP 4/2016 rd, pp. 38–40.

763 See further *Regeringens proposition till Riksdagen med förslag till lagar om ändring av 10 kap. i strafflagen och av 6 och 7 kap. i tvångsmedelslagen*, RP 4/2016 rd, pp. 15 and 43–44.

764 Compare *Regeringens proposition till Riksdagen med förslag till revidering av lagstiftningen om förverkandepåföljder*, RP 80/2000 rd, pp. 11, 17 and 19 and *Regeringens proposition till Riksdagen med förslag till lagar om ändring av 10 kap. i strafflagen och av 6 och 7 kap. i tvångsmedelslagen*, RP 4/2016 rd, p. 5.

765 See para. 18, *Effektiviserat åtgärdsprogram för bekämpning av grå ekonomi och ekonomisk brottslighet 2012–2015*, Statsrådet 19.1.2012.

CHAPTER 7

DIRECTIVE 2014/42/EU: A REFORM WITH SIGNIFICANT LEGAL CHANGES?

7.1. THE NECESSITY OF A NEW EU INSTRUMENT ON CONFISCATION

At the adoption of Directive 2014/42/EU, the EU legislator primarily argued that the national and international confiscation regimes were "underdeveloped and underutilised".[766] This conclusion was reached even though it was admitted during the legislative procedure that only limited statistical evidence is available for the actual confiscation practices.[767] In Recital (4) of Directive 2014/42/EU it is therefore stated that the amounts recovered from proceeds of crime in the Union *seem* insufficient compared to the *estimated* proceeds.[768] It can be questioned whether it is acceptable that the Union legislator justifies a new instrument with stronger confiscation powers on such a poor statistical basis.[769] In fact, if the instruments on confiscation presently in force have been "poorly

---

[766] Compare Section 2.2 above.

[767] In fact, the researchers who performed a study by *Matrix* commissioned by the European Commission on the effectiveness of the confiscation systems in the EU had to abandon their original intention to review operational statistics and recommend ways of measuring effectiveness. The main reason was that there were no sufficient statistical records in the Member States. The conclusion from the study was that this circumstance makes it very difficult to diagnose and remedy system defects. See *Assessing the Effectiveness of EU Member States' Practices in the Identification, Tracing, Freezing and Confiscation of Criminal Assets*, Final Report 2009, p. 12.

[768] Already in 2006, it was argued by *Vettori* within the framework of a study of the confiscation practices in the Member States that there is very little quantitative and qualitative information on how confiscation provisions are enforced within the Union. Accordingly, there was a lack of a significant platform for analysis. See further B. Vettori, *Tough on Criminal Wealth: Exploring the Practice of Proceeds from Crime Confiscation in the EU*, Springer, 2006, p. XI and pp. 13–21.

[769] See for a similar conclusion, the *European Criminal Bar Association* (ECBA), Statement on the proposal for a directive, p. 3, available at: http:77www.ecba.org/extdocserv/2012 10assetseizureECBAstatement.pdf, and *Bundesrechtsanwaltskammer*, Stellungnahme Nr. 38/2012, pp. 2–4. For a general discussion of the evidence base in EU criminal policy, see W. de Bondt, "Evidence Based EU Criminal Policy Making: In Search of Matching Data" (2014) 20 *European Journal on Criminal Policy and Research*, pp. 23–49.

implemented" and seldom used in the Member States, it is quite difficult to argue that the existing rules are insufficient *per se*.[770] In this respect one must agree with the German *Bundesrechtsanwaltskammer*:

> Es wäre ohne weiteres möglich, in den Mitgliedstaaten Daten dazu zu erheben, welche Erträge aus Straftaten dort anfallen und in welcher Höhe diese Erträge eingezogen werden. Dass dies in der Vergangenheit nicht geschehen ist, berechtigt die Kommission nicht dazu, allein aufgrund eines gefühlten Defizits eine neue Maßnahme vorzuschlagen. Mangels Daten ist in keiner Weise feststellbar, ob die Maßnahme überhaupt erforderlich und damit verhältnismäßig ist.[771]

The difficulties in assessing the real extent of what criminal proceeds are actually being confiscated with the EU in the area of organised crime were further confirmed in the OCP project (Organised Crime Portfolio), which was funded with support from the European Commission. This research project published its final report in 2015, and *inter alia* concluded that the lack of statistics as well as the differences among the confiscation regimes make it almost impossible to assess and compare the extent of the recovery of criminal assets and to produce a solid statistical analysis.[772]

The European Commission is, on the other hand, aware of the shortcomings regarding a reliable statistical basis, and the Member States have been obligated in Article 11 of the new directive to collect and forward certain statistical data.[773] This is to be welcomed in order to permit a proper evaluation of the confiscation practices in the future.[774] However, it is important to underline that even if sufficient statistics on confiscation measures in different Member States had been kept, a proper analysis of the *underlying reasons for a sparing utilisation* would also have been necessary. In fact, there may be other explanations for the difficulties in practice than any shortcomings of the national and international legislative instruments. A study of confiscation practices within the EU in 2009, for example, concluded that law enforcement agencies in different Member

---

770 See generally on the difficulties to implement international standards at national level particularily when it comes to overcoming internal obstacles, P. Faraldo Cabana, "Improving the Recovery of Assets Resulting from Organised Crime" (2014) 22 *European Journal of Crime, Criminal Law and Criminal Justice*, pp. 13–32.

771 *Bundesrechtsanwaltskammer*, Stellungnahme Nr. 38/2012, p. 3.

772 See further E. Savona and M. Riccardi (eds.), *From Illegal Markets to Legitimate Businesses: the Portfolio of Organised Crime in Europe*, Final Report of Project OCP (Organised Crime Portfolio), Trento, 2015, especially pp. 15–17 and Chapter 10.

773 Compare Recitals (36)–(37) of Directive 2014/42/EU. This obligation of the states was however limited in some respects in comparison to the original proposal from the European Commission, as several Member States argued that it would lead to unreasonably high costs. Compare Article 11, COM(2012) 85 final.

774 The inquiry on extended confiscation practices in Sweden in 2015 (compare Section 5.1 above) also met certain problems regarding the statistics kept by the Swedish authorities, see SOU 2015:67 pp. 63–64.

States are often *sceptical per se* about the *value* of criminal asset recovery.[775] The underlying reasons for such scepticism or a poor usage in practice may of course derive from complicated rules on confiscation, but there may also be other reasons, for example the additional workload which follows from financial investigations. The development of asset confiscation measures has presented "a paradigm shift" in the criminal justice systems, and it seems that the law enforcement authorities sometimes prefer to remain focused upon their traditional roles.[776] This has, for example, been seen in the Swedish, German and English practice.[777] As rightly argued, it is not sufficient that the legislator establishes a legislative framework, but real implementation plans must also be given regarding training for the public officials and sufficient human and material resources.[778]

Consequently, a study of the confiscation measures in *daily practice* must not be neglected, as it can show that there may be other factors which have influenced the efficiency of confiscation measures in different States. An increase in the use of national provisions on confiscation can, for example, be achieved by measures targeting the practice of the law enforcement agencies. In Sweden, certain guidelines have in this respect been issued which focus on the issue of confiscation in daily practice.[779] Furthermore, the *incentive* for law enforcement authorities to use the instrument of confiscation can be influenced by how the confiscated assets are disposed of. In States where the law enforcement agency receives all or a part of the assets collected, the confiscation scheme may be more attractive.[780] In the same way, rules on asset sharing of confiscated property between States in cross-border cases may stimulate international cooperation.

Against this background, the argument is not fully convincing that a new directive was needed in order to remedy the situation that the confiscation regimes are not being sufficiently utilised in the Member States.[781] Further,

---

775 See *Assessing the Effectiveness of EU Member States' Practices in the Identification, Tracing, Freezing and Confiscation of Criminal Assets*, Final Report 2009, p. 12. The same conclusion was drawn by Vettori within her study of the EU States in 2006, see Vettori, n 768 above, pp. 114 and 119.

776 *Study for an Impact Assessment on a Proposal for a New Legal Framework on the Confiscation and Recovery of Criminal Assets*, RAND Europe, 2012, p. xvii.

777 Compare Sections 5.5.6, 4.1, 4.4.1 and Section 3.6.1 above.

778 Faraldo Cabana, n 770 above, pp. 23–24.

779 See Section 5.5.6 above.

780 However, at the same time certain drawbacks of such a system are highlighted in Section 3.6.7 above, which analyses the confiscation regime in England and Wales, where the law enforcement agencies receive a part of the assets collected. See for a general discussion of refunding the law enforcement agencies, G. Stessens, *Money Laundering; A New International Law Enforcement Model*, Cambridge University Press, 2000, pp. 56–58. On the disposal policy of confiscated assets in the EU, see Center for the Study of Democracy, *Disposal of Confiscated Assets in the EU Member States, Laws and Practices*, 2014.

781 It can however be noted that the European Commission also argued that a new directive was needed in view of the importance to create binding rules on third party confiscation

harmonisation in the area of criminal law remains a sensitive matter for the Member States. The EU is, according to Article 5(3) TEU, only entitled to act if the proposed action cannot be sufficiently achieved by the Member States (i.e. the "principle of subsidiarity"). The Union legislator here claimed to be "better placed than individual Member States" to regulate this area, because confiscation is an important tool to combat organised crime "which is very often transnational in nature" and needs to be tackled on a common basis.[782] This argument in particular seems peculiar against the background that the specific link to organised crime in the current EU instrument has been removed.

In any case, the directive is based on Articles 83(1) and 82(2) TFEU. These provisions allow for the adoption of directives regarding "sanctions in the areas of particularly serious crime with a cross border dimension" and in specific areas of criminal procedure "to the extent necessary to facilitate mutual recognition of judgments and judicial decisions". It has been argued by some that the suggested legal basis under Article 82(2) TFEU is erroneous because there are no provisions in relation to mutual recognition.[783] However, an important aim of the new directive has been to enhance and facilitate mutual recognition by abolishing the various different legal approaches in national legislation to extended confiscation. This is in fact a convincing argument for the necessity of harmonising EU measures in this area. On the other hand, it can be questioned whether a similar effect could not have been achieved by abolishing the unfortunate link between national provisions and the duty to execute foreign confiscation orders? Accordingly, the particular refusal ground in the mutual recognition instrument could have been removed.

A more general issue which must be discussed in the context of the necessity of a new EU instrument concerns the *legislative technique* as such. Directive 2014/42/EU will *only partly* replace the current EU-instruments in the area of confiscation, as the directive is limited to certain offences. Accordingly, FD 2005/212/JHA will remain in force for all criminal offences punishable by deprivation of liberty for more than one year (Article 2).[784] This follows from the limited competence of the EU to harmonise in the area of all kinds of criminal

and non-conviction based confiscation. See Commission Staff Working Paper, *Accompanying Document to the Proposal for a Directive of the European Parliament and the Council on the Freezing and Confiscation of Proceeds of Crime in the European Union, SWD (2012) 31 final*, Brussels 12.3.2012, pp. 16–17.

782 COM(2012) 85 final, p. 8.

783 See p. 2 in the statement of the proposal for a new directive on confiscation from the *European Criminal Bar Association*, at http:77www.ecba.org/extdocserv/201210assetseizureECBAstatement.pdf. The association of German judges is also sceptical towards the suggested legal basis for EU action, see *Stellungnahme des Deutschen Richterbundes zum Vorschlag für eine Richtlinie des Europäischen Parlaments und des Rates über die Sicherstellung und Einziehung von Erträgen aus Straftaten in der Europäischen Union*, COM(2012) 85, Nr. 23/12, August 2012, p. 3.

784 See Section 2.3.1 above.

offences. From the practitioner's point of view difficulties may arise, because there might be different criteria for confiscation in one case depending on which offence is being handled. This may occur in cases already today, but it may be expected that such situations will increase as a result of the proposal.[785] The lack of coherence of EU legislation may therefore actually hinder an efficient application of the instruments in practice and lead to a fragmentation of the rules. *Eurojust* has, for example, argued that the difficulties which practitioners could encounter in applying such a "multi-fold fragmented legal framework" should not be underestimated.[786] Accordingly, it is not evident that the new directive will fulfill its general aim to *simplify* the existing rules.

In this chapter, I will discuss whether the provisions of Directive 2014/42/EU may lead to the expected changes of the national confiscation regimes. First, however, it addresses some general challenges for the EU legislator when new legislation is drafted in this area.

7.2. THE CHALLENGES TO A MORE HARMONISED EU REGIME

A common statement is that effective confiscation measures are hindered by the differences regarding substantive and procedural provisions between the Member States.[787] Different legislative schemes for extended confiscation have been shown above in Chapters 3–6. In general, differences may, for example, be noted in the following areas:

- the triggering offences for extended confiscation,
- the assets which may be confiscated,
- the division of the burden of proof,
- the standard of proof,
- monetary- or time-limits for confiscation,
- requirements of a criminal lifestyle,
- the scope of procedural safeguards for the person affected,

785 See in *Stellungnahme des Deutschen Richterbundes zum Vorschlag für eine Richtlinie des Europäischen Parlaments und des Rates über die Sicherstellung und Einziehung von Erträgen aus Straftaten in der Europäischen Union*, COM(2012) 85, Nr. 23/12, August 2012, pp. 1–2 and D. Brodowski, "Strafrechtsrelevante Entwicklungen in der Europäischen Union - ein Überblick" (2012) 11 *ZIS*, pp. 558, pp. 563–64.

786 *Eurojust's Opinion on the Proposal of the European Commission for a Directive on the Freezing and Confiscation of Proceeds of Crime in the European Union*, 2012, pp. 5–6.

787 See for example Recital (8) in Directive 2014/42/EU and *Eurojust Annual Report 2010*, p. 30, available at: www.eurojust.org. Compare also *Commission Staff Working Paper, Accompanying Document to the Proposal for a Directive of the European Parliament and the Council on the Freezing and Confiscation of Proceeds of Crime in the European Union*, SWD(2012) 31 final, Brussels 12.3.2012, pp. 16–17.

- the availability of a hardship clause, and/or
- the scope for third party confiscation.[788]

In addition, there are not only differences in legislation, but also in *general approaches* to the measure of confiscation.[789] There are, for example, different views on the legal character of the measure. In most States a penal character is denied and confiscation is instead seen as a special consequence or measure with a preventive aim,[790] but there are also States, for example France and Belgium, which view confiscation as a sanction of a penal character.[791] In some States (for example Sweden and Germany) extended confiscation is used subsidiarily to ordinary confiscation,[792] whereas according to the English system the first main issue for the court to decide is whether a defendant has a *criminal lifestyle* which triggers its provisions on extended confiscation.[793]

Shifting approaches to the importance of powerful national confiscation legislation have different explanations. It may, *inter alia*, be influenced by the character of criminality within States. One underlying reason for the far-reaching approach towards proceeds of crime in the UK is, for example, the importance of London as a centre for the global banking sector and the threat of money

788 For a comparative analysis of the confiscation regimes in the Member States in the EU, see European Commission, JUST/2011/JPEN/PR/0153/A4, *Comparative Law Study of the Implementation of Mutual Recognition of Orders to Freeze and Confiscate Criminal Assets in the European Union*, Final Finding Report. See also Vettori, n 768 above and the project on Bulgaria, Romania and Italy which is presented in the Report, *Legislation Meets Practice: National and European Perspectives in Confiscation and Forfeiture of Assets*, Transparency International, 2015.

789 See generally *Assessing the Effectiveness of EU Member States' Practices in the Identification, Tracing, Freezing and Confiscation of Criminal Assets*, Final Report 2009 and *Study for an Impact Assessment on a Proposal for a New Legal Framework on the Confiscation and Recovery of Criminal Assets*, RAND Europe, 2012. For an overview on some national legislation and systems for confiscation, compare M. Kilchling, "Comparative Perspectives on Forfeiture Legislation in Europe and the United States" (1997) 5 *European Journal of Crime, Criminal Law and Criminal Justice*, pp. 314–33 and M. Kilchling, "Tracing, Seizing and Confiscating Proceeds from Corruption (and other Illegal Conduct) within or outside the Criminal Justice System" (2001) 9 *European Journal of Crime, Criminal Law and Criminal Justice*, pp. 264–80, as well as Directorate-General for Internal Policies, Policy Department Citizens' Rights and Constitutional Affairs, *The Need for New EU Legislation Allowing the Assets Confiscated from Criminal Organisations to be used for Civil Society and in particular for Social Purposes*, 2012. For numerous references to national law and a discussion of different models of asset recovery, see also F. Meyer, "'Reformiert die Rückgewinnungshilfe!' – Denkanstöße für eine Generalüberholung der Vermögensabschöpfung" (2015) 2 *ZStW*, pp. 241–83.

790 Compare for example Section 5.2 on Sweden or Section 4.2 on Germany above.

791 See for example *Proposal for a Directive of the European Parliament and the Council on the Freezing and Confiscation of Proceeds of Crime in the European Union, Compilation of Replies to Questionnaire*, 12219/2/12, REV 2, Brussels 20.7.2012, p. 3 and 63. See also Kilchling, n 789 above, pp. 270–71.

792 See Section 5.3.1 and Section 4.3.1 above.

793 See Section 3.3.2 above.

laundering.[794] Considering that powers of extended confiscation have primarily been developed as a measure to fight organised crime, it is obvious that in States with a high percentage of such criminality (for example Italy), the development of more far-reaching confiscation regimes has been more evident.[795] The rate of organised crime is, however, not *per se* a decisive factor for how advancedly the national legislation on confiscation is drafted. Some of the Scandinavian States (with a lower rate of organised crime) have also developed relatively strict confiscation regimes.[796]

More important factors to explain different national approaches to confiscation are fundamental differences in the criminal justice systems and the legal culture of States, which lead to differences in the choice of law enforcement measures to be utilised. If a State, for example, has got advanced forms of non-conviction-based confiscation measures, the use of extended confiscation may in practice be less important.[797] The same may be the case if criminalisation is used in order to target situations in which other States use extended confiscation.[798] An example is France which has – in addition to provisions on extended confiscation – criminalised the very ownership of unjustified assets or sustaining a lifestyle without being able to justify its origins. This law criminalises persons who have regular relations with persons who commit serious criminal offences.[799] Furthermore, as is pointed out in the *Study for an Impact Assessment*, the design of general procedural rules may also influence the national scope of extended

---

794 N. Ryder, "To Confiscate or not to Confiscate? A Comparative Analysis of the Confiscation of the Proceeds of Crime Legislation in the United States and the United Kingdom" (2013) 8 *Journal of Business Law*, pp. 767, pp. 784–86.

795 A specific feature of the Italian system is the so-called "preventive" or precautionary confiscation regime, which is separate from the criminal proceedings and operates regardless of a criminal conviction by the court. This special regime for non-conviction-based confiscation concerns persons listed in the so-called *Anti-mafia Code*. Compare *Illicit Assets Recovery in Italy, Enhancing Integrity and Effectiveness of Illegal Asset Confiscation*, Transparency International Italia, 2013, pp. 11–12, A.M. Maugeri, "The Criminal Sanctions against the Illicit Proceeds of Criminal Organisations" (2012) 3 *New Journal of European Criminal Law*, p. 257, pp. 275–78 and R. Polidori, "General Overview and Critical Analysis of Italian Preventive Measures and ECtHR Case Law" (2016) 4 *Journal of Law and Criminal Justice*, pp. 97–106.

796 See for example the systems in Norway and Denmark, Sections 6.1 and 6.2 above.

797 States may also use powerful money laundering legislation to complement confiscation measures. One example of such a State is the UK. See further *Study for an Impact Assessment on a Proposal for a New Legal Framework on the Confiscation and Recovery of Criminal Assets*, RAND Europe, 2012, p. 46.

798 Compare the proposal made from the *European Commission* in 2008 to create a new criminal offence for owning "unjustified" assets, *Communication from the Commission to the European Parliament and the Council, Proceeds of Organised Crime; Ensuring that "Crime does not Pay"*, 20.11.2008, COM(2008) 766 final, pp. 6–7.

799 The offence of "illicit enrichment" is punishable by three years' imprisonment and a €75,000 fine. See Arts. 321–326 of the Criminal Code Law No. 2006-64 of 23 January 2006. The legislation has been challenged before the ECtHR, see *Aboufadda v. France*, Appl. No. 28457/10, Decision on 4 November 2014. This case is described in Section 7.4.2 below.

confiscation and the criteria for proving illicit origin. Evidence gathering may, for example, be easier in a State with strong coercive measures for the law enforcement agencies during the investigative stage, and accordingly there may be less need for a lowered burden of proof regarding the matter of confiscation. The same applies to differences in the rules of evidence. Evidentiary problems may be expected to be higher in States where there are strict rules of evidence. As a consequence, the view on which evidentiary standard is to be chosen may vary.[800]

Consequently, national differences and approaches may be problematic for the EU legislator, whose aim is to create the most harmonised confiscation regime possible. The *underlying reasons* for specific features in the legal systems of the Member States are, however, seldom taken into full consideration within the EU when new instruments are prepared and negotiated. Often it seems to be argued that "new" legislation is always a good cure for any malfunctioning of the old ones. However, it is obvious that the Member States have different needs of legislative changes both when it comes to the necessity of a new confiscation directive (at all), and also when it comes to which changes are brought. The States simply expect different things to be achieved. This was, for example, evident during the negotiations of Directive 2014/42/EU in the Council and the European Parliament. It is also paradoxically shown by fact that the UK and Denmark – which already have rather developed confiscation laws – have chosen not to be bound by Directive 2014/42/EU.

Furthermore, there is another challenge when certain substantive criteria for confiscation are harmonised in order to create strong powers for law enforcement agencies. Within the domestic systems, the national legislator has adopted such provisions as are necessary to maintain the delicate balance between law-enforcement powers and the respect for fundamental human rights. Consequently, it can be complicated to draft an EU instrument which is neither too general with little effect in practice, nor risks violating fundamental rights within Member States. Ambitiously drafted instruments by the European Commission are therefore often "watered down" during the negotiations in the Council, or lead to poor implementation practices by the States. Especially in the area of confiscation, there are several complicated legal problems which have proved to be difficult to solve *within* States, for example regarding the standard of proof. The task of creating a *European approach* and providing for harmonised definitions and a uniform application is thus challenging. On the same ground, it may be expected that it will be a difficult task for the CJEU in the future to solve potential questions on the interpretation of the new Directive and its compliance with the EU Charter on Fundamental Rights and the ECHR.

800 *Study for an Impact Assessment on a Proposal for a New Legal Framework on the Confiscation and Recovery of Criminal Assets*, RAND Europe, 2012, pp. 45–46.

In what follows, the legislative changes which have been brought to the regime of extended confiscation by Directive 2014/42/EU will be analysed. The differences in relation to the present regulation of FD 2005/212/JHA are thereby highlighted. The original *Proposal for a Directive from the European Commission* will be referred to in order to illustrate in which areas the directive has been "watered down" as a result of negotiations. A number of proposals which were dropped in the legislative process will be discussed and some requirements or legal criteria found in national legislation will be highlighted. In this respect, it can be observed that the legislation in the UK and Denmark will also be included although they will not be bound by the new directive. In order to simplify an understanding of the analysis, the provision on extended confiscation in FD 2005/212/JHA and in Directive 2014/42/EU is viewable in the following table:

Art. 3(2) FD 2005/212/JHA:	**Art. 5(1) Directive 2014/42/EU:**
Each Member State shall take the necessary measures to enable confiscation under this article at least: (a) where a national court based on specific facts is fully convinced that the property in question has been derived from criminal activities of the convicted person during a period prior to conviction for the offence referred to in paragraph 1 which is deemed reasonable by the court in the circumstances of the particular case, or, alternatively, (b) where a national court based on specific facts is fully convinced that the property in question has been derived from similar criminal activities of the convicted person during a period prior to conviction for the offence referred to in paragraph 1 which is deemed reasonable by the court in the circumstances of the particular case, or, alternatively, (c) where it is established that the value of the property is disproportionate to the lawful income of the convicted person and a national court based on specific facts is fully convinced that the property in question has been derived from the criminal activity of that convicted person.	Member States shall adopt the necessary measures to enable the confiscation, either in whole or in part, of property belonging to a person convicted of a criminal offence which is liable to give rise, directly or indirectly, to economic benefit, where a court, on the basis of the circumstances of the case, including the specific facts and available evidence, such as that the value of the property is disproportionate to the lawful income of the convicted person, is satisfied that the property in question is derived from criminal conduct.

7.3. TRIGGERING OFFENCES AND THE SCOPE OF DIRECTIVE 2014/42/EU

Directive 2014/42/EU has increased the scope for extended confiscation and applies to more crimes than FD 2005/212/JHA. As described in Section 2.3.3

above, the directive has abolished the link to the framework of a criminal organisation or terrorism, and provides that extended confiscation must be available at least for certain expressly listed offences, and for such offences in Article 3 Directive 2014/42/EU which are punishable (under an EU instrument or national law) by a custodial sentence of a maximum of *at least four years*. This means a change of legislation in many Member States, as more offences must be added to the list of triggering offences. This especially concerns the last mentioned group of criminal offences with a maximum custodial sentence of *at least four years'* imprisonment. The threshold in FD 2005/212/JHA is set at triggering offences with a maximum of at least between 5 and 10 years of imprisonment (with the exception of the offence of money laundering).

When it comes to the change in terms of the abolished link between extended confiscation and organised crime/terrorism, it can be concluded that many Member States have not limited the scope of the national legislation in this respect anyway.[801] However, for States like Germany it will mean a significant extension of the legislation, as the original aim of the national legislator has been to direct this measure towards criminal offences which are typically committed in the area of organised criminality.[802]

Like FD 2005/212/JHA, Directive 2014/42/EU restricts the scope by requiring that a triggering offence must be liable to give rise, directly or indirectly, to *economic benefit*. Such a requirement was originally lacking in the *Proposal for a Directive from the European Commission*, but was reintroduced during the negotiations. This criterion is reflected in many provisions currently available in national legislation, and is important in order to direct confiscation orders to offences which are capable of giving financial gain.[803] In such a way, the assumption is substantiated that a defendant may have committed other offences with a financial motive and therefore might possess assets of criminal origin.

The general scope of Directive 2014/42/EU was widely debated in the negotiations within the Council. The *Proposal for a Directive from the European Commission* was, for example, more widely drafted, applying to *all offences covered by the directive* and was not limited to particularly serious offences. This was criticised by, for example the European Union Agency for Fundamental Rights ("FRA"), which argued that while Article 83(1) TFEU specifies areas of serious crime; this does not mean that every single crime falling in these areas necessarily forms a particularly serious offence. Against this background, the proposal was considered disproportionate in this respect.[804] As a result of the

---

801 See for example Sweden (Section 5.3.2 above) or England and Wales (Section 3.4.1 above).

802 See further Sections 4.3.2, 4.4.3 and 4.4.4 above.

803 See for example, above, Sweden (Section 5.3.2), Norway (Section 6.1), Denmark (Section 6.2) and Finland (Section 6.3).

804 *Opinion of the European Union Agency for Fundamental Rights on the Confiscation of Proceeds of Crime*, FRA 03/2012, Vienna 4.12.2012, pp. 13–14.

negotiations the provision was thus in a first step changed into applying only to "serious" criminal offences.[805] However, this was not considered as sufficient and finally Article 5 was further limited in the way described above applying only to certain specifically listed offences and to offences with a certain penalty scale.

There were also other suggestions being made during the legislative process in order to especially *single out the triggering offences* so that the scope of the directive would be more restricted. As an example may be mentioned that FRA proposed that specific elements should be introduced in order to substantiate and corroborate the assumption that other assets in the possession of the offender stem from criminality similar to the triggering offence. In this way, not every triggering offence would qualify, but rather only offences which were particularly serious. It was suggested that extended confiscation would be restricted to situations:

> where such a court has sufficient evidence to assume that the offence was not committed as a singular event but only forms an instance in a series of similar offences, which the offender commits for a living or at least for recurrent gains amounting, over a certain period of time, to significant additional income.[806]

The suggestion to limit the triggering offences to offences committed on a *systematic basis* was not adopted in the EU instrument. However, in some States, the present legislation on extended confiscation is drafted in a way to single out persons who commit crime on a multiple basis or have a criminal lifestyle.[807]

The *Proposal for a Directive from the European Commission* had, however, one requirement which would have limited the scope for extended confiscation by a further qualification of the triggering offences. Article 4 in the proposal required that the property in question had derived from *similar* criminal activities.[808] This type of limiting requirement may, for example, be found in Article 3(2)(b) FD 2005/212/JHA. The criterion was, however, removed from the text during the negotiations, and Article 5 of Directive 2014/42/EU simply states that the property in question shall be "derived from criminal conduct". During the legislative process other approaches were also considered in order to limit the scope for extended confiscation. The introduction of a criterion based on an economic benefit filter was, for example, suggested, but was not considered sufficient to guarantee that the powers are only used in specific

---

805 See *Proposal for a Directive of the European Parliament and of the Council on the Freezing and Confiscation of Proceeds of Crime in the European Union*, General Approach, Council Document 17117/12, 3.12.2012, p. 17.

806 *Opinion of the European Union Agency for Fundamental Rights on the Confiscation of Proceeds of Crime*, FRA 03/2012, Vienna 4.12.2012, p. 14.

807 See for example England and Wales (Section 3.4.1 above) or the Norwegian legislation (Section 6.1.1 above).

808 Compare COM(2012) 85 final, p. 20.

(serious) cases.[809] The EU legislation thus does not limit the measure of extended confiscation to any monetary value of assets. Neither FD 2005/212/JHA nor Directive 2014/42/EU contains any rules in this respect. In contrast hereto restrictions in terms of the value of assets are found in some national legislation. As an example may be mentioned some provisions of the legislation in England and Wales, which require relevant benefit of not less than £5,000.[810] Other national legislation (for example the Swedish) does not contain any such limits at all.[811] Obviously, the legislative changes necessary in the Member States in order to implement Directive 2014/42/EU vary depending on the scope of the national regimes.

A general issue of interest is whether the particular group of defendants to be targeted with a measure of extended confiscation under Directive 2014/42/EU may be justified. As stated above, extended confiscation was originally restricted to cases where a presumption could be justified that if a defendant had committed a certain type of criminality, it could be inferred that also other offences have been committed and that any assets derive from such prior criminality. Against this background, it can be argued that the justification for such presumptions is weakened if the measure is increasingly being used for more and more triggering offences. Accordingly, it is of crucial importance – also within the Union – to discuss in which cases such intrusive powers are justified in order to prevent an unreasonable "expansion". As been rightly argued in the context of POCA 2002 "the small fry are simply easier to catch" and one must be cautious of a "process of net widening in which all sorts of trivial offenders are caught up".[812] When an express link to organised criminality is abandoned, some other restricting requirements may in fact be necessary.

As is seen in Chapters 3–6 above, there are different ways used in the national regimes to further classify the triggering offences and limit the scope for extended confiscation. Some States, for example, justify the financial investigations of certain defendants by setting up a condition that the triggering offences in question have been committed on a multiple or systematic basic. In England and Wales, it is for example argued that the motive for concentrating the application of the domestic legislation on the central decisive issue of establishing a *criminal lifestyle* is that such tests are designed to identify offenders who may be regarded as normally living off crime.[813] As described above, some proposals

809 See *Proposal for a Directive of the European Parliament and the Council on the Freezing and Confiscation of Proceeds of Crime in the European Union, State of Play and Orientation Debate*, 14826/12, Brussels 16.10.2012, p. 3.

810 See Section 3.4.1.

811 This is critically discussed in Section 5.5.1.

812 J. Lea, "Hitting Criminals Where It Hurts: Organised Crime and the Erosion of Due Process" (2004) 35 *Cambrian Law Review*, pp. 81, p. 88.

813 Explanatory Notes to POCA 2002, p. 23.

to set up limiting requirements in this respect were decided against during the negotiations of the new EU directive. The suitability of providing for more restrictive requirements for extended confiscation in order to exclude trivial triggering offences or offences committed on a one-off basis have been touched upon in Section 5.5.2 above. Against this background, I will here restrict myself to some general comments on the issue from the EU perspective.

It has, for example, been argued by Boucht that as extended confiscation is mainly justified by the threat of organised crime, this should also be "mirrored at EU level" in the sense that access to the measure is limited to this category of criminality. He is of the opinion that the general target area of the measure ought to be limited to offences committed within a criminal organisation as well as to habitually committed offences with the purpose to achieve gain. At EU level the provision "should probably only address the first type", because the Union is mainly concerned with "transitional crime".[814] I tend to agree to the extent that it is of significant importance that extended confiscation stays a measure of limited use, preferably *subsidiary* to an order for ordinary confiscation. It should not expand to become "the normal use". One must therefore be cautious and develop the measure in a legitimate and proportionate way in compliance of human rights law. As a general principle such a far-reaching measure must be reserved for cases where the criminal offence committed by a defendant in some way indicates previous criminal activity.

This being said, it is also to be acknowledged that it is indeed quite difficult to construct such requirements (especially in the EU legislative context). The requirement that an offence is to be committed within the framework of a criminal organisation is complicated, because there is no clear common definition of this[815] and some States do not domestically use such classifications at all.[816] In addition, there are often significant difficulties in practice in proving that a criminal offence has been committed within or is linked to a criminal organisation. On a national level, it has also been difficult to construct and apply reasonable requirements that offenders are living a "criminal lifestyle" or have committed crimes on a "systematic basis" or "habitually". As an example may be mentioned the criticism against the legislation in England and Wales discussed in Sections 3.6.1 and 3.6.2 above.

Against this background, it is vital that there is at least a *high custodial threshold* for triggering the scheme on extended confiscation in the first place.

814 J. Boucht, "Extended Confiscation and the Proposed Directive on Freezing and Confiscation of Criminal Proceeds in the EU: On Striking a Balance between Efficiency, Fairness and Legal Certainty" (2013) 21 *European Journal of Crime, Criminal Law and Criminal Justice*, p. 127, pp. 141–43 and 160.

815 See on this, L. Paoli, "How to Tackle (Organized) Crime in Europe? The EU Policy Cycle on Serious and Organized Crime and the New Emphasis on Harm" (2014) 22 *European Journal of Crime, Criminal Law and Criminal Justice*, p. 1, pp. 2–3.

816 See for example Sweden, Sec. 5.3.2.

From this perspective it can be questioned whether the limit of a maximum sentence of at least four years in Directive 2014/42/EU is really appropriate. If the instrument is successively expanded so that every culpable or loathsome criminal offence can classify as a triggering offence, the compatibility of the extended confiscation regime with the right of property is weakened. It is not obvious that legislation which allows for far-reaching forms of extended confiscation regarding all types of criminal offences will be considered as compliant with the human rights *acquis*.[817] An important guarantee for a reasonable and a fair application of the EU scheme is in this respect also that the domestic courts are allowed certain discretion in the form of a hardship rule. This is further discussed in Section 7.6 below.

7.4. THE ESTABLISHMENT OF ILLEGAL ORIGIN

7.4.1. SOME SPECIAL SUPPORTIVE LEGISLATIVE CRITERIA

There are various legislative criteria which may be used in order to establish that certain assets have an illegal origin. An aim of Directive 2014/42/EU has been to harmonise the national provisions and to simplify the EU regulation currently in force. Thereby the three alternative solutions for the formulation of national legislation in FD 2005/212/JHA have been abolished. In practice, the Member States have based their national legislation on one of these alternatives or on a combination of several of them. In addition, other criteria to support the establishment of illegal origin are used in national legislation and/or case-law.

The *Proposal for a Directive from the European Commission* did not specify any specific criteria for the design of the domestic legislation in this respect, but simply listed certain significant supportive circumstances in Recital (10).[818] This was criticised in the legislative process and especially the criterion referred to in Article 3(2)(c) FD 2005/212/JHA about disproportionate financial circumstances was omitted from the proposal. The European Economic and Social Committee (EESC) for example argued that this factor has decisive importance in those national laws that are the most advanced in terms of the fight against organised crime.[819] FRA held that an express requirement to establish a marked disparity between the lawful income of an offender and his or her property was especially called for. This was necessary in order to justify the necessity of confiscation, and would further give more detailed guidance for the courts in relation to the

817 Compare on this, Section 7.4.2 below.

818 Compare Art. 4 (which only stated "based on specific facts"), COM(2012) 85 final.

819 Section 4.4.2, *Opinion of the European Economic and Social Committee on the proposal for a Directive*, *OJ* C 299, 4.10.2012, pp. 128–132, at p. 131.

evidentiary standard.[820] Such views prevailed in the discussions in the Council, and Article 5 Directive 2014/42/EU now provides that the Court shall base its decision on the circumstances of the case "including the specific facts and available evidence, such as that the value of the property is disproportionate to the lawful income of the convicted person".

Some Member States have set up certain time-limits prior to conviction within which assets acquired may be considered as being derived from illegal sources. The legislative options of (a) and (b) in Article 3(2) FD 2005/212/JHA provide that national legislation may set such time-limits in order to identify the period within which to assess the property as well as the criminal activities of a convicted person. There are thus limitations in some national legislation regarding the assets which may be the object of confiscation. According to the legislation on "criminal lifestyle" confiscation in England and Wales, this period is six years before the confiscation proceedings start.[821] In other States, like Sweden and Germany, no time-limits apply at all. Directive 2014/42/EU does not contain any time-limit for extended confiscation. However, it has been added in Recital (21) that the Member States are allowed in national law to set up such a period of time during which the property can be deemed to have originated from criminal conduct. This means in this respect that the States will be able to continue to apply the domestic requirements available.

As follows from the study of national legislation in Chapters 3–6 above, the legal provisions and case-law show both similarities and differences when it comes to which supportive criteria are used to assess any illegal origin of property. Most States have not in their legal provisions explicitly stated any circumstances which especially support a conclusion that a certain asset is of illegal origin. Rather this has been developed in case-law. A circumstance of significant importance for the courts in all states when addressing the issue of illegal origin is a shown disparity between the lawful income of a defendant and the property at his or her disposal. However, it differs between national legislation whether the financial circumstances are the fundamental starting-point of the regime or not.

The abolishment of the alternative solutions for drafting the national provisions on extended confiscation was important, because FD 2005/212/JHA has in this respect led to certain practical difficulties. This is particularly true regarding mutual recognition of foreign confiscation orders, as the duty to execute such warrants only applies if the national confiscation rules are based on the same legislative option.[822] This may now be avoided. On the other hand, it must be doubted whether the confiscation regimes will be more "harmonised

[820] *Opinion of the European Union Agency for Fundamental Rights on the Confiscation of Proceeds of Crime*, FRA 03/2012, Vienna 4.12.2012, pp. 14–16. Compare also Amendment 31 of the *Report from the Committee on Civil Liberties, Justice and Home Affairs of the European Parliament on the proposal for a directive*, A7-0178/2013, 20.5.2013.

[821] See further Section 3.4.2.1 above.

[822] See further on this, Section 11.2.2 below.

as such", because obviously the Member States are allowed to continue to use different criteria for establishing criminal origin. Maybe it would have been sufficient in this respect to simply have abolished the link between the legislative option chosen by the executing State and the refusal ground in the instrument on mutual recognition.

7.4.2. THE EVIDENTIARY STANDARD AND BURDEN OF PROOF

The standard of evidence provided for by FD 2005/212/JHA is that a court is "*fully convinced*" that assets have an illegal origin. This is a rather high threshold, implying that a criminal standard of evidence is necessary.[823] An important aim of the European Commission was therefore to *lower* this burden. During the legislative process, the introduction of a civil standard of proof (in the form of a lower "balance of probabilities") was firstly considered. However, this had to be abandoned against the background of the proportionality principle and the problems of the incompatibility of such a standard with the national systems of some Member States.[824] Instead, Article 4 in the *Proposal for a Directive from the European Commission* provided that a court must find it "substantially more probable" that the property in question has been derived from criminal activities than not.[825] This standard resembled the evidentiary standard provided for in Swedish legislation.[826] It has been argued that the wording of this standard indicates a so-called qualified balance of probabilities with a certainty at 70–80 per cent.[827] The proposal was welcomed by many; *Eurojust* for example argued that the reduction of the burden of proof would "allow greater flexibility in applying extended confiscation".[828]

As seen in Chapters 3–6 above, there are at present many varying standards of evidence in the legislation on extended confiscation in the Member States. Differences may also be observed regarding the division of the burden of proof. In some States, the burden of proof is exclusively on the prosecutor and in others the burden of proof is divided or reversed. Against this background, it is not surprising that the issue proved to be extremely complicated in the negotiations in the Council. In fact, there was no consensus regarding such a low standard

---

823 Maugeri, n 795 above, p. 281.

824 See Commission Staff Working Paper, *Accompanying Document to the Proposal for a Directive of the European Parliament and the Council on the Freezing and Confiscation of Proceeds of Crime in the European Union*, SWD(2012) 31 final, Brussels 12.3.2012, p. 26 and Appendix H, *Study for an Impact Assessment on a Proposal for a New Legal Framework on the Confiscation and Recovery of Criminal Assets*, RAND Europe, 2012, pp. 199–200.

825 COM(2012) 85 final, p. 20.

826 Compare Section 5.3.4 above.

827 Boucht, n 814 above, p. 137.

828 *Eurojust's Opinion on the Proposal of the European Commission for a Directive on the Freezing and Confiscation of Proceeds of Crime in the European Union*, 2012, p. 6.

of proof as referred to in the proposal. The result was an adjustment in Article 5 Directive 2014/42/EU to a requirement that a court "*is satisfied*" that the property in question is derived from criminal conduct.[829] The removal of the standard of a balance of probabilities in the text from the European Commission was necessary as it was considered incompatible with some national legal systems.[830] In, for example Germany, a similar evidentiary standard had not been approved by the German Constitutional Court.[831]

The evidentiary standard of "satisfied" is rather vague. Recital (21) of the directive explains that:

> Extended confiscation should be possible where a court is satisfied that the property in question is derived from criminal conduct. This does not mean that it must be established that the property in question is derived from criminal conduct.

It is further emphasised that only *minimum* rules are set up, which means that the Member States can provide for more extensive powers in national law, for example in relation to their rules of evidence.[832] The formulation of the evidentiary standard thus gives the Member States significant freedom to redraft (or keep) their standards.[833]

Especially Member States with a low evidentiary standard were disappointed that the balance of probabilities proposed by the European Commission was not kept in the final version of the directive. However, it is very difficult to answer the question of how far the EU legislator can go when the evidentiary standard for extended confiscation is harmonised. There is no absolute uniformity regarding constitutional safeguards and procedural limits throughout the EU. As was pointed out in the *Study for an Impact Assessment*, the systems of extended confiscation are already "pressed against the limits of constitutionality" in some Member States, and:

> Although some concepts such as the presumption of innocence and the right to property are found in many places, uniform interpretations should not be expected. Furthermore, some constitutions contain more protections than others.[834]

---

829 Compare European Parliament, *Draft Report on the proposal for a directive of the European Parliament and of the Council on the freezing and confiscation of proceeds of crime in the European Union*, Amendments (30–177) 2012/0036(COD), pp. 39–41.

830 Proposal for a Directive of the European Parliament and of the Council on the Freezing and Confiscation of Proceeds of Crime in the European Union, *General Approach*, Council Document 17117/12, 3.12.2012, p. 3.

831 See further Section 4.3.3.

832 See also Recital (22) Directive 2014/42/EU.

833 See for example Boucht, n 814 above, p. 137, who argues that the wording of the standard indicates that whether a court is satisfied or not will be based on the evidentiary rules in each Member State.

834 *Study for an Impact Assessment on a Proposal for a New Legal Framework on the Confiscation and Recovery of Criminal Assets*, RAND Europe, 2012, p. 45.

This is shown by the fact that legislative proposals for stronger powers of extended confiscation have already given rise to constitutional concerns in some Member States.[835]

Another complication regarding a harmonisation of the evidentiary standard within the Union arises from the fact that there are no uniform formulations of proof or common approaches to the valuation of evidence. It is probably generally agreed that the standard formulated as "beyond reasonable doubt" is the highest standard for criminal proof, and that the balance of probabilities is a lower standard than this. However, the exact content and application of such standards may vary between States. As mentioned in Section 7.2 above, the national design of procedural law and the criminal justice system may lead to different needs regarding evidentiary standards. In addition, even if similar wording of the evidentiary standard exists in some States, its interpretation may still be very different according to legal traditions and procedural systems. Chapters 3–6 describe different evidentiary standards used in some national legislation.[836] A comparison of such national standards and evidentiary regimes is, though, very complicated.[837] The standard of proof applied in Germany is, for example, set at "*uneingeschränkte Überzeugung*", i.e. a judge must be absolutely convinced of the illegal origin of assets. This may be classified as a high standard.[838] In comparison, the Swedish standard of "substantially more probable" sounds much lower, but is not as low as a standard of a "balance of probabilities".[839]

On the other hand, one may doubt the usefulness of comparing the *formulations* of different national standards. As mentioned, there are always different interpretations domestically. Even if the highest criminal standard ("beyond reasonable doubt") sounds very rigid, it may in most States be met also by circumstantial evidence. Directive 2014/42/EU requires that a court is "satisfied", but underlines that such a conclusion may be based on "the circumstances of the case, including the specific facts and available evidence". Even if the evidentiary standards in the future may be differently formulated in the Member States, it may be expected that the courts often will pay attention

---

835 See further *Study for an Impact Assessment on a Proposal for a New Legal Framework on the Confiscation and Recovery of Criminal Assets*, RAND Europe, 2012, pp. 44–45.

836 See also Appendix F in *Study for an Impact Assessment on a Proposal for a New Legal Framework on the Confiscation and Recovery of Criminal Assets*, RAND Europe, 2012 which contains a table on some key aspects of the confiscation legislation in the Member States including evidentiary standard and burden of proof.

837 See for the same conclusion, *Study for an Impact Assessment on a Proposal for a New Legal Framework on the Confiscation and Recovery of Criminal Assets*, RAND Europe, 2012, p. 46.

838 In fact, it has been argued that this standard may be slightly lower than "beyond reasonable doubt". See *Study for an Impact Assessment on a Proposal for a New Legal Framework on the Confiscation and Recovery of Criminal Assets*, RAND Europe, 2012, Appendix F, p. 157.

839 The Swedish standard has in this respect been classified as a "medium" standard of proof, see *Study for an Impact Assessment on a Proposal for a New Legal Framework on the Confiscation and Recovery of Criminal Assets*, RAND Europe, 2012, p. 46.

to similar pieces of circumstantial evidence in order to establish whether assets have an illegal origin. Common factors are thereby, for example, an imbalance of assets in relation to legal income and "suspicious" locations of cash. The German courts are in this respect also allowed to consider circumstantial evidence.[840]

Against the background of the evidentiary difficulties in proving the illegal origin of assets in confiscation proceedings, the States have often at the international level been encouraged to consider a reversal of the burden of proof.[841] Even the second Council of Europe Convention on Laundering, Search, Seizure and Confiscation of the Proceeds from Crime and on the Financing of Terrorism from 2005 in principle *obligates* the ratifying States to require a defendant to demonstrate the lawful origin of assets.[842] However, this is demanded "to the extent that such a requirement is consistent with the principles of its domestic law", which means that such a provision may be left out if it is in conflict with the procedural principles of a State.[843] Only a few Member States have a reversal of the burden of proof, for example England and Wales,[844] Denmark,[845] Finland[846] and Ireland. Under the Italian system, the prosecutor must initially prove that there is a disproportion between the goods possessed and the legal income of a person convicted. Thereafter a reversal of the burden of proof operates, so that the defendant will have to prove the legitimate acquisition of the assets in question.[847] There have been many legal challenges both nationally and internationally towards such provisions in the area of

840 The application of the German standard is further described in Sections 4.3.3 and 4.4.2 above.

841 See for example Art. 5(7) United Nations Convention against Illicit Traffic in Narcotic Drugs and Psychotropic Substances, 1988, Art. 12(7) United Nations Convention against Transnational Organized Crime and *Best Practices on Confiscation (Recommendations 4 and 38)* and a *Framework for ongoing work on Asset Recovery*, FATF, October 2012. See for a discussion of the standard of proof and statutory legal presumptions in the area of extended confiscation, Boucht, n 814 above, pp. 146–52.

842 Compare Art. 3(4), ETS 198.

843 This conclusion was for example drawn in an inquiry regarding the Swedish implementation of the convention in this respect, SOU 2012:12 pp. 354–56.

844 See further Sections 3.4.2 and 3.6.5 above.

845 See Section 6.2.2 above.

846 See Section 6.3.2 above.

847 The Italian legislation on extended confiscation is found in Art. 12-*sexies* of Law Decree No. 399/94 converted into Act No. 501/94. This provision was introduced after the Italian Constitutional Court had overturned the former Art. 12-*quinquies* (Act No. 356/92), as it was found that this law infringed Art. 27 of the Constitution (the principle of non-guilt). See *Corte Costituzionale*, 17.2.1994, Decision nr 48, *Cassazione Penale* (1995) p. 1455 and L. Paoli, "Seizure and Confiscation Measures in Italy: An Evaluation of Their Effectiveness and Constitutionality" (1997) 5 *European Journal of Crime, Criminal Law and Criminal Justice*, pp. 256–72. Compare further *Illicit Assets Recovery in Italy*, Enhancing Integrity and Effectiveness of Illegal Asset Confiscation, Transparency International Italia, 2013, pp. 9 and 30, D. Piva, "Anti-Mafia Forfeiture in the Italian System" in C. King and C. Walker (eds.), *Dirty Assets: Emerging Issues in the Regulation of Criminal and Terrorist Assets*, Ashgate, 2014, pp. 71–91, Vettori, n 768 above, pp. 78–84 and Maugeri, n 795 above, pp. 263–65.

confiscation.[848] The English system has, for example, been confirmed in several cases by the ECtHR as compatible with Article 6 ECHR.[849] In many Member States a reversal of the burden of proof is, however, regarded as incompatible with the national Constitution or the traditions of the criminal justice system.[850]

On the other hand, the differences between systems with a reversal of the burden of proof, a division of the burden of proof and a lowered standard of evidence for the prosecutor are not always as significant or obvious as one might imagine. Obviously, one can generally conclude that a regime which *initially* places the burden of proof on the defendant is more burdensome. The obligation to explain the origin of property in order to avoid confiscation might very easily clash with the protection against self-incrimination which is part of the right to a fair trial. (This being said, this is not an absolute right and inferences may be drawn from a defendant's decision not to give information if there is sufficient evidence.)[851] The regime in England and Wales is often classified as providing for a "full" reversal of the burden of proof. Within this system, the prosecutor must though prove several facts before the burden shifts (i.e. that benefit has occurred and the amount of that benefit). Furthermore, in some systems with a reversed burden of proof, there may be a rather low evidentiary burden for the defendant when it comes to the legality of assets. In comparison to this, even in the systems where the burden of proof lies "exclusively" on the prosecutor, case-law from many States shows that a burden of explanation anyway at some stage falls on the defendant in order to rebut the evidence for illegal origin. Such an obligation might be quite demanding and if the defendant remains silent, the risk is that the courts will draw adverse inferences.[852]

Consequently, a harmonisation of national provisions on evidentiary standards as well as of the burden of proof is extremely difficult. It has been anticipated that there is a slow but observable trend towards a lowered standard of proof in confiscation regimes, and that although this is likely to continue, some Member States will never be affected by this.[853] The demands for an easing of the burden of proof in cases of confiscation are mainly motivated by the exceptional difficulties in obtaining evidence in the area of organised criminality, terrorism, drug offences or money laundering. This is also the area where the measure

[848] See for an interesting discussion of rules providing for a reversal of the burden of proof, Stessens, n 780 above, pp. 66–76.

[849] Such case-law is described in Sec. 3.6.6. See also generally, European Committee of Crime Problems, *Reversal of the Burden of Proof in Confiscation of the Proceeds of Crime: a Council of Europe Best Practice Survey*, Best Practice Survey No. 2, Strasbourg, 25.5.2000.

[850] See for example Sweden (Section 5.3.4) or Germany (Section 4.3.3.1).

[851] *Murray v. United Kingdom*, Appl. No. 18731/91, Judgment of 8 February 1996 and *Saunders v. United Kingdom*, Appl. No. 19187/91, Judgment of 17 December 1996.

[852] This has, for example, been discussed in the context of the Swedish legislation, see (Section 5.5.4 above).

[853] Appendix H, *Study for an Impact Assessment on a Proposal for a New Legal Framework on the Confiscation and Recovery of Criminal Assets*, RAND Europe, 2012, p. 200.

of extended confiscation initially was introduced. In order to safeguard that Directive 2014/42/EU was to be compatible with human rights; the European Commission drew the following conclusions from the case-law from the ECtHR:

> Reversals of the burden of proof concerning the legitimacy of assets have so far survived the scrutiny of the ECtHR, so long as they were applied fairly in the particular case, with adequate safeguards in place to allow the affected person to challenge these rebuttable presumptions. While the ECtHR has consistently upheld extended confiscation regimes in specific cases, their compatibility with the Convention is assessed on a case by case basis. Again, the degree of procedural safeguards afforded to the defendant plays a determinant role in assessing the proportionality of the measure.[854]

This means that the compatibility of the national regimes on confiscation with the human rights guarantees of the ECHR is always assessed in relation to the particular case in question.[855] The very far-reaching legislation on confiscation in Italy has, for example, been approved against the background of the special character of criminality in this State. In *Raimundo v. Italy* the ECtHR specifically emphasised "the difficulties encountered by the Italian State in the fight against the Mafia", and recognised that confiscation is an "effective and necessary weapon in the combat against this cancer". It was further emphasised that the confiscation measures pursued an aim that was in the general public interest, and that they were proportionate to the aim pursued.[856] In *Arcuri and Three Others v. Italy* the ECtHR explicitly granted the Italian legislator a wide margin of appreciation both with regard to the existence of a problem affecting the public interest, and the appropriate way to apply such measures.[857]

Similar reasoning is found in, for example, *Phillips v. United Kingdom*, where the national legislation on extended confiscation was considered as a proportionate response to the "scourge of drug trafficking".[858] In *Aboufadda v. France* the Court ruled on the French legislation on criminalisation of and confiscation of proceeds from individuals who cannot demonstrate resources corresponding to their lifestyle, and who have regular relations with persons who commit serious criminal offences.[859] The applicants in question, a married couple, had been convicted of this offence, and a building which belonged to them and in which they lived, had been confiscated. The French

854 Commission Staff Working Paper, *Executive Summary of the Impact Assessment, Accompanying the Proposal for a Directive of the European Parliament and the Council on the Freezing and Confiscation of Proceeds of Crime in the European Union*, SWD(2012) 32 final, Brussels 12.3.2012, p. 6. See further COM(2012) 85 final, p. 9.

855 See for some case-law, Section 3.6.6 above.

856 Para. 30, Appl. No. 12954/87, Judgment of 22 February 1994.

857 Appl. No. 52024/99, Decision of 5 July 2001.

858 Para. 52, Appl. No. 41087/98, Judgment of 5 July 2001. See on case-law from the ECtHR regarding the UK, Section 3.6.6 above.

859 This law was mentioned in Section 7.2 above.

courts had thereby determined that most of their assets had been obtained through the proceeds of drug trafficking engaged in by their son. The ECtHR in this respect underlined that States have a margin of appreciation to decide which infringements of the right to property are necessary and justified. Further, it was acknowledged that there is a legitimate wish and general public interest to punish and deter criminal offences which were akin to concealing illegally-obtained assets. Given the ravages caused by large-scale drug trafficking, the Court found it understandable that the Member States would want to act with great firmness. It was added that the applicants could have avoided conviction and confiscation if they had demonstrated the lawful origin of their assets.[860]

This case-law illustrates that the public interest in confiscation measures is generally measured against the individual's right to property. The issue of proportionality is of outmost importance, and the legislator must thus make sure that the rules are justified and proportionate to the aims that such measures seek to achieve. Another effect of this is, however, that measures of harmonisation which are inspired by the national legislation in one Member State may be risky from a human rights perspective if the circumstances and legal rules of other States differ significantly. Against this background, it is not to be automatically assumed that every piece of legislation on extended confiscation with a reversal of the burden of proof or a significantly lowered burden of proof will be measured in the same way by the ECtHR or CJEU in the future. This is especially the case if the application of the measure moves away from the areas of organised or drug-related criminality. An interesting reflection, which has been made generally, is that the EU institutions have since the beginning of the present century progressively accompanied, "or even *tout court* substituted", the expression "organized crime" with that of "serious crime".[861] Such a development is in fact seen within the legislative process related to Directive 2014/42/EU. However, one might in fact need stronger arguments than have been so far presented, in order to substantiate a position that an expansion of extended confiscation is a necessary measure which is proportionate to the right of property in Article 17 of the EU Charter of Fundamental Rights. The full limits of what is to be classified as a disproportionate interference with the right to property are yet to be decided.

7.5. EXCEPTIONS TO EXTENDED CONFISCATION

FD 2005/212/JHA does not contain any explicit exceptions to extended confiscation. In contrast thereto, the *Proposal for a Directive from the European*

860 *Aboufadda v. France*, Appl. No. 28457/10, Decision on 4 November 2014.

861 Paoli, n 815 above, p. 3.

Commission stated that extended confiscation should be excluded where the similar criminal activities could not be the subject of criminal proceedings due to statutory limitation under national law, had already been the subject of criminal proceedings which resulted in a final acquittal or in other cases where the *ne bis in idem* principle applies.[862] The exclusion of property originating from such criminal activity of which a defendant has been acquitted aimed at upholding the presumption of innocence (Article 48 of the EU Charter of Fundamental Rights).[863] These exceptions were, however, deleted during the negotiations and accordingly Directive 2014/42/EU lacks any express exceptions to confiscation.

Exceptions to extended confiscation in cases of prescription or *ne bis in idem* are not explicitly provided for in the regimes in Sweden, England and Wales or Germany. The suitability of an exception in this area regarding cases of prescription may be questioned. If it is not required that a prosecutor shows any link between the assets and any specific criminal offence, it might in practice be very difficult to test and apply such a provision. Furthermore, one might argue that if the general aim is to deprive the defendant of illicit proceeds from crime, it is of less importance whether the criminal activities in question cannot be the subject of criminal proceedings due to statutory limitations.

An exception to extended confiscation in some cases of *ne bis in idem* is on the other hand to be viewed differently. In, for example, the case of *Geerings v. The Netherlands* the applicant had been convicted of numerous counts of offences of dishonesty, but, on appeal, he had been acquitted of some of these because there was insufficient evidence.[864] In the confiscation proceedings, the prosecution sought a confiscation order regarding an illegally obtained advantage based on *all the offences charged*, i.e. including the offences of which he had been acquitted. The Dutch Court of Appeal ordered confiscation by arguing that, despite its own acquittal judgment, there were nevertheless sufficient indications that the defendant had committed the offences. The Supreme Court confirmed that also offences that have resulted in an acquittal can form the basis for the imposition of a confiscation measure. The ECtHR, on the other hand, found that the right to be presumed innocent had been violated. It was thereby argued that the confiscation order had related to the very offences of which the defendant had in fact been acquitted, and that Article 6(2) ECHR embodies a general rule which does not allow "even the voicing of suspicions" as to an accused's innocence once an acquittal is final. Accordingly, the findings of the national courts amounted to a determination of the applicant's guilt even though he had not been "found guilty according to law".[865]

---

862 Art. 4(2), COM(2012) 85 final.
863 COM(2012) 85 final, p. 11.
864 Appl. No. 30810/03, Judgment of 1 March 2007.
865 See K. Mahmutaj, "Cash Forfeiture Following Acquittal: 'An Affront to Public Perception' or a Breach of a Fundamental Human Right?", (2009) 11 *Criminal Law Review*, pp. 783–93, for a discussion of this case.

The ruling of the Court is to be welcomed. As a general principle, a confiscation order should not be based upon such conduct as has already been subject to criminal proceedings which resulted in a final acquittal. This being said, a *general* exception to extended confiscation regarding "other cases of *ne bis in idem*", which was originally proposed by the European Commission, must be further evaluated as it could give rise to certain difficulties in practice. Is there for example a situation of *ne bis in idem* if a defendant claims that certain cash derives from a robbery for which he has already been convicted in a previous trial? In such a case, a plea for confiscation could not be brought if a court has ruled on criminal responsibility for such criminal activity, but has neglected or decided against a confiscation order. Another area which must be further evaluated regards the risk of *double confiscation* (i.e. confiscation of the same proceeds twice). Especially in transnational cases, such situations may be especially tricky to investigate and consider. There is a need for clarification of the situation where several Member States are investigating the same triggering offences and there are pleas for confiscation related to such cases. Even if Directive 2014/42/EU does not contain any explicit exceptions in this respect, a presumption of innocence and the principle of *ne bis in idem* follows from the human rights *acquis*, and the limits of extended confiscation remain to be seen.

7.6. THE ABSENCE OF A HARDSHIP CLAUSE

The national confiscation regimes of many Member States contain a *hardship clause*, which provides that the measure of confiscation may be avoided in cases of undue hardship to the person affected. Under Swedish law, a court can decide against a motion for extended confiscation if such an order would be *unreasonable*.[866] The German legislation also provides for a hardship clause.[867] Such provisions have been adopted in order to ensure that there is room for considerations of proportionality. Neither the *Proposal for a Directive from the European Commission* nor the FD 2005/212/JHA contains any express hardship clause, which led to certain criticism during the legislative process.[868] This shortcoming was partly corrected in Directive 2014/42/EU, but only in the form of a statement in Recital (18). This states that the Member States may provide that confiscation should, in exceptional circumstances, not be ordered in cases of undue hardship for the affected person, whereby the circumstances of the

866 Ch. 36 Sec. 1b Subsec. 4 SPC. See further on this rule, Section 5.3.1 above. A hardship rule is also present in the Finnish legislation, see Ch. 10 Sec. 10 of the Finnish Penal Code.

867 Sec. 73d Subsec. 4 and Sec. 73c *StGB*.

868 See for example *Stellungnahme des Deutschen Richterbundes zum Vorschlag für eine Richtlinie des Europäischen Parlaments und des Rates über die Sicherstellung und Einziehung von Erträgen aus Straftaten in der Europäischen Union*, COM(2012) 85, Nr. 23/12, August 2012, p. 3.

respective individual case should be decisive. It is left to the courts to decide what would represent an undue hardship. However, it has been added that only a "very restricted use" of this possibility should be made, and that the courts should only be allowed to waive a confiscation order in cases where it would "put the person concerned in a situation in which it would be very difficult for him to survive". This is a rather rigorous interpretation of the rule.

The importance of having a rule which gives certain discretion to the courts may differ from State to State, and depends partly on the design of the particular provision of extended confiscation. From an international perspective, the range of discretion given to the courts in the area of confiscation differs. In, for example, Sweden the introduction of a hardship rule was motivated by the need to provide a counterweight to the lack of some limiting requirements there which were found in other States.[869] The Swedish provision therefore gives rather wide discretion, whereas, for example, the development of the legislation in England and Wales has gone towards practically no judicial discretion. Even if a hardship rule is provided for, it has a very limited procedural application and is not directed towards any possible *personal* hardship on a defendant.[870] Against the background of the rather restrictive statements expressed in Recital (18) of Directive 2014/42/EU, it could be questioned whether the Swedish courts can keep their wide discretion in such cases. In the *Report on Extended Confiscation* in 2015, it was, however, pointed out that the recital allows that undue hardship is decided "in accordance with national law" and that it is anyway not clear to what extent statements in a recital are legally binding. It was therefore concluded that no changes to the domestic hardship rule were necessary in Sweden.[871]

A provision which seeks to prevent disproportionate confiscation orders is an important safety break. The lack of a specific hardship rule (in a provision in the directive and not merely in the form of a recital) is therefore regrettable. However, the omission is not surprising against the background that it was even proposed during the legislative proceedings within the EU to create a *compulsory* obligation for the judges to confiscate. Thereby the Member States would have been required to provide for mandatory assets investigations and to limit the judicial discretion by providing that confiscation *shall* be ordered. Luckily, these policy actions had to be discarded due to the anticipated problems with the conferral of powers to the EU, as well as complications following from the proportionality principle and the compatibility of the Member States' legislation.[872]

---

869 See, however, on the low application of the Swedish hardship rule in practice, Section 5.5.3 above.

870 Compare on this rule and for criticism against the lack of discretion, Section 3.4.2.1 and Section 3.6.4 above.

871 SOU 2015:67 pp. 151–53.

872 Compare *Commission Staff Working Paper, Accompanying Document to the Proposal for a Directive of the European Parliament and the Council on the Freezing and Confiscation of Proceeds of Crime in the European Union*, SWD(2012) 31 final, Brussels 12.3.2012, p. 26.

Obviously, this is an area of significant importance for an individual affected by a decision on confiscation. The existence of a hardship clause has been one important factor for the ECtHR when the Court has ruled on the compatibility of national legislation with the ECHR.[873] In the future, the CJEU might also have to rule on proportionality issues and successively develop an EU hardship rule in this area.[874]

7.7. PROCEDURAL SAFEGUARDS FOR THE INDIVIDUAL

One aim of the European Commission when the new Directive was drafted was to improve the respect for the rights guaranteed by the EU Charter on Fundamental Rights by *explicitly stating* certain procedural rights. In order to avoid human rights violations, the case-law from the ECtHR regarding measures of extended confiscation and non-conviction-based confiscation was considered.[875]An important condition following from such case-law is that any legal presumptions regarding illegal origin must be rebuttable.[876] The ambition to adopt detailed and specific procedural rights for individuals in an EU instrument on confiscation must be applauded. Article 8 Directive 2014/42/EU is thus to be welcomed, as the adoption of procedural rules which are adjusted to the practical reality of different judicial measures is of significant importance.[877] In comparison to the sparing provision in FD 2005/212/JHA (Article 4), the catalogue of rights stated by this new article is clearly an improvement.[878]

---

873 See for example the case-law described in Section 3.6.6 above.

874 The Member States are here bound by Art. 49(3) of the EU Charter of Fundamental Rights, which contains a proportionality principle. It is in this respect interesting to see that national courts are starting to interpret and apply EU instruments in the light of the Charter. In a German judgment, it was for example considered whether surrender on the basis of a European arrest warrant would breach Art. 49(3) of the Charter. The individual was eventually surrendered, but it was confirmed that the Charter is binding on Member States when assessing whether or not an EAW should be issued. See *General Public Prosecution Service v. C. Judges*, Higher Regional Court Stuttgart (OLG Stuttgart), Decision of 25 February 2010, 1 Ausl. (24) 1246/09. See for an English translation of the judgment and a commentary to the case, J. Vogel and J.R. Spencer, "Proportionality and the European Arrest Warrant" [2010] *Criminal Law Review*, pp. 474–82.

875 See for example COM(2012) 85 final, p. 9 and *Study for an Impact Assessment on a Proposal for a New Legal Framework on the Confiscation and Recovery of Criminal Assets*, RAND Europe, 2012, Appendix E, pp. 139–50.

876 Compare the rulings presented in Section 3.6.6 above.

877 See for example generally on the need for the adoption of fitted defence rights in the EU instruments on judicial cooperation, M. Thunberg Schunke, *Internationell rättslig hjälp i brottmål inom EU: Effektivitet v. rättssäkerhet*, Iustus förlag, 2004, pp. 309–13 and M. Thunberg Schunke, *Whose Responsibility? A Study of Transnational Defence Rights and Mutual Recognition of Judicial Decisions within the EU*, Intersentia, 2013, pp. 125–26.

878 Compare also Recitals (38)–(40), Directive 2014/42/EU.

This being said, it was rightly argued during the legislative process that many of the safeguards spelled out are only such procedural rights as already follow from the right to a fair trial, and that a more concrete approach was needed:

> Sofern in der Richtlinie die überaus schwierigen Fragen des Entscheidungs- und Rechtsmittelweges bei der Einziehung geregelt werden sollen, sind diese seriös anzugehen. Allein der Hinweis auf wirksame Rechtsbehelfe reicht hierzu nicht aus. Dabei ist insbesondere festzulegen, wie in Fällen grenzüberschreitender Einziehungen die Beteiligung aller Betroffener und deren Rechtsmittelweg auszugestalten ist. So müsste konkret festgeschrieben werden, welche Rechte und Pflichten z.B. einem Einziehungsbeteiligten in einem grenzüberschreitenden Verfahren zustehen und welche Rechtsmittel er gegen eine Einziehungsentscheidung im Ausstellungs- und im Vollstreckungsmitgliedstaat besitzt.[879]

When law enforcement agencies are given more far-reaching powers against individuals an efficient counterweight to such powers must be created. The prosecutor has in confiscation cases the assistance of financial investigators and may use coercive powers to search for information and assets. The only real way to guarantee a defendant a fair trial is to more clearly *improve* or *strengthen* the legal position of a defendant in confiscation matters.

Article 8(8) Directive 2014/42/EU states in this respect that an affected person shall in a case regarding extended confiscation "have an effective possibility" to challenge the circumstances of the case, including specific facts and available evidence regarding the basis on which property concerned is considered to derive from criminal conduct. According to Article 8(7), there is a right of access to a lawyer throughout the confiscation proceedings. These are important safeguards. However, the legislator should have clarified in more detail what is to be included in an "effective possibility".[880] Closely linked to this is obviously a right to legal aid. Such a right is, however, not expressly mentioned in Article 8.[881] Recital (38) of Directive 2014/42/EU even states that:

> This Directive should be without prejudice to national law in relation to legal aid and does not create any obligations for Member States' legal aid systems, which should apply in accordance with the Charter and the ECHR.

---

879 *Stellungnahme des Deutschen Richterbundes zum Vorschlag für eine Richtlinie des Europäischen Parlaments und des Rates über die Sicherstellung und Einziehung von Erträgen aus Straftaten in der Europäischen Union*, COM(2012) 85, Nr. 23/12, August 2012, p. 6.

880 Compare the *Opinion of the European Union Agency for Fundamental Rights on the Confiscation of Proceeds of Crime*, FRA 03/2012, Vienna 4.12.2012, p. 15.

881 Such a right was recommended by the European Economic and Social Committee, see Section 4.7.2 of the *Opinion of the European Economic and Social Committee on the proposal for a Directive*, *OJ* C 299, 4.10.2012, pp. 128–32.

Obviously, this was done in order to reassure some Member States that there would be no additional costs in this part from implementing the new Directive. The statement is anyway remarkable, as in most cases legal aid will be necessary in order to ensure that individuals have the right of effective remedy and a fair trial.[882]

7.8. THE RELATIONSHIP BETWEEN CONFISCATION AND COMPENSATION FOR VICTIMS

The *Proposal for a Directive from the European Commission* lacked any provision on the relationship between a confiscation order and any compensation for a victim of crime. This was criticised during the legislative process, and it was suggested that a provision must be included that highlighted the fair trial rights of victims.[883] National legislation often contains provisions which give the victim's right to compensation *priority* over a confiscation order.[884] It is obvious that the EU legislator often lacks a holistic approach when legislation is drafted in the area of criminal procedural law. According to the Directive on victims' rights in 2012, there is an obligation for the Member States to ensure that recoverable property which is seized in the course of criminal proceedings is returned to victims without delay (Article 15). Additionally, there is an obligation to ensure that those victims are entitled to obtain a decision on compensation from the offender (Article 16).[885] Even if there are many offences in Directive 2014/42/EU which normally do not violate the rights of individuals, such offences are also included, for example trafficking in human beings and sexual exploitation of women and children.

---

882 It can be added that given that an issue of extended confiscation is handled within criminal proceedings, the right to a lawyer and other procedural rights may also be fulfilled in accordance with other EU instruments, for example *Directive 2013/48/EU of the European Parliament and of the Council of 22 October 2013 on the Right of Access to a lawyer in Criminal Proceedings and in European Arrest Warrant Proceedings, and on the Right to have a Third Party informed upon Deprivation of Liberty and to Communicate with Third Persons and with Consular authorities while Deprived of Liberty*, *OJ* L 294, 6.11.2013, pp. 1–12.

883 *Opinion of the European Union Agency for Fundamental Rights on the Confiscation of Proceeds of Crime*, FRA 03/2012, Vienna 4.12.2012, pp. 17–18. Compare also the statement from the ECBA on the proposal for a new directive on confiscation, at: http:77www.ecba.org/extdocserv/201210assetseizureECBAstatement.pdf, at p. 4.

884 An example is Germany, see Sec. 73 Subsec. 1 Para. 2 and Sec. 73d Subsec. 1 Para. 3 *StGB*. See further Sections 4.1 and 4.3.1 above. In the system in England and Wales, the court has been given discretion whether to make a confiscation order in cases where a victim of the criminal conduct has started or intends to bring civil proceedings against a defendant (Secs. 6(6) and 7(3) POCA 2002).

885 *Directive 2012/29/EU of the European Parliament and of the Council of 25 October 2012 establishing minimum standards on the rights, support and protection of victims of crime, and replacing Council Framework Decision 2001/220/JHA*, *OJ* L 315, 14.11.2012, pp. 57–73.

The silence on the rights of victims in the *Proposal for a Directive from the European Commission* therefore contradicted the work done by the EU in this area, and was corrected in the final draft. Article 8(10) of Directive 2014/42/EU now states that the Member States shall take the necessary measures to ensure that the confiscation measure under the directive does not prevent any victims from seeking compensation for their claims. The exact content of this wording is not entirely clear, as it is stated that victims should not be prevented from "*seeking*" compensation (rather than from "*obtaining*" compensation). However, in order to be in line with the Directive on victims' rights, it *ought* to mean that the claims of an injured party have *priority* over a decision of extended confiscation by the State.[886]

7.9. THIRD PARTY CONFISCATION

FD 2005/212/JHA does not contain any binding obligations for the Member States regarding third party confiscation.[887] This has been regretted, as criminal proceeds may very easily be transferred to other persons in order to avoid a decision on confiscation. Obviously, international cooperation in confiscation cases is also hindered due to differences in legislation regarding third party confiscation in the Member States.[888] Even if many States provide for confiscation regarding third persons, there is to a certain extent a different scope of national legislation for example regarding under which circumstances third party confiscation is allowed.

Against this background, the possibility of third party confiscation was an important issue when Directive 2014/42/EU was negotiated. Article 6 now obligates the Member States to enable third party confiscation *at least* in cases where those third parties "knew or ought to have known" that the purpose of the transfer was to avoid confiscation.[889] The interpretation of such "bad faith" is left to the national courts. The provision does not, however, specifically mention whether the obligation regarding third party confiscation also concerns extended confiscation, or if the provision is only applicable regarding ordinary confiscation. In the context of the Swedish legislative inquiry regarding the implementation of the new directive, the *Report on Extended Confiscation* in 2015 concluded that Article 6 does not apply to extended confiscation.[890] This was based on the argument that this provision specifically concerns the confiscation of "proceeds", which is the term used in Article 4 (ordinary confiscation) whereas

886 Compare on this, Section 12.9 below.
887 Compare Section 2.3.1 above.
888 COM(2012) 85 final, 12.3.2012, p. 12.
889 Compare also Recitals (24)–(25), Directive 2014/42/EU.
890 SOU 2015:67 pp. 110–12, pp. 129–33 and pp. 150–51.

Article 5 (extended confiscation) concerns the confiscation of "property". Further reference was made to Article 2(1) Directive 2014/42/EU which defines "proceeds" as any economic advantage derived directly or indirectly from a criminal offence. However, it was concluded that Sweden in any case fulfils the obligations regarding extended confiscation too.[891]

It is not entirely clear from the provisions of Directive 2014/42/EU whether the obligation regarding third party confiscation also applies to extended confiscation. The interpretation made by the Swedish inquiry is, however, not entirely convincing. One may question whether the choice of terms in Article 6 should be interpreted in this way. Recitals (24)–(25) of the directive, for example, use the term "property" and not "proceeds" in the context of third party confiscation. Furthermore, the placement of the provision after the provisions on ordinary confiscation and extended confiscation may indicate that it applies to both these provisions. In fact, the motives for being able to confiscate property or proceeds which have been transferred to third parties are equally strong both regarding ordinary and extended confiscation. Against this background, it is a bit unfortunate that the exact scope of the obligation has not been explicitly set. It therefore remains to be seen how the Member States will implement the Directive in national legislation. The legislative choices in this respect may have significant consequences for the efficiency of confiscation both nationally and internationally.

7.10. CONCLUDING REMARKS: WHAT HAS BEEN ACHIEVED AND WHAT STILL NEEDS TO BE DONE?

During the EU legislative process regarding the reform of the confiscation regime, different policy options were studied. Thereby various degrees of intervention were considered: no legal action; the minimal legislative option (i.e. only correcting certain deficits in the existing EU provisions); and the maximal legislative option (i.e. going beyond the existing rules). The European Commission thereby decided to go for the last option in order to considerably harmonise the national rules on confiscation.[892] In line with this, Directive 2014/42/EU has the fundamental aim to *facilitate* confiscation and *streamline the existing rules*. It remains to be seen if this will be achieved. A careful prognosis is that the directive may lead to some harmonisation, but that the Member States will also keep many different national approaches.

---

891 SOU 2015:67 pp. 150–51.

892 See COM(2012) 85 final, pp. 7–8 and Appendix H, *Study for an Impact Assessment on a Proposal for a New Legal Framework on the Confiscation and Recovery of Criminal Assets*, RAND Europe, 2012.

Obviously, a more significant broadening of the regime for extended confiscation would have been achieved if the *Proposal for a Directive from the European Commission* had been adopted. What has been left after the negotiations is a more weakened and watered down directive.[893] This being said, it is clear that the scope for extended confiscation will increase as more triggering offences are targeted by the new directive. In view of the abolishment of the three different ways to implement the provision on extended confiscation and the creation of a clearer legal framework, it can further be anticipated that Directive 2014/42/EU may to a certain extent facilitate international cooperation between the Member States.[894]

The comparative analysis in Chapters 3–6 above shows that there are many similarities, but also some significant conceptual differences and legal approaches to confiscation as a procedural measure *per se*. It is in fact very difficult to properly assess which of the national regimes on confiscation is the most severe. The legislation on extended confiscation in Norway seems, for example, at first glance more extensive than the Swedish, for example regarding the reversed burden of proof and the possibility to confiscate the value of assets of the offender's present or previous spouse or partner. However, a further study also reveals that the Swedish regime lacks some limiting requirements which are present in the Norwegian. Accordingly, it must be acknowledged to a greater extent that different designs of national legislative provisions may *in practice* lead to the same or similar results. Against this background, it may be doubted whether all States should be forced into the same schedule for confiscation. I fully agree with the conclusions of Kilchling in this respect:

> The concept of confiscation of illegal proceeds provides a range of legislative options for concrete implementation. International comparison suggests that each country should refer to those instruments that are in accordance with their legal traditions on which their criminal justice systems are built. This is also true in light of the fact that until now scientific evaluation has not brought any findings according to which specific types of legislation bring significantly better results than others; each system has its particular strengths and weaknesses.[895]

In the beginning of this chapter (Section 7.1), it was argued that the adoption of a new EU directive on confiscation could be justified from the perspective of the difficulties which have arisen in the area of mutual recognition following from

---

893 As pointed out, this directive, though, appears to be the maximum that the Member States could achieve in terms of mutual consent on the topic. See Comparative Report, *Legislation Meets Practice: National and European Perspectives in Confiscation and Forfeiture of Assets*, Transparency International, 2015, p. 68.

894 Compare further on this, Chapter 12 below.

895 Kilchling, n 789 above, p. 280. Compare also M. Fazekas and E. Nanopoulos, "The Effectiveness of EU Law: Insights from the EU Legal Framework on Asset Confiscation" (2016) 24 *European Journal of Crime, Criminal Law and Criminal Justice*, p. 39, p. 50.

FD 2005/212/JHA. *A first general conclusion of this chapter* is nevertheless that caution must be paid to placing too much faith in the process of harmonisation. A common approach to the confiscation of criminal proceeds can be promoted. However, if the main motive is to facilitate cooperation regarding cross-border crime, other measures may be more effective than the difficult path of pushing the States into adopting the same view!

A *second general conclusion of this chapter* is that one must be careful in the future not to expand the instrument of extended confiscation in such a way that the justifications for its use are completely lost. There is no doubt that effective confiscation regimes for serious forms of criminality are needed and justified. However, it must not be forgotten that certain substantive requirements have the aim to protect a defendant against violations of human rights, for example the need for a criminal conviction, a restriction of triggering offences, a stringent standard of proof, etc. The figure of extended confiscation principally allows that previous criminal activity of a defendant may be *assumed*. A fundamental issue – not only for the EU legislator but also for the national legislator – is therefore to more thoroughly consider which criminal offences may be justified as triggering offences. It is also necessary to reconsider whether every defendant who commits a triggering offence should be targeted by such a far-reaching measure or whether it should be reserved for criminal offences with specific "grave" characteristics.

Consequently, it is of significant importance that a proper balance is kept between the State's interests in combatting crime and the rights of the individual. Article 5(4) TEU generally demands that EU action shall not exceed what is necessary in order to achieve the objectives of the Treaties. It is a pity that there have been so few attempts during the years to really evaluate the functioning and efficiency of the confiscation regimes in different States. Obviously, severe and extensive legislation on confiscation is no guarantee of a high number of confiscation orders.

A *third general conclusion* is that any future legislation must be shaped with a view of all stages of the proceedings.[896] Directive 2014/42/EU brought high expectations for significant changes to confiscation practice, but this instrument is mostly concentrated on the substantive criteria for extended confiscation.[897] A successful strategy of "*going for the money*" must though involve all of the four different stages of the confiscation process referred to in Section 1.3.2 above. Even with the most far-reaching substantive provisions, there is no confiscation

---

[896] For the need of a holistic approach to measures of confiscation and international cooperation, compare Sections 1.4 and 3.5.2 of *Opinion of the European Economic and Social Committee on the proposal for a Directive*, *OJ* C 299, 4.10.2012, pp. 128–32.

[897] See for an interesting discussion on the effectiveness of the EU legal framework on asset confiscation, Fazekas and Nanopoulos, n 895 above. The authors argue *inter alia* that despite the adoption of new EU legislation, the effectiveness of the EU's action is unlikely to significantly improve.

if assets are not investigated and secured at an early stage, or if there are no efficient routines for the execution of warrants. As was pointed out:

> Proceeds of crime only rarely fall into the lap of the courts or government like ripe fruits from the tree or vine. What is not investigated by financial intelligence or other personnel may never be learned about at all, for it is very difficult to reconstruct financial flows from crime long after they have occurred, and harder still to get the money back.[898]

In this respect, much more needs to be done. In practice, successful confiscation of criminal proceeds depends on the structure and administrative support for the law enforcement agencies. Efficient freezing and seizure of assets depend on rapid access to centralised information and swift procedures. Decisive in the area of transnational cases are well-functioning instruments and arrangements for international cooperation.

Obviously, the development of a comprehensive EU regime for confiscation is not completed with the adoption of Directive 2014/42/EU, but must be continued. In the next part of this study, I will outline some other measures which may influence the success of the national and international confiscation regimes, and highlight to what extent there has already been legislative action nationally or from the EU.

898 *Reversal of the Burden of Proof in Confiscation of the Proceeds of Crime: a Council of Europe Best Practice Survey*, Best Practice Survey No. 2, European Committee of Crime Problems, Strasbourg, 25.5.2000, p. 6.

PART III

THE LEGAL FRAMEWORK FOR INTERNATIONAL COOPERATION

"One country's forfeiture efforts, however effective and comprehensive, may not be enough to take the profit out of international crime. Thus, the countries of the world must apply and enforce their domestic confiscation schemes in increasingly multinational settings".[899]

---

[899] W.J. Snider, "International Cooperation in the Forfeiture of Illegal Drug Proceeds" (1995) 6 *Criminal Law Forum*, p. 377, p. 378.

CHAPTER 8

INTERNATIONAL COOPERATION IN THE AREA OF CONFISCATION

8.1. INTRODUCTION

Obviously, close international cooperation is a fundamental key to a successful policy of asset recovery, as strong national powers of confiscation are significantly weakened if they cannot be enforced abroad. Technological developments (for example instant electronic transactions and banking) and the increasing internationalisation of society in general, render it absolute necessary that law enforcement agencies may investigate and search for assets across borders in an efficient and speedy way. The EU area is in this respect particularly vulnerable against the background of the free movement and the abolishment of internal border controls. Consequently, it is relatively easy for criminals to transfer and hide illegal proceeds in other Member States.

Various instruments on international cooperation in criminal matters have been adopted over the years. Some of them generally regulate the area of requests for legal assistance, whereas others are specifically drafted with respect to cooperation within asset recovery or regarding certain types of criminality. Traditionally, international cooperation in criminal matters is built upon the system of *mutual legal assistance* ("MLA").[900] Hereby a requesting State sends a formal request for legal assistance to a *requested State*, which will decide whether such a measure may be executed on the behalf of another State.[901] It is based on reciprocity. Common grounds for refusal of such requests are, for example, a lack of double criminality, *ordre public* or exceptions for fiscal and political offences. Generally speaking, the regime of MLA is considered to be slow and cumbersome, as requests usually go through diplomatic channels or

---

900 See generally on the development and structure of the European cooperation in criminal matters, A. Klip, *European Criminal Law: An Integrative Approach*, 2nd edn, Intersentia, 2012, p. 335–56.

901 Another term often used for international requests for legal assistance is "*letters rogatory*", which is the traditional term for a mandate given by a judicial authority of one State to a judicial authority of a foreign State to perform in its place one or more specified procedural measures.

central authorities (often the Ministry of Justice).[902] Even if there have been improvements in this area in recent years to facilitate the execution of requests and provide for faster procedures, many difficulties remain.[903] Within the EU, some legal instruments have therefore been adopted in order to provide for improved and more advanced forms of MLA between the Member States. The international and EU instruments on MLA which may be applied for requests in the area of asset recovery will be described in Section 8.2.

In addition to instruments on MLA, the EU legislator has also developed a special legal framework for cross-border cooperation which builds on the principle of *mutual recognition and execution of judicial decisions*.[904] This concept has been promoted as the cornerstone of judicial cooperation in both civil and criminal matters within the Union. In short, this cooperation model is based on mutual trust and provides that domestic orders on procedural measures shall in principle be recognised and executed abroad without any further formality. This different way of cooperation in comparison to the traditional system of MLA is reflected in the new terminology of the States involved: "an *issuing*" and "an *executing*" State. Even if a regime of *absolute* mutual recognition in the area of criminal law has not yet been adopted, the scope for refusing to execute orders has been significantly restricted in comparison to traditional MLA requests. There are currently many EU instruments on mutual recognition of different procedural measures during the preliminary criminal investigation, criminal proceedings and after criminal conviction. Some of these concern matters of confiscation. The EU instruments on mutual recognition will be described in Section 8.3 below.

8.2. INTERNATIONAL INSTRUMENTS ON MLA

The United Nations Convention against Illicit Traffic in Narcotic Drugs and Psychotropic Substances (1988) was the first multilateral instrument which

[902] MLA requests have been found to take about a year on average. See Commission Staff Working Document, *Impact Assessment*, accompanying the document *Proposal for a Regulation of the European Parliament and of the Council on the Mutual Recognition of Freezing and Confiscation Orders*, SWD(2016) 468 final, Brussels 21.12.2016, p. 12.

[903] See for the experiences of several States regarding the functionuing of the MLA conventions adopted by the Council of Europe, European Committee of Crime Problems, *Questionnaire on the Use and Efficiency of Council of Europe Instruments as regards International Cooperation in the field of Seizure and Confiscation of Proceeds of Crime, including the Management of Confiscated Goods and Asset Sharing*, PC-OC Mod (2015) 06Rev4 Bil.

[904] See generally on this principle, Klip, n 900 above, pp. 356–95, A. Suominen, *The Principle of Mutual Recognition in Cooperation in Criminal Matters: A Study of the Principle in Four Framework Decisions and in the Implementing Legislation in the Nordic Member States*, Intersentia, 2011, pp. 19–66 and M. Fichera, *The Implementation of the European Arrest Warrant in the European Union: Law, Policy and Practice*, Intersentia, 2011, pp. 41–64.

provided a comprehensive set of international rules on confiscation, for example regarding tracing, freezing and seizure of assets. Other international instruments followed, and provisions on MLA which especially target matters of confiscation are now also found in, for example, the United Nations Convention against Transnational Organized Crime (2000), the United Nations Convention against Corruption (2003), the European Convention on Laundering, Search, Seizure and Confiscation of the Proceeds from Crime (1990) and the European Convention on Laundering, Search, Seizure and Confiscation of the Proceeds from Crime and on the Financing of Terrorism (2005). International requests for MLA in this area can also be based on the European Convention on Mutual Assistance in Criminal Matters from 1959 (hereafter "the 1959 Convention") and its two additional protocols from 1978 and 2001.[905] The 1959 Convention is often referred to as the "Mother Convention" of MLA, as many of the other instruments on judicial cooperation refer to or build upon its provisions.

The EU Member States have ratified all of the above-mentioned international conventions, except for the European Convention on Laundering, Search, Seizure and Confiscation of the Proceeds from Crime and on the Financing of Terrorism (2005), which has so far only been ratified by 17 Member States. Among the ratifying States are, for example, Sweden, the Netherlands, the United Kingdom and Belgium.

Legislative instruments have additionally been developed within the EU for cases of MLA between the Member States. These mainly build upon the above mentioned treaties within the Council of Europe, but provide for a more advanced cooperation. The Schengen Convention of 1990, for example, provides for direct communication of requests between a requesting and a requested State, and limits the refusal grounds for certain coercive measures like search and seizure.[906] In 2000, the Council Act of 29 May 2000 establishing the Convention on Mutual Assistance in Criminal Matters between the Member States of the European Union (hereafter the "2000 EU Convention") was adopted, which facilitates and speeds up requests in different ways.[907] Further, the Council Act of 16 October 2001 establishing the Protocol to the Convention on Mutual Assistance in Criminal Matters between the Member States of the European Union (hereafter the "2001 EU Protocol") provides for specific provisions, especially regarding requests for banking information.[908] These instruments are described in more detail in the following chapters.

---

905 *Additional Protocol to the European Convention on Mutual Assistance in Criminal Matters*, 1978, ETS 99 and *Second Additional Protocol to the European Convention on Mutual Assistance in Criminal Matters*, 2001, ETS 182.

906 See for the Schengen *Acquis*, *OJ* L 239, 22.9.2000, pp. 1–473.

907 *OJ* C 197, 12.7.2000, pp. 1–23.

908 *OJ* C 326, 21.11.2001, pp. 1–8.

The 2000 EU Convention has been adopted in all Member States, except for Greece, Italy, Ireland and Croatia. The non-EU States of Gibraltar, Norway and Iceland have acceded to it. The 2001 EU Protocol has not yet been ratified by Croatia, Greece, Estonia, Ireland and Italy. As a result of its character as being a development of the Schengen *Acquis*, it applies to Iceland and Norway.[909]

The international instruments mentioned above are mostly concerned with the cooperation in criminal matters between judicial authorities, as requests for MLA are often exclusively reserved for such channels. In contrast to judicial cooperation, the framework of international police cooperation may also be of interest in the area of asset recovery. This is especially the case at the investigatory stage of the proceedings, which is further highlighted in Chapter 9 below.

Apart from the instruments regarding requests for MLA, the EU legislator has also in other ways taken measures in order to enhance international cooperation in asset recovery cases.[910] One example is the FD on Asset Recovery Offices.[911] This instrument is further discussed in Sections 9.1.3 and 9.2.2 below.

8.3. EU INSTRUMENTS ON MUTUAL RECOGNITION

In 2003, the Council Framework Decision 2003/577/JHA on the Execution in the European Union of Orders Freezing Property or Evidence (hereafter the "FD on Freezing Orders") was adopted within the EU.[912] This framework decision extends the mutual recognition principle to certain pre-trial orders and provides for more swift procedures in order to secure evidence and to seize property which are easily movable. This instrument, which especially concerns issues in the area of confiscation, will be described and evaluated in Chapter 10. The EU legislator has in the area of confiscation also extended the mutual recognition principle to final confiscation orders. The Council Framework Decision 2006/783/JHA of 6 October 2006 on the application of the principle of mutual recognition to confiscation orders (hereafter the "FD on Confiscation Orders") provides the rules under which a Member State shall recognise and execute in its territory a confiscation order issued by a court competent in criminal matters of another Member State.[913] This instrument is discussed in Chapter 11 below.

---

909 See Recital (2) and Art. 15 2001 EU Protocol.

910 See generally on asset recovery in the EU, A. Bacarese, "Advancing International Understanding and Cooperation in Combating Fraud and Corruption: Recovering Stolen Assets – A New Issue?" (2009) 10 *ERA Forum*, p. 421, especially pp. 429–33.

911 *OJ* L 332, 18.12.2007, pp. 103–05.

912 *OJ* L 196, 02.8.2003, pp. 45–55.

913 *OJ* L 328, 24.11.2006, pp. 59–78 and an Amending Act thereto (Framework Decision 2009/299/JHA), *OJ* L 81, 27.3.2009, pp. 24–36.

In 2008, another initiative in order to implement the principle of mutual recognition in the field of evidence gathering was adopted: the Council Framework Decision 2008/978/JHA on the European evidence warrant for the purpose of obtaining objects, documents and data for use in proceedings in criminal matters (hereafter the "FD on EEW").[914] This instrument allows that a State issues a European evidence warrant ("EEW") in order to obtain pieces of evidence for use in proceedings in criminal matters. However, the FD on EEW has a very limited scope, as it may only be applied in order to obtain evidence already gathered in an executing State at the time when the EEW is issued. Accordingly, it is only applicable to a limited part of the evidence gathering, and practitioners will still have to use requests for MLA for all other evidentiary matters. The framework decision has therefore had no real impact in practice, and has only been implemented by Denmark and Finland. In any case, it will in the future be replaced by Directive 2014/41/EU of the European Parliament and of the Council of 3 April 2014 regarding the European Investigation Order in criminal matters (hereafter the "Directive on EIO").[915] The Member States must comply with this new instrument by 22 May 2017.

The Directive on EIO will replace also other instruments regarding MLA and mutual recognition between the Member States. Against the background that the Directive will significantly change the regime of cooperation in criminal matters within the EU in the future, it seems reasonable to describe the system in some detail. The outline is primarily concentrated on provisions which may be of interest regarding international requests in the area of asset recovery.

---

914 *OJ* L 350, 30.12.2008, pp. 72–92. See on this instrument, B. Hecker, "Mutual Recognition and Transfer of Evidence: The European Evidence Order" in S. Ruggeri (ed.), *Transnational Inquiries and the Protection of Fundamental Rights in Criminal Proceedings*, Springer, 2013, pp. 269–78.

915 *OJ* L 130, 1.5.2014, pp. 1–36. This instrument was adopted after lengthy discussions between the Member States. See for the original proposal, *Initiative for a Directive of the European Parliament and of the Council regarding the European Investigation Order in Criminal Matters from the Kingdom of Belgium, the Republic of Bulgaria, the Republic of Estonia, the Kingdom of Spain, the Grand Duthy of Luxembourg, the Republic of Austria, the Republic of Slovenia and the Kingdom of Sweden*, 9145/10, COPEN 115, Brussels 29.4.2010. On its background and the negotiations, see for example L. Bachmaier Winter, "European Investigation Order for Obtaining Evidence in the Criminal Proceedings, Study of the Proposal for a European Directive" (2010) 9 *ZIS*, pp. 580–89, S. Ruggeri, "Horizontal Cooperation, Obtaining Evidence Overseas and the Respect for Fundamental Rights in the EU. From the European Commission's Proposals to the Proposal for a Directive on a European Investigation Order: Towards a Single Tool of Evidence Gathering in the EU?" in S. Ruggeri (ed.), *Transnational Inquiries and the Protection of Fundamental Rights in Criminal Proceedings*, Springer, 2013, pp. 279–310 and A. Mangiaracina, "A New and Controversial Scenario in the Gathering of Evidence at the European Level: The Proposal for a Directive on the European Investigation Order" (2014) 10 *Utrecht Law Review*, pp. 113–33.

8.4. THE DIRECTIVE ON EIO

The Directive on EIO will provide for one unified and single instrument for the gathering and transfer of evidence between the Member States.[916] Thereby it will replace the existing provisions on cross-border evidence gathering between the Member States bound by the Directive; namely the 1959 Convention and its two additional protocols, the Schengen Convention, the 2000 EU Convention, the 2001 EU Protocol, the FD on EEW and partly the FD on Freezing Orders (as regards freezing of evidence).[917] The UK has opted into it, whereas Ireland and Denmark have chosen not to take part.

An European Investigation Order is a judicial decision "issued or validated by a judicial authority" of a Member State to have one or several specific investigative measure(s) carried out in another Member State to obtain evidence in accordance with the directive.[918] An order may also concern the obtaining of evidence that is already in the possession of the competent authorities of the executing State. Article 2(b)–(c) defines that an 'issuing authority' means a judge, a court, an investigating judge, a public prosecutor and also any other investigating authority that has the power to order the gathering of evidence in accordance with national law. In the last case, the EIO must be validated by a judge, court, investigating judge or a public prosecutor in the issuing State.

An EIO is not restricted to certain criminal offences and may be issued in respect of criminal proceedings as well as certain administrative proceedings in criminal matters.[919] The directive covers requests for any kind of investigative measures except the setting up of a joint investigation team (Article 3). Judicial authorities may, for example, issue an EIO in order to interview witnesses, to carry out a search or seizure or to monitor bank accounts. Specific provisions have been given on particular investigative measures, for example the hearing by videoconference, requests for banking information and interception of telecommunications.[920]

The judicial authorities of an issuing State may only issue an EIO where it is "necessary and proportionate" and where the investigative measures in question could have been ordered "under the same conditions in a similar domestic case" (Article 6). The underlying philosophy of the directive is that the EIO focuses on the investigative measure to be carried out. In principle, an issuing authority is supposed to be best placed to decide which investigative measure is to be used.

---

916 See on the instrument, for example L. Bachmaier, "Transnational Evidence: Towards the Transposition of Directive 2014/41 regarding the European Investigation Order in Criminal Matters" (2015) 2 *eucrim*, pp. 47–60.

917 Art. 34 Directive on EIO.

918 Art. 1 Directive on EIO.

919 See further Art. 4 Directive on EIO.

920 See further Chapter IV Directive on EIO.

However, an executing authority may have recourse to an investigative measure other than that provided for in the EIO in the following cases where:

(a) the investigative measure indicated in the EIO does not exist under the law of the executing State; or
(b) the investigative measure indicated in the EIO would not be available in a similar domestic case.[921]

According to Article 10(2) the following investigative measures must always be available under the law of the executing State:

(a) the obtaining of information or evidence which is already in the possession of the executing authority and the information or evidence could have been obtained, in accordance with the law of the executing State, in the framework of criminal proceedings or for the purposes of the EIO;
(b) the obtaining of information contained in databases held by police or judicial authorities and directly accessible by the executing authority in the framework of criminal proceedings;
(c) the hearing of a witness, expert, victim, suspected or accused person or third party in the territory of the executing State;
(d) any non-coercive investigative measure as defined under the law of the executing State;[922] and
(e) the identification of persons holding a subscription of a specified phone number or IP address.

An executing authority may also opt for an investigative measure other than that indicated in the EIO if such a measure would be less intrusive and still achieve the same result (Article 10(3)).

The executing authority shall recognise the EIO "without any further formality" and ensure its execution in the same way and under the same modalities as in a domestic case, unless any of the grounds for non-recognition or non-execution apply.[923] The original *Proposal for a Directive on EIO* presented in 2010 contained a very significant restriction of the grounds for refusal of an order. For the first time in a mutual recognition instrument in criminal matters it was, for example, proposed that a requirement of double criminality would be fully dropped.[924] The proposal resulted in lengthy negotiations in the Council,

921 Recital (10) and Art. 10(1) Directive on EIO.

922 According to Recital (16) non-coercive measures could be, for example, such measures that do not infringe the right to privacy or the right to property, depending on national law.

923 Art. 9 Directive on EIO.

924 Compare Art. 10 in the *Initiative for a Directive of the European Parliament and of the Council regarding the European Investigation Order in Criminal Matters from the Kingdom of Belgium, the Republic of Bulgaria, the Republic of Estonia, the Kingdom of Spain, the Grand Duthy of Luxembourg, the Republic of Austria, the Republic of Slovenia and the Kingdom of Sweden,*

and many of its provisions were widely criticised from the perspective of legal certainty and human rights implications.[925] The text was significantly amended during the process and when it comes to the grounds for refusal, an executing State may now on the basis of Article 11 Directive on EIO refuse to recognise and execute an EIO where:

(a) there is an immunity or a privilege under the law of the executing State;
(b) there is a risk of harm of essential national security interests;
(c) the EIO has been issued in proceedings brought by administrative or judicial authorities referred to in Art. 4(b) and (c) of the Directive and the investigative measure would not be authorised under the law of the executing State in a similar domestic case;
(d) the execution of the EIO would be contrary to the principle of *ne bis in idem*;
(e) the EIO relates to a criminal offence which is alleged to have been committed outside the territory of the issuing State and wholly or partially on the territory of the executing State, and the conduct in connection with which the EIO is issued is not an offence in the executing State;
(f) there are substantial grounds to believe that the execution of the investigative measure would be incompatible with the executing State's human rights obligations;
(g) the conduct for which the EIO has been issued does not constitute an offence under the law of the executing State, unless it concerns an offence listed within the categories of offences set out in Annex D,[926] as indicated by the issuing authority in the EIO, if it is punishable in the issuing State by a custodial sentence or a detention order for a maximum period of at least three years; or
(h) the use of the investigative measure indicated in the EIO is restricted under the law of the executing State to a list or category of offences or to offences punishable by a certain threshold, which does not include the offence covered by the EIO.[927]

All but the last two refusal grounds apply to any EIO irrespective of the investigative measure in question. The requirement of double criminality

---

9145/10, COPEN 115, Brussels 29.4.2010 and the *Explanatory Memorandum* thereto, 9288/10 ADD 1, COPEN 117, Brussels 3.6.2010, pp. 11–12.

925 See for example Bachmaier Winter, n 915 above, C. Heard and D. Mansell, "The European Investigation Order: Changing the Face of Evidence-gathering in EU Cross Border Cases" (2011) 2 *New Journal of European Criminal Law*, pp. 353–67 and Mangiaracina, n 915 above.

926 Examples of criminal offences listed in Annex D are: participation in a criminal organisation, terrorism, trafficking in human beings, drug offences, corruption, fraud, money laundering and organised or armed robbery.

927 Art. 11(3) provides that where the EIO concerns an offence in connection with taxes or duties, customs and exchange, the executing authority shall not refuse recognition or execution on the ground that the law of the executing State does not impose the same kind of tax or duty or does not contain a tax, duty, customs and exchange regulation of the same kind as the law of the issuing State.

expressed in (g) and (h) above do *not apply* to the investigative measures which have been listed above which are referred to in Article 10(2).

There is a standardised form for the EIO provided for in Annex A to the Directive on EIO, and the order is to be sent directly between the issuing and the executing authorities.[928] The investigative measures shall be carried out with the "same celerity and priority" as for a similar domestic case and within certain deadlines. The decision on the recognition or execution of a EIO must be taken in principle no later than 30 days from the receipt of the order by the competent executing authority. The investigative measure shall be carried out without delay and not later than within 90 days. Both deadlines can be extended in specific cases by a maximum of 30 days.[929] There is a more strict deadline regarding provisional measures (see further Section 10.1.2.2 below).

8.5. AN OUTLINE OF THE FOLLOWING CHAPTERS

To sum up, within the EU requests for cross-border assistance in the area of confiscation may be based on either:

- multinational or EU instruments which specifically regulate issues of confiscation, and/or
- multinational or EU instruments which more generally provide for MLA.

Within the EU, in both these areas, some of these instruments are built upon the principle of mutual recognition. Accordingly, there are various, partly overlapping, instruments which may be applied, meaning that a practitioner has in many cases a choice between different legal frameworks. The use of a legal basis for a request or an order depends on *inter alia* ratifying/implementing States, criminal offences and the procedural measure in question. The States have also made numerous reservations and declarations regarding, for example, the 1959 Convention and the 2000 EU Convention, which must be taken into consideration before a request is made. The international regime can therefore be characterised as fragmented and complicated, and there is different scope and requirements depending on which instrument is used.

In order to provide for an efficient regime on asset recovery, there is a need for international cooperation in all stages of the confiscation process, which

928 Arts. 5 and 7 Directive on EIO. Art. 20 of the Directive further contains certain rules on the data protection of information transmitted in execution of an EIO. Compare Recital (40)–(42) Directive on EIO.

929 Art. 12 Directive on EIO.

was identified in Section 1.3.2 above. Accordingly, transnational regulation is necessary during the:

(1) *investigation stage*, where the proceeds from criminal offences are investigated, identified, traced and seized,
(2) *judicial stage* involving evidence gathering, the preparation of a plea for confiscation and the court proceedings handling the motion,
(3) *maintenance stage* during which the seized asset is stored, managed and maintained, and/or
(4) *execution stage* where the confiscation order is to be executed and the asset disposed of.

The following chapters give an overview of the current EU legal framework for cross-border cooperation in confiscation matters. The main focus is on the investigation of assets, the seizure and confiscation thereof, which means that stages 1–2 and 4 above will be included. There is no space for inclusion of the maintenance stage, even if it must be acknowledged that the issue of how a seized asset is stored, managed and maintained is also of significant importance in the international context. The costs for storing and maintaining certain property (for example yachts, vehicles or animals) may be significant and there may be a need for rules dividing this cost between the States.

It is often argued that cross-border cooperation within the area of asset recovery is hindered by different national approaches and requirements for confiscation.[930] The measure of extended confiscation is hereby especially complicated. Even if Directive 2014/42/EU does not address the issue of international cooperation directly, it aims to improve mutual recognition by providing for common rules. In the following chapters, the directive is therefore put in a broader international context. The aim is to consider to what extent it may boost the handling of transnational cases.

The following chapters have been divided into *cross-border asset tracing and exchange of information* (Chapter 9), *international cooperation in order to seize or freeze assets* (Chapter 10) and *international cooperation in order to execute final confiscation orders* (Chapter 11). In the framework of each chapter, some of the overarching difficulties of the legal framework will be highlighted, discussed or illustrated by some selected issues from the viewpoint of some national approaches to confiscation. Thereby the national provisions discussed represent either a certain amount of "best practice" or are used to illustrate an area where the national system has particular difficulties. Accordingly, German legislation

930 See for example United Nations Office on Drugs and Crime, *Digest of Organized Crime Cases: A Compilation of Cases with Commentaries and Lessons Learned*, 2012, p. 96 or Council of the European Union, *Report on Eurojust's Experience in the Field of Asset Recovery, including Freezing and Confiscation*, 10179/15, COPEN 162, Brussels 22.6.2015, p. 4.

will be highlighted in Section 9.2.3, the Swedish legislation in Section 10.2.2 as well as in Section 11.2.2.2 and the English legislation in Section 11.2.3.

In the context of the adoption of Directive 2014/42/EU, the need for a consolidated legal framework for freezing and confiscation orders was acknowledged by the European Parliament and the Council. The European Commission was therefore called upon to prepare a new legislative proposal on a comprehensive system of mutual recognition of freezing and confiscation orders, including a further examination of "the concept of freezing". In addition, any possible difficulties in the implementation of mutual recognition instruments following from the new provision of extended confiscation should be specifically considered.[931] In December 2016, a proposal for a Regulation of the European Parliament and of the Council on the Mutual Recognition of Freezing and Confiscation Orders (hereafter the "*Proposal for a Regulation on Mutual Recognition*") was presented.[932] If adopted, this instrument would create one single legal instrument by replacing the FD on Freezing Orders and the FD on Confiscation Orders for the Member States that are bound by these instruments. A reform of this area is crucial for the development of the transnational confiscation regime within the EU. The draft proposal for a regulation is described and discussed in Chapter 12.

[931] *Joint Statement by the European Parliament and the Council issued upon the adoption of Directive 2014/42/EU*, Council of the European Union, 7329/1/14, COPEN 83, Brussels 31.3.2014.

[932] COM(2016) 819 final, Brussels 21.12.2016.

CHAPTER 9

CROSS-BORDER ASSET TRACING AND EXCHANGE OF INFORMATION

9.1. THE LEGAL FRAMEWORK

9.1.1. REQUESTS WITHIN THE FRAMEWORK OF INTERNATIONAL POLICE COOPERATION

During the investigative stage any assets must be identified, searched for, located and documented. This is a multifaceted activity with overlapping objectives as criminal assets must not only be found, but it may also be necessary to acquire sufficient evidence to link the asset to an unlawful activity or to the criminal offence.[933] A request for assistance at the investigative stage may be of varied character, but common requests concern for example:

- to obtain information on whether any assets are present in another State,
- to trace and search for specific assets abroad, and/or
- to gather evidence needed to support a confiscation order.

The tracing of criminal assets is not an easy task in itself, and there is a significant need for specialised and trained units:

> the multiple forms assets can take means that investigators must have an understanding of a wide range of spheres, including financial markets, corporate and commercial structures, banking practices, property and insolvency law, and online currencies in order to successfully trace the path of a converted asset.[934]

---

933 See further on this, C. Monteith and A. Dornbierer, "Tracking and Tracing Stolen Assets in Foreign Jurisdictions" (2013) 2 *eucrim*, p. 51, p 51. Compare also generally on the investigative process, *Tracing Stolen Assets: A Practitioner's Handbook*, International Centre for Asset Recovery, Basel 2009, and for a useful guide for practitioners in this area, *Tracing Illegal Assets, Basel Institute on Governance International Centre for Asset Recovery*, 2015.

934 Monteith and Dornbierer, n 933 above, p. 52.

Financial investigations are conducted by different authorities, for example police forces, prosecutors or investigating magistrates. These authorities may need access to different types of information regarding property, for example land registers, company registers, records on vehicles and data from insurance companies or tax authorities.[935] Transnational exchange of information or intelligence in confiscation cases may take place in many different ways, but a significant part of the initial investigation takes place within the framework of international cooperation between *police forces*. Often it is possible to directly share intelligence or data which is legally available to the agencies through domestic databases. There are currently numerous channels for informal and formal police-cooperation, which may be used in order to search for assets abroad. Examples are liaison officers, *Europol*, *Interpol* or the CARIN network.[936] The specialised framework of the national asset recovery offices set up by the FD on Asset Recovery Offices is also an important cooperation channel. Also the Financial Intelligence Units ("FIUs") may be useful. These initiatives are further described in Section 9.1.3 below.

An important basis for exchange of information and intelligence between law enforcement authorities is the Council Framework Decision 2006/960/JHA of 18 December 2006 on simplifying the exchange of information and intelligence between law enforcement authorities of the Member States of the European Union.[937] As the framework decision was initiated by Sweden it is usually referred to as the "Swedish Initiative", which will be used also in the following.[938] This instrument was adopted against the background of a need to improve the existing ways of exchanging information and intelligence. The EU legislator argued that the current regime was "seriously hampered by formal procedures, administrative structures and legal obstacles".[939] The purpose was therefore to:

> establish the rules under which Member States' law enforcement authorities may exchange existing information and intelligence effectively and expeditiously

---

935 See generally on asset tracking and tracing, A. Kennedy, "Winning the Information Wars: Collecting, Sharing and Analysing Information in Asset Recovery Investigations" (2007) 14 *Journal of Financial Crime*, pp. 372–404 and Monteith and Dornbierer, n 933 above.

936 Information from foreign jurisdictions may also in specific cases be obtained through participation in a Joint Investigation Team ("JIT"). The CARIN network is described further in Section 9.1.3 below.

937 *OJ* L 386, 29.12.2006, pp. 89–100. Compare the *Guidelines to the Implementation of Council Framework Decision 2006/960/JHA of 18 December 2006 on Simplifying the Exchange of Information and Intelligence between Law Enforcement Authorities of the Member States of the European Union*, Council of the European Union, 9512/1/10, REV 1, Brussels 17.12.2010.

938 See for the original proposal, *Initiative of the Kingdom of Sweden with a view to adopting a Framework Decision on simplifying the exchange of information and intelligence between law enforcement authorities of the Member States of the European Union, in particular as regards serious offences including terrorist acts*, *OJ* 281, 18.11.2004, pp. 5–10.

939 Compare Recital (6) in the Swedish Initiative.

for the purpose of conducting criminal investigations or criminal intelligence operations.[940]

Obviously, the aim was not to centralise all exchange of information, but to *facilitate the existing cooperation* by providing common rules on procedure, time-limits and grounds for refusal. The framework decision thereby replaced some provisions of the Schengen Convention.[941] All Member States have implemented the instrument. As it is classified as a development of the Schengen *Acquis*, the framework decision also applies to Iceland, Norway and Switzerland.[942]

In the *Hague Programme* the *principle of availability* was propounded as a new principle for cooperation between law enforcement agencies within the EU.[943] The Swedish Initiative aimed at realising this by adopting the *principle of equivalent access.* Accordingly, the conditions for providing information and intelligence to law enforcement authorities of other Member States must not be stricter than the conditions which apply in purely national cases.[944] Access to available information must thus be equivalent for both domestic and foreign authorities, and where a judicial authorisation is needed prior to providing information, the authority must apply to its decision the same rules as in a national case.[945] This means, for example, that it is not allowed to demand a request for MLA in a cross-border case if such judicial authorisation is not needed in a domestic case.

According to Article 2(d) the terms "information" and "intelligence" cover any type of information or data which is held by law enforcement authorities or public authorities or private entities and which is available to law enforcement authorities without taking coercive measures. There are thus certain limits to the obligation to exchange information. First, there is no obligation to *gather and store* information and intelligence purely for the purpose of providing it to law enforcement authorities of other Member States or to obtain any information or intelligence *by means of coercive measures.*[946] Secondly, there is no obligation to provide information and intelligence to be used as *evidence before a judicial authority* nor is there any right to use information or intelligence for that purpose.

---

940 Art. 1(1) in the Swedish Initiative. For the definition of a "law enforcement authority", compare Art. 2(a).

941 See further Art. 12(1) in the Swedish Initiative.

942 See Recitals (13) and (14) in the Swedish Initiative.

943 European Council, *The Hague Programme*, Presidency Conclusions 4–5 November 2004.

944 Art. 3(3) in the Swedish Initiative.

945 Art. 3(4) in the Swedish Initiative. See further Council Framework Decision 2006/960/JHA – Assessment of compliance according to Article 11(2), Council Document 14755/1/12 REV 1, CRIMORG 114, 15 November 2012, p. 2.

946 Art. 1(3) and (5) in the Swedish Initiative. The meaning of "coercive measures" is to be defined in accordance with national law of the Member State receiving the request for information or intelligence.

In a case where a Member State wishes to use information or intelligence as evidence before a judicial authority, it has to obtain consent from the requested Member State. When required under national law of this State, this must take place on the basis of the instruments on MLA. (On the other hand, such consent is not required where the requested Member State has already given its consent for the use of information as evidence at the time of the transmittal.)[947]

States have generally different requirements under national law regarding in which cases a formal request for MLA is needed. The need for the involvement of a judicial authority at different stages of a criminal proceeding varies. Some States, for example, allow that information is provided although it was previously obtained by means of coercive measures.[948]

Article 10 in the Swedish Initiative contains certain rights for a requested State to withhold information and intelligence:

(1) if providing the information would be likely to "harm essential national security interests of the requested Member State", or "jeopardise the success of a current investigation or a criminal intelligence operation, or the safety of individuals", or if the information would "clearly be disproportionate or irrelevant with regard to the purposes for which it has been requested";
(2) if "the request pertains to an offence punishable by a term of imprisonment of one year or less under the law of the requested Member State"; or
(3) "if the ... judicial authority has not authorised the access and exchange of the information".

A request may be sent in cases where there are *factual reasons* to believe that relevant information and intelligence is available in another Member State.[949] The law enforcement authorities may thereby use any existing channel of international law enforcement cooperation, for example via bilateral liaison officers, *Europol*, the SIRENE Bureaux[950] or via *Interpol*.[951] Each of these channels has its own purpose, special requirements and ways of communication. The Member States have been recommended to structure the police cooperation nationally so that there is one Single Point of Contact ("SPOC") in order to gather all requests and determine the most appropriate channel for cooperation.

947 Art. 1(4) in the Swedish Initiative.
948 Compare Art. 1(6) in the Swedish Initiative.
949 Art. 5(1) in the Swedish Initiative.
950 Supplementary Information Request at the National Entry.
951 For a general analysis of transnational intelligence sharing in the EU especially from the perspective of fundamental rights, see J. Ballaschk, "In the Unseen Realm: Transnational Intelligence Sharing in the European Union – Challenges to Fundamental Rights and Democratic Legitimacy" (2015) 51 *Stanford Journal of International Law*, pp. 19–52.

Certain time-limits have been set up for cooperation. Any requests regarding the criminal offences referred to in Article 2(2) of the Framework Decision 2002/584/JHA on the European arrest warrant[952] should be responded to within one week if the requested information or intelligence is held in a database directly accessible by a law enforcement authority. An urgent request shall be responded to within eight hours. In all other cases, the maximum period for response is 14 days. The notion of "urgency" has been left to national practice.[953] In order to encourage a speedy handling of cases, a standard form for requests has been provided in an annex to the framework decision. However, these forms are rarely used in practice, as they are considered to be time-consuming and difficult to use.[954]

A significant part of the initial investigatory measures in confiscation cases, in order to search for assets and obtain information from abroad, takes place within the framework of international cooperation between police forces or other law enforcement authorities. Such channels of informal and direct assistance may in practice be very smooth and speedy. However, the use of this regime is, as already mentioned, sometimes restricted by various requirements that such requests must be processed through the cooperation channels of judicial authorities. In the following, this legal framework will be outlined.

9.1.2. REQUESTS WITHIN THE FRAMEWORK OF INTERNATIONAL COOPERATION BETWEEN JUDICIAL AUTHORITIES

The channels of judicial cooperation in criminal matters are usually *required* to be used in the following situations:

(1) if the information is to be used as *evidence* in order to support a confiscation order in a criminal trial. An example of this is when pieces of evidence are needed in order to prove that certain assets exist and belong to a defendant, or in order to link an asset to an unlawful activity or to a criminal offence. It can, for example, be necessary to obtain documents to be presented in court or to initiate hearings of witnesses. Another task of judicial authorities in this respect is to consider

---

952 *OJ* L 190, 18.7.2002, pp. 1–18.

953 Art. 4 in the Swedish Initiative. Some interpretation and examples of such situations are given in *Guidelines to the Implementation of Council Framework Decision 2006/960/JHA of 18 December 2006 on Simplifying the Exchange of Information and Intelligence between Law Enforcement Authorities of the Member States of the European Union*, Council of the European Union, 9512/1/10, REV 1, Brussels 17.12.2010, p. 7.

954 European Commission, Directorate-General Migration and Home Affairs, *Study on the Implementation of the European Information Exchange Model (EIXM) for Strengthening Law Enforcement Cooperation*, Final Report, 26.1.2015, p. 28.

whether information *already collected and obtained* via the channels of police cooperation (for example on the basis of the Swedish Initiative) may be used as evidence in the judicial proceedings. This usually depends on the international instrument in question and on the national legislation of the requested State;

(2) if different coercive measures (for example a house search) are necessary in order to *search* for assets to be confiscated or in order to *gather evidence* and to obtain documents which are not delivered voluntarily. (It is here thus not a matter of taking coercive measures in order to secure the asset in support of the execution of a final confiscation order.);[955]

(3) if the information in question can only be obtained after *approval* by a judicial authority; or

(4) if the information in question can only be obtained after a *request* from such an authority. An example of this is information regarding banking issues.

It can be added that, when it comes to evidentiary issues, the regime of extended confiscation is somewhat peculiar. In a case regarding ordinary confiscation where the motion for confiscation concerns the criminal proceeds of a particular offence, evidence may be needed in order both to investigate and prove the criminal offence and to support a confiscation order. In cases of extended confiscation, there may be a need to gather and transmit evidence in order to support alleged criminal activity of the defendant, which is not specifically connected to the triggering offence.

A request for MLA with the purpose to identify, locate and search for assets abroad may be based on different treaties. The general obligation to execute international requests in Articles 1–5 of the European Convention on Mutual Assistance in Criminal Matters (hereafter the "1959 Convention") does not expressly extend to MLA with the purpose *only* of confiscation. The provisions regulate "letters rogatory relating to a criminal matter" and "for the purpose of procuring evidence or transmitting articles to be produced in evidence, records and documents".[956] This formulation suggests that a request should concern property which is needed as *evidence* in a trial and should not be made with the purpose only to trace property to be confiscated.[957] On the other hand, the 1959 Convention also obligates the States to give each other the "widest measure of mutual assistance" (Article 1(1)), and in the end it is up to national States how they interpret and implement the provisions. Accordingly, many States execute such requests within the framework of the 1959 Convention.

---

955 This is primarily discussed in Chapter 10 below.

956 See for example Art. 3(1) of the 1959 Convention.

957 See further on this, G. Stessens, *Money Laundering; A New International Law Enforcement Model*, Cambridge University Press, 2000, pp. 370–71 and D. McClean, *International Cooperation in Civil and Criminal Matters*, Oxford University Press, 2002 p. 177.

In any case, the European Convention on Laundering, Search, Seizure and Confiscation of the Proceeds from Crime (1990) expressly provides for MLA in these cases. Article 7 obligates the Parties to cooperate with each other to the "widest extent possible for the purposes of investigations and proceedings aiming at the confiscation of instrumentalities and proceeds". Article 8 specifies that MLA shall be given regarding "the identification and tracing of instrumentalities, proceeds and other property liable to confiscation", and that this shall include any measure providing and securing evidence as to the existence, location or movement of property. The United Nations Convention against Illicit Traffic in Narcotic Drugs and Psychotropic Substances (1988) also contains clear obligations in this respect (Article 5). Between ratifying Member States, a request may further be based on the 2000 EU Convention. Such requests may be sent directly between the judicial authorities within the EU. In general, it is decided by *national legislation of the requested State* under what circumstances requests are executed and whether (and which) coercive measures may be taken in order to identify and search for assets to be confiscated.

Of significant importance in the area of confiscation are obviously international requests for information regarding bank accounts and banking transactions. Such information is often necessary at an initial stage of the preliminary investigation in order to prepare a request for seizure or freezing. This type of information can usually only be obtained after a request from a judicial authority. Within the EU the 2001 EU Protocol provides for a specific regime that significantly facilitates the transfer of such information.[958] The following three measures are included:

1. *Information on bank accounts*: Article 1(1) obligates the Member States to provide each other assistance in determination of:

> whether a natural or legal person that is the subject of a criminal investigation holds or controls one or more accounts, of whatever nature, in any bank located in its territory and, if so, provide all the details of the identified accounts.

The obligation relates to "any bank" in the territory of the requested State, and a Member State is thus required to be able to perform this task. This means that if there is no central bank register, it might be necessary to address all banks located in the territory in order to comply with such a request.[959] The

---

958 With regard to formalities and procedure, the provisions in Art. 3 of 1959 Convention and Art. 4 of the 2000 EU Convention apply.

959 This means that this article cannot be interpreted as stating an obligation *per se* to set up centralised bank registers. See *Explanatory Report to the Protocol to the 2000 Convention on Mutual Assistance in Criminal Matters between the Member States of the European Union*, OJ C 257, 24.10.2002, pp. 1–9, at p. 2.

information in question must, though, be in the possession of the bank keeping the account.[960] The obligation to give information only applies for the following criminal offences:

- an offence punishable by a penalty of a maximum period of at least four years of imprisonment in the requesting State and at least two years in the requested State, or
- an offence within the area of Europol's competence,[961] or
- an offence referred to in the 1995 Convention on the Protection of the European Communities' Financial Interests, and its protocols from 1996 and 1997.[962]

The limitation of this form of MLA to certain offences was *inter alia* motivated by the fact that such requests amount to a lot of work in a requested State.[963] A requested State may make the execution of a request dependent on the same conditions as apply to requests for search and seizure (Article 1(5)). This means that there can be further requirements that there is double criminality, an extraditable offence or that execution is consistent with the law of the requested State.[964] It must be specified in a request why the requested information is likely to be of substantial value for the purpose of the investigation into the offence. In order to facilitate the execution and prevent any "fishing expeditions", it is also required that it is indicated on what grounds it can be presumed that banks in the requested State hold the account and, to the extent possible, which banks may be involved (Article 1(4)).
2. *Information on banking transactions that have taken place in the past*: Article 2 of the 2001 EU Protocol states that the requested State:

> shall provide the particulars of specified bank accounts and of banking operations which have been carried out during a specified period through one or more accounts specified in the request, including the particulars of any sending or recipient account.

---

960 Art. 1(2) 2001 EU Protocol.

961 Offences referred to in Art. 2 of the *Council Act of 26 July 1995 drawing up the Convention based on Article K.3 of the Treaty on European Union, on the Establishment of a European Police Office*, *OJ* C 316, 27.11.1995, pp. 1–32 or in the Annex to that Convention.

962 *Council Act of 26 July 1995 drawing up the Convention on the Protection of the European Communities' Financial Interests*, *OJ* C 316, 27.11.1995, pp. 48–57, *Council Act of 27 September 1996 drawing up a Protocol to the Convention on the Protection of the European Communities' Financial Interests*, *OJ* C 313, 23.10.1996, pp. 1–10 and *Council Act of 19 June 1997 drawing up the Second Protocol of the Convention on the Protection of the European Communities' Financial Interests*, *OJ* C 221, 19.7.1997, pp. 11–22.

963 *Explanatory Report to the Protocol to the 2000 Convention on Mutual Assistance in Criminal Matters between the Member States of the European Union*, *OJ* C 257, 24.10.2002, pp. 1–9, at p. 3.

964 See further *Explanatory Report to the Protocol to the 2000 Convention on Mutual Assistance in Criminal Matters between the Member States of the European Union*, *OJ* C 257, 24.10.2002, pp. 1–9, at p. 4.

This article is different to Article 1, because it does not make any references to accounts linked to the person that is subject to the criminal investigation. This means that such requests may also concern accounts held by third persons.[965] Any obligation applies only to the extent that the information is in the possession of the bank keeping the account. A requesting State is obligated to state in the request why it considers that the requested information is likely to be of substantial value for the purpose of the investigation into the offence. The Member States may make the execution dependent on the same conditions as apply to requests for search and seizure.[966]

3. *Monitoring of future banking transactions:* According to Article 3 a requested State shall:

> Monitor, during a specified period, the banking operations that are being carried out through one or more accounts specified in the request and communicate the results thereof to the requesting Member State.

A requesting State shall indicate in the request why it considers the requested information to be relevant for the purpose of the investigation into the offence. The Member States are obligated to set up a mechanism for such requests. However, a decision to monitor is to be taken in each individual case by the competent authorities of the requested Member State, with due regard for its national law. This means that a State may apply requirements such as, for example, double criminality or a certain minimum penalty threshold.[967]

An important provision of the 2001 EU Protocol is the obligation for the Member States to ensure that banks do not disclose to the bank customer concerned or to third persons that information has been transmitted to the requesting State, or that an investigation is being carried out (Article 4). The Protocol also abolishes some traditional refusal grounds, as Article 7 states that banking secrecy shall not be invoked as a reason for refusing any cooperation.[968] Neither shall a request be refused solely on the ground that it concerns a fiscal

---

965 *Explanatory Report to the Protocol to the 2000 Convention on Mutual Assistance in Criminal Matters between the Member States of the European Union*, OJ C 257, 24.10.2002, pp. 1–9, at p. 5.

966 Art. 2(2)–(4) 2001 EU Protocol.

967 See further *Explanatory Report to the Protocol to the 2000 Convention on Mutual Assistance in Criminal Matters between the Member States of the European Union*, OJ C 257, 24.10.2002, pp. 1–9, at p. 6.

968 This was no novelty as this ground for refusal had already been abolished or restricted in other international instruments, see for example Art. 18(7) European Convention on Laundering, Search, Seizure and Confiscation of the Proceeds from Crime (1990) and Art. 7(5) United Nations Convention against Illicit Traffic in Narcotic Drugs and Psychotropic Substances (1988).

or political offence.[969] A spontaneous exchange of information is encouraged in cases where a requested State considers that it may be appropriate to undertake an investigation not initially foreseen (Article 5).

On 22 May 2017, the 2001 EU Protocol will be replaced by the provisions of the Directive on EIO. This directive (described briefly in Section 8.4 above) allows a judicial authority in an issuing State to issue an EIO in order to obtain information or evidence abroad. The Directive contains specific provisions allowing an EIO to be issued in order to obtain information on bank and other financial accounts (Article 26), information on banking and other financial operations in the past (Article 27) and the monitoring of future banking and other financial operations (Article 28). The corresponding rules in the 2001 EU Protocol have been used as a basis for the text of the new provisions, but there have also been different changes.[970] Some of these are editorial, but there are also some changes in substance to the regime.

As described above, Article 1(3) of the 2001 EU Protocol limits the obligation to provide information on bank accounts to certain listed criminal offences. This limitation to a list of offences has been deleted in Article 26 Directive on EIO, and the obligation to provide such assistance therefore in principle includes all types of criminal offences. This is an important improvement of the conditions for a request for banking information. Further, Articles 1(5) and 2(4) of the 2001 EU Protocol at present allow a requested State to make the execution of a request dependent on the same conditions as applied for requests for search and seizure. These paragraphs are missing from Articles 26 and 27 Directive on EIO. The execution of such an order may instead in general be refused in accordance with the grounds given in Article 11.[971] An executing State may, for example, only set up a requirement of double criminality if the conduct for which the EIO has been issued does not concern an offence listed in Annex D, as indicated by the issuing authority and punishable in the issuing State by a custodial sentence or a detention order for a maximum period of at least three years.[972] It is also possible to refuse an order if the use of an investigative measure indicated in the EIO is restricted under the law of the executing State to a list or category of

---

969 See Arts. 8 and 9 2001 EU Protocol. The abolishment of a refusal ground related to cases of fiscal offences had already been accomplished in, for example, Art. 1 of the *Additional Protocol to the European Convention on Mutual Assistance in Criminal Matters*, 1978, ETS 99.

970 As an example may be mentioned that Art. 4 of the 2001 EU Protocol on the obligation of the banks to keep the confidentiality of investigations corresponds to Art. 19(4) Directive on EIO.

971 See further Section 8.4 above.

972 Art. 11(g) of the Directive on EIO. Art. 11(3) further provides that "where the EIO concerns an offence in connection with taxes or duties, customs and exchange, the executing authority shall not refuse recognition or execution on the ground that the law of the executing State does not impose the same kind of tax or duty or does not contain a tax, duty, customs and exchange regulation of the same kind as the law of the issuing State".

offences or to offences punishable by imprisonment above a certain threshold, which does not include the offence covered by the EIO.[973]

Another difference in the Directive on EIO is that an EIO in order to obtain information on bank accounts and information on banking transactions in the past (Articles 26 and 27) may also be made in relation to *non-bank financial institutions* located in the territory of the executing State.[974] In such a case, the execution of an EIO may (in addition to the refusal grounds in Article 11 of the Directive) also be refused if the execution of the investigative measure would not be authorised in a similar domestic case.[975] Further, Recital (27) Directive on EIO states that an EIO may be issued in order to obtain evidence concerning the accounts, of whatever nature, held in any bank or any non-banking financial institution by a person subject to criminal proceedings. It is in this respect provided that this possibility "is to be understood broadly" as comprising not only suspected or accused persons, but also any other person in respect of whom such information is found necessary by the competent authorities in the course of criminal proceedings.[976] When it comes to the monitoring of bank transactions (Article 28(1)) it is provided that – in addition to the refusal grounds in Article 11 – an EIO may also be refused if the execution of the investigative measure concerned would not be authorised in a similar domestic case.

Alongside the EU instruments, there are also some other international treaties which specifically contain provisions which support requests for MLA regarding banking information, for example Article 6 United Nations Convention against Illicit Traffic in Narcotic Drugs and Psychotropic Substances (1988). Articles 17–19 of the European Convention on Laundering, Search, Seizure and Confiscation of the Proceeds from Crime and on the Financing of Terrorism (2005) contain similar provisions on requests as in the 2001 EU Protocol. This Convention also broadens the application, as the ratifying States may apply it in relation to non-bank financial institutions. As some EU Member States have not ratified the 2001 EU Protocol and/or will not take part in the Directive on EIO, the provisions may in relation to such States be important.[977]

---

973 Art. 11(h) of the Directive on EIO.

974 Recital (28) Directive on EIO further clarifies that the term "financial institutions" shall be understood according to the relevant definition of Art. 3 of Directive 2005/60/EC of the European Parliament and of the Council of 26 October 2005 on the prevention of the use of the financial system for the purpose of money laundering and terrorist financing, *OJ* L 309, 25.11.2005, pp. 15–36.

975 See further Arts. 26(6) and 27(5) Directive on EIO.

976 Recital (29) Directive on EIO provides that when an EIO is issued to obtain "details" of a specified account, this should be understood to include at least the name and address of the account holder, details of any powers of attorney held over the account, and any other details or documents regarding when the account was opened.

977 Compare on the States in question, Sections 8.2 and 8.4 above.

9.1.3. THE FD ON ASSET RECOVERY OFFICES

In addition to legislative initiatives regarding harmonisation of legal criteria for confiscation and different instruments on cross-border cooperation, legal action has also been taken in order to facilitate transnational cases by improving the institutional framework and practice of national agencies. Obviously, the EU legislator has acknowledged that a rapid exchange of information requires that the law enforcement agencies have the necessary skills to investigate and analyse financial data, as well as being able to cooperate closely with other authorities. In practice e.g. *Europol* and *Eurojust* may assist national authorities in cases regarding asset recovery in order to overcome differences in national legislation or assist with practical solutions.

In 2007, the Commission adopted the FD on Asset Recovery Offices.[978] This instrument obligates the Member States to set up or designate a centralised national Asset Recovery Office ("ARO") and ensure that these offices can exchange information rapidly.[979] The purpose of an ARO is to facilitate:

> the tracing and identification of proceeds of crime and other crime related property which may become the object of a freezing, seizure or confiscation order made by a competent judicial authority in the course of criminal or, as far as possible under the national law of the Member State concerned, civil proceedings.[980]

It has been left to the Member States to indicate the authorities which are to function as AROs and decide whether the authority forms part of an administrative authority, a law enforcement authority or a judicial authority.[981] The majority of the AROs in the Member States are police-based. Some Member States have in accordance with Article 1(2) designated two AROs, for example Germany, Lithuania and Bulgaria. In Sweden, the National Criminal Intelligence Police Service and the National Economic Crimes Bureau ("*Ekobrottsmyndigheten*") have been designated.

The AROs shall cooperate directly with each other "by exchanging information and best practices, both upon request and spontaneously".[982] An ARO of a Member State, or another authority charged with the facilitation of the tracing of proceeds of crime, may send a *request* for information to an ARO of another Member State. The procedure and the conditions for cooperation

---

978 *OJ* L 332, 18.12.2007, pp. 103–05.

979 Art. 1(1) FD on Asset Recovery Offices.

980 Art. 1(1) FD on Asset Recovery Offices.

981 Art. 1(3) and Art. 2(2) FD on Asset Recovery Offices.

982 Art. 2(1) FD on Asset Recovery Offices. A centre of excellence on asset recovery and training of financial investigators has been set up (the so-called CEART Project). This is financed by the European Commission.

take place on the basis of the provisions in the Swedish Initiative.[983] Within the limits of applicable national law, the AROs may also exchange information spontaneously.[984] Any exchange of information must be made in compliance with applicable data protection provisions and the use of information shall be subject to the national data protection provisions of the receiving Member State.[985] A concern of the operating AROs, which was expressed in the mutual evaluation process, was the lack of support of a fully secure information exchange system.[986] At present, many AROs are connected to *Europol*'s communication system SIENA ("Secure Information Exchange Network Application"), which provides for secure and swift information exchange.[987]

The aim is thus that an ARO shall function as a "central contact point for confiscation activities at national level".[988] At the adoption of the framework decision, some other networks and contact points existed. One of them was the informal global network of judicial and law-enforcement authorities; the Camden Assets Recovery Inter-Agency Network ("CARIN"). This network of contacts was established at The Hague in 2004 by Austria, Belgium, Germany, Ireland, the Netherlands and the United Kingdom and aims at improving and facilitating cross-border cooperation in all aspects of asset recovery. The European Commission supports the network, and practitioners from 53 jurisdictions and nine international organisations are included. The purpose is that the FD on Asset Recovery Offices will support and complete the CARIN network by providing a legal basis for the exchange of information between the AROs of all the Member States (compare Recital (5)). The CARIN network will thus continue to operate between and in relation to non-EU Member States. The Europol Criminal Assets Bureau ("ECAB") – which holds the CARIN secretariat – also functions as a focal point and supports the Member States in the identification and confiscation of criminal proceeds.

Other national institutions which may be used in some cases regarding cross-border exchange of information are the national Financial Intelligence Units

---

983 Compare Art. 3 and Recital (7) FD on Asset Recovery Offices. See on the Swedish Initiative, Section 9.1.1 above.

984 Art. 4 FD on Asset Recovery Offices.

985 Art. 5 FD on Asset Recovery Offices.

986 *Report from the European Commission based on Article 8 of the Council Decision 2007/845/JHA of 6 December 2007 concerning cooperation between Asset Recovery Offices of the Member States in the field of tracing and identification of proceeds from, or other property related to, crime*, COM(2011) 176 final, p. 8.

987 Cross-border asset tracing requests through SIENA increased from 472 in 2012 to over 2,000 in 2013. See further *Communication from the Commission to the European Parliament and the Council, The Final Implementation Report of the EU Internal Security Strategy 2010–2014*, COM(2014) 365 final, 20.6.2014, p. 5.

988 *Proceeds of Organised Crime; Ensuring that "Crime does not Pay"*, 20.11.2008, COM(2008) 766 final, p. 7.

("FIUs").[989] These units collect, analyse and investigate financial information provided by financial and non-banking institutions regarding suspicious or unusual financial transactions in the area of money laundering, associated offences and the financing of terrorism. They also build up profiles of individuals and money laundering practices. The structure and powers of the national FIUs differ between States. The units may be set up within administrative authorities, police forces, and judicial authorities or as a multi-disciplinary agency. In the UK, Sweden and Germany, the FIUs are all placed within the police organisation. In Luxembourg, the FIU is judicial and staffed by prosecutors. This means that it has far-reaching powers and is not limited in its investigations to the suspicious transaction reports. All FIUs are connected to the computer network FIU.NET. In 1995, the *Egmont Group of Financial Intelligence Units* was created, which provides a forum for FIUs of different States to share financial intelligence. It has currently 151 Member FIUs, including all EU FIUs. In January 2016, the FIU.NET was embedded into *Europol*. At present, a proposal to enhance the role and power of the FIUs is being discussed. This has been made in the context of a revision of the EU regime of measures against money laundering and terrorist financing.[990] This initiative is shortly described and discussed in Section 10.2.3 below.

9.2. COMMENTARIES TO THE REGIME OF INTERNATIONAL COOPERATION REGARDING THE TRACING OF ASSETS

9.2.1. THE SCOPE AND PRACTICAL APPLICATION OF THE LEGAL FRAMEWORK

The identification and tracking of assets is often the most difficult phase of the confiscation procedure. The need for proper forms for transnational cooperation is evident, especially if one considers that "information is the lifeblood of a financial investigation".[991] However, an overarching conclusion is that the international legal framework to be used for cases of cross-border cooperation at the investigatory stage is fragmented, complicated and user-unfriendly. There is on one hand a dividing line between requests based on the regime for

---

989 Within the EU, these are regulated by for example the Council Decision 2000/642/JHA of 17 October 2000 concerning arrangements for cooperation between financial intelligence units of the Member States in exchanging information, *OJ* L 271, 24.10.2000, pp. 4–6.

990 See the *Proposal for a Directive of the European Parliament and of the Council amending Directive (EU) 2015/849 on the Prevention of the use of the Financial System for the Purposes of Money Laundering or Terrorist Financing and amending Directive 2009/101/EC*, COM(2016) 450 final, Strasbourg 5.7.2016.

991 Kennedy, n 935 above, p. 395.

international police cooperation and international judicial cooperation. On the other hand, there are also not only numerous different forms and channels for police cooperation, but above all there are (too) many and partly overlapping instruments on judicial cooperation. In practice, this situation leads to difficulties and delays.

As already noted, the exchange of information via international police cooperation is of significant importance at the investigative stage of the confiscation process. In order to improve cross-border cooperation, the development of the system of a direct exchange of information is of high priority. The question of how to promote a speedy *and* proper handling of information at the international level in criminal matters is complicated. Specific factors to take account of are *inter alia* data protection rules, technical issues (i.e. secure platforms for transmitting information) and how to coordinate the many different channels of national and international police cooperation.[992] Such a far-reaching analysis cannot be provided within the framework of this study.[993] Instead I will mainly focus on the provisions and practical application of the Swedish Initiative and comment on its use in the area of confiscation.

A general conclusion is that exchange of information or intelligence on the basis of the Swedish Initiative provides significant advantages and lead to informal and smooth procedures. Often, a request only concerns the assistance with a simple check on whether a defendant owns certain real estate or vehicles in another State. The *principle of equivalent access* seems to be a reasonable method for international cooperation, as the conditions for providing information must not be stricter in a transnational case. In that way, the law enforcement agencies in principle apply "familiar provisions" and do not have to check any additional rules in cross-border cases. This being said, it can be noted that two reports have been published on the general operation of the Swedish Initiative, which both have concluded that the instrument is not yet fully applied between the Member States.[994] Certain impediments to the application of the principle of equivalent access have also been found, which seem to result from differences in the legal and administrative systems of the Member States.

---

992 It has in this respect been concluded that the tension between the need for transnational data exchange by police authorities and intelligence agencies and the need for data privacy is increasing. It has been criticised that there is no overall EU concept on data protection. See K. Lachmayer, "Rethinking Privacy Beyond Borders, Developing Transnational Rights on Data Privacy" (2015) 20 *Tilburg Law Review*, pp. 78–102.

993 For an interesting analysis which involves some of these issues, see *European Commission, Directorate-General Migration and Home Affairs, Study on the Implementation of the European Information Exchange Model (EIXM) for Strengthening Law Enforcement Cooperation*, Final Report, 26.1.2015.

994 See *Commission Staff Working Paper, Operation of the Council Framework Decision 2006/960/ JHA of 18 December 2006*, SEC(2011) 593 final, 13.5.2011 and *Council Framework Decision 2006/960/JHA – Assessment of compliance according to Article 11(2)*, Council Document 14755/1/12 REV 1, CRIMORG 114, 15.11.2012.

It is important to note that the Swedish Initiative is not an instrument which has been specifically drafted for the area of confiscation, but is a *general* instrument for exchange of information in investigations regarding various types of issues. This is evident in different areas. A first example concerns the time-limits for responding to a request. The time-limits are themselves generally an important improvement of the exchange of information, and they seem to be kept in practice in most cases.[995] However, the limits are not really drafted with consideration of the realities of international electronic transactions, where assets may be transferred to another jurisdiction within seconds. An eight-hour limit to respond to requests in urgent cases may in some cases simply be too slow. Further, it is not obvious that all requests in confiscation cases are automatically viewed as urgent.

Another difficulty in practice is the traditional limitations of transnational police cooperation. Obviously, cooperation on the basis of the Swedish Initiative may be useful to locate any assets abroad in order to decide whether to issue a confiscation order in the first place. However, as described above, a significant part of cross-border cooperation in confiscation cases at the investigatory stage *must* take place via judicial authorities. This practice is sometimes criticised by law enforcement agencies, because it is considered to slow down and complicate the exchange of information, and hinder the application of the *principle of equivalent access*.[996] One may agree that the present international regime of MLA often leads to time-consuming and cumbersome procedures. However, even if there has been a certain blur between different forms of police, administrative and judicial cooperation in criminal matters in the last years, the established principles for drawing the borderline between the competences of such authorities should be kept. It is wise in terms of legal safety to keep transnational cooperation regarding the use of coercive measures within the realm of judicial authorities.

This being said, the international framework supporting a request for MLA at the investigatory stage of a confiscation proceeding is definitely in need of reform in order to provide for more efficient and speedy procedures. Even if direct communication between the EU Member States is allowed in many cases in order to speed up the handling of cases, the overall impression is that the regulation is too fragmented. The 2001 EU Protocol is obviously a fundamental tool within a strategy of "going for the money". However, a drawback of its

995 European Commission, Directorate-General Migration and Home Affairs, *Study on the Implementation of the European Information Exchange Model (EIXM) for Strengthening Law Enforcement Cooperation*, Final Report, 26.1.2015, pp. 26–38.

996 See, for example, the views of the interviewees in European Commission, Directorate-General Migration and Home Affairs, *Study on the Implementation of the European Information Exchange Model (EIXM) for Strengthening Law Enforcement Cooperation*, Final Report, 26.1.2015, pp. 30–33.

application in practice is that not all Member States have ratified it.[997] Low rates of ratification are also seen when it comes to the European Convention on Laundering, Search, Seizure and Confiscation of the Proceeds from Crime and on the Financing of Terrorism (2005).[998]

A further general difficulty regarding requests for banking information is that not all States have central registers of bank accounts. The necessity of requests to numerous different banks and financial institutions may lead to unreasonable time delay for asset tracing nationally as well as internationally. It is not surprising that the access to banking data has been identified as the weak link in the investigation and tracing of criminal proceeds.[999] Central bank registers are available in some Member States, for example, France, Germany, Italy, Romania, Slovenia and Portugal.[1000] The system in Germany is regarded as best practice in respect of access to bank data, because it both functions quickly and is efficient.[1001] The Member States are in several international instruments obligated to render speedy information, and identify and transmit information held by financial institutions. At the same time, it is up to every State to organise how to access such information. One must agree with the conclusion that – without a centralised bank account register – the identification of bank accounts is usually "a cumbersome and lengthy procedure" and "sometimes not possible at all".[1002]

It is not surprising that there are many international recommendations to consider the setting up of central registers containing financial information.[1003]

---

997 Compare Section 8.2 above.

998 See Section 8.2 above.

999 Europol, ARO Platform Sub Working Group, *Report on the Establishment of Centralised Bank Account Registers as an Effective Tool for Financial Investigations and Asset Recovery*, 5 December 2012, p. 4.

1000 For the structure of the central bank account registers in France, Germany, Italy, Portugal and Romania, see Council of the European Union, *Manual of Best Practices in the fight against Financial Crime: A Collection of Good Examples of Well-Developed Systems in the Member States to fight Financial Crime*, 9741/13, CRIMORG 75, Brussels 4.6.2013, pp. 39–45. See also for a description of some EU systems for the identification of bank accounts, Europol, ARO Platform Sub Working Group, *Report on the Establishment of Centralised Bank Account Registers as an Effective Tool for Financial Investigations and Asset Recovery*, 5 December 2012, pp. 11–30.

1001 *Evaluation Report on the Fifth Round of Mutual Evaluations, Financial Crime and Financial Investigations, Report on Germany*, 16269/2/11, REV 2, Brussels, 19.1.2012, pp. 31–32 and 55.

1002 Europol, ARO Platform Sub Working Group, *Report on the Establishment of Centralised Bank Account Registers as an Effective Tool for Financial Investigations and Asset Recovery*, 5 December 2012, p. 5.

1003 See for example Recital (57) of Directive (EU) 2015/849 of the European Parliament and of the Council of 20 May 2015 on the Prevention of the Use of the Financial System for the Purposes of Money Laundering or Terrorist Financing, amending Regulation (EU) No. 648/2012 of the European Parliament and of the Council, and repealing Directive 2005/60/EC of the European Parliament and of the Council and Commission Directive 2006/70/EC, *OJ* L 141, 5.6.2015,

In July 2016, a proposal for a directive in order to amend the fourth EU Anti-Money Laundering directive was presented.[1004] This new instrument is a response to the increased threats of money laundering and terrorist financing, and is at present being discussed. In the draft directive, the Member States are *inter alia* required to set up centralised national bank and payment account registers, or other similar mechanisms such as central "data retrieval systems". The registers would at national level allow for identification of all bank accounts belonging to one person, and such information would be directly accessible at national level to "FIUs and competent authorities for fulfilling their obligations under this Directive".[1005] In the context of drafting the proposal, it was proposed that the instrument should permit wider access to such registers for other purposes, i.e. that it might be directly accessible by a broader range of national law enforcement authorities. However, it was concluded that this would go beyond the objectives of this instrument, as its scope is limited to the area of money laundering and terrorism. The European Commission has envisaged that the issue of broadening the scope will be further considered within the framework of another legal instrument.[1006]

If the proposal for a directive were adopted, the data-gathering powers of the national FIUs would thus be significantly expanded. Another change would be that the obligations for the FIUs to cooperate with other FIUs would be

---

pp. 73–117. Compare recommendation 16, Section 4.1.3, *Final Report on the Fifth Round of Mutual Evaluations, Financial Crime and Financial Investigations*, 12657/2/12, Brussels 3.10.2012, p. 26 and Section 6(e) p. 2 in *Best Practices on Confiscation (Recommendations 4 and 38) and a framework for ongoing work on asset recovery*, Financial Action Task Force, October 2012. Compare also the conclusions from the *Meeting of the Consultative Forum of Prosecutors General and Directors of Public Prosecutions of the Member States of the European Union at Eurojust*, 12 December 2014, published by the Council of the European Union, 8552/15, COPEN 108, Brussels 5.5.2015, p. 3.

1004 *Proposal for a Directive of the European Parliament and of the Council amending Directive (EU) 2015/849 on the Prevention of the use of the Financial System for the Purposes of Money Laundering or Terrorist Financing and amending Directive 2009/101/EC*, COM(2016) 450 final, Strasbourg 5.7.2016. See on this proposal, A. Met-Domestici, "The Fight against Money Laundering in the EU: The Framework Set by the Fourth Directive and its Proposed Enhancements" (2016) 4 *eucrim*, pp. 170–78 and B. Vogel and J.B. Maillart, "Recent Developments in EU Anti-Money Laundering: Some Critical Observations" (2016) 4 *eucrim*, pp. 179–83.

1005 Art. 1(12) *Proposal for a Directive of the European Parliament and of the Council amending Directive (EU) 2015/849 on the Prevention of the use of the Financial System for the Purposes of Money Laundering or Terrorist Financing and amending Directive 2009/101/EC*, COM (2016) 450 final, Strasbourg 5.7.2016.

1006 Compare *Commission Staff Working Document, Impact Assessment*, Accompanying the document, *Proposal for a Directive of the European Parliament and of the Council amending Directive (EU) 2015/849 on the Prevention of the use of the Financial System for the Purposes of Money Laundering or Terrorist Financing and amending Directive 2009/101/EC*, SWD(2016) 223 final, Strasbourg 5.7.2016, especially p. 39 and pp. 69–70.

strengthened, as the Member States would be required to ensure a cross-border exchange of such information. Even if the European Commission has concluded that the scope of the new directive would be limited to the authorities competent in the specific scope of the directive, such information might also become more easily accessible for law enforcment authorities in general. This is especially the case because the exact definition of a crime may still be open at the beginning of a criminal investigation.

As argued in the beginning of this section, there are presently too many partially overlapping instruments on judicial cooperation. Before issuing a request for MLA, a practitioner has to consider not only the scope and prerequisites of a legal instrument, but also check on ratifying/implementing States and any reservations or declarations to the instrument in question. It is obvious that such a system is not very efficient. When the Directive on EIO takes force in May 2017, an important reform of judicial cooperation at the investigatory stage will take place. The new instrument ought to enhance cooperation and render cross-border investigations faster and more efficient. A significant improvement is that the practitioners of the Member States will in many cases be able to apply one single instrument using a standardised form for the order.[1007] It will then be possible for the judicial authority in the issuing State to issue an EIO in order to obtain information or evidence needed for a motion related to confiscation. The delays in the execution of requests for MLA may hopefully be overcome by the provisions in the Directive on EIO that the investigative measures shall be carried out with the same priority as in a similar domestic case and within certain deadlines.

Many of the difficulties which are at present evident in practice (both regarding the deficits in the legal framework and the dividing line between different forms of cooperation) may partly be counteracted through the establishment of national and international *institutional structures*, where officials from police forces, administrative authorities and judicial agencies work together within specialised units or contact points. In order to perform all tasks necessary in confiscation proceedings, there are at least four main requirements for such a structure:

- the unit has a multidisciplinary organisation within States consisting of investigators, financial experts and prosecutors sitting together;
- the unit has the competence to, *inter alia*, exchange and gather information, decide on coercive measures and process different requests for MLA or warrants for judicial recognition;

1007 However, in the area of freezing, the FD on Freezing Orders will remain in force. See further Section 10.1.2.2.

- the members of the unit have special training and specialisation regarding asset recovery *and* the international instruments on cooperation in criminal matters, and
- the unit has access to relevant information and data bases.[1008]

Within the EU an important initiative in this respect has been the instrument setting up national AROs in order to improve international cooperation by way of *influencing the daily practice* of the law enforcement agencies. In the following, it will be discussed whether the AROs presently in place function satisfactorily and to what extent they fulfil the requirements set up above.

9.2.2. THE SETTING UP OF EFFICIENT AROs

The FD on Asset Recovery Offices was the first legally binding instrument which sets up a network of specialised criminal asset intelligence units obligated to directly cooperate with each other. The aim was to facilitate "the fastest possible EU-wide tracing of assets derived from crime".[1009] There are good reasons to believe that the establishment of such units may enhance the investigation capacities of the authorities and promote a fast handling of transnational exchange of information. Accordingly, this EU initiative was a very significant step to improve cross-border cooperation. In 2011, the European Commission published a mutual evaluation report which generally concluded that the implementation of the framework decision had been moderately satisfactory. The AROs established so far had expressed satisfaction with the degree of cooperation, but there were also certain major challenges.[1010]

Not all AROs function in the same way, but the structure varies widely when it comes to administration, legal powers and practices.[1011] It has been

---

1008 Compare the recommendations to the States in order to set up effective AROs given in *Communication from the Commission to the European Parliament and the Council, Proceeds of Organised Crime; Ensuring that "Crime does not Pay"*, 20.11.2008, COM(2008) 766 final, pp. 8–9.

1009 *Report from the Commission based on Article 8 of the Council Decision 2007/845/JHA of 6 December 2007 concerning cooperation between Asset Recovery Offices of the Member States in the field of tracing and identification of proceeds from, or other property related to, crime*, COM(2011) 176 final, p. 2.

1010 *Report from the Commission based on Article 8 of the Council Decision 2007/845/JHA of 6 December 2007 concerning cooperation between Asset Recovery Offices of the Member States in the field of tracing and identification of proceeds from, or other property related to, crime*, COM(2011) 176 final.

1011 The Spanish Centre of Excellence on Asset Recovery and Training has finalised a White Paper on best practices in the field of asset recovery. This compendium contains descriptions of the structure and activities of some AROs in different States. See *White Paper on Best Practices in Asset Recovery*, CEART Project, Prevention of and fight against Crime 2009.

left to the Member States to decide on such issues as long as "the status chosen under national law" does not "hamper an efficient cooperation".[1012] This can be compared to the CARIN network which foresees two operational contact points (one law enforcement, one judicial) per country. As already mentioned in Section 9.2.1, the most preferable structure would perhaps be a "hybrid" of police forces, administrative authorities and judicial agencies because such offices would also be able to handle requests for coercive measures and MLA. As expressed in Recital (5) of the Swedish Initiative:

> It is important that the possibilities for law enforcement authorities to obtain information and intelligence concerning serious crime and terrorist acts from other Member States be viewed horizontally and not in terms of differences with regard to type of crime or division of competencies between law enforcement or judicial authorities.

According to the FD on Asset Recovery Offices the conditions and procedure for requests shall be ruled by the provisions in the Swedish Initiative.[1013] As further described in Section 9.1.1 above, this instrument relates to the exchange of information between police forces. Accordingly, information obtained with the use of coercive powers and information to be used as evidence in criminal proceedings are excluded (Article 1(4)). The reference to the Swedish Initiative in the framework decision seems to indicate that the exchange of information between the AROs is restricted to investigative cooperation at the police level. Such a limitation of application has been questioned, because the offices then only play a restricted role. It has thereby been argued that the tasks of the AROs are "explicitly limited to exchanging information at police level, whereas international cooperation takes place largely at judicial level".[1014] This is an important observation. In the first draft for the framework decision, it was stated that the AROs should cooperate in the "widest possible degree", both in accordance with the framework decision and with national law.[1015] During the discussions of this proposal, it was however pointed out that the intention was that it should solely concern investigative (i.e. police) cooperation, and that the existing arrangements for judicial cooperation should continue to apply. In order to make clear that the

---

1012 Arts. 1(3) and 2(2) FD on Asset Recovery Offices.

1013 Compare Art. 3 and Recital (7) FD on Asset Recovery Offices.

1014 See M.J. Borgers, "Confiscation of the Proceeds of Crime: The European Union Framework" in C. King and C. Walker (eds.), *Dirty Assets: Emerging Issues in the Regulation of Criminal and Terrorist Assets*, Ashgate, 2014, p. 27, pp. 36–38 and M.J. Borgers and J.A. Moors, "Targeting the Proceeds of Crime: Bottlenecks in International Cooperation" (2007) 1 *European Journal of Crime, Criminal Law and Criminal Justice*, p. 1, p. 21.

1015 Compare Arts. 1, 2 and 4, *Initiative of the Republic of Austria, Belgium and Finland with a view to the adoption of a Council Decision concerning arrangements for cooperation between Asset Recovery Offices of the Member States*, 15628/05 CRIMORG 156, Brussels 14.12.2005.

framework decision was not to modify the existing police cooperation, a reference to the newly adopted Swedish Initiative was therefore added.[1016]

Against this background, it seems that the FD on Asset Recovery Offices only applies to "requests for *information*" (see Article 3(1)). This can be compared to the CARIN network, whose purpose is to establish assistance during the whole confiscation process from asset tracing, through freezing/seizure, execution of a final order up until even the storage/management stage. The reason for this limitation of the framework decision can be that the EU legislator did not wish to obligate the Member States to give the AROs legal powers to handle requests for coercive measures or other measures in the area of judicial cooperation.[1017]

This being said, the Member States may obviously choose to give the AROs more legal powers and expand the mandate nationally. In fact, this has also been recommended by the European Commission. In a Communication from 2008 it is, for example, stated that the Member States:

> should decide the best practical ways of setting up AROs at national level, their powers to trace *and freeze* assets efficiently, *and* their possibilities to exchange data (emphasis added).

In this context, it was also suggested that the AROs should have coercive powers to obtain information, and have powers to provisionally freeze assets for at least 72 hours in order to prevent dissipation of the criminal proceeds.[1018] It seems helpful if a national ARO is at least so organised that it is able to rely on the necessary execution capacity of the police and judicial authorities. As has been pointed out, if it only acts as a "mailbox", there will be no adequate guarantee that requests are executed with the necessary expedition.[1019]

Turning to the practical work of the AROs, the mutual evaluation report found that they had few resources and that specialised training of the personnel was lacking. According to the statements from the operating AROs, the most

---

1016 See *Draft Council Decision concerning arrangements for cooperation between Asset Recovery Offices of the Member States*, Council of the European Union, 5644/06, CRIMORG 19, Brussels 26.1.2006.

1017 Accordingly, it is set down in Art. 7 and Recital (8) that the framework decision is without prejudice to the obligations resulting from EU instruments on MLA or on mutual recognition of decisions, from bilateral or multilateral agreements in relation to third States and from Council Decision 2000/642/JHA of 17 October 2000 concerning arrangements for cooperation between financial intelligence units of the Member States in exchanging information. Also the Swedish Initiative is hereby added.

1018 *Communication from the Commission to the European Parliament and the Council, Proceeds of Organised Crime; Ensuring that "Crime does not Pay"*, 20.11.2008, COM(2008) 766 final, pp. 8 and 9. Compare similar conclusions regarding the desirable features of AROs, *Manual on International Cooperation for the Purposes of Confiscation of Proceeds of Crime, United Nations Office on Drugs and Crime*, United Nations 2012, p. 12.

1019 Borgers and Moors, n 1014 above, pp. 18–22.

important challenge that they faced was the difficulty to get access to financial information (notably to bank account information). Only one ARO had at this time access to a national register of bank accounts. While access to company registers was allowed in all AROs, centralised land registers did not exist in all Member States.[1020] Considering that the key function of these offices is to assist in order to trace assets of a criminal origin within their borders, it seems absurd that most of the authorities do not have direct or indirect access to all relevant databases. The Member States must establish AROs that are equipped with the necessary resources, powers and training, and the ability to exchange information.[1021]

In recent years, one trend within the development of criminal cooperation has been to *decentralise* the handling of international requests, for example by the abolition of transmission of requests via a central authority. Such reforms have surely many advantages and may avoid unnecessary bureaucracy. Direct contact between the authorities deciding on the measures may generally speed up the handling of cases. On the other hand, it presupposes that the judicial authorities concerned have all necessary skills (for example regarding the international instruments in force). A further important prerequisite is that the requesting State has adequate information about the competent authority abroad.[1022] It has been argued, in the context of the Directive on EIO, that it will not always be easy in practice to identify the authority competent to execute an EIO.[1023] An example would be a case where an issuing State issues an EIO in order to obtain information of the bank accounts of a defendant, and does not know exactly where the banks are located. It can also be difficult in a case where assets are located in different parts of the executing State's territory.

The building of networks and personal trust is of significant importance for international cases. It has in this respect been observed that:

> Successful cooperation in executing a mutual assistance request – in all stages of the confiscation procedure, but particularly in the seizure and execution stages – is linked to personal contacts.[1024]

1020 Compare *Report from the Commission based on Article 8 of the Council Decision 2007/845/JHA of 6 December 2007 concerning cooperation between Asset Recovery Offices of the Member States in the field of tracing and identification of proceeds from, or other property related to, crime*, COM(2011) 176 final, pp. 8–9.

1021 *Communication from the Commission to the European Parliament and the Council, The EU Internal Security Strategy in Action: Five steps towards a more secure Europe*, COM(2010) 673 final, Brussels, 22.11.2010, p. 6.

1022 See further I. Cameron, M. Thunberg Schunke, K. Påle-Bartes, C. Wong and P. Asp, *International Criminal Law from a Swedish Perspective*, Intersentia, 2011, pp. 129–30.

1023 L. Bachmaier, "Transnational Evidence, Towards the Transposition of Directive 2014/41 regarding the European Investigation Order in Criminal Matters" (2015) 2 *eucrim*, p. 47, pp. 49–50.

1024 Borgers and Moors, n 1014 above, p. 10.

In practice, the competent authorities seldom use the services of different specialised international organisations.[1025] The objectives of *Eurojust* are, *inter alia*, to facilitate the execution of requests for judicial cooperation. In many cases, this agency may be very helpful and can assist in the clarification of legal requirements in different jurisdictions. In spite of this, the requests for assistance by *Eurojust* are rather limited, and it has been recommended that the Member States should increasingly use this opportunity.[1026]

Obviously, effective *national agencies* charged with the tracing of assets are not only a precondition for successful confiscation rates, but also for efficient international cooperation.[1027] In this respect, the organisation of asset recovery at the federal level in Germany is often referred to as good or even best practice.[1028] This chapter therefore closes with a broad outline of the organisation and powers of the German ARO, which has been called "an active and cooperative international partner".[1029]

9.2.3. THE GERMAN ASSET RECOVERY OFFICES

In July 2009, Germany designated two AROs under the FD on Asset Recovery Offices; the dual structure consists of:

- a national *judicial* ARO embedded in Division III 1 of the *Bundesamt für Justiz* (Federal Office of Justice), and
- a national *police* ARO embedded in Unit SO 35 of the *Bundeskriminalamt*, BKA (Federal Criminal Police Office).[1030]

The national *judicial* ARO has no operational tasks, but a more advisory role. It serves as the central point for national and international requests by judicial

---

1025 Borgers and Moors, n 1014 above, pp. 10 and 17.

1026 See for example Council of the European Union, *Report on Eurojust's Experience in the Field of Asset Recovery, including Freezing and Confiscation*, 10179/15, COPEN 162, Brussels 22.6.2015, p. 13.

1027 *Communication from the Commission to the European Parliament and the Council, Proceeds of Organised Crime; Ensuring that "Crime does not Pay"*, 20.11.2008, COM(2008) 766 final, p. 3.

1028 Evaluation Report on the Fifth Round of Mutual Evaluations, *Financial Crime and Financial Investigations, Report on Germany*, 16269/2/11, REV 2, Brussels 19.1.2012, p. 29.

1029 Council of the European Union, *Manual of Best Practices in the fight against Financial Crime: A Collection of Good Examples of Well-Developed Systems in the Member States to fight Financial Crime*, 9741/13, CRIMORG 75, Brussels 4.6.2013, p. 51.

1030 See generally on the structure of the German AROs, *White Paper on Best Practices in Asset Recovery*, CEART Project, Prevention of and fight against Crime 2009, pp. 241–45 and Evaluation Report on the Fifth Round of Mutual Evaluations, *Financial Crime and Financial Investigations, Report on Germany*, 16269/2/11, REV 2, Brussels 19.1.2012 especially pp. 18–21.

authorities, and may assist in different issues. However, it is not responsible for any decisions regarding requests for MLA or warrants regarding mutual recognition.[1031] The Federal Ministry of Justice has transferred this competence to the local prosecuting offices in the Federal States. Domestic and international authorities may therefore consult the *judicial* ARO, and send requests to this unit in cases where they are unsure which local authority is responsible. The *judicial* ARO cooperates closely with the *police* ARO and supports the operational activities of the BKA. Further, it is a CARIN contact point. The *judicial* ARO conducts several training sessions each year regarding asset recovery both at the national and international level.

The national *police* ARO has an operational function and is responsible for practical cooperation between law enforcement authorities.[1032] Unit SO 35 is a specialised department for asset recovery within the BKA, and it supports all those investigations of serious and organised crime which are initiated within this department. The *police* ARO gives advice to national or foreign law enforcement agencies regarding legal provisions and asset recovery practices, as well as supporting asset tracing in Germany and abroad. The unit is also responsible for information-sharing on the basis of the FD on Asset Recovery Offices, and is a central point of contact with the various foreign police offices for the purpose of asset recovery. The *police* ARO uses the channel of SIENA for this purpose. It also hosts the FIU for Germany, and initiates training and education.[1033]

The *police* ARO has access *inter alia* to the following registers: registers of Notary acts concerning real estate, central company registers and central land registers of all of the 16 Federal States. It has further direct access to police information systems in Germany and to vehicle, car and ship ownership registers. The *police* ARO may receive information directly from the centralised bank register regarding information on bank account-holders and opening and closing dates of an account.[1034] However, this does not include information on bank account movements or account balances, because such requests must be

1031 Evaluation Report on the Fifth Round of Mutual Evaluations, *Financial Crime and Financial Investigations, Report on Germany*, 16269/2/11, REV 2, Brussels 19.1.2012, p. 19.

1032 Evaluation Report on the Fifth Round of Mutual Evaluations, *Financial Crime and Financial Investigations, Report on Germany*, 16269/2/11, REV 2, Brussels 19.1.2012, p. 19.

1033 The BKA has also established a specialist service on financial analysis (the "*Wirtschaftsprüfdienst*"). This unit is specialised in company structures and bank account analysis. This support in financial investigations along with the relatively easy and fast access to several sources of financial information provide for efficient handling of cases. See further *White Paper on Best Practices in Asset Recovery*, CEART Project, Prevention of and fight against Crime 2009, pp. 95–96.

1034 See further on available information and databases, Evaluation Report on the Fifth Round of Mutual Evaluations, *Financial Crime and Financial Investigations, Report on Germany*, 16269/2/11, REV 2, Brussels 19.1.2012, pp. 21 and 31–41.

made by judicial authorities.[1035] The *judicial* ARO has in principle no direct access to national or international databases.

The German system provides for efficient and flexible cooperation in asset recovery cases within the EU. To reconnect to the requirements for successful units mentioned in Section 9.2.1, it can be concluded that the dual structure of the judicial and the police AROs provides for a smooth multidisciplinary cooperation. The interplay between the offices seems to function very well and there is a clear division of roles and responsibility.[1036] Even if the *judicial* ARO does not decide on coercive measures or carry out the international requests or warrants, it provides comprehensive assistance in such cases and transmits requests to the competent authorities. The *police* ARO may assist actively in the tracing of assets. In this respect, the exchange of information is very expeditious, as the unit is operational and has access to many databases. The German *police* ARO may, at the request of a law enforcement authority in another Member State, find out whether a person has any bank accounts in Germany. There is no need for a judicial request for MLA; the only prerequisite is that there is an ongoing criminal investigation in the requesting Member State. As already concluded, this possibility of international cooperation "goes well beyond" what is required under the 2001 EU Protocol.[1037] This practice should be endorsed in all Member States, as it facilitates a competent authority to initially check whether there are any assets in a State before a formal request is issued.

1035 *White Paper on Best Practices in Asset Recovery*, CEART Project, Prevention of and fight against Crime 2009, pp. 242–43. See also *Europol*, ARO Platform Sub Working Group, *Report on the Establishment of Centralised Bank Account Registers as an Effective Tool for Financial Investigations and Asset Recovery*, 5 December 2012 pp. 21–22.

1036 Evaluation Report on the Fifth Round of Mutual Evaluations, *Financial Crime and Financial Investigations, Report on Germany*, 16269/2/11, REV 2, Brussels 19.1.2012, p. 29.

1037 Evaluation Report on the Fifth Round of Mutual Evaluations, *Financial Crime and Financial Investigations, Report on Germany*, 16269/2/11, REV 2, Brussels 19.1.2012, p. 55.

CHAPTER 10

INTERNATIONAL COOPERATION IN ORDER TO SEIZE OR FREEZE ASSETS

10.1. THE LEGAL FRAMEWORK

10.1.1. REQUESTS FOR MLA

When assets have been identified and located, provisional coercive measures may be necessary in order to avoid that a suspect disposes of the assets before the court has made a final decision on confiscation. An efficient regime of cross-border seizure or freezing of any assets identified as criminal proceeds is crucial.[1038] The seizure/freezing of property may be necessary in order both to secure evidence needed to support a motion for confiscation and/or to secure property in order to be able to execute a final confiscation order.

International provisions allowing for requests regarding coercive measures are found in a number of instruments on cooperation in criminal matters, for example Articles 1 and 5 of the European Convention on Mutual Assistance in Criminal Matters (1959) (hereafter the "1959 Convention"), Article 13(2) United Nations Convention against Transnational Organized Crime (2000), Article 11 European Convention on Laundering, Search, Seizure and Confiscation of the Proceeds from Crime (1990) and Article 21 Council of Europe Convention on Laundering, Search, Seizure and Confiscation of the Proceeds from Crime and on the Financing of Terrorism (2005). There is often a rather broad range of refusal grounds regarding such requests, and a common requirement in international conventions on MLA is that a demand for double criminality is set up for coercive measures like seizure. According to Article 5 of the 1959 Convention, the States are allowed to set up the following requirements for the execution of a request for search or seizure of property:

- a requirement of double criminality,
- a requirement that the criminal offence is an extraditable offence in the requested State, and/or

1038 The terms "seizure" or "freezing" are often used interchangeably in order to refer to an order to temporarily take control of assets to prevent their transferral or movement.

- that the execution of the request is compatible with the law of the requested State.[1039]

Within the EU, the Schengen Convention has modified the right to reservations regarding Article 5 of the 1959 Convention, and has limited the scope for refusing requests for international requests for MLA in this respect. According to Article 51 of this convention the States may not make the admissibility of letters rogatory for search or seizure dependent on conditions other than the following:

- the offence giving rise to the letters rogatory is punishable under the law of both Contracting Parties by a penalty involving deprivation of liberty or a detention order of a maximum period of at least six months, or is punishable under the law of one of the two Contracting Parties by an equivalent penalty and under the law of the other Contracting Party by virtue of being an infringement of the rules of law which is being prosecuted by the administrative authorities, and where the decision may give rise to proceedings before the court having jurisdiction in particular in criminal matters; or
- the execution of the letters rogatory is consistent with the law of the Requested Contracting Party.

The Schengen Convention thus facilitates cross-border cooperation in this area, as the requirement of double criminality has been limited and it is not possible to set up a requirement of an extraditable offence. Between the EU Member States the 2000 EU Convention is also applicable. This instrument does not provide for any changes regarding the permitted refusal grounds regarding search or seizure, but it facilitates the application of, for example, the 1959 Convention by permitting that the requests may be transmitted directly between the judicial authorities.

Requests for seizure may also be based on Article 11 in the European Convention on Laundering, Search, Seizure and Confiscation of the Proceeds from Crime (1990). However, a clear gap in this convention is that there is no obligation for a requested State during the initial investigation stage, but only when a requesting State has "instituted criminal proceedings or proceedings for the purpose of confiscation".[1040] Alongside the legal framework for MLA, there is a specific EU regime for the freezing of assets based on mutual recognition.

1039 Compare also Arts. 1–2 of the *Additional Protocol to the European Convention on Mutual Assistance in Criminal Matters*, 1978, ETS 99 which restricts this right regarding fiscal offences.

1040 *Study for an Impact Assessment on a Proposal for a New Legal Framework on the Confiscation and Recovery of Criminal Assets*, RAND Europe, 2012, p. 40.

10.1.2. ORDERS FOR SEIZURE OR FREEZING BASED ON MUTUAL RECOGNITION

10.1.2.1. The FD on Freezing Orders

The FD on Freezing Orders was adopted in 2003 in order to provide for a more efficient and advanced system of seizure and freezing within the Union.[1041] The framework decision builds upon an *initiative from France, Sweden and Belgium*,[1042] and provides for the application of mutual recognition to certain pre-trial orders. The aim has been to set up speedy transnational procedures, and permit the national authorities to more efficiently secure evidence and seize property which are easily movable.[1043] The framework decision has not created any new EU safety measure, and the Member States are allowed to keep their own national systems on coercive measures, as long as the purpose of the decision is to provisionally prevent the destruction or transfer of assets, to hand over evidence or to confiscate property at foreign request.[1044] It is generally applicable in proceedings concerning all types of offences in which assets may be located abroad. The Member States are obligated to recognise and execute in their territory "a freezing order issued by a judicial authority of another Member State in the framework of criminal proceedings" for purposes either of *securing evidence* or of *securing the subsequent confiscation of property*.[1045] A freezing order may relate to any kind of property. In what follows, orders with the purpose of a subsequent confiscation will be primarily addressed.

In short, the procedure is as follows. A judicial authority in a Member State issues a domestic order on freezing which has to be supplemented by a special *certificate*. The latter is supposed to reproduce the content in the original freezing order and contain all information needed for an executing State.[1046]

1041 Compare Section 8.3 above.

1042 *OJ* C 75, 7.3.2001, p. 3. See on this original proposal, G. Stessens, "The Joint Initiative of France, Sweden and Belgium for the Adoption of a Council Framework Decision on the Execution in the European Union of Orders Freezing Assets or Evidence" in G. de Kerchove and A. Weyembergh (eds.), *La reconnaissance mutuelle des décisions judiciaires pénales dans l'Union européenne*, Editions de l'Université de Bruxelles, 2001, pp. 91–100.

1043 Recital (2) of FD on Freezing Orders.

1044 The European Commission has prepared a handbook with guidelines to help the authorities to handle freezing orders in accordance with the FD on Freezing Orders, see European Commission, JUST/2010/JPEN/PR/1004/B3, *Handbook for Judges, Prosecutors and other Competent Authorities on how to issue and execute a request for enforcement of a Freezing Order, in accordance with Council Framework Decision 2003/577/JHA of 22 July 2003*, available at: http://e-justice.europa.eu/content_criminal_law-255-en.do.

1045 Arts. 1 and 3(1) FD on Freezing Orders. It does not apply to orders which aim at the restitution of property to the rightful owner.

1046 A standard form for the certificate is given in an Annex to the framework decision, see further Art. 9 FD on Freezing Orders. Official translation of the certificate in all EU languages have been provided. For issues regarding requirements of translation, see Art. 9(2)–(3).

Thereby the execution can take place on the basis of the certificate, which aims to provide for a more swift and efficient handling of cases. The freezing order and the certificate are to be transmitted *directly* between the judicial authorities of the Member States.[1047] In accordance with the principle of mutual recognition the examination of a foreign freezing order shall be of limited extent and any substantive reasons must not be reconsidered. Accordingly, Article 5(1) states that an executing State shall recognise a freezing order:

> without any further formality being required and shall forthwith take the necessary measures for its immediate execution in the same way as for a freezing order made by an authority of the executing State.

This means that there is in principle an obligation to execute if the formal requirements are fulfilled, but certain *optional* grounds for refusing to recognise or execute an order are also given. These are exhaustively contained in Article 7 FD on Freezing Orders and include cases:

(a) where there is no certificate or it is inadequate in form or content,
(b) where an order would violate provisions on immunity or privilege under the law of the executing State,
(c) where it is instantly clear that the order would infringe the principle of *ne bis in idem*, and
(d) where, if applicable, there is no double criminality.[1048]

A requirement of double criminality is thus partly abolished. According to Article 3 FD on Freezing Orders several serious offences are listed, which are not to be subjected to any verification of double criminality if they are punishable in the issuing State by a custodial sentence of a maximum period of at least three years. These offences are, for example, participation in a criminal organisation, terrorism, fraud, trafficking in human beings and drug offences. The legal classification of these offences lies exclusively within national law of the issuing State. For offences not included in this list, the executing State may require that the acts for which the freezing order was issued must constitute an offence which, under the laws of that State, allows for such freezing, whatever the constituent elements or however described under the law of the issuing State.[1049]

1047 See further Art. 4 FD on Freezing Orders. The definition of judicial authorities is left to national law (Art. 2(a) and (b)). In, for example Sweden, the prosecutor has a central role, see Ch. 3 Sec. 2 Para. 1 of the Act (2005:500) on Recognition and Execution of European Freezing Decisions.

1048 In relation to offences concerning taxes or duties, customs and exchange the execution of an order may not be refused on the ground that the law of the executing State does not impose the same kind of tax or duty or does not contain a tax, duty, customs and exchange regulation of the same kind as the law of the issuing State.

1049 Art. 3(4) FD on Freezing Orders.

The handling of a foreign order in the executing State is supposed to take place promptly; Article 5(3) states that, if possible, the freezing order shall be *decided* and *communicated* within 24 hours. The procedure and prerequisites (for example if any optional grounds are set up) are primarily regulated by national legislation in this State. The framework decision provides that execution shall take place "in the same way" as a freezing order made by an authority in the executing State (*locus regit actum*).[1050] If any additional coercive measures are necessary, they are also to be executed in accordance with such procedural rules.[1051]

A freezing order is not an independent measure, but only a *preliminary* coercive measure. This means that a freezing order must always be *accompanied* by a request for confiscation requiring either enforcement of a confiscation order that has been issued in the issuing State or confiscation in the executing State and subsequent enforcement of any such order.[1052] It is also possible to request that the property remain in the executing State *pending* such a request.[1053] The subsequent requests are to be decided by the executing State in accordance with the rules applicable to international cooperation relating to confiscation.[1054] This means that any treaty on judicial assistance in such cases, for example the provisions regarding confiscation in the European Convention on Laundering, Search, Seizure and Confiscation of the Proceeds from Crime (1990) can be used. Between the EU States, it is also possible to proceed on the basis of a mutual recognition instrument, i.e. Council Framework Decision 2006/783/JHA of 6 October 2006 on the application of the principle of mutual recognition to confiscation orders. This instrument is further described in Chapter 11 below.

The property shall in principle remain frozen in the executing State until that State has responded definitely to a subsequent request for assistance.[1055] Legal remedies for a person affected by a freezing order are provided for in Article 11 FD on Freezing Orders. In principle, an appeal concerning the *execution* of a freezing order shall take place in an executing State, whereas the substantive reasons for issuing the order in the first place may only be challenged before a court in the issuing State.[1056] From the human rights perspective, there are obviously substantial difficulties for an individual to challenge a judicial

1050 Art. 5(1) FD on Freezing Orders.

1051 Art. 5(2) FD on Freezing Orders.

1052 Art. 10(1)(b) FD on Freezing Orders. In the case of a freezing order regarding evidence, it must be followed by a request for the evidence to be transferred to the issuing State (Art. 10(1)(a)). In the last case, there is a special rule regarding double criminality, see Art. 10(3) FD on Freezing Orders.

1053 Art. 10(1)(c) FD on Freezing Orders.

1054 Art. 10(2) FD on Freezing Orders.

1055 Art. 6(1) FD on Freezing Orders. There is a possibility for the executing State to limit this period, compare Art. 6(2).

1056 Art. 11(2) FD on Freezing Orders.

decision that has been taken abroad. In many cases, it is necessary to engage the legal assistance of a lawyer specialised in such issues and with knowledge of the foreign legal system.[1057]

As mentioned in Section 8.3 above, the FD on EEW (adopted in 2008) contains certain provisions on mutual recognition of orders regarding evidence gathering. This framework decision partly overlaps with the FD on Freezing Orders when it comes to a freezing order with the purpose to secure evidence, but the FD on EEW is hardly used in practice. At present, a request for seizure or freezing of property with the purpose to secure evidence (for a confiscation matter) or with the purpose to safeguard a subsequent final confiscation order is made either on the basis of MLA instruments or by applying the FD on Freezing Orders. However, the FD on Freezing Orders has so far had a rather limited use in practice, and the requests have been mainly based on the instruments on MLA. This will be further discussed in Section 10.2.1 below. When the Directive on EIO takes legal force in May 2017, certain changes to this system will anyway occur, as the practitioners will then have to choose a legal framework depending on the *objectives* of a seizure or a freezing order. This will be explained in what follows.

10.1.2.2. The Directive on EIO

As described in Section 8.4 above, the Directive on EIO will replace the FD on Freezing Orders when it comes to the freezing of evidence.[1058] This means that it will then be possible for an issuing State to issue an EIO in order to gather evidence, for example to secure or freeze evidence in an executing State. Such an order may be subjected to a requirement of double criminality only if the criminal offence is not on the list of especially enumerated offences for which this demand has been abolished.[1059]

Article 32 of the Directive on EIO also contains a provision on "provisional measures". It allows a State to issue an EIO in order to take any measure with a view to "provisionally preventing" the destruction, transformation, removal, transfer or disposal of an item that may be used as evidence. An executing State shall decide and communicate a decision on the provisional measure as soon as possible and, wherever practicable, within 24 hours.[1060] This article will thus replace the "freezing of evidence" which at present is regulated by the FD on

---

1057 See for a critical study of the human rights responsibility within mutual recognition, M. Thunberg Schunke, *Whose Responsibility? A Study of Transnational Defence Rights and Mutual Recognition of Judicial Decisions within the EU*, Intersentia, 2013. The provisions on the legal remedies are also discussed in Section 12.10 below.

1058 Art. 34 Directive on EIO.

1059 See further Art. 11 Directive on EIO and Section 8.4 above.

1060 As in the case with the FD on Freezing Orders, the time-limit for the actual execution of the measure is not given. Compare Sections 10.1.2.1 and 10.2.3.

Freezing Orders, and the result will be a more smooth procedure as it will be possible to issue one single EIO in order to secure the item *and* to hand over the evidence.[1061]

When it comes to freezing orders with the purpose of a subsequent confiscation, the FD on Freezing Orders will continue to apply. This fragmentation of the rules pre-supposes that the purpose of a coercive measure can always be clearly identified at the beginning of investigations. In practice, the distinction between a provisional measure to secure evidence and to secure confiscation is not always as clear-cut. This has also been acknowledged in Recital (34) of the Directive on EIO:

> This Directive, by virtue of its scope, deals with provisional measures only with a view to gathering evidence. In this respect, it should be underlined that any item, including financial assets, may be subject to various provisional measures in the course of criminal proceedings, not only with a view to gathering evidence but also with a view to confiscation. The distinction between the two objectives of provisional measures is not always obvious and the objective of the provisional measure may change in the course of the proceedings. For this reason, it is crucial to maintain a smooth relationship between the various instruments applicable in this field. Furthermore, for the same reason, the assessment of whether the item is to be used as evidence and therefore be the object of an EIO should be left to the issuing authority.[1062]

10.2. A COMMENTARY TO THE EU REGIME ON CROSS-BORDER SEIZURE OF ASSETS

10.2.1. THE FD ON FREEZING ORDERS: A LACK OF APPLICATION IN LEGAL PRACTICE

The FD on Freezing Orders should have been implemented into national legislation before 2 August 2005.[1063] However, the national processes have been slow and incomplete. In a mutual evaluation report published in 2008 (hereafter the "*Report on Freezing*"), the European Commission concluded that by the end of this year only 19 States had implementing legislation.[1064] It was further found that the national laws which had been adopted so far contained

1061 L. Bachmaier, "Transnational Evidence, Towards the Transposition of Directive 2014/41 regarding the European Investigation Order in Criminal Matters" (2015) 2 *eucrim*, p. 47, p. 56.

1062 Compare on this, Section 12.2 below.

1063 Art. 14 FD on Freezing Orders.

1064 *Report from the Commission based on Article 14 of the Council Framework Decision 2003/577/JHA of 22 July 2003 on the execution in the EU of orders freezing property or evidence*, COM(2008) 885 final, p. 2.

numerous omissions and misinterpretations. Many States (for example the UK) had provided that a freezing order must be sent via a central authority, and in some national legislation (for example the Swedish), additional (not permitted) grounds for refusal had been added.[1065] At present all Member States except Greece and Luxembourg have implemented the framework decision (as of December 2016). The UK initially only implemented those parts of the framework decision which relate to the freezing of evidence. National provisions on freezing orders in relation to a subsequent confiscation order came into force as late as in December 2014 by Part 2 and Schedules 1 and 2 to the Criminal Justice and Data Protection (Protocol No. 36) Regulations 2014. However, the UK could freeze property in response to requests prior to this act on the basis of legislation on general international cooperation regarding freezing and confiscation of criminal assets (so-called "Restraint Orders").

In general, there seem to be many advantages with the freezing regime provided for by the FD on Freezing Orders. The execution of pre-trial decisions on the basis of mutual recognition may promote swift cooperation, as the time-consuming procedure of MLA may be avoided. The measures may be executed with restricted possibilities of refusal, and direct communication ought to lead to faster and more efficient cross-border seizures. The procedure is simplified, as a unified document (the certificate) translated into all EU languages may be used. In addition, short deadlines for execution of the order are given.

Accordingly, one would assume that the framework decision has led to a significant improvement of the possibilities for law enforcement agencies to quickly freeze assets situated in other EU States. However, in practice, it seems as if the FD on Freezing Orders has had only limited use so far.[1066] As mentioned above, the instrument does not replace MLA, and the law enforcement agencies have so far preferred to use traditional requests for assistance instead of freezing orders.[1067] Many reasons for this situation have been stressed. A common explanation is the construction of the framework decision itself, i.e. that the scope does not allow for the identification, freezing and confiscation of assets in one request.[1068] Its application means only a first step which must be followed

---

1065 See further on the Swedish implementing legislation, Section 10.2.2 below.

1066 See for example Commisssion Staff Working Document, *Impact Assessment*, Accompanying the document *Proposal for a Regulation of the European Parliament and of the Council on the Mutual Recognition of Freezing and Confiscation Orders*, SWD(2016) 468 final, Brussels 21.12.2016, p. 16.

1067 See for example *Communication from the Commission to the European Parliament and the Council, Proceeds of Organised Crime; Ensuring that "Crime does not Pay"*, 20.11.2008, COM (2008) 766 final, p. 4, I. Cameron, M. Thunberg Schunke, K. Påle-Bartes, C. Wong and P. Asp, *International Criminal Law from a Swedish Perspective*, Intersentia, 2011, p. 147, *Eurojust Annual Report 2012*, p. 23 and Council of the European Union, *Report on Eurojust's Experience in the Field of Asset Recovery, including Freezing and Confiscation*, 10179/15, COPEN 162, Brussels 22.6.2015, pp. 5–6.

1068 See for example *Eurojust Annual Report 2012*, p. 23.

by subsequent requests. Practitioners therefore find the procedure cumbersome and too complex, and seem to argue that "there is little purpose in going through two different sets of proceedings".[1069] This attitude did not really change after the adoption of Framework Decision on the Application of the Principle of Mutual Recognition to Confiscation Orders in 2006, which extended the mutual recognition principle to the subsequent stage. This could be due to the fact that the implementation process regarding the latter instrument has also been very slow, and some Member States still have no implementing legislation in place.[1070]

Other reasons seem to be of a more practical nature. Many judicial authorities find that the certificate is difficult to complete and argue that it does not contain all the necessary fields.[1071] This may in fact be a hindrance, because an improperly filled out certificate may then be refused. The European Commission has in this respect acknowledged certain flaws and has suggested a redraft of the certificate.[1072] A further problem in practice has concerned the provisions on direct communication of orders. In some cases, there have been difficulties in identifying the competent authorities abroad, and the fact that some States have kept a requirement for transmission via a central authority has led to confusion.[1073] In addition to this, it has been pointed out that there is insufficient knowledge among practitioners about the framework decision itself.[1074]

There are in fact some drawbacks of the regime of freezing set up by the FD on Freezing Orders. First, as mentioned above, the fragmentation of the provisions leads to practical difficulties. The instrument can *only* be used in order to freeze property, but it cannot be used in order to investigate or search for assets. Mostly, there is thus a need for the use of a "previous" and "subsequent" instrument. Initially, the legal framework of police or judicial cooperation described in

---

1069 Cameron, Thunberg Schunke, Påle-Bartes, Wong and Asp, n 1067 above, p. 147. See also *Study for an Impact Assessment on a Proposal for a New Legal Framework on the Confiscation and Recovery of Criminal Assets*, RAND Europe, 2012, pp. 50–51.

1070 Compare further Section 11.1.2.1 below. Several reasons for the limited use of the FD on Freezing Orders are given in Council of the European Union, *Report on Eurojust's Experience in the Field of Asset Recovery, including Freezing and Confiscation*, 10179/15, COPEN 162, Brussels 22.6.2015, pp. 5–7.

1071 *Communication from the Commission to the European Parliament and the Council, Proceeds of Organised Crime; Ensuring that "Crime does not Pay"*, 20.11.2008, COM(2008) 766 final, p. 4.

1072 European Commission, JUST/2010/JPEN/PR/1004/B3, *Handbook for Judges, Prosecutors and other Competent Authorities on how to issue and execute a request for enforcement of a Freezing Order, in accordance with Council Framework Decision 2003/577/JHA of 22 July 2003*, pp. 113–15, available under: http://e-justice.europa.eu/content_criminal_law-255-en.do.

1073 See further the *Report on Freezing*, compare pp. 3 and 7.

1074 See further European Commission, JUST/2010/JPEN/PR/1004/B3, *Handbook for Judges, Prosecutors and other Competent Authorities on how to issue and execute a request for enforcement of a Freezing Order, in accordance with Council Framework Decision 2003/577/JHA of 22 July 2003*, pp. 111–12 (available at: http://e-justice.europa.eu/content_criminal_law-255-en.do.).

Chapter 9 above must be used in order to determine whether property exists and to find its location. After securing the property on the basis of the framework decision, international instruments on the enforcement of a final confiscation order must be applied. It is not strange that the practitioners then prefer to use requests for MLA, given that they can request all such measures concurrently. The Directive on EIO will in this respect not improve the situation in the area of confiscation, because it will still be necessary to use three separate sets of instruments in order to identify, trace, freeze and confiscate criminal assets. At present, a reform of the EU regime on the basis of the *Proposal for a Regulation on Mutual Recognition* is being discussed. According to the draft, the FD on Freezing Orders and the FD on Confiscation Orders would be integrated into one single legislative instrument. In such a way, the measures of freezing and subsequent confiscation could be used jointly and not successively, and provide for faster proceedings. The proposal is discussed in Chapter 12 below.

Obviously, the FD on Freezing Orders is in need of a "freshen up".[1075] One problem that has occurred in the current practice is connected to the requirement of the FD on Freezing Orders that an issuing State must know the *exact* location of property to be frozen, i.e. in which State the property is located. A common situation in practice is that an issuing State intends to freeze a specifically identified asset belonging to a defendant, but it is not definitively clarified where the asset is located. This can require that several measures of investigation be undertaken in many jurisdictions in order to specify the State in question. In order to improve this situation, it has been proposed that the EU legislator should consider the possibility of allowing a freezing order without a specification of the receiving authority.[1076] This would in fact be an important improvement in order to efficiently locate property within the EU. However, it is crucial in this context to make a distinction between different situations. There are cases where the issuing State does not know whether a defendant *has any assets at all* in any State. It is then appropriate to restrict the risk of "fishing expeditions" in order to prevent that law enforcement authorities are unnecessary drowned in requests to check all sorts of registers. Nevertheless, it seems reasonable that an authority – which intends to freeze *particularly identified* property with an unknown location – is allowed to send out a freezing order to several Member States. This is comparable to the system of the European Arrest Warrants. Accordingly, the SIS system for locating stolen property (for example cars or other vehicles) could be used.

1075 See for a similar conclusion, *Eurojust's Opinion on the Proposal for a Directive on the European Investigative Order*, published in Council of the European Union, Document 6814/11, COPEN 26, Brussels 4.3.2011, pp. 4–7.

1076 European Commission, *Handbook for Judges, Prosecutors and other Competent Authorities on how to issue and execute a request for enforcement of a Freezing Order, in accordance with Council Framework Decision 2003/577/JHA of 22 July 2003*, p. 115, available at: http://e-justice.europa.eu/content_criminal_law-255-en.do.

Another difficulty of the present freezing system is that an order must exactly specify the property to be frozen. A common situation in practice is that the property specified in the freezing order is not found, but other assets are located which could cover the amount to be frozen. Under the current system, the freezing of this other property is impossible if the issuing State does not issue a new freezing order. In the meanwhile, the accused might easily dispose of the property. In order to make the instrument more efficient, the European Commission has proposed that the seizure of a certain determined amount of unspecified property could be allowed.[1077] This is a reasonable suggestion, which needs to be further considered.[1078]

When it comes to freezing orders in the area of extended confiscation, it has on occasions been argued that the FD on Freezing Orders does not support this form of confiscation.[1079] This has been justified with reference to the definition of "property". In Article 2(d) FD on Freezing Orders, property is defined as:

> property of any description, whether ... which the competent judicial authority in the issuing State considers is the proceeds of an offence referred to in Article 3, or is equivalent ... of the value of such proceeds.

This definition is compared to the FD on Confiscation Orders where this definition of "property" has been expanded to include also anything liable to confiscation according to Article 3(1) and (2) of FD 2005/212/JHA. It has been acknowledged that the reason for this difference of definition might be that the FD on Freezing Orders was drafted before the measure of extended confiscation was introduced at EU level. Nevertheless, it has been concluded that this "in any event" effectively limits mutual recognition of freezing orders to cases of ordinary confiscation.[1080] It may be doubted whether such a far-reaching conclusion can be drawn in this respect. In fact, a different view is expressed in the handbook

---

1077 European Commission, *Handbook for Judges, Prosecutors and other Competent Authorities on how to issue and execute a request for enforcement of a Freezing Order, in accordance with Council Framework Decision 2003/577/JHA of 22 July 2003*, p. 116, available at: http://e-justice.europa.eu/content_criminal_law-255-en.do. Compare also European Commission, JUST/2011/JPEN/PR/0153/A4, *Comparative Law Study of the Implementation of Mutual Recognition of Orders to Freeze and Confiscate Criminal Assets in the European Union*, Final Finding Report, p. 78.

1078 Compare Section 12.7 below.

1079 See Commission Staff Working Paper, *Accompanying Document to the Proposal for a Directive of the European Parliament and the Council on the Freezing and Confiscation of Proceeds of Crime in the European Union*, SWD(2012) 31 final, Brussels 12.3.2012, p. 19 and *Study for an Impact Assessment on a Proposal for a New Legal Framework on the Confiscation and Recovery of Criminal Assets*, RAND Europe, 2012, p. 71. Compare also M. Fazekas and E. Nanopoulos, "The Effectiveness of EU Law: Insights from the EU Legal Framework on Asset Confiscation" (2016) 24 *European Journal of Crime, Criminal Law and Criminal Justice*, p. 39, p. 52.

1080 Compare *Study for an Impact Assessment on a Proposal for a New Legal Framework on the Confiscation and Recovery of Criminal Assets*, RAND Europe, 2012, p. 42.

from the European Commission, which provides guidelines regarding freezing orders. Here it is stated that the definition of property in the FD on Freezing Orders is very broad, and that "this concept of property" is compatible with the progressive extending of property subject to confiscation in EU legislation. The examples of such "extending" instruments are: the FD 2001/500/JHA, which reinforced the concept of value confiscation, and the FD 2005/212/JHA, which refers to the powers of extended confiscation.[1081]

This being said, such issues may in practice perhaps not lead to difficulties, because in the beginning of an investigation it is sometimes not to be clearly distinguished whether an asset may be the object of ordinary or extended confiscation. Furthermore, in some cases, property may during the preliminary investigation function both as the object of a possible measure of confiscation and as a piece of evidence. In any case, this situation would be corrected by the adoption of the new EU instrument on mutual recognition.[1082]

As mentioned above, Article 5 of the 1959 Convention allows that a request for MLA involving search and seizure is executed only on the basis of double criminality. The FD on Freezing Orders has in this respect abolished this requirement for the criminal offences specifically listed provided that they are punishable in the issuing State by a custodial sentence of a maximum period of at least three years. This is a significant improvement of cross-border cooperation regarding coercive measures. In this respect, the Swedish legislation on freezing orders is innovating as it goes further in some areas than what is required by the EU instruments. This will be described in what follows.

10.2.2. AN ABOLITION OF DOUBLE CRIMINALITY: THE EXAMPLE OF SWEDEN

Sweden implemented the FD on Freezing Orders through the Act (2005:500) on Recognition and Execution of EU Freezing Decisions and the Ordinance (2005:501).[1083] Both came into force on 1 July 2005. In principle, a freezing

---

1081 European Commission, JUST/2010/JPEN/PR/1004/B3, *Handbook for Judges, Prosecutors and other Competent Authorities on how to issue and execute a request for enforcement of a Freezing Order, in accordance with Council Framework Decision 2003/577/JHA of 22 July 2003*, available at: http://e-justice.europa.eu/content_criminal_law-255-en.do, p. 10.

1082 The current proposal for a new EU instrument on mutual recognition is described and discussed in Chapter 12 below.

1083 *Lag (2005:500) om erkännande och verkställighet inom Europeiska Unionen av frysningsbeslut.* See on this Act, Cameron, Thunberg Schunke, Påle-Bartes, Wong and Asp, n 1067 above, pp. 147–58 and A. Suominen, *The Principle of Mutual Recognition in Cooperation in Criminal Matters: A Study of the Principle in Four Framework Decisions and in the Implementing Legislation in the Nordic Member States*, Intersentia, 2011. See Bills 2002/03:67 and 2004/05:115.

order which is to be executed in Sweden is executed in accordance with the provisions which apply for equivalent national decisions. This means that it may be executed either according to the Swedish procedural rules on seizure which apply to confiscation of property (object confiscation) or according to the rules on provisional attachment (sequestration) when it comes to value confiscation. The Swedish legislator has, in the context of refusal grounds, chosen to draft the national legislation more generously than the framework decision and has abolished the requirement of double criminality for *all types of offences*. There is thus no opportunity to refuse to recognise or execute a foreign freezing order due to a lack of double criminality.[1084] It was argued during the legislative process that an expeditious examination of a freezing order is of significant importance, and it was emphasised that at this stage it is not decided whether the property will be transferred to another State or be confiscated. It would needlessly slow down and complicate the handling of cases if the authorities had to check double criminality.[1085]

Sweden may also assist other Member States with requests for MLA regarding seizure, searches or provisional attachment on the basis of the International Legal Assistance in Criminal Matters Act 2000:562 (hereafter the "ILA Act").[1086] Also this Act has been drafted in order to provide for more generous assistance than the international obligations would require. This is especially the case in relation to other EU States. The underlying principle has been to "put international legal assistance on an equal footing" with domestic criminal investigations.[1087] Even if the MLA procedure may take place relatively speedily, the handling of the cases is in many areas more thorough than under the Act (2005:500) on Recognition and Execution of EU Freezing Decisions.[1088] There is no demand for double criminality concerning a request from another EU Member State for search of premises or seizure if the request concerns an offence which is punishable

1084 See Ch. 3 Sec. 5 Act (2005:500) on Recognition and Execution of European Union Freezing Decisions.

1085 See for the reasons to abolish double criminality, Bill 2004/05:115 pp. 51–54. It can be added that Sweden has introduced two grounds for refusing the execution of a freezing order, which has been criticised by the European Commission. These grounds are that it would be in conflict with Swedish constitutional law or that it is in conflict with the ECHR and its protocols. These additional safeguards are not explicitly provided for by the FD on Freezing Orders, but the Swedish legislator considered that both of these obstacles follow implicitly from Recital (6). See further *Report on Freezing*, pp. 5 and 7. Compare also Cameron, Thunberg Schunke, Påle-Bartes, Wong and Asp, n 1067 above, p. 152.

1086 *Lag (2000:562) om internationell rättslig hjälp i brottmål.*

1087 See further on this legislation, Cameron, Thunberg Schunke, Påle-Bartes, Wong and Asp, n 1067 above, pp. 104–35.

1088 See for example for a description of the specific procedural requirements under Swedish law, Cameron, Thunberg Schunke, Påle-Bartes, Wong and Asp, n 1067 above, pp. 113–15.

by imprisonment in the requesting State.[1089] However, where seizure is made, it must be with the aim of transferring the property to a requesting State. If a request for MLA concerns provisional attachment or seizure with the purpose to secure enforcement in Sweden of a foreign confiscation order, a requirement of double criminality is set up.[1090]

The Swedish initiative to domestically abolish the requirement of double criminality for all freezing orders and to significantly restrict it regarding some requests for coercive measures in the area of MLA must be applauded. Against the background that a freezing order is only meant to be a temporary measure, executed only for a limited duration of time, it may be possible to execute such orders without a requirement of double criminality within the EU. However, there seem to be great difficulties in achieving this. In the negotiations of the Directive on the EIO, such a proposal regarding EIOs for search and seizure was defeated.[1091]

10.2.3. THE NEED FOR URGENT MEASURES: IS THE PRESENT LEGAL FRAMEWORK SUFFICIENT?

If the strategy *to go for the money* is to have any success, the authorities must be able to take urgent action and initiate rapid measures in order to secure evidence or assets. This is obviously a requirement both domestically and internationally. An essential question is thus whether the present regime for asset recovery is sufficient. It can be noted in this respect that in practice certain forms of transnational cooperation regarding urgent freezing of assets have developed. Thereby it may be possible for authorities to more urgently obtain a *preliminary* seizure or freezing of property *prior* to the delivery of a formal request for assistance.[1092] The judicial authorities may, for example, for the seizure or freezing of money on a bank account be allowed to use the cooperation channels of the financial intelligence units ("FIUs") located in other States in order to obtain provisional decisions.[1093] Some national FIUs are, for example, allowed to

---

1089 Chapter 2 Sec. 2 and Ch. 4 Sec. 20 Para. 1 ILA Act. However, in exceptional cases a request may be denied due to a lack of double criminality if it would be offensive from Swedish perspective on the basis of Ch. 2 Sec. 14 Para. 2 Item 4 ILA Act.

1090 Ch. 4 Sec. 23 ILA Act.

1091 See Section 8.4 above. Compare on the requirement of double criminality in the *Proposal for a Regulation on Mutual Recognition*, Section 12.5 below.

1092 Compare for example European Commission, JUST/2011/JPEN/PR/0153/A4, *Comparative Law Study of the Implementation of Mutual Recognition of Orders to Freeze and Confiscate Criminal Assets in the European Union*, Final Finding Report, p. 78.

1093 See further on FIUs, Section 9.1.3 above.

temporarily freeze or block assets for a maximum of 72 hours as an emergency measure, based on telephone and fax information, if the originating authorities undertake to send an official follow-up request in a timely manner.[1094] The powers are usually limited in time, because such coercive measures normally require a decision by judicial authorities.

Such administrative rapid freezing of money in a bank account is in some States also used in international asset recovery cases. In, for example, the Czech Republic, the FIU has a power to on its own initiative postpone the execution of a transaction for up to 72 hours (to be prolonged for a further three days in special cases). In such a case, the FIU submits a report to the police and if a preliminary investigation is started, the prosecutor may decide on a longer seizure/freezing of the assets. This coordination between the powers of FIUs and police and judicial authorities may also be used in favour of international cooperation in criminal matters. In such a case, a judicial authority in one State must give notice to the FIU that criminal investigations have been initiated, that there is a suspicion that the suspect has gained assets from crime and that this amount is held in a bank account in the Czech Republic. It must also be indicated that the authority will send a request for MLA regarding seizure. In this way the FIU can postpone transactions on the account for a maximum of six days, giving the judicial authority an opportunity to deliver the formal request.[1095]

As described in Section 9.1.3 above, the national FIUs have at present very different structures, powers and functions. Within the EU, not all FIUs have the power to freeze bank account transactions. If there is a power, the prerequisites for any such decisions vary. It might, for example, differ whether it may be used for all offences or only for money laundering cases. Furthermore, it is not always possible to use such coercive measures on behalf of other States regarding criminal proceedings. Some international instruments relating to the operation of FIUs obligate the States to allow the national FIU to take urgent action at the request of a foreign FIU in order to suspend or withhold transactions.[1096] Sweden has long lagged behind other States in this area. However, on 1 July 2014 new legislation on measures against money laundering was adopted, which included a new provision on a prohibition on disposals of property ("*dispositionsförbud*").

1094 K. Stephenson, L. Gray, R. Power, J.P. Brun, G. Dunker and M. Panjer, *Barriers to Asset Recovery: An Analysis of the Key Barriers and Recommendations for Action*, The International Bank for Reconstruction and Development/The World Bank, 2011, p. 20.

1095 JUST/2011/JPEN/AG/2956, *Fostering Mutual Understanding in order to Strengthen Mutual Trust between the Judicial Authorities of Member States*, Handbook, October 2014, pp. 61–62.

1096 See for example regarding transactions related to *money laundering*, Art. 47 Council of Europe Convention on Laundering, Search, Seizure and Confiscation of the Proceeds from Crime and on the Financing of Terrorism (2005).

The Swedish FIU may now temporarily secure property. The decision does not apply for more than two working days from the order, and must as soon as possible be reported to a prosecutor. Such a measure may also be taken on behalf of a foreign FIU.[1097]

It has been proposed that all States should create a mechanism allowing assets to be frozen *on an urgent basis*, so that freezing should be permitted in emergencies on the basis of information provided by fax or, where there is a high level of trust, on the basis of direct communication through e-mail or a phone call. Even if a formal MLA request would be required, the initial orders would be made under domestic law.[1098] On the one hand, this is a good proposal. However, when it comes to the use of the FIUs, certain caution may be required as several difficulties related to legal safety and accountability may arise. National FIUs have different roles and competences within the Member States. There are administrative FIUs as well as police-based or judicial FIUs. One fundamental principle within transnational cooperation in criminal matters is that a request for legal assistance must be made (and decided) by a *judicial authority* if it concerns a coercive measure. Even if the borderlines between police and administrative and judicial authorities have been blurred to a certain extent within cross-border cooperation in the last years, this important principle has been kept. It is therefore important to ensure that the criminal procedural requirements for the use of coercive measures are not circumvented. Even if it is required in the above described cases that a foreign authority will later transmit a request for MLA regarding seizure, the *initial* (preliminary) decision on a coercive measure may be taken on the basis of national administrative procedure. Such legislation may in some cases lack the sufficient judicial safeguards necessary for upholding criminal procedural rights.

This being said, there is also in practice another way to obtain a *preliminary* seizure of bank accounts prior to a formal request for cooperation. This practice is entirely within the realm of criminal procedural law. In some States, it is, for example, possible for the national investigative judges or prosecutors to make a provisional order pending a request for assistance. In, for example, Germany the prosecutors and/or law enforcement officials are in urgent cases entitled to freeze or decide on preliminary seizure without judicial authorisation. Such decisions must be based on reliable information, and may be made on behalf of

---

1097 See Ch. 3 Secs. 8–9 in the Act (2009:62) on measures against money laundering and terrorist financing. Compare further Bill 2013/14:121 and SOU 2012:12. The Swedish provisions in the area of money laundering are described in a booklet; *Money Laundering*, Legal Memorandum 2015:2 from the *Prosecution Development Centre*, Stockholm and the *Swedish Economic Crime Authority*.

1098 Stephenson, Gray, Power, Brun, Dunker and Panjer, n 1094 above, p 55.

other States. A necessary precondition is that a formal MLA request is sent as soon as possible.[1099]

Against this background, it is obvious that the competent authorities of the Member States are in need of more urgent forms of freezing within cross-border cooperation. With regard to the respect for fundamental rights and the interests of clarity and accountability, such measures should, though, be provided for within the system of judicial cooperation. In this respect, it may be noted that the FD on Freezing Orders provides a time-limit of 24 hours (Article 5(3)). This is a strict deadline with the purpose of providing for a speedy handling of freezing orders. The formulation of the framework decision is, however, rather vague as it states that an order shall, if possible, be *decided* and *communicated* within this time-period. The Swedish implementing legislation provides instead that a freezing order *shall be executed* expeditiously and, if possible, within 24 hours from when the prosecutor received the order and a sufficiently filled in certificate.[1100] To link the time-limit to the actual *execution* of orders seems to be a better way to provide for faster procedures.

The European Commission seems aware of the significant importance of efficient freezing mechanisms. Article 7 of Directive 2014/42/EU states in this respect that the Member States shall take the necessary measures to enable the freezing of property with a view to possible subsequent confiscation. Such measures shall include "urgent action to be taken when necessary in order to preserve property". The term "freezing" is defined as "the temporary prohibition of the transfer, destruction, conversion, disposal or movement of property or temporarily assuming custody or control of property".[1101] It has been highlighted that the purpose of including these rules in the directive has been "without prejudice to" the FD on Freezing Orders to "approximate some aspects of the national systems of freezing for the purposes of confiscation".[1102] Obviously, this might succeed when it comes to the implementation of the more specific and detailed legal safeguards which have been given to individuals affected by a freezing order.[1103] However, as a whole, the provision is so generally formulated

1099 Compare Sec. 67 of the Act on International Cooperation in Criminal Matters of 23 December 1982 (*Gesetz über die internationale Rechtshilfe in Strafsachen*). See also JUST/2011/JPEN/AG/2956, *Fostering Mutual Understanding in order to Strengthen Mutual Trust between the Judicial Authorities of Member States*, Handbook, October 2014, p. 64. Some information on different forms of assistance to foreign States in asset recovery cases is also given in *Vermögensabschöpfung im deutschen Recht, Hinweise für Praktiker*, Bundesministerium der Justiz und für Verbraucherschutz, October 2015.

1100 Ch. 3 Sec. 8 Act (2005:500) on Recognition and Execution of EU Freezing Decisions.

1101 Art. 2(5) Directive 2014/42/EU. According to Art. 7(2) freezing measures can also regard property in the possession of a third party.

1102 Recitals (27)–(32) Directive 2014/42/EU.

1103 The legal safeguards are described in Section 2.3.5 above.

that any more far-reaching harmonisation of the freezing powers and any "urgent action" cannot really be expected. The Member States are already obligated by many international instruments on MLA and by the FD on Freezing Orders to have legal provisions in place in order to be able to efficiently freeze assets.[1104]

Consequently, one cannot hope for a more significant change of the Member States' routines regarding the possibilities for "urgent action" based on these provisions in Directive 2014/42/EU. Accordingly, the expectations are high for a major reform within the framework of the present legislative process of adopting a single instrument on *mutual recognition*. This issue is noted in Section 12.6 below.

[1104] In the Swedish legislative process it was concluded that there was no need for changes to Swedish law following from Art. 7 Directive 2014/42/EU, as there were already provisions on different coercive measures to be used. See the *Report on Extended Confiscation*, SOU 2015:67, pp. 153–57.

CHAPTER 11

INTERNATIONAL COOPERATION IN ORDER TO EXECUTE FINAL CONFISCATION ORDERS

11.1. THE LEGAL FRAMEWORK

11.1.1. REQUESTS FOR MLA

An international basis to request judicial assistance from other States in order to recognise and enforce the execution of a final confiscation order can be found in several treaties, for example Article 13 of the European Convention on Laundering, Search, Seizure and Confiscation of the Proceeds from Crime (1990), Article 13 of the United Nations Convention against Transnational Organized Crime (2000), Article 5 of the United Nations Convention against Illicit Traffic in Narcotic Drugs and Psychotropic Substances (1988) and Article 23 of the Council of Europe Convention on Laundering, Search, Seizure and Confiscation of the Proceeds from Crime and on the Financing of Terrorism (2005).[1105] In general, the provisions on cooperation on the basis of MLA obligate a requested State *either* to enforce a confiscation order made by a court of a requesting State or to submit the request to its own competent authorities for the purpose of obtaining a domestic order of confiscation and, if such order is granted, enforce it.[1106] The traditional procedure for MLA applies, and common grounds for refusal of such assistance are, for example, a lack of double criminality, violations of *ordre public* or concern for the principle of *ne bis in idem*.[1107]

1105 For the status regarding ratifying States within the EU, see Section 8.2 above.

1106 See generally on international cooperation mechanisms for the enforcement of confiscation orders, G. Stessens, *Money Laundering; A New International Law Enforcement Model*, Cambridge University Press, 2000, pp. 381–419.

1107 See, for example, Art. 28 Council of Europe Convention on Laundering, Search, Seizure and Confiscation of the Proceeds from Crime and on the Financing of Terrorism (2005) and Art. 18 European Convention on Laundering, Search, Seizure and Confiscation of the Proceeds from Crime (1990).

11.1.2. THE FD ON CONFISCATION ORDERS

11.1.2.1. General Provisions

Within the EU more advanced cooperation based on mutual recognition has been introduced within the area of final confiscation orders by the FD on Confiscation Orders.[1108] The purpose of this instrument is to establish the rules under which a Member State must recognise and execute in its territory a confiscation order issued by a court competent in criminal matters of another Member State.[1109] In this way, the FD on Freezing Orders has been complemented with an instrument which regulates also the handling of transnational *final* confiscation orders in accordance with the criteria of mutual recognition. The instrument should have been implemented by 24 November 2008. In 2010, the European Commission concluded in a mutual evaluation report that the degree of implementation was not satisfactory, as only 13 Member States had implemented the instrument.[1110] Since then the situation has improved, although the instrument has not yet been implemented by Greece, Slovakia, Ireland and Luxembourg (as of February 2017). In some of these States, the implementation process is ongoing. In relation to the States in which the FD on Confiscation Orders is not yet in force, an application of any of the international instruments mentioned in Section 11.1.1 above might be possible.

The FD on Confiscation Orders is in principle applicable to any offence in relation to which confiscation orders may be issued.[1111] Article 2(c) defines a "confiscation order" as a final penalty or measure imposed by a court following proceedings in relation to a criminal offence or offences, resulting in the definitive deprivation of property. This means that if an order is not

---

1108 Framework Decision 2006/783/JHA, *OJ* L 328, 24.11.2006, pp. 59–78 and an Amending Act thereto (Framework Decision 2009/299/JHA), *OJ* L 81, 27.3.2009, pp. 24–36. For an overview of the framework decision especially from the perspective of the protection of the rights of the parties, see F. Gascón Inchausti, "Mutual Recognition and Transnational Confiscation Orders" in S. Ruggeri (ed.), *Transnational Inquiries and the Protection of Fundamental Rights in Criminal Proceedings*, Springer, 2013, pp. 253–67. See generally on mutual recognition in the area of final decisions, *Communication from the Commission to the Council and the European Parliament, Mutual recognition of Final Decisions in Criminal Matters*, COM(2000) 495 final, Brussels 26.7.2000.

1109 Art. 1(1) FD on Confiscation Orders.

1110 *Report from the European Commission to the European Parliament and the Council based on Article 22 of the Council Framework Decision 2006/783/JHA of 6 October 2006 on the application of the principle of mutual recognition to confiscation orders*, 23.8.2010, COM(2010) 428 final, p. 2.

1111 *Report from the Commission to the European Parliament and the Council based on Article 22 of the Council Framework Decision 2006/783/JHA of 6 October 2006 on the application of the principle of mutual recognition to confiscation orders*, 23.8.2010, COM(2010) 428 final, p. 2. See also Gascón Inchausti, n 1108 above, p. 257.

final, precautionary measures (for example under the FD on Freezing Orders) will be used. In short, the procedure is as follows. The issuing State issues a domestic confiscation order supplemented by a special *certificate*, which should reproduce all information needed for an executing State.[1112] These documents are sent *directly* to a competent authority of the executing State.[1113] In certain cases, the Member States have been allowed to designate a central authority for administrative transmission and assistance.[1114]

A confiscation order may be sent to a Member State, where there are "reasonable grounds" to believe that property is located, or in the case of money, where a natural or legal person has property or income. It is thus not possible to send out the order to several States in the hope of assets in any of them. This prevention of "fishing expeditions" shows the importance of having efficient channels for the tracing of assets before a confiscation order is made. If there are no indications of assets in a particular State, an order may be sent to a Member State where the natural or legal person is normally resident or has its registered seat.[1115] In principle, a confiscation order may only be sent to one executing State at a time.[1116] There are, however, certain exceptions to this and simultaneous transmission of a confiscation order to several States is allowed regarding *specific property* in the following cases:

(1) if the issuing State has reasonable grounds to believe that different items of property are located in different executing States,
(2) if the confiscation of a specific item of property involves action in more than one executing State, or
(3) if the issuing State has reasonable grounds to believe that a specific item of property is located in one of two or more specified executing States.[1117]

A confiscation order regarding *an amount of money* may be transmitted to more than one executing State at the same time, in cases where there is a specific need to do so. This might be so in urgent cases, if the property concerned has not been frozen under the FD on Freezing Orders, or where the value of the property is likely to be insufficient for the execution of the full amount covered by the confiscation order.[1118] The transmission of a confiscation order to another State

1112 A standard form for the certificate is given in an *Annex* to the framework decision, see also Art. 4(1)–(3) FD on Confiscation Orders. Official translations of the certificate in all EU languages have been provided. For issues regarding requirements of translation, see Art. 19.
1113 Art. 4(2) FD on Confiscation Orders. The definition of competent authorities is left to national law (Art. 3).
1114 Art 3(2) FD on Confiscation Orders.
1115 Art. 4(1) FD on Confiscation Orders.
1116 Art. 5(1) FD on Confiscation Orders.
1117 Art. 5(2) FD on Confiscation Orders.
1118 Art. 5(3) FD on Confiscation Orders.

does not prevent the issuing State from executing the confiscation order itself. In such a case, it must inform the executing State of this as soon as possible.[1119]

The executing State shall recognise a confiscation order "without further formality" and shall "forthwith take all the necessary measures for its execution".[1120] This means that when a foreign confiscation order has been recognised, the property must be found and seized (if it is not already frozen on the basis of the FD on Freezing Orders).[1121] In accordance with the principle of mutual recognition, the examination shall be of limited extent and any substantive reasons shall not be reconsidered. The executing State may though, according to Article 8, invoke certain grounds for refusal. As these grounds are *optional*, it differs from State to State which (if any) grounds for refusal are applicable. In short, the reasons for non-recognition and non-execution of an order are:

(1) if the certificate is missing, is incomplete, or manifestly does not correspond to the order;
(2) if it is established that:
    (a) the execution of the confiscation order would be contrary to the principle of *ne bis in idem*;
    (b) where applicable, there is no double criminality;
    (c) the executing State provides for immunity or privileges that prevent execution;
    (d) the rights of the parties concerned including third parties acting in good faith make it impossible to execute the order under the law of the executing State;
    (e) according to the certificate the person affected by the confiscation order was not present or represented in the proceedings resulting in the confiscation order;[1122]
    (f) the criminal offences were committed wholly or partly within the territory of the executing State or outside the territory of the issuing State, and the law of the executing State does not permit legal proceedings to be taken in respect of such offences;

1119 See further Art. 14 FD on Confiscation Orders.

1120 Art. 7(1) FD on Confiscation Orders. The European Commission has found that implementing laws which provide for an obligation to convene a hearing in every case in the executing State are not in compliance with this provision because it usually represents a significant formality. See *Report from the Commission to the European Parliament and the Council based on Article 22 of the Council Framework Decision 2006/783/JHA of 6 October 2006 on the application of the principle of mutual recognition to confiscation orders*, 23.8.2010, COM(2010) 428 final, p. 7.

1121 Gascón Inchausti, n 1108 above, p. 260.

1122 This was introduced by the Amending Act to the framework decision, see Framework Decision 2009/299/JHA, *OJ* L 81, 27.3.2009, pp. 24–36.

(g) the confiscation order was issued in circumstances where confiscation of property was ordered under extended powers of confiscation *which are not those* specified in FD 2005/212/JHA; or
(h) the confiscation order is statute-barred under the national law of the executing State.

There is a *partial abolition* of the requirement of double criminality regarding 32 criminal offences listed in Article 6, provided that these offences are punishable in the issuing State by a custodial sentence of a maximum of at least three years.[1123] The legal classification of these offences lies exclusively within national law of the issuing State. Accordingly, the executing State must execute such orders and cannot refuse to recognise an order on this ground. It is allowed to require double criminality for crimes other than those listed in the framework decision.[1124]

The confiscation order is in principle executed in accordance with the national law of the executing State.[1125] There is no deadline given for the handling of a case. Provisions on legal remedies for the person affected by a confiscation order and third parties are given in Article 9 FD on Confiscation Orders.[1126] In principle, an appeal against the execution of a foreign order takes place in the executing State, but the substantive reasons for issuing the order in the first place may only be challenged before a court in the issuing State.[1127] The provisions are similar to those in the FD on Freezing Orders (compare Section 10.1.2.1 above). There are further certain rules regarding asset sharing (Article 16). Unless otherwise agreed between the States in question, amounts below €10,000 accrue to the executing State, and in all other cases, 50 per cent of the amount is to be transferred to the issuing State.[1128]

An executing State may in certain cases postpone the execution of a confiscation order, for example if there is a risk that the execution might damage an ongoing criminal investigation or proceeding in the executing State.[1129] It can happen that an executing State receives *multiple confiscation orders*, i.e. orders from two or more Member States against the same natural or legal person. If such confiscation orders clash, because they concern the same property or

1123 This list of criminal offences corresponds to the list in the FD on Freezing Orders.
1124 Compare Arts. 6(3) and 8(2)(b) FD on Confiscation Orders.
1125 Art. 12 FD on Confiscation Orders. A confiscation order issued against a legal person shall be executed even if the executing State does not recognise the principle of criminal liability of legal persons (Art. 12(3)).
1126 See on the protection of the parties involved, Gascón Inchausti, n 1108 above, pp. 261–67.
1127 Art. 9(2) FD on Confiscation Orders.
1128 See further for rules on the disposal of property, Art. 16(2)–(4) FD on Confiscation Orders.
1129 Art. 10 FD on Confiscation Orders.

because the person concerned does not have sufficient means, it is up to the executing State to decide which confiscation order is to be executed. Hereby due consideration shall be given to all circumstances, for example the seriousness of the offences and the dates of the respective orders.[1130]

11.1.2.2. Mutual Recognition of Orders on Extended Confiscation

Specific provisions concern the powers of extended confiscation. The FD on Confiscation Orders differs between such orders on extended confiscation which have been based on Article 3(1) and (2) of FD 2005/212/JHA (see Article 2(d)(iii)) and orders based on any other provisions of extended powers of confiscation under the law in the issuing State (Article 2(d)(iv)). It has been left to the Member States to decide whether they recognise and execute the latter type of confiscation orders at all. The possibility of such a *declaration* to the European Council is further described in Section 11.2.2.1 below. In any case, as seen above, there is for the latter category of confiscation orders also an optional ground for refusal in Article 8(2)(g).

Mutual recognition of final confiscation orders regarding extended confiscation based on FD 2005/212/JHA is in principle covered by the FD on Confiscation Orders. However, there is one important exception to this in cases where it "appears to the competent authority" of the executing State that a foreign confiscation order was issued under the extended powers of confiscation in FD 2005/212/JHA, but the order "falls outside the scope of the option adopted by the executing State" under Article 3(2). In such a case, the executing State must execute the confiscation order at least to the extent provided for in a similar domestic case under national law.[1131] This provision thus limits the principle of mutual recognition so that an executing State must only execute such orders on extended confiscation as are based on the same legislative solution as its own national law. This construction of the FD on Confiscation Orders has led to practical problems, and has been widely criticised (see further Section 11.2.2.1 below).

In October 2016, when Directive 2014/42/EU came into force, the directive replaced FD 2005/212/JHA between the States which have implemented the directive. The framework decision, however, continues to apply in relation to the States that are not participating in the Directive (i.e. the UK and Denmark). As seen above, the FD on Confiscation Orders refers on several matters to the

---

1130 Art. 11 FD on Confiscation Orders. Compare also the possibility to postpone the execution in a case where there is a risk of confiscation of an amount in excess of that established in the order, Art. 10(1)(a).

1131 Art. 8(3) FD on Confiscation Orders.

FD 2005/212/JHA. In this respect, Article 14 Directive 2014/42/EU now provides the following:

1. Joint Action 98/699/JHA, point (a) of Article 1 and Articles 3 and 4 of Framework Decision 2001/500/JHA, and the first four indents of Article 1 and Article 3 of Framework Decision 2005/212/JHA, are replaced by this Directive for the Member States bound by this Directive, without prejudice to the obligations of those Member States relating to the time limits for transposition of those Framework Decisions into national law.
2. For the Member States bound by this Directive, references to Joint Action 98/699/JHA and to the provisions of Framework Decisions 2001/500/JHA and 2005/212/JHA referred to in paragraph 1 shall be construed as references to this Directive.

This means that Article 2(d)(iii) FD on Confiscation Orders now also refers to the extended powers of confiscation which have been implemented on the basis of Article 5 Directive 2014/42/EU.[1132] The provisions regarding the powers of extended confiscation, which are not based on these EU instruments, i.e. Articles 2(d)(iv), 7(5) and 8(2)(g) remain unchanged. Article 8(3) seems to become obsolete *in relation to Article 5*, as this provision does not contain any different options for legislation.

11.2. A COMMENTARY ON THE EU REGIME ON CROSS-BORDER EXECUTION OF FINAL CONFISCATION ORDERS

11.2.1. GENERALLY ON THE LEGAL CONSTRUCTION OF THE FD ON CONFISCATION ORDERS

According to the mutual evaluation report in 2010, the national implementation of the framework decision have been generally satisfactory, especially regarding the most important issues such as the abolition of double criminality and the recognition procedure. However, the report states that almost all Member States had at this time included additional grounds for refusal of recognition, which was found to be in breach of Article 8 FD on Confiscation Orders. Many States had added violations of constitutional or human rights law as mandatory grounds for refusal.[1133]

1132 The reference to Art. 3(1) and (2) FD 2005/212/JHA will thus remain in relation to the UK and Denmark.

1133 *Report from the Commission to the European Parliament and the Council based on Article 22 of the Council Framework Decision 2006/783/JHA of 6 October 2006 on the application of*

Similarly to the FD on Freezing Orders, the FD on Confiscation Orders has not replaced any existing instruments. This means that the competent authorities of the Member States may choose to base a request on instruments on MLA or to issue an order under the framework decision. There are many advantages with the last mentioned system. Cooperation on the basis of mutual recognition provides for more swift procedures in comparison to the time-consuming and complicated regime of MLA. In addition, the Member States are *obligated* to execute final confiscation orders regarding several criminal offences on the list without a requirement of double criminality. Nevertheless, in practice, the choice of MLA or mutual recognition will depend on the national regime for confiscation and the implementation status of the international instruments in the requested/executing State in question. This situation may improve in the future if a comprehensive instrument on mutual recognition is adopted.[1134]

Obviously, it is mostly in two areas where the current legal construction of the FD on Confiscation Orders leads to significant difficulties. The first concerns the execution of final orders based on the extended confiscation powers. This will be discussed in the following section. The second area concerns the execution of final orders on non-conviction-based confiscation (hereafter "NCB confiscation orders"). This is addressed in Section 11.2.3 below.

11.2.2. THE EXECUTION OF FINAL ORDERS BASED ON THE POWERS OF EXTENDED CONFISCATION

11.2.2.1. Mutual Recognition and the FD on Confiscation Orders

The general starting-point of the FD on Confiscation Orders is that also final confiscation orders on extended confiscation will be recognised and enforced in other Member States. This now applies to orders of extended confiscation based on FD 2005/212/JHA as well as on Directive 2014/42/EU. Recital (8) of the FD on Confiscation Orders proclaims that this instrument is "linked to" FD 2005/212/JHA, which *inter alia* obligates the Member States to have powers of extended confiscation. As further described in Section 2.1.2 above, the latter framework decision has allowed the States to choose between *three alternative options* for the construction of the national provisions on extended confiscation (Article 3(2)). In this respect, the optional refusal ground (Article 8(3) FD on Confiscation Orders) has been very unfortunate. The decision of execution is to depend on whether States have chosen the same legislative construction. This

the principle of mutual recognition to confiscation orders, 23.8.2010, COM(2010) 428 final, pp. 8–10 and 13.

1134 See further Chapter 12 below.

means that the national choice of model for extended confiscation has in some cases become an obstacle to cooperation. This limited recognition of final orders of extended confiscation has led to practical problems, and has been widely criticised. It has, for example, in this respect been argued that the relationship to the FD 2005/212/HJA is "tortuous".[1135] One may in fact wonder why this generous ground for refusing recognition was drafted in the first place. Why should a Member State not be obligated to enforce an order of confiscation which is based on one of the *accepted* options in a harmonising framework decision drafted in accordance with the human rights guarantees? Such an exception contradicts the whole idea of mutual recognition.

Between the Member States that have implemented Directive 2014/42/EU, the provision of Article 2(d)(iii) FD on Confiscation Orders now refers to the extended powers of confiscation which have been implemented on the basis of Article 5 of this directive. Article 8(3) seems to have become obsolete in relation to Article 5, because this article does not allow for any different options for legislation. Quite the opposite, Directive 2014/42/EU has introduced one single standard for the national construction of extended confiscation. This ought to mean that a Member State is obligated to execute orders based on Article 5 Directive 2014/42/EU without any consideration of its own legislative model. As seen in Chapters 3–6, there are at present many different regimes of extended confiscation. One important motive for adopting the directive was that divergence hampers cross-border cooperation, and that the transnational execution of warrants in the area of extended confiscation must be improved.[1136] However, as discussed in Chapter 7, even if Directive 2014/42/EU may achieve a degree of harmonisation, the Member States have still been left much space for adopting different provisions. In certain matters, they may also be able to keep the old regimes on extended confiscation. It might therefore be expected that the various regimes will also in the future have different characteristics. It remains to be seen how mutual recognition regarding such orders will function on the basis of the FD on Confiscation Orders. This matter will be further discussed in Section 12.4 in the framework of the new *Proposal for a new EU regulation on mutual recognition*.

Another area where the construction of the FD on Confiscation Orders has been critically discussed concerns orders for extended confiscation which are based on any other provisions of extended powers of confiscation under the law in the issuing State (Article 2(d)(iv)). According to the FD on Confiscation

1135 *Study for an Impact Assessment on a Proposal for a New Legal Framework on the Confiscation and Recovery of Criminal Assets*, RAND Europe, 2012, pp. 43 and 71.

1136 Recital (19) Directive 2014/42/EU. See also Commission Staff Working Paper, *Accompanying Document to the Proposal for a Directive of the European Parliament and the Council on the Freezing and Confiscation of Proceeds of Crime in the European Union*, SWD(2012) 31 final, Brussels 12.3.2012, pp. 12–18.

Orders such confiscation orders may be completely excluded from mutual recognition. The taking force of Directive 2014/42/EU has in this respect left Article 2(d)(iv), Article 7(5) and Article 8(2)(g) of the FD on Confiscation Orders unchanged. The Member States may therefore keep any declarations that they do not recognise or execute such orders. Examples of such States are Germany, Belgium, Bulgaria, the Czech Republic, Croatia, Slovenia, Luxembourg, Austria, Poland and Romania.[1137] This was the case also in Sweden until 2014, when new legislation took force (see further Section 11.2.2.2 below). For the States that have not made such a general declaration, Article 8(2)(g) contains an optional ground for refusal to recognise or execute such orders in individual cases.

National authorities confront several difficulties when they apply the FD on Confiscation Orders in this respect. It is first of all complicated to decide whether a national confiscation order is to be classified under Article 2(d)(iii) or (iv). In order to do that, it may be necessary to analyse national legislation in a foreign State from the perspective of the framework decision or the directive. In practice, the starting-point for such considerations is the *certificate* which is transmitted to an executing State. The issuing State is obligated to indicate in Section (i) Subsection 1.2 box (iii) of the certificate whether a confiscation order is to be classified under Article 2(d)(iii) or (iv). Accordingly, the issuing State sets the framework for application by indicating which type of confiscation order it sends for execution. The authority in the executing State should in principle not question this information. However, some provisions of the FD on Confiscation Orders indicate that the *executing State* has the final say in some situations.[1138] There is further a right to refuse to execute an order based on Article 8(1) FD on Confiscation Orders in cases where there are anomalies. Inconsistencies could, for example, follow from the information given by an issuing State regarding the description and legal classification of the criminal offence being the basis of the confiscation order.[1139]

This being said, one must also acknowledge that also for the issuing State, it is not always an easy task to decide the status of its own national legislation. There may be different views on whether the powers in national law are based on FD 2005/212/JHA, Directive 2014/42/EU or arise from any other provisions. Many States had, for example, regimes on extended confiscation long before the framework decision was adopted. Some of these were based on other international

1137 For a list of the declarations based on Art. 7(5) FD on Confiscation Orders, see Council of the European Union, *Implementation of the Framework Decision 2006/783/JHA of the Council of the European Union of 6 October 2006 on the Application of the Principle of Mutual Recognition to Confiscation Orders, Information provided to the General Secretariat*, 7574/1/15, REV 1, Brussels 3.6.2015.

1138 Compare the phrase “in the view of that authority” in Art. 8(2)(g). See also Bill 2013/14:66 p. 43.

1139 Compare the information necessary according to Sec. (i) Subsec. 2 of the certificate.

conventions or have resulted from purely national initiatives. In Sweden, the instrument of extended confiscation was adopted as a result of the framework decision, but more far-reaching rules were decided upon. Accordingly, there was some uncertainty in the legislative process about the status of these decisions under the FD on Confiscation Orders. The position finally prevailed that they are classified as belonging to Article 2(d)(iv).[1140] This position did not change after the implementation of Directive 2014/42/EU.[1141] In this context, the Swedish interpretation given to Article 2(d)(iii) is that the implementing national legislation must "exactly correspond" to Article 3 FD 2005/212/JHA or Article 5 Directive 2014/42/EU in order to fall under this paragraph.[1142] In principle, this would mean that every little difference from the minimum requirements would lead to a classification under Article 2(d)(iv). One must doubt whether all States really use the same thresholds for deciding this issue.

The principal exclusion in the FD on Confiscation Orders of such orders on extended confiscation, which are based on other provisions than the EU instruments, has been criticised. In this respect, *Eurojust* has, for example, proposed to delete Article 8(2)(g) in the framework decision.[1143] However, this is a complicated area of cross-border cooperation. The scope of FD 2005/212/JHA as well as Directive 2014/42/EU are restricted to certain criminal offences, and the obligation to execute orders has been linked to this criminality. In contrast to this, the confiscation orders which may be transmitted under Article 2(d)(iv) have not been the object of measures of harmonisation. They may thus concern any criminal offence, any standard of evidence and very different criteria (if any) regarding the link to criminal activity. There is thus a significant risk of constitutional problems in an issuing State if some confiscation orders based on very far-reaching legislation must be recognised. At present, a reform of the EU regime is being discussed, and the issue of mutual recognition of orders regarding extended confiscation will be further discussed in Section 12.4 below within the context of the draft for a new Regulation.

In what follows, the Swedish legislative process regarding the implementation of the FD on Confiscation Orders in light of the EU instruments on extended confiscation is described. The purpose is to highlight some general difficulties that the national legislator has met in this area, and to illustrate how certain criteria may be found in order to be able to deal with the extended confiscation powers under Article 2(d)(iv).

1140 See on this, Section 11.2.2.2 below.

1141 Compare Section 11.2.2.2 as well as Bill 2015/16:155 pp. 34–36 and pp. 42–44.

1142 Compare SOU 2015:67 p. 179.

1143 *Eurojust's Opinion on the Proposal of the European Commission for a Directive on the Freezing and Confiscation of Proceeds of Crime in the European Union*, 2012, p. 7.

11.2.2.2. *The Example of Sweden: Execution of Foreign Orders Regarding Extended Confiscation*

The FD on Confiscation Orders has been implemented into Swedish law through legislation which came into force in 2011; the Act (2011:423) on recognition and execution of confiscation orders within the European Union (hereafter "Act 2011:423"). Supplementary rules are also given in the Ordinance (2011:578) on recognition and execution of confiscation orders within the European Union.[1144] During the preparatory legislative process, it had been concluded that the Swedish orders on extended confiscation would fall under Article 2(d)(iii). It had further been recommended that foreign orders based on Article 2(d)(iv) should be excluded from the Act through a declaration according to Article 7(5).[1145] However, the Swedish legislator took a different position. First, it was argued that Article 2(d)(iv) should include confiscation orders which:

1) have been drafted more extensively in national legislation than the legislative alternatives in Article 3(2) FD 2005/212/JHA, or
2) are based on other national provisions on extended confiscation.[1146]

Accordingly, it was held that the Swedish decisions on extended confiscation (Chapter 36 Section 1b SPC) must fall within Article 2(d)(iv) because they are based on FD 2005/212/JHA, but are more extensively drafted.[1147] It was further concluded that – in order to get such domestic decisions recognised abroad – it was necessary for Sweden to execute foreign orders on extended confiscation falling within Article 2(d)(iv). However, legislative provisions on this matter were at this stage postponed, because it was considered necessary to more thoroughly analyse under which requirements this could be possible. Consequently, Sweden initially made a declaration according to Article 7(5). This also had the consequence that it was not possible at this stage to send any Swedish orders on extended confiscation for execution abroad.[1148]

The Act 2011:423 was thus initially only applicable to (foreign) confiscation orders based on Article 2(d)(iii). The Act provides that such orders are to be recognised and executed without any specific requirements, and the same general grounds for refusal as for orders regarding ordinary confiscation are applied.[1149] Sweden has not made use of the right of refusal given in Article 8(3)

1144 For the legislative works, see Bills 2004/05:55 and 2010/11:43.
1145 Ds 2007:18 pp. 140–49.
1146 Bill 2010/11:43 p. 51.
1147 Bill 2010/11:43 p. 51. This is further described in Section 5.3.2 above.
1148 Bill 2010/11:43 pp. 51–53.
1149 See Ch. 3 Secs. 10 and 11 Act 2011:423. These refusal grounds concern *inter alia* deficiencies regarding the certificate, situations of *ne bis in idem*, immunity or privilege and certain cases

FD on Confiscation Orders, so that foreign orders are executed without any consideration of what legislative solution is applied by such a State. The motives for this legislative solution were that it was considered to be difficult for an executing State to decide which legislative model a foreign decision is based upon. Further, it was emphasised that the purpose of FD 2005/212/JHA was to give the Member States different legislative alternatives and to provide for flexibility within the national implementation. It would therefore not be compatible with the principal motives of mutual recognition to execute only such orders which correspond to one's own domestic model.[1150]

On 1 July 2014, provisions took force which made the Act 2011:423 applicable also to orders referred to in Article 2(d)(iv).[1151] Sweden therefore withdrew its declaration based on Article 7(5). The guiding principle during the legislative process was that such legislative changes were in line with the purpose of mutual recognition. However, it was acknowledged that there are significant differences in the legislation of the Member States, and that it may be difficult to foresee which types of orders may be sent under this provision. The setting up of certain limits was therefore considered necessary in order to prevent the execution of such orders, which strongly deviate from Swedish legislation and practice on confiscation. In accordance with Article 8(2)(g) FD on Confiscation Orders, some limiting requirements for the execution have been provided in Chapter 3 Section 11a of the Act 2011:423.[1152] This provision stipulates certain specific refusal grounds regarding foreign orders referred to in Article 2(d)(iv). They apply in addition to the general obstacles to execution given in Chapter 3 Sections 10–11.

The general principle is that Sweden shall execute foreign orders to the same extent as domestic orders for extended confiscation in such a case. Chapter 3 Section 11a of the Act 2011:423 states that an order may not be executed if:

(1) the triggering offence which is the basis of the foreign confiscation order neither corresponds to a criminal offence for which according to Swedish law is prescribed imprisonment for four years or more nor is any of the offences listed in Chapter 36 Section 1b Subsection 2 and 3 SPC,
(2) the crime is not of such nature as to lead to proceeds,
(3) it follows neither from the confiscation order nor from the conditions laid down in national legislation of the issuing State that the property to be confiscated derives from criminal activity,

of prescription. The execution of an order may also be refused if it would violate constitutional laws or the instruments on human rights. See further Bill 2013/14:66 p. 13.

1150 Bill 2010/11:43 pp. 86–91.

1151 See Ch. 1 Sec. 2 Subsec. 2 and Ch. 1 Sec. 3 Subsec. 1 Para. 4. See for legislative works, Bill 2013/14:66 and Ds 2012:51.

1152 See Bill 2013/14:66 pp. 16–18 and pp. 46–48.

(4) the confiscation order is not directed towards any of the persons mentioned in Chapter 36 Section 5a SPC, or
(5) the execution of an order would be unreasonable.[1153]

These obstacles correspond to the requirements given in Chapter 36 Section 1b SPC and have been explained in detail in Chapter 5 above.[1154] Accordingly, only a few short comments are here necessary. It can be noted that the scope of the triggering offences for extended confiscation according to Swedish law will be decisive. Further, the obstacle to execution given under (3) has been introduced in order to prevent the execution of foreign confiscation orders in cases where there is no link between the property which has been confiscated and criminal activity. The Swedish authority shall thus decide on the basis of the foreign confiscation order whether there is a link to criminal activity. The legislative works state in this respect that if it is not evident from the foreign confiscation order that the court has made such a ruling, the national legislation in the issuing State must be studied in order to decide if there is such a requirement at all.[1155] However, there is no requirement that the standard of evidence applied in the issuing State corresponds to the standard of Chapter 36 Section 1b SPC (that is "substantially more probable"). It was argued that such a provision would be difficult to operate, because it would mean that the Swedish authority would have to assess the evidence presented in the foreign procedure.

The obstacle expressed under (5) above clarifies that an execution may not take place if this would be unreasonable. This rather unusual exception to mutual recognition was adopted in order to function as a "safety net" for cases where the foreign confiscation order significantly deviates from the Swedish legal system.[1156] It is stated in the legislative works that this provision may, for example, be applied when it is evident from the foreign confiscation order or from national legislation in an issuing State that the standard of evidence is particularly low. This might be the case when the burden of proof is reversed, or is lower than the balance of probabilities.[1157]

The general position of the Swedish legislation to also execute foreign confiscation orders based on Article 2(d)(iv) of the FD on Confiscation Orders is to be recommended. It also seems reasonable to somewhat link the execution to the condition that the Swedish authorities could have made a confiscation order under similar circumstances. This being said, some practical difficulties

1153 This requirement does not follow from Ch. 3 Sec. 11a Act 2011:423, but is a requirement for extended confiscation under Swedish law according to Ch. 36 Sec. 1b Subsec. 4 SPC. Compare on this condition, Section 5.3.1 above.
1154 Compare also Bill 2013/14:66 pp. 19–26.
1155 Bill 2013/14:66 pp. 22–23.
1156 See for the motives, Bill 2013/14:66 pp. 24–26.
1157 Bill 2013/14:66 p. 25.

regarding the procedure may be expected. It may in fact not be easy for the national authorities to control and consider such issues based on the rather spare information given in a certificate. In addition, there is no general requirement that the foreign confiscation order shall be translated. It has in this respect been stated in the legislative works that it might be necessary more often in these cases to translate the order and to ask for complementary information. At the same time, it has been emphasised that there must be no review of the decision of a foreign authority.[1158] It can be doubted whether it will be possible in all cases to judge on the basis of a foreign confiscation order and national legislation in other States whether such orders would be unreasonable to execute. It is not as easy as one might think to consider legal issues on the basis of foreign legislation, because this mostly presupposes a further knowledge of the functioning of the criminal justice system, especially when it comes to procedural law.

When Directive 2014/42/EU was implemented into Swedish law, it was in principle concluded that the present EU regime on the recognition and execution of confiscation orders may be applied also in relation to the new rule of extended confiscation in Article 5. Act 2011:423 was thus only changed in order to include such orders regarding extended confiscation which are based on this directive. Chapter 3 Section 11a in Act 2001:423 was also changed in order to adjust the provision to the change in the Swedish provision on extended confiscation regarding the threshold for the triggering offences.[1159] It was generally noted during the legislative process that the Swedish decisions on extended confiscation will also in the future be classified to the group referred to in Article 2(d)(iv).[1160]

The Swedish legislation clearly illustrates the difficulties that States have encountered when they implement the FD on Confiscation Orders. Obviously, the Swedish generosity, regarding the foreign orders based on Article 2(d)(iv), is to a large extent based on its own interest to be able to execute its domestic orders abroad. With regards to the large amount of States, which have made declarations excluding such orders, it can be expected that Sweden will anyway have difficulties when such orders must be executed abroad.[1161] This being said, it seems like a reasonable starting-point to give other States the possibility to send such domestic orders for execution. It remains to be seen whether the Swedish requirements will function in practice.[1162]

1158 Bill 2013/14:66 p. 26 and p. 47.
1159 Bill 2015/16:155 pp. 34–36 and pp. 42–44. Compare Section 5.3.2 above.
1160 Bill 2015/16:155 p. 36.
1161 Other States may also have set up far-reaching domestic requirements for the execution (Art 8(2)(g) FD on Confiscation Orders).
1162 Compare further Section 12.4 on the new proposal for an EU regulation on mutual recognition.

11.2.3. SPECIAL DIFFICULTIES FOR THE UK: RECOGNITION AND EXECUTION OF NCB CONFISCATION ORDERS

As seen in Section 3.2 above, the legal regime in the UK provides for rather far-reaching powers of confiscation including for example both conviction-based confiscation (Parts 2–4 POCA 2002) and NCB confiscation (Part 5 POCA 2002). The domestic civil recovery provisions are though significantly weakened due to the fact that there are difficulties in such cases to obtain international assistance in order to trace or freeze assets, or to enforce such confiscation orders abroad. As concluded in the evaluation report on the UK regarding financial crime and financial investigations;

> POCA provides the UK authorities with numerous and very effective tools to address criminal assets. Civil recovery seems to be a highly valuable instrument that may be applied in cases where penal procedure and confiscation are not efficient ... However, the specific nature of the solution, which is uncommon and not well understood in many EU Member States, poses numerous practical problems in international cooperation as civil recovery orders issued by the UK are not recognised.[1163]

The UK is not alone in confronting such problems. This is also the experience of some other Member States that provide for NCB confiscation orders, for example Ireland and Italy.

In principle, the international framework for cooperation in confiscation matters is drafted to provide for assistance in the context of criminal proceedings and the investigation of a criminal offence.[1164] This is the case both regarding MLA and mutual recognition. Requests for MLA according to the 1959 Convention must relate to "a criminal matter" (Article 2). The 2000 EU Convention and the 2001 EU Protocol are also drafted in order to apply to the framework of criminal proceedings.[1165] According to Article 1 FD on Freezing Orders it only concerns an order issued by a judicial authority "in the framework of criminal proceedings". Accordingly, it cannot be used in civil or administrative proceedings.[1166] The same goes for the FD on Confiscation

---

1163 Council of the European Union, *Report on the United Kingdom*, 9636/2/10, REV 2, CRIMORG 94, Brussels 7.9.2010, p. 67.

1164 The possibilities to execute NCB confiscation orders on the basis of international instruments regarding the enforcement or recognition of *civil judgments* will not be discussed here. See further on this, for example *Study for an Impact Assessment on a Proposal for a New Legal Framework on the Confiscation and Recovery of Criminal Assets*, RAND Europe, 2012, pp. 39–40 and p. 50.

1165 The *Directive on EIO*, which will take force in 2017, provides that an EIO may be issued in respect to criminal proceedings as well as certain administrative proceedings in criminal matters. See further Art. 4 Directive on EIO.

1166 European Commission, JUST/2010/JPEN/PR/1004/B3, *Handbook for Judges, Prosecutors and other Competent Authorities on how to issue and execute a request for enforcement of a*

Orders, which only applies to confiscation orders issued by a court "competent in criminal matters" (Article 1).[1167] Consequently, domestic orders or requests for MLA regarding seizure and freezing of assets, or in order to obtain information on bank accounts, which are needed in the context of civil proceedings, are not executed on the basis of these instruments. The EU regime is not fully coherent in this respect, however. Article 1(1) FD on Asset Recovery Offices, for example, provides that national AROs may facilitate the tracing and identification of criminal proceeds, which may become the object of an order made by a judicial authority "in the course of criminal or, as far as possible under the national law of the Member State concerned, civil proceedings". This thus includes civil recovery proceedings.

During the negotiations on Directive 2014/42/EU many States with an NCB confiscation regime hoped for the adoption of an EU wide regime of civil recovery. However, the result was a very limited provision on confiscation without a final conviction in cases where a suspect or accused person is ill or has absconded.[1168] The issue of mutual recognition of such orders is not addressed at all in the directive. The FD on Confiscation Orders is not applicable to such orders based on Article 4(2).[1169] A proposal to change this situation, and to allow for the recognition of some forms of NCB confiscation, has recently been made within the framework of the new proposal on a Regulation on mutual recognition.[1170] Further, the possibilities for a more extensive NCB confiscation regime are at present studied by the European Commission.[1171] A feasibility analysis has been envisaged in 2017.[1172]

This being said, there are at present two international instruments which may be applied regarding NCB confiscation orders. Article 11 in the European Convention on Laundering, Search, Seizure and Confiscation of the Proceeds from Crime (1990) states that the obligation to take provisional measures concerns "criminal proceedings or proceedings for the purpose of confiscation".[1173]

Freezing Order, in accordance with Council Framework Decision 2003/577/JHA of 22 July 2003, available at: http://e-justice.europa.eu/content_criminal_law-255-en.do, p. 8.

1167 Compare the definition of a confiscation order in Art. 2(c), which relates to a criminal offence. See also *Proceeds of Organised Crime; Ensuring that "Crime does not Pay"*, 20.11.2008, COM(2008) 766 final, p. 5.

1168 Compare Section 2.3.2 above.

1169 See for example See SOU 2015:67 pp. 176 and 178–79.

1170 See further Section 12.4.

1171 See Joint Statement by the European Parliament and the Council issued upon the adoption of Directive 2014/42/EU, Council of the European Union, 7329/1/14, COPEN 83, Brussels 31.3.2014, p. 1.

1172 See COM(2016) 819 final, Brussels 21.12.2016, p. 3.

1173 Compare also Art. 13 in the same Convention, which states an obligation to confiscate "concerning instrumentalities or proceeds". This formulation has been interpreted as to include non-conviction-based civil recovery. See M. Egan, "Non-conviction Based Sanctions: The Court of Justice v. the European Court of Human Rights, Who Decides?" (2011) 19 *European Journal of Crime, Criminal Law and Criminal Justice*, pp. 167–82, p. 172.

Article 23(5) of the Council of Europe Convention on Laundering, Search, Seizure and Confiscation of the Proceeds from Crime and on the Financing of Terrorism (2005) states that the Parties *shall* cooperate to the widest extent possible regarding the execution of:

> measures equivalent to confiscation leading to the deprivation of property, which are not criminal sanctions, in so far as such measures are ordered by a judicial authority of the requesting Party in relation to a criminal offence.

This is expressed as a mandatory obligation, but at the same time there are grounds for refusal of cooperation for a requested State.[1174] Both of these Conventions thus give a basis for cooperation regarding NCB confiscation orders if this is compatible with the domestic judicial systems in question. However, neither instrument contains an absolute obligation for the Parties to recognise such orders.[1175] Further, as mentioned in Section 8.2 above, many Member States have not ratified the 2005 Convention.

There are at present different views within the EU on whether foreign NCB confiscation orders may be executed domestically or not.[1176] Most States are not executing such orders at all (for example Belgium,[1177] Spain[1178] and Sweden[1179]), whereas some may be willing to execute the orders in cases where there is a definite link to a criminal matter.[1180] France is often used as an example of a State

1174 See for example Art. 28(1)(a) and (b) Council of Europe Convention on Laundering, Search, Seizure and Confiscation of the Proceeds from Crime and on the Financing of Terrorism (2005).

1175 Parties have the right to refuse to cooperate, for example, in cases of *ordre public* (Art. 18(1)(a)) and, more specifically, in some cases if the request does not relate to a previous conviction (Art. 18(4)(d) *European Convention on Laundering, Search, Seizure and Confiscation of the Proceeds from Crime* (1990)). Compare also *Study for an Impact Assessment on a Proposal for a New Legal Framework on the Confiscation and Recovery of Criminal Assets*, RAND Europe, 2012, p. 40.

1176 For an overview of different position, see European Commission, JUST/2011/JPEN/PR/0153/A4, *Comparative Law Study of the Implementation of Mutual Recognition of Orders to Freeze and Confiscate Criminal Assets in the European Union*, Final Finding Report, pp. 266–97.

1177 See *Mutual Evaluation Report on Belgium*, Anti-money laundering and Counter-terrorist Financing Measures, Financial Action Task Force ("FATF"), April 2015, p. 140 and *Proposal for a Directive of the European Parliament and the Council on the Freezing and Confiscation of Proceeds of Crime in the European Union, Compilation of replies to questionnaire*, 12219/2/12, REV 2, Brussels 20.7.2012, p. 4.

1178 Compare Commission Staff Working Document, *Impact Assessment*, Accompanying the document *proposal for a Regulation of the European Parliament and of the Council on the Mutual Recognition of Freezing and Confiscation Orders*, SWD(2016) 468 final, Brussels 21.12.2016, p. 18.

1179 Compare *Proposal for a Directive of the European Parliament and the Council on the Freezing and Confiscation of Proceeds of Crime in the European Union, Compilation of replies to questionnaire*, 12219/2/12, REV 2, Brussels 20.7.2012, p. 125.

1180 See for different positions in *Proposal for a Directive of the European Parliament and the Council on the Freezing and Confiscation of Proceeds of Crime in the European Union,*

that may execute foreign civil forfeiture orders in spite of the fact that its own legal justice system only provides for conviction-based criminal confiscation. In, for example, the *Crisafulli* case, the French Court of Cassation recognised and executed an Italian NCB confiscation order pursuant to the 1990 Council of Europe Convention on Laundering, Search, Seizure and Confiscation of the Proceeds of Crime (1990).[1181] The Court ruled that, although the foreign order had not been issued by a criminal court, confiscation could have been possible according to French law under similar circumstances.[1182] A common requirement in practice, when such orders are executed, seems to be that the evidence that establishes that the property is the proceeds of an offence can "be considered sufficient to approximate to a decision of a criminal nature".[1183]

There are at present a variety of different confiscation regimes within the Union, and it is in some cases difficult to make a sharp distinction between them.[1184] In principle, NCB confiscation orders and criminal confiscation orders share the same objective (to remove the gain from criminal offences), but they differ in the procedures used.[1185] It has in this respect been argued that the non-applicability of the FD on Freezing Orders and the FD on Confiscation Orders to civil recovery orders "handicap the ability of Member States to combat organised crime".[1186] Obviously, if the Union has an aim to target criminal proceeds, then something has to be done about this. Nevertheless, the issue is very complex, and space only allows a few comments on the possible legislative

Compilation of replies to questionnaire, 12219/2/12, REV 2, Brussels 20.7.2012. Information on some States is also found in K. Stephenson, L. Gray, R. Power, J.P. Brun, G. Dunker and M. Panjer, *Barriers to Asset Recovery: An Analysis of the Key Barriers and Recommendations for Action*, The International Bank for Reconstruction and Development/The World Bank, 2011, p. 113–79. Compare *Mutual Evaluation Report on Spain*, Anti-money laundering and Counter-terrorist Financing Measures, FATF, December 2014, p. 126.

1181 Cour de Cassation, 13 November 2003, No. 3 03-80371.

1182 It has been argued that decisive for granting the enforcement of the order was in fact that there was a parallel criminal conviction. See for a critical commentary of this case and some others involving the enforcement of NCB confiscation orders, F. Alagna, "Non-conviction Based Confiscation: Why the EU Directive is a Missed Opportunity" (2015) 21 *European Journal on Criminal Policy and Research*, pp. 447–64.

1183 *Proposal for a Directive of the European Parliament and the Council on the Freezing and Confiscation of Proceeds of Crime in the European Union, Compilation of replies to questionnaire*, 12219/2/12, REV 2, Brussels 20.7.2012, p. 67.

1184 See, for example, the study by *Eurojust* regarding the systems of confiscation within the EU and the difficulties regarding international cooperation, *Report on Non-Conviction-based Confiscation*, General Case 751/NMSK-2012, 2.4.2013.

1185 T.S. Greenberg, L. Samuel, W. Grant, and L. Gray, *Stolen Asset Recovery: A Good Practices Guide for Non-Conviction Based Asset Forfeiture*, STAR Initiative, The World Bank, 2009, p. 13.

1186 *Study for an Impact Assessment on a Proposal for a New Legal Framework on the Confiscation and Recovery of Criminal Assets*, RAND Europe, 2012, p. 71. See for similar opinions, Alagna, n 1182 above and *Eurojust, Report on Non-Conviction-based Confiscation*, General Case 751/NMSK-2012, 2.4.2013, p. 15.

paths. One way to solve the difficulties would be to introduce a fully harmonised system for NCB confiscation in all Member States. Such an option seems at present unrealistic. It might also not be the most suitable way ahead. In short, the concept of NCB confiscation is alien to many legal systems in the EU, does not fit into the national procedural systems and may present constitutional problems. Accordingly, it ought to be very difficult to design a comprehensive common civil asset recovery regime. Even if this path may be tested, it can be expected that the extent of harmonisation will be modest and – for the purposes of international cooperation – of limited value.

A more reasonable method would be to investigate to what extent the Member States could be prepared to cooperate in proceedings based on NCB confiscation. This issue has, for example, been considered in the legislative process regarding the new regulation on mutual recognition of freezing and confiscation orders (see further Section 12.4). The matter is, though, rather complicated. It is internationally often recommended that States should recognise and be able to cooperate also regarding foreign NCB confiscation orders.[1187] However, there are many different models of civil recovery.[1188] Against this background, it must be carefully assessed under which circumstances such orders may be recognised by other States. Some Member States generally hesitate to recognise orders of this character, arguing that they may violate the human rights guarantees of the person involved. Common objections are that such procedures may provide for a civil or reversed burden of proof and that this might violate the presumption of innocence.[1189] In contrast, the States operating a system of NCB confiscation highlight the fact that such orders are issued by judicial authorities with the due process rights contained in the ECHR.

The discussion will continue within the EU. Therefore it should be acknowledged that the dividing line between different national regimes is often not as clear as one thinks. As was rightly pointed out in this respect:

> Der Grat, der *in personam*-Verfahren und *in rem*-Verfahren voneinander trennt, ist freilich schmal, und es ist nicht auszuschließen, dass Instrumente, die sich in der Sache gegen die Person richten, in den jeweiligen nationalen Gefilden formell als *in rem*-Verfahren klassifiziert werden.[1190]

1187 Compare for example recommendation 4 and 38, The FATF Recommendations, *International Standards on Combating Money Laundering and the Financing of Terrorism & Proliferation*, October 2012 and Stephenson, Gray, Power, Brun, Dunker and Panjer, n 1180 above, Recommendation 3 at p. 7.

1188 See in this respect *Eurojust, Report on Non-Conviction-based Confiscation*, General Case 751/NMSK-2012, 2.4.2013 and J.P. Brun, L. Gray, C. Scott and K.M. Stephenson, *Asset Recovery Handbook: A Guide for Practitioners*, STAR Initiative, The World Bank, 2011, p. 156.

1189 See on human rights implications, Egan, n 1173 above and Greenberg, Samuel, Grant and Gray, n 1185 above, pp. 19–21.

1190 F. Meyer, "Reformiert die Rückgewinnungshilfe!" – Denkanstöße für eine Generalüberholung der Vermögensabschöpfung (2015) 2 *ZStW*, pp. 241–83, p. 271.

As a consequence of this, it cannot be taken for granted that all NCB confiscation regimes are by definition more intrusive than certain provisions allowing for far-reaching powers of extended confiscation. Even if the latter measure requires evidence beyond a reasonable doubt that a person has committed a crime, the criminal proceeds to be confiscated may derive from other criminal activity not fully proven. Furthermore, as is evident from the comparative study (Chapters 3–6), such legislation sometimes operates with a civil standard of proof. The system of extended confiscation has in this respect been classified as a "criminal non-conviction-based system", as it is linked to criminal proceedings but there is no criminal conviction (i.e. only for the triggering offence).[1191] In this respect, it may be noted that Member States with a more far-reaching regime on extended confiscation may also encounter difficulties in the area of mutual recognition.[1192]

At present, mutual recognition is influenced by the traditional approach to confiscation that a criminal conviction is needed. However, the instrument of confiscation has changed its face during recent decades, and mixed forms of criminal and civil recovery as well as extended confiscation have emerged. In the end, a more flexible and practical application of mutual recognition may be needed. In any case, a better understanding of the national solutions of other States could prevent a categorical refusal of cooperation regarding specific types of confiscation orders. This concerns NCB confiscation orders, as well as extensive forms of extended confiscation. In this area, a significant reform of the regime for mutual recognition is at present being discussed within the negotiations on the *Proposal for a Regulation on Mutual Recognition*. This initiative is addressed in the following chapter.

1191 *Eurojust, Report on Non-Conviction-based Confiscation*, General Case 751/NMSK-2012, 2.4.2013, pp. 9–10.

1192 Compare further Sections 11.2.2.1 and 11.2.2.2.

CHAPTER 12

THE PROPOSAL FOR A REGULATION ON MUTUAL RECOGNITION

12.1. THE BACKGROUND TO THE PROPOSAL

On 21 December 2016, the European Commission issued a package of legislative measures aimed at strengthening the EU's capacity to fight the financing of terrorism and organised crime. The focus of this action was three pieces of legislation in the area of money laundering, illicit cash movement and the freezing and confiscation of assets.[1193]

In this context, the *Proposal for a Regulation on Mutual Recognition* was presented.[1194] The purpose of this proposal is to provide for one single legal instrument on the recognition and execution of freezing orders and confiscation orders within the EU. The *Proposal for a Regulation on Mutual Recognition* is therefore intended to establish a comprehensive framework for international cooperation covering both the freezing and confiscation of proceeds of crime. It lays down the rules under which a Member State must recognise and execute foreign freezing and confiscation orders issued within the framework of criminal proceedings (Article 1). Accordingly, the regulation would replace the FD on Freezing Orders and the FD on Confiscation Orders for the Member States that are bound by these instruments. The framework decisions would, though, continue to apply in relation to those Member States that are not bound by this Regulation.[1195] Denmark has announced that it will not take part in the Regulation, and the UK and Ireland may choose whether to opt in.[1196]

1193 Compare the *Communication from the Commission to the European Parliament, the Council, the European Economic and Social Committee and the Committee of the Regions, The European Agenda on Security*, COM(2015) 185 final and *Communication from the Commission to the European Parliament and the Council on an Action Plan for strengthening the fight against terrorist financing*, COM(2016) 50 final.

1194 COM(2016) 819 final, Brussels 21.12.2016. Compare Section 8.5 above.

1195 See Art. 39 of the *Proposal for a Regulation on Mutual Recognition* and COM(2016) 819 final, Brussels 21.12.2016, p. 18.

1196 Compare for the situation of the UK after Brexit, Section 1.5 above.

12.2. THE MOTIVES FOR EU ACTION

At the adoption of Directive 2014/42/EU, the Council and the European Parliament both called for further legislative action in order to improve the cross-border enforcement of freezing and confiscation orders. The *Proposal for a Regulation on Mutual Recognition* is thus a direct answer to these calls. There are many other reasons given by the European Commission for a new instrument. It is *inter alia* highlighted that:

> However, and although existing statistics are limited, the amount of money currently being recovered from proceeds of crime within the EU is only a small proportion: 98.9% of estimated criminal profits are not confiscated and remain at the disposal of criminals. A functioning asset recovery regime is a precondition if more criminal assets are to be seized. This includes an efficient mutual recognition framework for freezing and confiscation orders. Although legislation on mutual recognition of freezing and confiscation orders does exist at EU level, it is patchy, out of date, and leaves lacunae which can be exploited by criminals.[1197]

The existing EU regime on mutual recognition is considered "out of date" as it has not kept up with the recent developments in some Member States' national legislation and with recent EU legislation. It is further acknowledged that the procedures which are provided for in the current framework decisions are time-consuming and partly complicated. Sufficient protection of the right of victims to compensation or restitution is also lacking within the regime for transnational cooperation.

It may be observed that the EU legislator once again justifies new legislative action by arguing that the extent of (cross-border) confiscation of criminal assets is insufficient.[1198] This statement is not substantiated by any reliable statistics, and it is even admitted in the proposal that the statistical basis is poor.[1199] Nevertheless, there is no doubt that there is a need for legislative reform. The current regime is indeed "patchy", user-unfriendly and needs to be adjusted to new developments in the area of confiscation.[1200] The adoption of one single comprehensive instrument on the execution of freezing and confiscation orders on the basis of mutual recognition ought to provide for more clarity in order to simplify the handling of transnational orders.

This being said, it would also under this regime be necessary in some cases to go through two sets of legal instruments. A judicial authority in the issuing

---

1197 COM(2016) 819 final, Brussels 21.12.2016, p. 2.

1198 Compare Section 7.1 above.

1199 COM(2016) 819 final, Brussels 21.12.2016, p. 2. It is therefore to be welcomed that the Member States would be obligated to collect and maintain statistics. See Art. 35 of the proposal.

1200 For the difficulties of the current regimes, see Sections 10.2 and 11.2 above.

State would, for example, still have to rely on the Directive on the EIO in order to transmit orders relating to the tracing and location of an asset, or in order to obtain banking information and execute orders of search and seizure of evidence. In this respect it is necessary to take into consideration that, especially during the preliminary investigation of a criminal offence, there may be many different overlapping objectives of investigative actions. There might, for example, not always be a sharp distinction between the objectives of securing evidence and securing a subsequent confiscation order.[1201] This means that it will be crucial for the future handling of cases on mutual recognition to maintain a smooth relationship between the applicable instruments.

In general, it might be added that it is in many aspects rather challenging to draft a comprehensive instrument which is tailor-made for transnational confiscation proceedings. The area of confiscation is very complex and demands particular consideration. It remains to be seen how the draft proposal will be received in the Member States. In what follows, the main elements of the *Proposal for a Regulation on Mutual Recognition* will be presented. This description is not intended to be exhaustive. Instead, some of the major proposed amendments in relation to the current regime will be highlighted in order to evaluate whether the proposal might lead to improvements.

12.3. THE LEGAL BASIS, CHOICE OF INSTRUMENT AND GENERAL STRUCTURE

It is maintained that the legal basis for the instrument is Article 82(1) TFEU. This provision authorises the EU to adopt measures to establish rules and procedures for ensuring recognition throughout the Union of all forms of judgments and judicial decisions, and to facilitate cooperation between judicial or equivalent authorities in relation to proceedings in criminal matters and the enforcement of decisions.[1202]

For the first time since the entry into force of the Lisbon Treaty, the European Commission uses the legal instrument of a Regulation in the field of mutual recognition in criminal matters. Such an instrument is *directly applicable* in the Member States. The European Commission justifies the choice of instrument in the following way:

> As the proposal concerns cross-border procedures, where uniform rules are required, there is no need to leave a margin to Member States to transpose such rules. A regulation is directly applicable, provides clarity and greater legal certainty, and avoids the

[1201] Compare on this, Section 10.1.2.2 above.

[1202] COM(2016) 819 final, Brussels 21.12.2016, pp. 6–7.

> transposition problems that the Framework Decisions on mutual recognition of freezing and confiscation orders were subject to. For these reasons the most appropriate form to be used for this mutual recognition instrument is considered to be a regulation.[1203]

The choice of legal instrument is surprising, as the legislative instruments used previously within the area of mutual recognition have been directives (for example the Directive on the EIO). It seems as if the EU legislator is finally fed up with the time-consuming national implementation processes and wants to reduce the risk of late or incorrect transposition by the Member States.[1204] One may understand this position. Nevertheless, a challenge with the use of an instrument which is to be directly applied by practitioners in different Member States is that the provisions must be drafted as simply and distinctly as possible. There must be no room for misinterpretation; otherwise the regulation may become an obstacle to an efficient handling of cases.

It may be doubted whether it is fully appropriate to use this type of instrument for matters of cross-border cooperation in asset recovery matters. As mentioned earlier, this area is both complicated and complex. Whether this will succeed largely depends on whether it will be possible to draft a text which may be smoothly transferred into the different legal practices and be directly applied under time pressure. One must remember that in the area of asset recovery, there are significant differences in terminology and legal concepts. It might thus also be a demanding task to find accurate translations of terminology that function in different criminal justice systems. The draft for a *Proposal for a Regulation on Mutual Recognition* does not yet fulfil all requirements for clarity, and it remains to be seen if this may be corrected during the negotiations to come.

Turning to the general structure of the proposal, it can be noted that Chapter I contains some general provisions of the subject-matter, common definitions and scope. Chapter II deals with the transmission, recognition and execution of confiscation orders. Chapter III lays down the conditions for the transmission, recognition and execution of freezing orders. Chapter IV contains some general provisions, *inter alia* regarding the law governing execution, multiple orders and legal remedies. Finally, the final provisions in Chapter V regulate, for example, the replacement of earlier EU instruments and the date for entry into force.

As argued above, if the instrument will apply directly in the Member States, it is of crucial importance not only that the actual text is as clear as possible, but also that the structure of the instrument is comprehensible and logical. Consequently, the chapter on freezing orders should *precede* the chapter on confiscation orders, as the measure of freezing is mainly used before any order of confiscation is issued. Further, it seems necessary to simplify the legal text in certain parts, for example it may be discussed whether all of the 39 recitals need to be kept.

1203 COM(2016) 819 final, Brussels 21.12.2016, p. 7.

1204 Compare COM(2016) 819 final, Brussels 21.12.2016, p. 5.

It could be appropriate to use the terms "*European Asset Freezing Order*" and "*European Asset Confiscation Order*" in the future instrument. This would be in line with other instruments on mutual recognition which have been created in this area, for example the "*European Arrest Warrant*", the "*European Investigation Order*" and the "*European Supervision Order*".[1205]

12.4. THE SCOPE OF APPLICATION

Article 1 provides that the instrument would cover mutual recognition of all types of freezing and confiscation orders issued within the framework of *criminal proceedings*. It would not apply to such orders issued within the framework of civil and administrative proceedings.[1206] The new regulation would have an extended scope compared to the current mutual recognition instruments, as, in addition to the types of confiscation already covered by the existing Framework Decisions, it would also cover third-party confiscation and criminal non-conviction-based confiscation. The wide discretion in the FD on Confiscation Orders to refuse recognition in cases of extended confiscation would also be abolished.[1207] The *Explanatory memorandum* lists examples of circumstances giving rise to criminal non-conviction-based confiscation: death of a person, immunity, prescription, cases where the perpetrator of an offence cannot be identified, or cases where a criminal court can confiscate an asset without conviction when the court has decided that such asset is the proceeds of crime. It is underlined that this requires the court to establish that an advantage was derived from a criminal offence.[1208]

The regulation would cover all criminal offences. It is thus not restricted to the so-called "*Eurocrimes*" (particularly serious crimes likely to have a cross-border dimension). It is maintained that Article 82 TFEU (which is the basis of the proposal) does not require such a limitation for mutual recognition of judgments in criminal matters. Therefore, the proposal covers mutual recognition of freezing and confiscation orders related to offences "covered by Directive 2014/42/EU, as well as orders related to other offences which are not covered by that Directive".[1209] This scope for cooperation seems reasonable, and

1205 Compare for example, Commission Staff Working Document, *Impact Assessment*, Accompanying the document *Proposal for a Regulation of the European Parliament and of the Council on the Mutual Recognition of Freezing and Confiscation Orders*, SWD(2016) 468 final, Brussels 21.12.2016, p. 37.

1206 Compare Recital (13) of the proposal and COM(2016) 819 final, Brussels 21.12.2016, p. 11.

1207 COM(2016) 819 final, Brussels 21.12.2016, p. 5.

1208 COM(2016) 819 final, Brussels 21.12.2016, pp. 5–6.

1209 COM(2016) 819 final, Brussels 21.12.2016, p. 11. Compare Recital (14) of the proposal.

would be in line with the FD on Freezing Orders and the FD on Confiscation Orders, which apply to all criminal offences.[1210]

According to the *Impact assessment* which accompanies the proposal, four main policy options were considered within the legislative process. Different solutions were thereby considered; from retention of the *status quo* to maximal legislative action, which would have entailed obligations to recognise and execute freezing and confiscation orders issued in civil and administrative proceedings. In the end, it was concluded that most of the Member States preferred legislative action, but there were different positions as to what kind of measures the instrument should cover.[1211] Obviously, the legislative option to include also confiscation orders issued in civil and administrative proceedings had to be abandoned, because many Member States cited constitutional problems regarding such cooperation.[1212] The special difficulties regarding civil recovery and non-conviction-based confiscation from the perspective of transnational enforcement have been discussed in Section 11.2.3 above. It has *inter alia* been concluded that even if the non-conviction-based confiscation regimes and the confiscation-based regimes in principle share the same objectives, there are various forms of legislation within the Union. At present, most Member States do not execute such foreign orders. Against this background, it seems reasonable to restrict the application of the new instrument on mutual recognition to orders on confiscation which have been issued in the context of *criminal proceedings*. Nevertheless, it is important to continue to consider if and how a cooperation instrument may be drafted in order to include at least some of the orders which are issued in the framework of civil and administrative proceedings in the future. However, such regulation requires a more extensive and careful analysis of the different measures.[1213]

This being said, one significant amendment of the present regime regarding orders on non-conviction-based confiscation could be made if the *Proposal for a Regulation on Mutual Recognition* were adopted. Under this draft for regulation, there would be an obligation for the Member States to execute such orders on non-conviction-based confiscation which have been decided within criminal proceedings. This is an interesting innovation of the mutual recognition regime. First of all, it is obviously necessary and appropriate to secure the execution of

---

1210 Art. 3 FD on Freezing Orders and Art. 6 FD on Confiscation Orders. Compare further Sections 10.1.2.1 and 11.1.2.1 above.

1211 See further Commission Staff Working Document, *Impact Assessment*, Accompanying the document *Proposal for a Regulation of the European Parliament and of the Council on the Mutual Recognition of Freezing and Confiscation Orders*, SWD(2016) 468 final, Brussels 21.12.2016, pp. 34–56.

1212 Commisssion Staff Working Document, *Impact Assessment*, Accompanying the document *Proposal for a Regulation of the European Parliament and of the Council on the Mutual Recognition of Freezing and Confiscation Orders*, SWD(2016) 468 final, Brussels 21.12.2016, pp. 47–48.

1213 See further on this Section 11.2.3 above.

the orders on non-conviction-based confiscation which is based on Article 4(2) Directive 2014/42/EU. The framework decisions are at present not applicable to such orders.[1214] When it comes to the inclusion of other foreign orders on criminal non-conviction-based confiscation, the matter is though more difficult. Many Member States have in this respect experienced difficulties in enforcing such orders from other States. One must not forget that the national regimes of the Member States are yet only harmonised when it comes to non-conviction-based confiscation based on Article 4(2) Directive 2014/42/EU. This means that the scope and prerequisites for other orders may vary significantly. Even if the intention to open up the field for different models of asset recovery within mutual recognition is to be welcomed in principle, the draft regulation does not seem to be sufficiently balanced at the moment. If such orders are added to the regime of transnational enforcement, the Member States must exceptionally be able to refuse an order on the basis of *ordre public* or violations of fundamental human rights.[1215] It remains to be seen how the Member States will deal with this proposal in the further negotiations.

Mutual recognition of extended confiscation orders is an area where similar considerations must be made. At present, there is only an obligation for the Member States to recognise and execute the orders which are based on the harmonising EU instruments (FD 2005/212/JHA and Directive 2014/42/EU). Many Member States have made a declaration, that foreign orders which are based on any other extended confiscation powers are not executed at all.[1216]

The obligation to execute foreign orders on extended confiscation in the *Proposal for a Regulation on Mutual Recognition* seems to include all orders and not only such measures which have been harmonised on an EU basis. The *Explanatory memorandum* states, for example, that the draft regulation is intended to cover mutual recognition of all types of freezing and confiscation orders issued within the framework of criminal proceedings.[1217] In Article 2, which provides for certain definitions, it is further stated that:

> (3) "property" means property of any description, whether corporeal or incorporeal, movable or immovable, and legal documents or instruments evidencing title or interest in such property, which the issuing authority considers to be:
> (a) the proceeds of an offence, or its equivalent, to either the full value or part of the value of such proceeds,

1214 Commisssion Staff Working Document, *Impact Assessment*, Accompanying the document *Proposal for a Regulation of the European Parliament and of the Council on the Mutual Recognition of Freezing and Confiscation Orders*, SWD (2016) 468 final, Brussels 21.12.2016, p. 18.

1215 See further for the need for such a refusal ground, Section 12.10 below.

1216 See further Sections 11.1.2.1, 11.1.2.2 and 11.2.2 above.

1217 COM(2016) 819 final, Brussels 21.12.2016, p. 5.

(b) the instrumentalities of such an offence, or the value of such instrumentalities,
(c) liable to confiscation resulting from the application in the issuing State of any of the powers of confiscation provided for in Directive 2014/42/EU, or
(d) liable to confiscation under any other provisions.

In addition, the extensive refusal grounds for orders of extended confiscation in Article 8 of the FD on Confiscation Orders have been completely abolished in the draft regulation.

It is obviously a significant improvement of the regime for mutual recognition of orders of extended confiscation if the States are no longer allowed to only recognise and execute such orders as are similar to their own domestic legislative model. The peculiar legal construction of the FD 2005/212/JHA as well as the FD on Confiscation Orders in this respect has led to significant difficulties in recent years. Nevertheless, the scope for mutual recognition which seems to be introduced by the *Proposal for a Regulation on Mutual Recognition* would result in a considerable broadening of the obligation to cooperate. Even if some extention of the scope of the transnational enforcement is in principle to be welcomed, one must underline that the proposal is rather far-reaching. Even after the implementation of Directive 2014/42/EU, national regimes on extended confiscation remain very different. It must not be forgotten that the measures of harmonisation undertaken by the EU only concern certain minimum rules, and many Member States have chosen to adopt more far-reaching legislation, for example regarding the scope of application or evidentiary standards. Wide powers of extended confiscation also existed in many States before the EU instruments took force.[1218]

Against this background, it may be difficult to foresee which types of orders may be sent under the *Proposal for a Regulation on Mutual Recognition*. This means that there is a certain risk that some constitutional problems may arise in some Member States. The German Constitutional Court has, for example, upheld a relatively high evidentiary standard domestically for extended confiscation. Would it then be possible for its national authorities to execute Swedish orders for extended confiscation which apply a much lower evidentiary standard? Would it be possible to execute orders from States that operate a reversed burden of proof? In this respect, the Swedish regime for mutual recognition may be mentioned, where the general principle is that foreign orders based on all powers of extended confiscation can be executed. This may in fact be a reasonable starting-point under a system of mutual recognition based on mutual trust. Nevertheless, the Swedish legislator has considered it necessary to set up special preconditions for such enforcement. This has been done in order to prevent the execution of orders which strongly deviate from Swedish legislation

1218 See further on this, Section 11.2.2 above.

and practice on confiscation. The detailed requirements and the difficulties that may arise in practice have been discussed in Section 11.2.2.2 above.

Against this background, it must also here be concluded that the draft regulation does not seem to be sufficiently balanced. Even if a broadened scope for mutual recognition is a step towards a more efficient transnational asset recovery regime, it is evident that at the very least a refusal ground based on *ordre public* or violations of fundamental human rights must be added.[1219]

12.5. GROUNDS FOR NON-RECOGNITION AND NON-EXECUTION

The *Proposal for a Regulation on Mutual Recognition* contains a common rule on the requirement of double criminality for both freezing and confiscation orders. Article 3(1) provides that a requirement of double criminality cannot be invoked for a list of offences punishable by at least three years' imprisonment in the issuing State. This list contains several serious forms of criminality, and has the same content as the list contained in other mutual recognition instruments with the exception that "fraud and counterfeiting of noncash means of payment" has been added.[1220] In the case of offences not included in this list, recognition and execution can be refused if the crime to which the order relates is not a criminal offence under the laws of the executing State (Article 3(2)).

According to Article 17 an executing State would be required to recognise and execute a *freezing order* "without further formalities", unless there is a ground for non-recognition or postponement. Article 18(1) contains an exhaustive list of the optional refusal grounds for freezing orders:

> 1. The executing authority may decide not to recognise and not to execute the freezing order only if:
>   (a) the form provided for in Article 16 is incomplete or manifestly incorrect, and has not been completed following the consultation in accordance with paragraph 2;
>   (b) the execution of the order would be contrary to the *ne bis in idem* principle;
>   (c) there is immunity or privilege under the law of the executing State which would prevent the execution of a domestic freezing order on the property concerned;
>   (d) the order is based on a criminal offence committed outside the territory of the issuing State and wholly or partially on the territory of the executing State, and the conduct in connection with which the freezing order is issued is not an offence in the executing State;

1219 Compare on this, Section 12.10 below.
1220 COM(2016) 819 final, Brussels 21.12.2016, p. 12.

(e) in a case referred to in Article 3(2), the conduct on which the freezing order is based does not constitute an offence under the law of the executing State; however, in relation to taxes or duties, customs and exchange, execution of the freezing order shall not be refused on the grounds that the law of the executing State does not impose the same kind of tax or duty or does not contain the same type of rules as regards taxes, duties and customs and exchange regulations as the law of the issuing State.

According to Article 8(1) of the *Proposal for a Regulation on Mutual Recognition* an executing State would be required "without further formalities" to recognise and execute a foreign *confiscation order*, unless there is a ground for non-recognition or postponement. Article 9 contains an exhaustive list of the optional grounds for non-recognition and non-execution of confiscation orders. Some of them are the same as in the FD on Confiscation Orders, for example the ground based on the principle of *ne bis in idem* or immunity or privilege. A significant amendment is that the possibility to refuse execution of orders of extended confiscation has been removed.[1221]

It can be noted that according to the proposal the requirement of double criminality is not changed in comparison to the current regime. In this respect, it is interesting to note that the Swedish implementing Act regarding the FD on Freezing Orders has abolished the requirement of double criminality *for all freezing orders*. The legislator has justified this by reference to the interest of expeditious execution, and has underlined that it is not decided at the freezing stage whether the property will be transferred to another State or be confiscated.[1222] As argued in Section 10.2.2 above, this might be possible to consider also in the context of the EU regime.

Further, in Section 12.10 below, the lack of an explicit refusal ground for mutual recognition of freezing and confiscation orders based on human rights concerns is discussed.

12.6. TIME LIMITS FOR RECOGNITION AND EXECUTION OF ORDERS

The *Proposal for a Regulation on Mutual Recognition* sets up clear deadlines for the recognition and execution of freezing as well as confiscation orders. An initial decision on the recognition and execution of a *freezing order* must be taken as soon as possible and not later than 24 hours after the executing authority has received the freezing order. The freezing must be carried out without delay and not later than 24 hours after the decision to recognise and execute the freezing

1221 COM(2016) 819 final, Brussels 21.12.2016, p. 13.
1222 See further, Section 10.2.2 above.

order. An executing authority must communicate its decision without delay to the issuing authority.[1223]

The executing authority must take the decision on the recognition and execution of a *confiscation order* without delay and not later than 30 days after the executing authority has received the confiscation order. The confiscation order must be carried out without delay and not later than 30 days after taking the decision to recognise and execute the order.[1224]

Obviously, it is important to encourage the Member States to give the same priority to the execution of foreign freezing and confiscation orders as in domestic cases. In this respect, the proposed deadlines are crucial, and could lead to significant improvements of the current regime. This is especially the case as the FD on Confiscation Orders does not contain any time-limits whatsoever. The deadline set up by the FD on Freezing Orders is unclear, and is applied differently by the Member States.[1225] Some States have regrettably not set up any deadlines at all.[1226] The new provision in the *Proposal for a Regulation on Mutual Recognition* could therefore bring clarity.

This being said, it is of significant importance in the area of asset recovery that the different orders are responded to very quickly, as the "criminals are able to move assets across borders extremely quickly, sometimes with a few clicks on a computer or a phone".[1227] Against this background, it may be questioned whether a limit of 48 hours for deciding and executing a foreign freezing order will in all cases be sufficient. When property must be frozen more urgently, this mechanism might fail. The necessity of urgent freezing measures has already been discussed in Section 10.2.3 above. It could thus be appropriate to initiate a discussion of the possibility to develop a regime for *preliminary urgent* action in order to freeze property in exceptional cases.

12.7. GENERAL PROVISIONS ON PROCEDURE

Articles 4 and 14 of the *Proposal for a Regulation on Mutual Recognition* provide for a direct transmission of orders between the competent national

---

1223 See further Art. 19 and COM(2016) 819 final, Brussels 21.12.2016, pp. 14–15.

1224 Art. 10 and COM(2016) 819 final, Brussels 21.12.2016, p. 13.

1225 See for a discussion of the present time limit in the FD on Freezing Orders, Section 10.2.3 above.

1226 Commission Staff Working Document, *Impact Assessment*, Accompanying the document *Proposal for a Regulation of the European Parliament and of the Council on the Mutual Recognition of Freezing and Confiscation Orders*, SWD(2016) 468 final, Brussels 21.12.2016, p. 20.

1227 Commission Staff Working Document, *Impact Assessment*, Accompanying the document *Proposal for a Regulation of the European Parliament and of the Council on the Mutual Recognition of Freezing and Confiscation Orders*, SWD(2016) 468 final, Brussels 21.12.2016, p. 31.

authorities. It also allows for the possibility of assistance by central authorities. The execution of freezing and confiscation orders would be governed by the law of the executing Member State (Article 26). However, the executing Member State would be required to execute an order against a legal person even if its own domestic law did not provide for the criminal liability of legal persons.

The *Proposal for a Regulation on Mutual Recognition* maintains the general rule that a freezing or confiscation order may only be transmitted to one executing State at a time. Some exceptions, allowing for the transmission to several States, are provided for in Article 5 and Article 15 however. These exceptions are almost identical to those which are currently applied in Article 5 FD on Confiscation Orders.

In Section 10.2.1 above, a drawback of the current regime of freezing orders has been discussed. Difficulties arise when an issuing State intends to freeze a specifically identified asset belonging to a defendant but it is not definitely established where the asset is located. In such a case, where an issuing State cannot identify any States in question, an order of freezing may be impossible. It has in this respect been proposed that the EU legislator should consider the possibility of allowing a freezing order without a specification of the receiving authority.[1228] Such a system would function like the SIS system for locating stolen property and has been further discussed in Section 10.2.1 above. In any case, a legislative solution for this problem should be considered, as it may significantly raise the efficiency of the freezing orders.

Another difficulty of the present freezing system, which has also been discussed in Section 10.2.1 above, is that an order regarding "specific items" must exactly identify the property to be frozen. In practice, it may happen that such property is not found, but other assets are located which could cover the amount to be frozen. Under the current system, the freezing of this other property is impossible if the issuing State does not issue a new freezing order. It seems as if the *Proposal for a Regulation on Mutual Recognition* would not change this. It should be considered whether this flaw may be resolved in the further negotiations.

12.8. SOME SPECIAL PROVISIONS REGARDING FREEZING ORDERS

The *Proposal for a Regulation on Mutual Recognition* lays down certain conditions for issuing and transmitting a freezing order to another State. The aim is to

1228 See for example European Commission, *Handbook for Judges, Prosecutors and other Competent Authorities on how to issue and execute a request for enforcement of a Freezing Order, in accordance with Council Framework Decision 2003/577/JHA of 22 July 2003*, p. 115, available at: http://e-justice.europa.eu/content_criminal_law-255-en.do.

ensure that the proportionality principle is respected, and to make sure that the same conditions apply to the regime of freezing for evidence and freezing for subsequent confiscation.[1229] Article 13 provides that:

> 1. The issuing authority may issue a freezing order provided that the following conditions are met:
>   (a) the issuing of the order is necessary and proportionate in order to provisionally prevent the destruction, transformation, moving, transfer or disposal of property with a view to possible subsequent confiscation taking into account the rights of the person concerned;
>   (b) the order could have been ordered under the same conditions in a similar domestic case; and
>   (c) the reason or reasons for the order are properly indicated, at least briefly.
> 2. The conditions referred to in paragraph 1 shall be assessed by the issuing authority in each case.
> 3. Where the executing authority has reason to believe that the conditions referred to in paragraph 1 have not been met, it may, after executing the order, consult the issuing authority on the importance of continuing the freezing. Such consultation shall not delay the execution of the freezing order. After that consultation the issuing authority may decide to withdraw the order.

It is to be welcomed that it is expressly provided that freezing orders should be issued within national States with care and respect for the proportionality principle. Article 13 is in this respect an improvement in terms of human rights law. Nevertheless, one might doubt whether Article 13(3) will have any significant effects in practice. It must in many cases be very difficult for an executing State to assess – on the basis of the sparse information given in the freezing process – whether these conditions have been properly met.

Regarding the form of a freezing order, the *Proposal for a Regulation on Mutual Recognition* provides for a simplification of the mutual recognition procedure in comparison to the FD on Freezing Orders. Article 16 states that the freezing order shall be issued in the form set out in the Annex, which provides a standard form. The current procedure in the FD on Freezing Orders is that a certificate is attached to the national freezing order.[1230] According to the draft regulation the issuing authority would instead only have to complete, sign and certify the content of the standard form as accurate and correct. It must then be translated into an official or accepted language of the executing State.[1231]

1229 COM(2016) 819 final, Brussels 21.12.2016, pp. 13–14. Compare Art. 6 in the Directive on the EIO.

1230 Compare Section 10.1.2.1 above.

1231 In comparison, it may be mentioned that the confiscation order must be accompanied by a standard certificate, which is also provided for in an annex to the proposal. See Art. 4 and COM(2016) 819 final, Brussels 21.12.2016, p. 12.

The new procedure has been drafted with inspiration from the Directive on the EIO.[1232]

As mentioned in Section 10.2.1 above, the judicial authorities have tended not to use the FD on Freezing Orders, *inter alia* as the certificate is considered to be inadequate and difficult to complete. Against this background, it seems of crucial importance to simplify and change this procedure. The future will tell whether the new standard form will function better. In this respect, another new feature may be mentioned. Articles 36 and 37 of the *Proposal for a Regulation on Mutual Recognition* introduce a more flexible procedure for amending the standard certificate and the standard form given in the Annex. The European Commission would thereby be empowered to adopt any amendments necessary. This seems to be a smooth way to be able to react quickly and efficiently to any up-coming difficulties in practice regarding the contents.

Turning to the duration of a freezing order, the general rule would be that the property should remain frozen until a final decision on confiscation or discharge of the frozen property is issued (Article 23(1)). An improvement of the current regime for freezing is that the EU legislator has acknowledged that there might be cases where the measure of freezing seems to be excessive. Accordingly, Article 23(2) lays down certain rules in order to limit the duration based on consultation between the executing and the issuing authority. Even if there is no absolute time limit on a freezing measure, the issuing authority must provide reasons for a pro-longed freezing. If it does not do so within six weeks, the executing authority may even lift the freezing order.[1233] This attempt to control the duration of freezing orders must be applauded. It is absolutely necessary from a human rights perspective that the necessity and proportionality of an ongoing measure is tested.

12.9. THE PRIORITY OF THE RIGHTS OF VICTIMS

The European Commission intends to ensure that in cases where property is confiscated, the victim's right to compensation and restitution has priority over the executing and issuing States' interests.[1234] It is thus to be guaranteed that "victims are not losing their rights" in cases where the assets are located abroad.[1235] Article 31(3) provide that in cases where the victim has been granted a decision on compensation or restitution, this sum shall accrue to the

[1232] COM(2016) 819 final, Brussels 21.12.2016, p. 14.
[1233] COM(2016) 819 final, Brussels 21.12.2016, pp. 15–16.
[1234] COM(2016) 819 final, Brussels 21.12.2016, p. 6.
[1235] COM(2016) 819 final, Brussels 21.12.2016, p. 17.

issuing State for purposes of compensation or restitution to the victim.[1236] If a procedure regarding compensation or restitution is pending in the issuing State, the executing State must withhold the disposition of the confiscated property until the decision is communicated to the executing authority (Article 31(5)).

This is a significant improvement of the rights of victims of a crime, and is in line with the Directive on victims' rights in 2012 and Article 8(10) Directive 2014/42/EU.[1237] In several Member States, for example in Sweden or Finland, there is a possibility to receive a decision on compensation or restitution within the criminal proceedings. In practice, difficulties have arisen in this area in cross-border cases. Neither the FD on Freezing Orders nor the FD on Confiscation Orders contain any provisions on victims' rights to compensation or an obligation to take account of such claims.[1238]

12.10. MUTUAL RECOGNITION AND THE RESPECT FOR FUNDAMENTAL RIGHTS

The *Proposal for a Regulation on Mutual Recognition* would improve the current regime of mutual recognition of freezing and confiscation orders and make it more effective. The scope for cross-border cooperation would thereby increase significantly. The Member States would be obligated to recognise and execute foreign orders on third party confiscation and certain criminal non-conviction-based confiscation orders. In addition, the scope for executing orders of extended confiscation would increase. In principle, measures of freezing and confiscation of property constitute major interferences in people's lives. Against this background, it seems more important than ever that there is also a strong regime for safeguarding the fundamental rights of the individuals affected by such decisions.

The European Commission is naturally aware of the fact that measures of mutual recognition under the new instrument may interfere with the human rights *acquis*. The *Explanatory memorandum* therefore draws attention to case-law of the ECtHR, where different regimes of non-conviction-based confiscation

1236 The *Explanatory memorandum* underlines that Art. 31 do not "introduce any new right for victims where such right does not exist under national law". See COM(2016) 819 final, Brussels 21.12.2016, p. 17.

1237 See further on this, Section 7.8.

1238 See further on this problem, Commission Staff Working Document, *Impact Assessment*, Accompanying the document *Proposal for a Regulation of the European Parliament and of the Council on the Mutual Recognition of Freezing and Confiscation Orders*, SWD(2016) 468 final, Brussels 21.12.2016, pp. 22–23.

and extended confiscation have been found to be consistent with the ECHR. It is in this respect also pointed out that:

> Some important safeguards are included in the proposed Regulation: the principle of proportionality needs to be respected, there are grounds for refusal based on the non-respect of the principle of "ne bis in idem" and the rules on "in absentia" proceedings. Moreover, the rights of bona fide third parties have to be respected, there is an obligation to inform interested parties of the execution of a freezing order including of the reasons thereof and the legal remedies available, and there is an obligation for Member States to provide for legal remedies in the executing State.[1239]

Furthermore, it is added that as the Regulation would only apply to freezing and confiscation orders issued within the framework of criminal proceedings, all criminal law procedural safeguards provided for in EU legislation and the EU Charter of Fundamental Rights would also apply. It is especially underlined that several important safeguards are given in Article 8 Directive 2014/42/EU, Article 6 ECHR and in the specific EU instruments on criminal procedural rights.

When it comes to legal remedies against a foreign freezing or confiscation order, the regime in the *Proposal for a Regulation on Mutual Recognition* is similar to the current mutual recognition instruments. Article 33 provides that:

> 1. Any interested party, including bona fide third parties, shall have legal remedies, including those provided for in Article 8 of Directive 2014/42/EU, against the recognition and execution of an order pursuant to Article 8 and 17, in order to preserve their rights. The legal remedy shall be brought before a court in the executing State in accordance with its national law. The action may have suspensive effect under the law of the executing State.
> 2. The substantive reasons for issuing the freezing or confiscation order shall not be challenged before a court in the executing State.
> 3. The competent authority of the issuing State shall be informed of any legal remedy filed in accordance with paragraph 1.

Against this background, the European Commission seems satisfied that the proposed Regulation complies with fundamental rights.

Obviously, the EU Charter of Fundamental Rights guarantees the most important procedural rights in the area of asset recovery, for example the presumption of innocence, the right of access to justice, the right of defence, the principles of legality and *ne bis in idem* (Articles 47–50). Nevertheless, one must ask whether mere references to the human rights *acquis* in different areas will be sufficient to deal with all legal matters that may occur as a result of the increased scope for transnational cooperation.

1239 COM(2016) 819 final, Brussels 21.12.2016, p. 10.

Article 8 Directive 2014/42/EU intends to safeguard *inter alia* the respect for the general prerequisites set up by the ECtHR for the measures of extended confiscation and non-conviction-based confiscation. One of the most important of them is that any legal presumptions regarding illegal origin must be rebuttable.[1240] Several provisions of this article thus seek to ensure "an effective possibility" for an affected person to challenge orders of freezing and confiscation. However, as concluded earlier, in order to provide for an "effective possibility" in the daily application, one must provide for a factual "equality of arms".[1241] To start with, the right of access to a lawyer (Article 8(7)) is not regulated satisfactorily from the perspective of cross-border proceedings. In many cases of mutual recognition, the affected person will be forced to challenge an order of freezing or confiscation before a court in another State. In order to be able to challenge an order on substantive grounds, most persons will need the assistance of a lawyer with knowledge of the foreign legislation and legal system in this other State. It might even be necessary with the assistance of a lawyer in an issuing as well as in an executing State.

Another weakness of the current regime concerns the matter of legal aid. If one considers that a freezing or confiscation order might deprive a person of assets, legal aid might be a necessity in order to prevent that the individual is not also deprived of the opportunity to be represented. Difficulties regarding legal aid often arise in cross-border cases. It is therefore to be regretted that such a right is not expressly mentioned in Article 8.[1242] Obviously, if one intends to safeguard the right of effective remedy and a fair trial, the right to legal aid must be guaranteed. In close connection with this, a significant strengthening of the defence rights within the EU would be achieved if the following recommendation were to be followed:

> Create a European human rights defenders' system which would receive individual complaints, have complete access to files and report any relevant issues to EU institutions and national authorities. This system could be incorporated under the European Union Agency for Fundamental Rights ("FRA"). FRA does not currently intervene in individual cases but rather focuses on broad issues and trends. Whilst many bodies are focused on creating networks to facilitate cooperation between authorities in order to prosecute crime – including the possibility under Article 86 to create a European Public Prosecutor – none provide for assistance in the defence of human rights in individual cases. It is thus, suggested that in order to maintain some form of equilibrium, a system of European rights defenders be created.[1243]

1240 See further Section 3.6.6 above.

1241 Compare on this, Section 7.7 above.

1242 See further on this Section 7.7 above.

1243 European Commission, JUST/2011/JPEN/PR/0153/A4, *Comparative Law Study of the Implementation of Mutual Recognition of Orders to Freeze and Confiscate Criminal Assets in the European Union*, Final Finding Report, p. 472.

From a human rights perspective, it seems important to have rules that seek to limit the duration of a freezing order. Some freezing measures may of course be of limited duration, but others can stay in place until a trial starts or the order is finally executed. Article 8(3) Directive 2014/42/EU provides in this respect that a freezing order shall remain in force only for as long as it is necessary to preserve the property with a view to possible subsequent confiscation. In line with this, the *Proposal for a Regulation on Mutual Recognition* contains an improvement of the present EU regime as it requires that a prolonged duration is justified by the issuing State. Another positive development is that the importance of the principle of proportionality in confiscation cases has been emphasised in the draft regulation.[1244] Furthermore, grounds for refusal of cooperation based on the principle of *ne bis in idem* and regarding *in absentia* proceedings are included.

However, an apparent shortage of the draft regulation is the lack of a refusal ground on the basis of a violation of fundamental human rights. One reason for this might have been that neither the FD on Freezing Orders nor the FD on Confiscation Orders allow for such refusal. In fact, human rights clauses have traditionally not been a part of the instruments on mutual recognition. The EU legislator has based mutual recognition on the concept of mutual trust, and has argued that all Member States are anyway bound by the human rights *acquis*. Nevertheless, in the last few years a slow development may be seen in the other direction. It has, for example, been criticised that the FD on the EAW does not contain such a refusal ground.[1245] A significant step was taken in 2014, when an explicit refusal ground on the basis of human rights violations was included in the Directive on the EIO. Article 11(f) of this Directive provides that an EIO may be refused where:

> there are substantial grounds to believe that the execution of the investigative measure would be incompatible with the executing State's human rights obligations.

The Directive on the EIO is in this respect a good example of a cooperation instrument which seeks to balance the mutual recognition obligations with certain respect for the diversity of national legal systems and their constitutional frameworks. In comparison hereto, the *Proposal for a Regulation on Mutual Recognition* seems to represent a regrettable step back.

A refusal ground based on human rights should be added to the draft regulation in the further legislative proceedings. All Member States have an obligation under human rights law to safeguard that the rights under the EU

[1244] See Section 12.8 above.

[1245] See for example Recommendation 7(d), European Parliament, *Resolution of 27 February 2014 with recommendations to the Commission on the review of the European Arrest Warrant*, 2013/2109(INL).

Charter of Fundamental Rights and the ECHR are protected in cross-border cooperation with other States. Consequently, an executing State may not refer all violations of fundamental rights to the issuing State, but has its own independent responsibility.[1246] Against this background a "safety-clause" must be inserted in the new Regulation on mutual recognition in order to allow the national authorities to *exceptionally* check human rights issues. This is especially urgent in light of the broadened scope for mutual recognition as well as the extended use of orders of confiscation. As already argued in Section 12.4, the courts of an executing State would according to the draft proposal be obligated to execute foreign confiscation orders which might differ significantly from their own legal system, or even such measures which do not exist at all.

A refusal ground based on human rights violations is absolutely necessary in order to ensure the compliance of the future EU confiscation regime with the human rights *acquis*. In this respect, it may generally be added that it is not to be taken for granted that all regimes of extended confiscation or non-conviction-based confiscation will in the future be in compliance with the ECHR. The case-law of the ECtHR is based on the individual case in question, and the full limits for adopting more extensive figures of confiscation remain to be seen.[1247]

An objective to guarantee a defendant a fair trial may demand that the legal position of this person is *improved* or *strengthened*. The *acquis* of the EU confiscation law has in recent years increased significantly in scope. Against this background, the Member States must take the opportunity at the negotiations on the new proposal to insert some more provisions in order to provide for full coverage of human rights from the cross-border perspective. If this is neglected, it is a significant risk that the regulation will take the shape of a one-sided cooperation instrument which only serves the efficiency of law enforcement. A more balanced instrument could increase the mutual trust necessary in order for it to function satisfactorily in and between all Member States.

1246 See for a critical study of the human rights responsibility within mutual recognition in the EU, M. Thunberg Schunke, *Whose Responsibility? A Study of Transnational Defence Rights and Mutual Recognition of Judicial Decisions within the EU*, Intersentia, 2013.

1247 Compare further on this, Section 7.4.2 above.

CHAPTER 13

FINAL REMARKS: "TO GO FOR THE MONEY" – BUT HOW?

> "Absent a clear and sound legal framework, asset recovery becomes, in a best-case scenario, arduous and, in a worst-case scenario, impossible".[1248]

In this book, I have taken a comprehensive approach to the instrument of extended confiscation. The underlying idea has been that in order to set up an efficient strategy, one needs to address the different stages of the confiscation procedure as a whole and not view them separately. The international and national legislators have in recent years sought to justify more far-reaching measures with regard to the "low efficiency" of the confiscation regimes and the (anticipated) low figures of confiscated assets. Within the EU, wider powers on extended confiscation have been adopted under the argument that the harmonisation of the substantive provisions achieve more efficient national regimes and facilitate international cooperation. In order to assess the justifications for such assertions, this study has placed Directive 2014/42/EU in the broader context of the national and international legal framework and confiscation practice. The starting-point has been that any conclusions as to which legislative paths may be most efficient must be drawn on the basis of an understanding of *how the system works as a whole.*

So what is then the right path for the future? This study will be concluded with four general guidelines for the future development of extended confiscation. These are based on the findings of the comparative study and are intended to summarise this analysis.

(1) To avoid a disproportionate expansion of the powers on extended confiscation

There is reason to feel some concern about the expansion of the powers of extended confiscation. In fact, the instrument has expanded dramatically in the last few years. The trend both nationally and internationally has been towards more far-reaching legislation with a broadened range of triggering

1248 K. Stephenson, L. Gray, R. Power, J.P. Brun, G. Dunker and M. Panjer, *Barriers to Asset Recovery: An Analysis of the Key Barriers and Recommendations for Action*, The International Bank for Reconstruction and Development/The World Bank, 2011, p. 3.

offences and a lowered standard of evidence. Even if extended confiscation was originally only applied in cases of organised crime and serious drug offences, there has been a successive shift towards the inclusion of all types of criminal offences.

Even if Directive 2014/42/EU abolished the previous link to organised criminality for extended confiscation, this criminality is often used in order to justify more extensive powers. The European Commission stated, *inter alia*, the following in the context of the *Proposal for a Regulation on Mutual Recognition* in the area of freezing and confiscation orders:

> Freezing and confiscation of assets is also an important tool to combat terrorist financing. The terrorist attacks in 2015 and 2016 in the European Union and beyond underlined the urgent need to prevent and fight terrorism. The challenge to disrupt terrorist financing and its close link with organised crime networks requires determined, rapid and cohesive action to modernise relevant legislation, ensure its implementation and better cooperation between Member States and beyond.[1249]

It is of significant importance in the future to ensure that any further expansion of the instrument of extended confiscation does not take place without careful consideration. As is evident from the terminology, such confiscation measures *extend* to assets other than those which can be directly linked to the criminal conviction in question. Accordingly, if a suspect has committed certain offences for financial gain, it is presumed that there is more property of illegal origin to confiscate. It is often forgotten that this basic construction of the measure – i.e. the assumptions of previous criminality – must be legally *founded and justified*. A fundamental principle, when the instrument was originally developed, was that not all criminal offences were regarded as being of a nature to justify a criminological assumption that the defendants possess further assets of an illegal origin. As a consequence, certain prerequisites were set up in order to limit the classification of the triggering offences, for example in the form of a threshold of high custodial sentences or specific criteria regarding the offenders (i.e. criminal lifestyle or recidivist offenders).

Many limiting requirements for the instrument of extended confiscation have in the last years been weakened or even abolished. This has taken place on the international as well as the national level. The risk of a disproportionate "net-widening" is thereby significant, as the restricting criteria were originally set up in order to prevent violations of human rights. The present case-law of the ECtHR seems to give the States considerable freedom to decide which domestic measures are necessary in order to fight serious forms of criminality.

[1249] COM(2016) 819 final, Brussels 21.12.2016, p. 2.

However, it is not to be taken for granted that there are no limits to further expansion of the figure of extended confiscation. This is especially the case if every culpable or loathsome criminal offence will be classified as a triggering offence.

(2) To use the method of harmonisation of substantive rules with certain care

The EU legislator has in the past used measures harmonising national prerequisites and scope for extended confiscation in order to facilitate and streamline the practice of confiscation and improve the rates of confiscation orders. Nevertheless, in this study, various obstacles to an efficient confiscation regime have been identified and analysed. The difficulties have concerned the legal regimes, but also the institutional, practical and operational structures. It has been acknowledged that if the fundamental aim is to adopt an efficient confiscation regime (which includes enforcement of orders abroad), the harmonisation of substantive rules alone is obviously not sufficient.

In general, harmonisation of national rules may promote the smooth functioning of mutual recognition of foreign decisions. A fundamental requirement for mutual recognition is that States are confident that the foreign systems operate in compliance with the rule of law and with protection for human rights. Accordingly, the harmonisation and codification of minimum national procedural rights is an absolute necessity. However, when it comes to the substantive rules for the measure of extended confiscation, it seems extremely difficult to reach an agreement on a harmonised model that is neither too general nor too intrusive. There are at present many different models on confiscation, often classified into "conviction-based confiscation", "non-conviction-based confiscation" or "extended confiscation". However, the distinction between such systems may in practice be little, and a system which is operated in one State may not fit another. It would seem to be more useful in the future to try to find ways to be able to accept different domestic models, and to further develop the provisions which regulate the circumstances and procedural guarantees under which foreign orders may be recognised in the cross-border context.

(3) To create an efficient but balanced regime on cross-border asset recovery

It is obvious that national confiscation orders must also be enforced abroad. However, the current legal framework for international cooperation in confiscation cases is both fragmented and complicated. In fact, it is so user-unfriendly that it in many cases even hinders efficient asset recovery. This is unfortunately especially the case within the EU. This area is thus in desperate need of improvement. The adoption of a single consolidated instrument covering mutual recognition of freezing and confiscation orders would thus be a significant step forward. The *Proposal for a Regulation on Mutual Recognition* is in this respect to be welcomed, and could lead to improvements in many areas.

Nevertheless, it is not an easy task for the EU legislator to improve the confiscation regimes nationally and internationally, and at the same time find the right balance between efficiency and the human rights *acquis*. The initiative to widen the obligation to recognise and execute foreign orders is an improvement *per se*, because it encourages the Member States to cooperate to a larger extent in spite of the existence of different domestic models for confiscation. As a whole, the draft proposal for a regulation, though, lacks a proper assessment of the consequences of an increased scope for cooperation. Many difficulties may arise in practice, which do not seem to have been sufficiently considered. Above all, the lack of a human rights clause must be addressed and corrected in the further negotiations.

(4) To focus on institutional and administrative structures

Another important issue for the future concerns the operation of asset recovery in practice. How is it possible "to go for the money" if there are no specialised authorities with knowledge about *how* to search for assets or if there aren't any expeditious possibilities to gain information or quickly secure property? Surprisingly few efforts have been made so far to deal with such problems. Against this background, I will conclude by pointing to some improvements which *at least* must be taken in this area in the future:

(a) As shown in the chapters on domestic legislation on extended confiscation, the national systems contain different scope of legislation, various standards and burdens of proof, as well as different views on which persons to be targeted by extended confiscation. However, a common feature of all the States studied is that there is a concern that the systems do not function efficiently. This is often not due to the construction of the legislative framework *per se*, but follows from the application of the provisions in practice. Important factors are here the attitude of the law enforcement officers involved, the organisation of the agencies and the investigatory routines. Very important for the future are therefore *administrative reforms and measures* within the States in order to provide for education, the support of financial expertise and more efficient routines for handling cases especially in the cross-border perspective.

(b) One measure that would probably have considerable effect both nationally and internationally is the establishment of *central bank registers* in all Member States. The identification of bank accounts is often the key chain in the confiscation process, and at present the law enforcement officers encounter significant difficulties in this respect.

(c) A further weak feature in the present system concerns the *seizure or freezing of assets*. Obviously, the legal framework that provides for such measures must be used in practice in the early stage of the procedure. It must also be developed in terms of speed and efficiency.

These four guidelines which have been presented in this last chapter are important for the future development of the regime of extended confiscation. The method "*to go for the money*" has for a long time been very popular among international and national legislators. What is still lacking today is a coherent policy to do that.

BIBLIOGRAPHY

BOOKS AND REPORTS

Almkvist, G., *Förverkande av egendom*, Iustus förlag, 2014.

Beck'scher Online-Kommentar StGB/Heuchemer, 29. Auflage, 2015, available at www.beck-online.de.

Brun, J.P., Gray, L., Scott, C. and Stephenson, K.M., *Asset Recovery Handbook: A Guide for Practitioners*, STAR Initiative, The World Bank, 2011.

Cameron, I., Thunberg Schunke, M., Påle-Bartes, K., Wong, C. and Asp, P., *International Criminal Law from a Swedish Perspective*, Intersentia, 2011.

Eissa, A. and Barber, R., *Confiscation Law Handbook*, Bloomsbury Professional, 2011.

Fichera, M., *The Implementation of the European Arrest Warrant in the European Union: Law, Policy and Practice*, Intersentia, 2011.

Fischer, T., *Strafgesetzbuch mit Nebengesetze*, 60 Auflage, C.H. Beck, 2013.

Greenberg, T.S., Samuel, L., Grant, W. and Gray, L., *Stolen Asset Recovery: A Good Practices Guide for Non-Conviction Based Asset Forfeiture*, STAR Initiative, The World Bank, 2009.

Hunsicker, E., *Die Präventive Gewinnabschöpfung (PräGe) im Überblick*, GRIN Verlag, 2014.

Hunsicker, E., *Präventive Gewinnabschöpfung (PräGe). Entscheidungssammlung in Volltexten und mit Leitsätzen*, 3. überarbeitete & erweiterte Auflage, GRIN Verlag, 2014.

Jescheck, H.-H. and Weigend, T., *Lehrbuch des Strafrechts*, Allgemeiner Teil, 5. Auflage, Duncker & Humblot, 1996.

Kindhäuser, Neumann & Paeffgen, *Kommentar zum StGB*, 4. Auflage, 2013, available at www.beck-online.de.

King, C. and Walker, C. (eds.), *Dirty Assets: Emerging Issues in the Regulation of Criminal and Terrorist Assets*, Ashgate, 2014.

Klip, A., *European Criminal Law: An Integrative Approach*, 2nd Edition, Intersentia, 2012.

Kommers, D. and Russell, A., *The Constitutional Jurisprudence of the Federal Republic of Germany*, Duke University Press, 2012.

Matningsdal, M., *Straffeloven, Lagkommentar till §34a*, Oslo, 2015.

McClean, D., *International Cooperation in Civil and Criminal Matters*, Oxford University Press, 2002.

Millington, Sutherland and Williams, *On the Proceeds of Crime*, 4th Edition, Oxford University Press, 2013.

Mitchell, Taylor & Talbot, *On Confiscation and the Proceeds of Crime*, 3rd Edition, Sweet & Maxwell, 2016.

Münchener Kommentar zum StGB, 2. Auflage, 2012, available at www.beck-online.de.

Ruggeri, S. (ed.), *Transnational Inquiries and the Protection of Fundamental Rights in Criminal Proceedings*, Springer, 2013.

Rui, P. and Sieber, U. (eds.), *Non-Conviction-Based Confiscation in Europe: Possibilities and Limitations on Rules Enabling Confiscation without a Criminal Conviction*, Berlin, 2015.

Savona, E. and Riccardi, M. (eds.), *From Illegal Markets to Legitimate Businesses: the Portfolio of Organised Crime in Europe*, Final Report of Project OCP (Organised Crime Portfolio), Trento, 2015.

Schönke, Schröder and Eser, *Strafgesetzbuch, Kommentar*, 29. Auflage, C.H. Beck, 2014, available at www.beck-online.de.

Stephenson, K., Gray, L., Power, R., Brun, J.P., Dunker, G. and Panjer, M., *Barriers to Asset Recovery: An Analysis of the Key Barriers and Recommendations for Action*, The International Bank for Reconstruction and Development/The World Bank, 2011.

Stessens, G., *Money Laundering: A New International Law Enforcement Model*, Cambridge University Press, 2000.

Suominen, A., *The Principle of Mutual Recognition in Cooperation in Criminal Matters: A Study of the Principle in Four Framework Decisions and in the Implementing Legislation in the Nordic Member States*, Intersentia, 2011.

Thunberg Schunke, M., *Internationell rättslig hjälp i brottmål inom EU: Effektivitet v. rättssäkerhet*, Iustus förlag, 2004.

Thunberg Schunke, M., *Whose Responsibility? A Study of Transnational Defence Rights and Mutual Recognition of Judicial Decisions within the EU*, Intersentia, 2013.

Vettori, B., *Tough on Criminal Wealth: Exploring the Practice of Proceeds from Crime Confiscation in the EU*, Springer, 2006.

Wetter, A., *Making EU Legislation in the Area of Criminal Law: A Swedish Perspective*, Uppsala, 2013.

ARTICLES

Alagna, F., "Non-conviction Based Confiscation: Why the EU Directive is a Missed Opportunity", 21 *European Journal on Criminal Policy and Research* (2015), pp. 447–64.

Alexander, R., "Do the UK's Provisions for Confiscation Orders breach the European Convention on Human Rights?", 3 *Journal of Money Laundering Control* (2000), pp. 297–303.

Alldridge, P., "The Limits of Confiscation", [2011] *Crim. L.R.*, pp. 827–43.

Alldridge, P., "Proceeds of Crime Law since 2003 – two key areas", [2014] *Crim. L.R.*, pp. 171–88.

Bacarese, A., "Advancing International Understanding and Cooperation in Combating Fraud and Corruption: Recovering Stolen Assets – A New Issue?", 10 *ERA Forum* (2009), pp. 421–34.

Bachmaier Winter, L., "European Investigation Order for Obtaining Evidence in the Criminal Proceedings, Study of the Proposal for a European Directive", 9 *ZIS* (2010), pp. 580–89.

Bachmaier, L., "Transnational Evidence, Towards the Transposition of Directive 2014/41 regarding the European Investigation Order in Criminal Matters", 2 *eucrim* (2015), pp. 47–60.

Baker, E., "The United Kingdom and its Protocol 36 Opt-Out: Is Police and Judicial Cooperation in Criminal Matters within the EU Losing Momentum?", 21 *European Journal of Crime, Criminal Law and Criminal Justice* (2013), pp. 237–45.

Ballaschk, J., "In the Unseen Realm: Transnational Intelligence Sharing in the European Union – Challenges to Fundamental Rights and Democratic Legitimacy", 51 *Stanford Journal of International Law* (2015), pp. 19–52.

Balsamo, A., "The Delocalisation of Mafia Organisations and the Construction of a European Law against Organised Crime", 17 *Global Crime* (2016), pp. 99–121.

Bell, R.E., "An Evolving Series of Proceeds of Crime Models", 8 *Journal of Financial Crime* (2000), pp. 21–31.

Benseler, J., "Forfeiture Legislation in Germany: Legal Basis and Prosecution Practice", 5 *European Journal of Crime, Criminal Law and Criminal Justice* (1997), pp. 203–09.

Bittmann, F., "Zum Regierungsentwurf der Reform der Vermögensabschöpfung", 2 *KriPoZ* (2016), pp. 120–32.

Borgers, M.J., "Confiscation of the Proceeds of Crime: The European Union Framework", in King, C. and Walker, C. (eds.), *Dirty Assets, Emerging Issues in the Regulation of Criminal and Terrorist Assets*, Ashgate, 2014, pp. 27–47.

Borgers, M.J. and Moors, J.A., "Targeting the Proceeds of Crime: Bottlenecks in International Cooperation", 1 *European Journal of Crime, Criminal Law and Criminal Justice* (2007), pp. 1–22.

Boucht, J., "Utvidgat förverkande enligt strl. §34a – ny modell för ökad funktionalitet eller obefogat avsteg från hävdvunna rättssäkerhetskrav?", 4 *Tidsskrift for Strafferett* (2012), pp. 382–423.

Boucht, J., "Extended Confiscation and the Proposed Directive on Freezing and Confiscation of Criminal Proceeds in the EU: On Striking a Balance between Efficiency, Fairness and Legal Certainty", 21 *European Journal of Crime, Criminal Law and Criminal Justice* (2013), pp. 127–62.

Brodowski, D., "Strafrechtsrelevante Entwicklungen in der Europäischen Union – ein Überblick", 11 *ZIS* (2012), pp. 558–70.

Brodowski, D., "Strafrechtsrelevante Entwicklungen in der Europäischen Union – ein Überblick", 1 *ZIS* (2015), pp. 79–101.

Bullock, K., "Criminal Benefit, the Confiscation Order and the Post-conviction Confiscation Regime", 62 *Crime, Law and Social Change* (2014), pp. 45–64.

Cassella, S., "The Case for Civil Forfeiture, Why in Rem Proceedings are an Essential Tool for Recovering the Proceeds of Crime", 11 *Journal of Money Laundering Control* (2008), pp. 8–14.

Cribb, N., "Tracing and Confiscating the Proceeds of Crime", 11 *Journal of Financial Crime* (2003), pp. 168–84.

de Bondt, W., "Evidence Based EU Criminal Policy Making: In Search of Matching Data", 20 *European Journal on Criminal Policy and Research* (2014), pp. 23–49.

de Busser, "The Lisbon after-burn effect", 16 *ERA Forum* (2015), pp. 1–13.

Dickson, D., "Towards More Effective Asset Recovery in Member States – the UK example", 10 *ERA Forum* (2009), pp. 435–51.

Dyrnes, A.-M., "Inndragning – Hva må gøras?", Oslo, 2004.

Egan, M., "Non-conviction Based Sanctions: The Court of Justice v. the European Court of Human Rights, Who Decides?", 19 *European Journal of Crime, Criminal Law and Criminal Justice* (2011), pp. 167–82.

Elholm, T., "Does EU Criminal Cooperation Necessarily Mean Increased Repression?", 17 *European Journal of Crime, Criminal Law and Criminal Justice*, (2009), pp. 191–226.

Eser, A., "Neue Wege der Gewinnabschöpfung im Kampf gegen die organisierte Kriminalität? Kritische Bemerkungen zu aktuellen Reformbemühungen", in Küper, W. (ed.), *Beiträge zur Rechtswissenschaft: Festschrift für Walter Stree und Johannes Wessels zum 70. Geburtstag*, C.F. Müller, 1993, pp. 833–53.

Fazekas, M. and Nanopoulos, E., "The Effectiveness of EU Law: Insights from the EU Legal Framework on Asset Confiscation", 24 *European Journal of Crime, Criminal Law and Criminal Justice* (2016), pp. 39–64.

Faraldo Cabana, P., "Improving the Recovery of Assets Resulting from Organised Crime", 22 *European Journal of Crime, Criminal Law and Criminal Justice* (2014), pp. 13–32.

Fisher, J., "Time Bomb of Confiscating Criminals' Assets", *The Times*, 23 August 2012.

Fortson, R., "Case Comment, *R v Ahmad and Fields*: Proceeds of Crime – Confiscation Orders – Whether Value of the Benefit Obtained Jointly Is to be Shared between Parties to the Joint Criminal Venture", 10 *Criminal Law Review* (2014), pp. 756–60.

Gardner, D., "Closing Loopholes to Take the Cash Out of Crime – Practical Changes in Legislation to Improve Confiscation Order Enforcement", [2009] *Criminal Law Review*, pp. 90–99.

Gascón Inchausti, F., "Mutual Recognition and Transnational Confiscation Orders", in Ruggeri, S. (ed.), *Transnational Inquiries and the Protection of Fundamental Rights in Criminal Proceedings*, Springer, 2013, pp. 253–67.

Gibb, F., "Bonuses for Lawyers who Seize Criminal Assets 'risk Undermining Justice'", *The Times*, 31 October 2009.

Giles, A., "The Assessment of Benefit under Part 2 of the Proceeds of Crime Act 2002: a Sledgehammer to Crack a Nut?", 1 *Plymouth Law and Criminal Justice Review* (2013), pp. 85–109.

Harvey, J., "Asset Recovery: Substantive or Symbolic?", in King, C. and Walker, C. (eds.), *Dirty Assets: Emerging Issues in the Regulation of Criminal and Terrorist Assets*, Ashgate, 2014, pp. 183–203.

Heard, C. and Mansell, D., "The European Investigation Order: Changing the Face of Evidence-gathering in EU Cross Border Cases", 2 *New Journal of European Criminal Law* (2011), pp. 353–67.

Hecker, B., "Mutual Recognition and Transfer of Evidence, The European Evidence Order", in Ruggeri, S. (ed.), *Transnational Inquiries and the Protection of Fundamental Rights in Criminal Proceedings*, Springer, 2013, pp. 269–78.

Herzog, F., "Gewinnabschöpfung unter der Flagge der positiven Generalprävention", 12 *Juristische Rundschau* (2004), pp. 494–98.

Hunsicker, E., "Präventive Gewinnabschöpfung (PräGe), Entgegnung auf Philipp Thiée in StV 2/2009, S. 102 ff.", 4 *Strafverteidiger* (2010), pp. 212–15.

Jacobsen, J. and Hallgren Sandvik, V., "An outline of the New Norwegian Criminal Code", 3 *Bergen Journal of Criminal Law and Criminal Justice* (2015), pp. 162–83.

Julius, K.P., "Einziehung, Verfall und Art. 14 GG", 109 *ZStW* (1997), pp. 58–102.

Katholnigg, O., "Die Neuregelungen beim Verfall", 9 *Juristische Rundschau* (1994), pp. 353–56.

Kaye, N., "Freezing and Confiscation of Criminal Proceeds", 77 *International Review of Penal Law* (2006), pp. 323–31.

Kennedy, A., "Justifying the Civil Recovery of Criminal Proceeds", 12 *Journal of Financial Crime* (2004), pp. 8–23.

Kennedy, A. (2007), "An Evaluation of the Recovery of Criminal Proceeds in the United Kingdom", 10 *Journal of Money Laundering Control* (2007), pp. 33–46.

Kennedy, A. (2007), "Winning the Information Wars, Collecting, Sharing and Analysing Information in Asset Recovery Investigations", 14 *Journal of Financial Crime* (2007), pp. 372–404.

Kilchling, M., "Comparative Perspectives on Forfeiture Legislation in Europe and the United States", 5 *European Journal of Crime, Criminal Law and Criminal Justice* (1997), pp. 314–33.

Kilchling, M., "Tracing, Seizing and Confiscating Proceeds from Corruption (and other Illegal Conduct) within or outside the Criminal Justice System", 9 *European Journal of Crime, Criminal Law and Criminal Justice* (2001), pp. 264–80.

Köhler, M., and Beck, W., "Gerechte Geldstrafe statt konfiskatorischer Vermögenssanktionen", 17 *Juristen Zeitung* (1991), pp. 797–804.

Lachmayer, K., "Rethinking Privacy Beyond Borders, Developing Transnational Rights on Data Privacy", 20 *Tilburg Law Review* (2015), pp. 78–102.

Lawrence, I., "Draconian and Manifestly Unjust: How the Confiscation Regime has Developed", 76 *Amicus Curiae* (2008), pp. 22–24.

Lea, J., "Hitting Criminals Where It Hurts: Organised Crime and the Erosion of Due Process", 35 *Cambrian Law Review* (2004), pp. 81–95.

Levi, M. and Osofsky, L., "Investigating, Seizing and Confiscating the Proceeds of Crime", *Crime Detection & Prevention Series Paper 61*, Police Research Group, 1995.

Levi, M., "Taking the Profit Out of Crime: The UK Experience", 5 *European Journal of Crime, Criminal Law and Criminal Justice* (1997), pp. 228–39.

Mahmutaj, K., "Cash forfeiture following Acquittal: 'An Affront to Public Perception' or a Breach of a Fundamental Human Right?", 11 *Criminal Law Review* (2009), pp. 783–93.

Mangiaracina, A., "A New and Controversial Scenario in the Gathering of Evidence at the European Level: The Proposal for a Directive on the European Investigation Order", 10 *Utrecht Law Review* (2014), pp. 113–33.

Maugeri, A.M., "The Criminal Sanctions against the Illicit Proceeds of Criminal Organisations", 3 *New Journal of European Criminal Law* (2012), pp. 257–97.

Met-Domestici, A., "The Fight against Money Laundering in the EU: The Framework set by the Fourth Directive and its Proposed Enhancements", 4 *eucrim* (2016), pp. 170–78.

Meyer, F. (2015), "Zivilgesellschaftliche Nutzung konfiszierter Vermögenswerte – ein zukunftsträchtiges Paradigma?", 8 *ZRP* (2015), pp. 244–47.

Meyer, F. (2015), ""Reformiert die Rückgewinnungshilfe! – Denkanstöße für eine Generalüberholung der Vermögensabschöpfung", 2 *ZStW* (2015), pp. 241–83.

Montaldo, S., "Directive 2014/42/EU and Social Reuse of Confiscated Assets in the EU: Advancing a Culture of Legality", 6 *New Journal of European Criminal Law* (2015), pp. 195–212.

Monteith, C., and Dornbierer, A., "Tracking and Tracing Stolen Assets in Foreign Jurisdictions", 2 *eucrim* (2013), pp. 51–54.

Naylor, R.T., "Wash-out: A Critique of Follow-the Money Methods in Crime Control Policy", 32 *Crime, Law and Social Change* (1999), pp. 1–57.

Nestler, N. "Zur Reichweite von §73d StGB: Der erweiterte Verfall vor neuen Legitimationsdefiziten?", *HRRS Onlinezeitschrift für Höchstrichterliche Rechtsprechung zum Strafrecht*, http://www.hrr-strafrecht.de, Ausgabe 12/2011, pp. 519–27.

Nicol, A., "Confiscation of the Profits of Crime", 52 *Journal of Criminal Law* (1988), pp. 75–83.

Nikolov, N., "General Characteristics of Civil Forfeiture", 14 *Journal of Money Laundering Control* (2011), pp. 16–31.

Paoli, L., "Seizure and Confiscation Measures in Italy: An Evaluation of Their Effectiveness and Constitutionality", 5 *European Journal of Crime, Criminal Law and Criminal Justice* (1997), pp. 256–72.

Paoli, L., "How to Tackle (Organized) Crime in Europe? The EU Policy Cycle on Serious and Organized Crime and the New Emphasis on Harm", 22 *European Journal of Crime, Criminal Law and Criminal Justice* (2014), pp. 1–12.

Perron, W., "Vermögensstrafe und Erweiterter Verfall – im Spannungsfeld zwischen öffentlichen Strafverfolgungsintressen und privaten Eigentumsrechten", 19 *Juristen Zeitung* (1993), pp. 918–25.

Pieth, M., "Gewinnabschöpfung bei Betäubungsmitteldelikten: Zu den Hintergründen und Risiken der neuen Gesetzgebung", 12 *Strafverteidiger* (1990), pp. 558–62.

Piva, D., "Anti-Mafia Forfeiture in the Italian System", in King, C. and Walker, C. (eds.), *Dirty Assets: Emerging Issues in the Regulation of Criminal and Terrorist Assets*, Ashgate, 2014, pp. 71–91.

Polidori, R., "General Overview and Critical Analysis of Italian Preventive Measures and ECtHR Case Law", 4 *Journal of Law and Criminal Justice* (2016), pp. 97–106.

Rahmatian, A., "A Comparison of German Moveable Property Law and English Personal Property Law", 3 *Journal of Comparative Law* (2010), pp. 197–248.

Raphael, M., "Tracing and Confiscating Illicit Proceeds: the Perspective of the Defence", 11 *ERA Forum* (2011), pp. 545–70.

Rieß, P., "Neue Gesetze zur Bekämpfung der Organisierten Kriminalität", 11 *Neue Justiz* (1992), pp. 491–97.

Rui, J.P., "The Civil Asset Forfeiture Approach to Organised Crime", 4 *eucrim* (2011), pp. 153–61.

Rui, J.P, "Non-conviction based Confiscation in the European Union – an Assessment of Art. 5 of the Proposal for a Directive of the European Parliament and of the Council on the Freezing and Confiscation of Proceeds of Crime in the European Union", 13 *ERA Forum* (2012), pp. 349–60.

Ruggeri, S., "Horizontal Cooperation, Obtaining Evidence Overseas and the Respect for Fundamental Rights in the EU. From the European Commission's Proposals to the Proposal for a Directive on a European Investigation Order: Towards a Single Tool of Evidence Gathering in the EU?", in Ruggeri, S. (ed.), *Transnational Inquiries and the Protection of Fundamental Rights in Criminal Proceedings*, Springer 2013, pp. 279–310.

Ryder, N., "To Confiscate or not to Confiscate? A Comparative Analysis of the Confiscation of the Proceeds of Crime Legislation in the United States and the United Kingdom", 8 *Journal of Business Law* (2013), pp. 767–98.

Simonato, M., "Directive 2014/42/EU and Non-Conviction based Confiscation: a Step Forward on Asset Recovery?", 6 *New Journal of European Criminal Law* (2015), pp. 213–28.

Snider, W.J., "International Cooperation in the Forfeiture of Illegal Drug Proceeds", 6 *Criminal Law Forum* (1995), pp. 377–89.

Sproat, P., "An Evaluation of the UK's Anti-Money Laundering and Asset Recovery Regime", 47 *Crime, Law and Social Change* (2007), pp. 169–84.

Sproat, P., "The New Policing of Assets and the new Assets of Policing, a Tentative Financial Cost-Benefit Analysis of the UK's Anti-Money Laundering and Asset Recovery Regime", 3 *Journal of Money Laundering Control* (2007), pp. 277–99.

Sproat, P., "To what Extent is the UK's Anti-Money Laundering and Asset Recovery Regime used against Organised Crime?", 12 *Journal of Money Laundering Control* (2009), pp. 134–50.

Sproat, P., "A Critique of the Official Discourse on Drug and Sex Trafficking by Organised Crime Using Data on Asset Recovery", 2 *Journal of Financial Crime* (2012), pp. 149–62.

Stessens, G., "The Joint Initiative of France, Sweden and Belgium for the Adoption of a Council Framework Decision on the Execution in the European Union of Orders Freezing Assets or Evidence", in de Kerchove, G., and Weyembergh, A. (eds.), *La reconnaissance mutuelle des décisions judiciaires pénales dans l'Union européenne*, Editions de l'Université de Bruxelles, 2001, pp. 91–100.

Summers, J., "We're innocent until proved guilty … Or until our assets are seized", *The Times*, 25 November 2003.

Theile, H., "Grundprobleme der Strafrechtlichen Verfallsvorschriften nach den §§73 ff. StGB", 4–5 *ZJS* (2011), pp. 333–41.

Thiée, P., "'Präventive Gewinnabschöpfung: Wenn Polizeibeamte Winkeladvokaten spielen", 2 *Strafverteidiger* (2009), pp. 102–04.

Thiée, P., "Polizeirechtliche Sicherstellung nach Freigabe gem. §98 StPO – Erwiderung auf die Erwiderung", 4 *Strafverteidiger* (2010), pp. 215–18.

Ulph, J., "Confiscation Orders, Human Rights and Penal Measures", 126 *Law Quarterly Review* (2010), pp. 251–78.

Ulväng, M., "Utvidgat förverkande och skattebrott", 4:10 *Ny Juridik* (2010), pp. 85–97.

van Dijck, M., "Dutch Anti-Money Laundering Policy in International Perspective", 13 *Tilburg Foreign Law Review* (2006), pp. 6–30.

Vogel, J. and Spencer, J.R., "Proportionality and the European Arrest Warrant", [2010] *Criminal Law Review*, pp. 474–82.

Vogel, B. and Maillart, J.B, "Recent Developments in EU Anti-Money Laundering, Some Critical Observations", 4 *eucrim* (2016), pp. 179–83.

Waechter, K., "Präventive Gewinnabschöpfung", 11 *NordÖR Zeitschrift für Öffentliches Recht in Norddeutschland* (2008), pp. 473–79.

Walter, T., "Die Beweislast im Strafprozeß", 7 *JuristenZeitung* (2006), pp. 340–49.

Weßlau, E., "Neue Methoden der Gewinnabschöpfung? – Vermögensstrafe – Beweislastumkehr", 5 *Strafverteidiger* (1991), pp. 226–35.

EU SOURCES

LEGISLATION AND TREATIES

Council Act of 26 July 1995 drawing up the Convention on the Protection of the European Communities' Financial Interests, *OJ* C 316, 27.11.1995, pp. 48–57.

Council Act of 27 September 1996 drawing up a Protocol to the Convention on the Protection of the European Communities' Financial Interests, *OJ* C 313, 23.10.1996, pp. 1–10.

Council Act of 19 June 1997 drawing up the Second Protocol of the Convention on the Protection of the European Communities' Financial Interests, *OJ* C 221, 19.7.1997, pp. 11–22.

Joint Action of 3 December 1998 on Money Laundering, the Identification, Tracing, Freezing, Seizing and Confiscation of Instrumentalities and the Proceeds from Crime, *OJ* L 333, 9.12.1998, pp. 1–3.

Joint Action 98/733/JHA of 21 December 1998 on Making it a Criminal Offence to Participate in a Criminal Organisation in the Member States of the European Union, *OJ* L 351, 29.12.1998, p. 1.

Council Framework Decision 2000/383/JHA of 29 May 2000 on Increasing Protection by Criminal Penalties and other Sanctions against Counterfeiting in Connection with the Introduction of the Euro, *OJ* L 140, 14.6.2000, p. 1.

Council Act of 29 May 2000 establishing in accordance with Article 34 of the Treaty on European Union the Convention on Mutual Assistance in Criminal Matters between the Member States of the European Union, *OJ* C 197, 12.7.2000, pp. 1–23.

Council Decision 2000/642/JHA of 17 October 2000 concerning Arrangements for Cooperation between Financial Intelligence Units of the Member States in Exchanging Information, *OJ* L 271, 24.10.2000, pp. 4–6.

Council Framework Decision 2001/500/JHA of 26 June 2001 on Money Laundering, the Identification, Tracing, Freezing, Seizing and Confiscation of Instrumentalities and the Proceeds of Crime, *OJ* L 182, 5.7.2001, pp. 1–2.

Council Act of 16 October 2001 establishing in accordance with Article 34 of the Treaty on European Union the Protocol to the Convention on Mutual Assistance in Criminal Matters between the Member States of the European Union, *OJ* C 326, 21.11.2001, pp. 1–8.

Council Framework Decision 2002/475/JHA of 13 June 2002 on Combating Terrorism, *OJ* L 164, 22.6.2002, p. 3.

Council Framework Decision of 13 June 2002 on the European Arrest Warrant and the Surrender Procedures between Member States, *OJ* L 190, 18.7.2002, pp. 1–18.

Council Framework Decision 2002/629/JHA of 19 July 2002 on Combating Trafficking in Human Beings, *OJ* L 203, 1.8.2002, p. 1.

Council Framework Decision 2002/946/JHA of 28 November 2002 on the Strengthening of the Penal Framework to Prevent the Facilitation of Unauthorised Entry, Transit and Residence, *OJ* L 328, 5.12.2002, p. 1.

Council Framework Decision 2003/577/JHA on the Execution in the European Union of Orders Freezing Property or Evidence, *OJ* L 196, 2.8.2003, pp. 45–55.

Council Framework Decision 2004/68/JHA of 22 December 2003 on Combating the Sexual Exploitation of Children and Child Pornography, *OJ* L 13, 20.1.2004, p. 44.

Council Framework Decision 2004/757/JHA of 25 October 2004 Laying down Minimum Provisions on the Constituent Elements of Criminal Acts and Penalties in the Field of Illicit Drug Trafficking, *OJ* L 335, 11.11.2004, p. 8.

Council Framework Decision 2005/212/JHA of 24 February 2005 on Confiscation of Crime-Related Proceeds, Instrumentalities and Property, *OJ* L 68, 15.3.2005, pp. 49–51.

Directive 2005/60/EC of the European Parliament and of the Council of 26 October 2005 on the Prevention of the Use of the Financial System for the Purpose of Money Laundering and Terrorist Financing, *OJ* L 309, 25.11.2005, pp. 15–36.

Council Framework Decision 2006/783/JHA on the Application of the Principle of Mutual Recognition to Confiscation Orders, *OJ* L 328, 24.11.2006, pp. 59–78 and an Amending Act thereto (Framework Decision 2009/299/JHA), *OJ* L 81, 27.3.2009, pp. 24–36.

Council Framework Decision 2006/960/JHA of 18 December 2006 on Simplifying the Exchange of Information and Intelligence between Law Enforcement Authorities of the Member States of the European Union, *OJ* L 386, 29.12.2006, pp. 89–100.

Council Framework Decision 2007/845/JHA on the Exchange of Information and Cooperation between Asset Recovery Offices, *OJ* L 332, 18.12.2007, pp. 103–05.

Council Framework Decision 2008/978/JHA on the European Evidence Warrant, *OJ* L 350, 30.12.2008, p. 72–92.

Directive on the Right to Information in Criminal Proceedings, *OJ* L 142, 1.6.2012, pp. 1–10.

Directive 2012/29/EU of the European Parliament and of the Council of 25 October 2012 establishing Minimum Standards on the Rights, Support and Protection of Victims of Crime, and replacing Council Framework Decision 2001/220/JHA, *OJ* L 315, 14.11.2012, pp. 57–73.

Directive 2013/48/EU of the European Parliament and of the Council of 22 October 2013 on the Right of Access to a Lawyer in Criminal Proceedings and in European Arrest Warrant Proceedings, and on the Right to have a Third Party informed upon Deprivation of Liberty and to Communicate with Third Persons and with Consular Authorities while Deprived of Liberty, *OJ* L 294, 6.11.2013, pp. 1–12.

Directive 2014/42/EU of the European Parliament and of the Council on the Freezing and Confiscation of Instrumentalities and Proceeds of Crime in the European Union, *OJ* L 127, 29.4.2014, pp. 39–50 and Corrigendum to the Directive published on 29 April 2014.

Directive 2014/41/EU of the European Parliament and of the Council of 3 April 2014 regarding the European Investigation Order in Criminal Matters, *OJ* L 130, 1.5.2014, pp. 1–36.

Directive (EU) 2015/849 of the European Parliament and of the Council of 20 May 2015 on the Prevention of the Use of the Financial System for the Purposes of Money Laundering or Terrorist Financing, amending Regulation (EU) No. 648/2012 of the European Parliament and of the Council, and repealing Directive 2005/60/EC of the European Parliament and of the Council and Commission Directive 2006/70/EC, *OJ* L 141, 5.6.2015, pp. 73–117.

COUNCIL DOCUMENTS

EU Action Plan to combat organized crime, *OJ* C 251, 15.8.1997, pp. 1–16.

Vienna Action Plan of December 1998, *OJ* C 19, 23.1.1999, pp. 1–15.

Prevention and Control of Organised Crime: a European Union Strategy for the Beginning of the new Millenium, *OJ* C 124, 3.5.2000, pp. 1–33.

European Council, The Hague Programme, Presidency Conclusions 4–5 November 2004.

Initiative of the Republic of Austria, Belgium and Finland with a view to the Adoption of a Council Decision concerning Arrangements for Cooperation between Asset Recovery Offices of the Member States, 15628/05 CRIMORG 156, Brussels 14.12.2005.

Draft Council Decision concerning Arrangements for Cooperation between Asset Recovery Offices of the Member States, Council of the European Union, 5644/06, CRIMORG 19, Brussels 26.1.2006.

Roadmap on Procedural Rights, *OJ* C 295, 4.12.2009, pp. 1–3.

An Open and Secure Europe Serving and Protecting the Citizens, Council Document 17024/09, 10–11 December 2009.

Initiative for a Directive of the European Parliament and of the Council regarding the European Investigation Order in Criminal Matters from the Kingdom of Belgium, the Republic of Bulgaria, the Republic of Estonia, the Kingdom of Spain, the Grand Duthy of Luxembourg, the Republic of Austria, the Republic of Slovenia and the Kingdom of Sweden, 9145/10, COPEN 115, Brussels 29.4.2010.

Explanatory Memorandum to the Initiative for a Directive of the European Parliament and of the Council regarding the European Investigation Order in Criminal Matters from the Kingdom of Belgium, the Republic of Bulgaria, the Republic of Estonia, the Kingdom of Spain, the Grand Duthy of Luxembourg, the Republic of Austria, the Republic of Slovenia and the Kingdom of Sweden, 9288/10 ADD 1, COPEN 117, Brussels 3.6.2010.

Justice and Home Affairs, Council Conclusions on Confiscation and Asset Recovery adopted in June 2010, Council Document 7769/10.

Council of the European Union, Report on the United Kingdom, Brussels 7.9.2010, 9636/2/10, REV 2, CRIMORG 94.

Guidelines to the Implementation of Council Framework Decision 2006/960/JHA of 18 December 2006 on Simplifying the Exchange of Information and Intelligence between Law Enforcement Authorities of the Member States of the European Union, Council of the European Union, 9512/1/10, REV 1, Brussels 17.12.2010.

Eurojust's Opinion on the Proposal for a Directive on the European Investigative Order, published in the Council of the European Union, Document 6814/11, COPEN 26, Brussels 4.3.2011.

Evaluation Report on the Fifth Round of Mutual Evaluations, Financial Crime and Financial Investigations, Report on Germany, 16269/2/11, REV 2, Brussels 19.1.2012.

Proposal for a Directive of the European Parliament and the Council on the Freezing and Confiscation of Proceeds of Crime in the European Union, Compilation of replies to questionnaire, 12219/2/12, REV 2, Brussels 20.7.2012.

Council of European Union, Final Report on the Fifth Round of Mutual Evaluations, Financial Crime and Financial Investigations, 12657/2/12, Brussels 3.10.2012.

Proposal for a Directive of the European Parliament and the Council on the Freezing and Confiscation of Proceeds of Crime in the European Union, State of Play and Orientation Debate, 14826/12, Brussels 16.10.2012.

Council of the European Union, Evaluation Report on the Fifth Round of Mutual Evaluations, Financial Crime and Financial Investigations, Report on Denmark, 12659/2/12, REV 2, Brussels 14.11.2012.

Council Framework Decision 2006/960/JHA – Assessment of Compliance according to Article 11 (2), Council Document 14755/1/12 REV 1, CRIMORG 114, 15.11.2012.

Mutual Evaluation Report on Sweden, Financial Crime and Financial Investigations, Council Document 8639/1/12, Brussels 20.11.2012.

Proposal for a Directive of the European Parliament and of the Council on the Freezing and Confiscation of Proceeds of Crime in the European Union, General Approach, Council Document 17117/12, 3.12.2012.

Council of the European Union, Manual of Best Practices in the Fight against Financial Crime: A Collection of Good Examples of Well-Developed Systems in the Member States to Fight Financial Crime, 9741/13, CRIMORG 75, Brussels 4.6.2013.

Joint Statements by the European Parliament and the Council issued upon the adoption of Directive 2014/42/EU, Council of the European Union, 7329/1/14, COPEN 83, Brussels 31.3.2014.

Council of the European Union, Conclusions from the Meeting of the Consultative Forum of Prosecutors General and Directors of Public Prosecutions of the Member States of the European Union Eurojust, The Hague, 12.12.2014, 8552/15, COPEN 108, Brussels 5.5.2015.

Council of the European Union, Implementation of the Framework Decision 2006/783/JHA of the Council of the European Union of 6 October 2006 on the Application of the Principle of Mutual Recognition to Confiscation Orders, Information provided to the General Secretariat, 7574/1/15, REV 1, Brussels 3.6.2015.

Council of the European Union, Report on Eurojust's Experience in the Field of Asset Recovery, including Freezing and Confiscation, 10179/15, COPEN 162, Brussels 22.6.2015.

COMMISSION DOCUMENTS AND STAFF WORKING PAPERS

Communication from the Commission to the Council and the European Parliament, Mutual Recognition of Final Decisions in Criminal Matters, COM(2000) 495 final, Brussels 26.7.2000.

Report from the Commission based on Article 6 of the Council Framework Decision of 26 June 2001 on Money Laundering, the Identification, Tracing, Freezing, Seizing and Confiscation of Instrumentalities and the Proceeds of Crime, COM(2004) 230 final.

Communication from the Commission to the Council and the European Parliament, Developing a Strategic Concept on Tackling Organised Crime, 2.6.2005, COM(2005) 232 final.

Report from the Commission pursuant to Article 6 of the Council Framework Decision of 24 February 2005 on Confiscation of Crime-related Proceeds, Instrumentalities and Property (2005/212/JHA), COM(2007) 805.

Communication from the Commission to the European Parliament and the Council, Proceeds of Organised Crime; Ensuring that "Crime does not Pay", COM(2008) 766 final, 20.11.2008.

Report from the Commission based on Art. 14 of the Council Framework Decision 2003/577/JHA of 22 July 2003 on the Execution in the EU of Orders Freezing Property or Evidence, COM(2008) 885 final.

Report from the Commission to the European Parliament and the Council based on Article 22 of the Council Framework Decision 2006/783/JHA of 6 October 2006 on the

Application of the Principle of Mutual Recognition to Confiscation Orders, COM(2010) 428 final, 23.8.2010.
Communication from the Commission to the European Parliament and the Council, "An Internal Security Strategy in Action", COM(2010) 673 final, 22.11.2010.
Commission Staff Working Paper, Operation of the Council Framework Decision 2006/960/JHA of 18 December 2006, SEC(2011) 593 final, 13.5.2011.
Report from the Commission based on Article 8 of the Council Decision 2007/845/JHA of 6 December 2007 concerning Cooperation between Asset Recovery Offices of the Member States in the Field of Tracing and Identification of Proceeds from, or other Property related to, Crime, COM(2011) 176 final.
Commission Staff Working Paper, Accompanying Document to the Proposal for a Directive of the European Parliament and the Council on the Freezing and Confiscation of Proceeds of Crime in the European Union, SWD(2012) 31 final, Brussels 12.3.2012.
Proposal for a Directive of the European Parliament and of the Council on the Freezing and Confiscation of Proceeds of Crime in the European Union, COM(2012) 85 final.
Communication from the Commission to the European Parliament and the Council, The Final Implementation Report of the EU Internal Security Strategy 2010–2014, COM(2014) 365 final, 20.6.2014.
European Commission, JUST/2010/JPEN/PR/1004/B3, Handbook for Judges, Prosecutors and other Competent Authorities on how to issue and execute a request for enforcement of a Freezing Order, in accordance with Council Framework Decision 2003/577/JHA of 22 July 2003, available under http://e-justice.europa.eu/content_criminal_law-255-en.do.
European Commission, JUST/2011/JPEN/PR/0153/A4, Comparative Law Study of the Implementation of Mutual Recognition of Orders to Freeze and Confiscate Criminal Assets in the European Union, Final Finding Report.
European Commission, JUST/2011/JPEN/AG/2956, Fostering Mutual Understanding in order to Strengthen Mutual Trust between the Judicial Authorities of Member States, Handbook, October 2014.
European Commission, Directorate-General Migration and Home Affairs, Study on the Implementation of the European Information Exchange Model (EIXM) for Strengthening Law Enforcement Cooperation, Final Report, 26.1.2015.
Communication from the Commission to the European Parliament, the Council, the European Economic and Social Committee and the Committee of the Regions, The European Agenda on Security, COM(2015) 185 final.
Commission Staff Working Document, Impact Assessment, Accompanying the document, Proposal for a Directive of the European Parliament and of the Council amending Directive (EU) 2015/849 on the Prevention of the use of the Financial System for the Purposes of Money Laundering or Terrorist Financing and amending Directive 2009/101/EC, SWD(2016) 223 final, Strasbourg 5.7.2016.
Proposal for a Directive of the European Parliament and of the Council amending Directive (EU) 2015/849 on the Prevention of the use of the Financial System for the Purposes of Money Laundering or Terrorist Financing and amending Directive 2009/101/EC, COM(2016) 450 final, Strasbourg 5.7.2016.
Communication from the Commission to the European Parliament and the Council on an Action Plan for strengthening the fight against terrorist financing, COM(2016) 50 final.

Commission Staff Working Document, Impact Assessment, Accompanying the document proposal for a Regulation of the European Parliament and of the Council on the Mutual Recognition of Freezing and Confiscation Orders, SWD(2016) 468 final, Brussels 21.12.2016.

Proposal for a Regulation of the European Parliament and of the Council on the Mutual Recognition of Freezing and Confiscation Orders, COM(2016) 819 final, Brussels 21.12.2016.

OTHER EU DOCUMENTS

The Joint Initiative of France, Sweden and Belgium for the Adoption of a Council Framework Decision on the Execution in the European Union of Orders Freezing Assets or Evidence, *OJ* C 75, 07.3.2001 p. 3.

Explanatory Report to the Protocol to the 2000 Convention on Mutual Assistance in Criminal Matters between the Member States of the European Union, *OJ* C 257, 24.10.2002, pp. 1–9.

Initiative of the Kingdom of Sweden with a view to Adopting a Framework Decision on Simplifying the Exchange of Information and Intelligence between Law Enforcement Authorities of the Member States of the European Union, in particular as regards Serious Offences including Terrorist Acts, *OJ* 281, 18.11.2004, pp. 5–10.

Matrix Study, Assessing the Effectiveness of EU Member States' Practices in the Identification, Tracing, Freezing and Confiscation of Criminal Assets, Final Report 2009.

Eurojust Annual Report 2010, available at: www.eurojust.org.

European Parliament, Report on Organised Crime in the European Union, 25.10.2011.

European Parliament, Resolution of 25 October 2011 on Organised Crime in the European Union.

Eurojust Annual Report 2012, available at www.eurojust.org.

Study for an Impact Assessment on a Proposal for a New Legal Framework on the Confiscation and Recovery of Criminal Assets, RAND Europe, 2012.

Directorate-General for Internal Policies, Policy Department Citizens' Rights and Constitutional Affairs, The Need for New EU Legislation Allowing the Assets Confiscated from Criminal Organisations to be used for Civil Society and in Particular for Social Purposes, 2012.

Opinion of the European Economic and Social Committee on the Proposal for a Directive, *OJ* C 299, 4.10.2012, pp. 128–32.

Opinion of the European Union Agency for Fundamental Rights on the Confiscation of Proceeds of Crime, FRA 03/2012, Vienna 4.12.2012, pp. 13–14.

Europol, ARO Platform Sub Working Group, Report on the Establishment of Centralised Bank Account Registers as an Effective Tool for Financial Investigations and Asset Recovery, 5.12.2012.

Eurojust's Opinion on the Proposal of the European Commission for a Directive on the Freezing and Confiscation of Proceeds of Crime in the European Union, 2012.

European Parliament, Draft Report on the Proposal for a Directive of the European Parliament and of the Council on the Freezing and Confiscation of Proceeds of Crime in the European Union, Amendments (30–177) 2012/0036(COD), pp. 39–41.
European Parliament, Resolution of 27 February 2014 with recommendations to the Commission on the review of the European Arrest Warrant, 2013/2109(INL).
Eurojust, Report on Non-Conviction-Based Confiscation, General Case 751/NMSK-2012, 2.4.2013.
Report from the Committee on Civil Liberties, Justice and Home Affairs of the European Parliament on the Proposal for a Directive of the European Parliament and of the Council on the Freezing and Confiscation of Proceeds of Crime in the European Union, COM(2012) 85, A7-0178/2013, 20.5.2013.
Center for the Study of Democracy, Disposal of Confiscated Assets in the EU Member States, Laws and Practices, 2014.
Eurojust, Report from the Strategic Seminar, Towards Greater Cooperation in Freezing and Confiscation of the Proceeds of Crime: A Practitioner' Approach, The Hague 11.12.2014, www.eurojust.europa.eu.
Statement from the European Criminal Bar Association on the Proposal for a Directive of the European Parliament and of the Council on the Freezing and Confiscation of Proceeds of Crime in the European Union, at http:77www.ecba.org/extdocserv/201210assetseizureECBAstatement.pdf.

INTERNATIONAL CONVENTIONS

European Convention on Mutual Assistance in Criminal Matters, 1959.
Additional Protocol to the European Convention on Mutual Assistance in Criminal Matters, 1978.
United Nations Convention against Illicit Traffic in Narcotic Drugs and Psychotropic Substances, 1988.
Council of Europe Convention on Laundering, Search, Seizure and Confiscation of the Proceeds from Crime, 1990.
United Nations Convention against Transnational Organized Crime, 2000.
Second Additional Protocol to the European Convention on Mutual Assistance in Criminal Matters, 2001.
United Nations Convention against Corruption, 2003.
Council of Europe Convention on Laundering, Search, Seizure and Confiscation of the Proceeds from Crime and on the Financing of Terrorism, 2005.

INTERNATIONAL REPORTS AND PUBLICATIONS

Reversal of the Burden of Proof in Confiscation of the Proceeds of Crime: a Council of Europe Best Practice Survey, Best Practice Survey No. 2, European Committee of Crime Problems, Strasbourg, 25 May 2000.

White Paper on Best Practices in Asset Recovery, CEART Project, Prevention of and Fight against Crime, 2009.
Tracing Stolen Assets, A Practitioner's Handbook, International Centre for Asset Recovery, Basel 2009.
United Nations Office on Drugs and Crime, Estimating Illicit Financial Flows Resulting from Drug Trafficking and other Transnational Organised Crime, October 2011.
Best Practices on Confiscation (Recommendations 4 and 38) and a Framework for Ongoing Work on Asset Recovery, FATF, October 2012.
The FATF Recommendations, International Standards on Combating Money Laundering and the Financing of Terrorism & Proliferation, October 2012.
United Nations Office on Drugs and Crime, Manual on International Cooperation for the Purposes of Confiscation of Proceeds of Crime, New York 2012.
United Nations Office on Drugs and Crime, Digest of Organized Crime Cases, A Compilation of Cases with Commentaries and Lessons Learned, 2012.
Assets Recovery in Italy, Enhancing Integrity and Effectiveness of Illegal Asset Confiscation, Transparency International Italia, 2013.
Mutual Evaluation Report on Spain, Anti-money Laundering and Counter-terrorist Financing Measures, FATF, December 2014.
Mutual Evaluation Report regarding Norway on Anti-money Laundering and Counter-terrorist Financing Measures, FATF, December 2014.
Mutual Evaluation Report on Belgium, Anti-Money Laundering and Counter-terrorist Financing Measures, FATF, April 2015.
Tracing Illegal Assets, Basel Institute on Governance International Centre for Asset Recovery, 2015.
Comparative Report, Legislation Meets Practice: National and European Perspectives in Confiscation and Forfeiture of Assets, Transparency International, 2015.
Council of Europe, European Committee of Crime Problems, Questionnaire on the Use and Efficiency of Council of Europe Instruments as regards International Cooperation in the field of Seizure and Confiscation of Proceeds of Crime, including the Management of Confiscated Goods and Asset Sharing, PC-OC Mod (2015) 06Rev4 Bil.

ENGLISH SOURCES

ACTS

Drug Trafficking Offences Act 1986.
Criminal Justice Act 1988.
Criminal Justice (International Cooperation) Act 1990.
Drug Trafficking Act 1994. Proceeds of Crime Act 1995.
Human Rights Act 1998.
Proceeds of Crime Act 2002.
Serious Organised Crime and Police Act 2005.
Serious Crime Act 2007.
Crime and Courts Act 2013.
Serious Crime Act 2015.

REPORTS AND OFFICAL PUBLICATIONS

Report from the Hodgson Committee, Hodgson, D., Profits of Crime and Their Recovery, Heinemann, London, 1984.

Recovering the Proceeds of Crime, A Performance and Innovation Unit Report, June 2000.

Criminal Justice: The Way Ahead, Secretary of State for the Home Department, February 2001, CM 5074.

Liberty, Proceeds of Crime: Consultation on Draft Legislation, May 2001.

Payback Time: Joint Review of Asset Recovery since the Proceeds of Crime Act 2002, published on 1 November 2004.

Joint Thematic Review of Asset Recovery: Restraint and Confiscation Casework, Criminal Justice Joint Inspection, March 2010.

HM Government, Serious and Organised Crime Strategy, Cm 8715, October 2013.

House of Commons Committee of Public Accounts, Confiscation Orders, Forty-ninth Report of Session 2013–14, HC 942, published on 21 March 2014.

Crown Prosecution Service, Improvement Plan, March 2014.

Crown Prosecution Service, Asset Recovery Strategy, June 2014.

Report on the Performance of the Ministry of Justice 2013–2014, October 2014.

House of Lords, Joint Committee on Human Rights, Second Report of Session 2014–15, HL Paper 49 HC 746.

National Audit Office, Confiscation Orders: Progress Review, HC 886, March 2016.

House of Commons, Home Affairs Committee, Proceeds of Crime, Fifth Report of Session 2016–2017.

House of Lords, European Union Committee, 7th Report of Session 2016–17, Brexit: Future UK-EU Security and Police Cooperation, December 2016.

Explanatory Notes to the Proceeds of Crime Act 2002, Home Office, www.legislation.gov.uk.

Explanatory Notes to the Serious Crime Act 2015, Home Office, www.legislation.gov.uk.

National Best Practice Guide to Confiscation Order Enforcement, www.legislation.gov.uk.

Crown Prosecution Service, Legal Guidance on the Proceeds of Crime, www.cps.gov.uk.

GERMAN SOURCES

ACTS

Strafgesetzbuch, BGBl. I S. 3322.

Strafproceßordnung, BGBl. I S. 1074, 1319.

Gesetz über die internationale Rechtshilfe in Strafsachen, 23.12.1982.

Gesetz zur Bekämpfung des illegalen Rauschgiftshandels und anderer Erscheinungsformen der Organisierten Kriminalität (OrgKG), 15.7.1992, BGBl. I 1992, p. 1302.

Gesetz zur Stärkung der Rückgewinnungshilfe und der Vermögensabschöpfung bei Straftaten, 24.10.2006, BGBl. I, 2350.

Niedersächsisches Gesetz über die öffentliche Sicherheit und Ordnung (Nds. SOG).

GOVERNMENTAL BILLS AND OFFICIAL DOCUMENTATION

Drucksache 16/90, 5.1.1990, Gesetzentwurf der Bundesregierung, Entwurf eines ... Strafrechtsänderungsgesetzes – Erweiterter Verfall – (... StrÄndG).
Drucksache 11/6623, 9.3.1990, Gesetzentwurf der Bundesregierung, Entwurf eines ... Strafrechtsänderungsgesetzes – Erweiterter Verfall – (... StrÄndG).
Drucksache 12/989, 25.7.1991, Gesetzentwurf des Bundesrates, Entwurf eines Gesetztes zur Bekämpfung des illegalen Rauschgifthandels und anderer Erscheinungsformen der Organisierten Kriminalität (OrgKG).
Drucksache 12/3346, 5.10.1992, Gesetzentwurf der Bundesregierung, Entwurf eines Gesetztes zu dem Übereinkommen der Vereinten Nationen vom 20. Dezember 1988 gegen den unerlaubten Verkehr mit Suchtstoffen und psychotropen Stoffen (Vertrags Gesetz Suchtstoffübereinkommen 1988).
Drucksache 12/6784, 4.2.1994, Gesetzentwurf der Fraktion der SPD, Entwurf eines Zweiten Gesetztes zur Bekämpfung des illegalen Rauschgifthandels und anderer Erscheinungsformen der Organisierten Kriminalität (2. OrgKG).
Drucksache 135/12, 11.5.2012, Beschluss des Bundesrates, Vorschlag für eine Richtlinie des Europäischen Parlaments und des Rates über die Sicherstellung und Einziehung von Erträgen aus Straftaten in der Europäischen Union, COM(2012) 85 final.
Drucksache 17/13087, 16.4.2013, Antrag Wirtschaftskriminalität effektiv bekämpfen.
Runderlass 15.2.2015, Präventive Gewinnabschöpfung; Hinweise zum Verfahren der Sicherstellung nach §26 Nds. SOG vor strafprozessualer Herausgabe offensichtlich nicht rechtmäßig erlangter Sachen, Niedersächsiges Minestrial Blatt Nr. 10, 2015, pp. 258–60.
Vermögensabschöpfung im deutschen Recht, Hinweise für Praktiker, Bundesministerium der Justiz und für Verbraucherschutz, October 2015.
Referentenentwurf des Bundesministeriums der Justiz und für Verbraucherschutz, Entwurf eines Gesetzes zur Reform der strafrechtlichen Vermögensabschöpfung, March 2016.
Gesetzentwurf der Bundesregierung, Entwurf eines Gesetzes zur Reform der strafrechtlichen Vermögensabschöpfung, BT-Drucksache 18/9525, 5.9.2016.
Bundesrat 418/16, Entwurf eines Gesetzes zur Reform der strafrechtlichen Vermögensabschöpfung, 23 September 2016.
Unterrichtung durch die Bundesregierung, Entwurf eines Gesetzes zur Reform der strafrechtlichen Vermögensabschöpfung – Drucksache 18/9525 –, Stellungnahme des Bundesrates und Gegenäußerung der Bundesregierung, BT-Drucksache 18/10146, 26.10.2016.
Koalitionsvertrag zwischen CDU, CSU und SPD, "Deutschlands Zukunft gestalten", 18. Legislaturperiode.

OTHER REPORTS AND PUBLICATIONS

Bundesrechtsanwaltskammer, Stellungnahme zum Vorschlag für eine Richtlinie des Europäischen Parlaments und des Rates über die Sicherstellung und Einziehung von Erträgen aus Straftaten in der Europäischen Union vom 12.3.2012 (2012/0036 (COD)), Stellungnahme Nr. 38/2012, June 2012.

Stellungnahme des Deutschen Anwaltsvereins durch den Strafrechtsausschuss zum Vorschlag der Kommission für eine Richtlinie des Europäischen Parlaments und des Rates über die Sicherstellung und Einziehung von Erträgen aus Straftaten in der Europäischen Union, COM(2012) 85, Nr. 70/2012, August 2012.
Stellungnahme des Deutschen Richterbundes zum Vorschlag für eine Richtlinie des Europäischen Parlaments und des Rates über die Sicherstellung und Einziehung von Erträgen aus Straftaten in der Europäischen Union, COM(2012) 85, Nr. 23/12, August 2012.
Stellungnahme der Strafverteidigervereingungen zum Entwurf eines Gesetzes zur strafrechtlichen Vermögensabschöpfung, May 2016.
Stellungnahme des Deutschen Anwalt Vereins zum Referentenentwurf des Bundesministeriums der Justiz und für Verbraucherschutz, Entwurf eines Gesetzes zur Reform der strafrechtlichen Vermögensabschöpfung, June 2016.
Bundesrechtsanwaltskammer, Stellungnahme Nr. 15/2016, zum Referentenentwurf zur Reform der strafrechtlichen Vermögensabschöpfung, June 2016.
Deutscher Richterbund, Stellungnahme zum Referentenentwurf eines Gesetzes zur Reform der strafrechtlichen Vermögensabschöpfung, June 2016.
Ergänzende Stellungnahme der Strafverteidigervereingungen zum Entwurf eines Gesetzes zur strafrechtlichen Vermögensabschöpfung (Gesetzentwurf der Bundesregierung), September 2016.
Stellungnahme des Deutschen Anwalt Vereins durch den Ausschuss Strafrecht zum Entwurf eines Gesetzes zur Reform der strafrechtlichen Vermögensabschöpfung – Empfehlungen der Ausschüsse des Bundesrates (Bundesrat-Drucksache 418/1/16 vom 12.9.2016), Nr. 59/2016, September 2016.
Deutscher Richterbund, Zweite Stellungnahme zum Gesetzentwurf zur Reform der strafrechtlichen Vermögensabschöpfung, Nr. 19/16, October 2016.
Bundesrechtsanwaltskammer, Stellungnahme Nr. 39/2016, zum Regierungsentwurf eines Gesetzes zur Reform der strafrechtlichen Vermögensabschöpfung, November 2016.

SWEDISH SOURCES

ACTS AND ORDINANCES

Swedish Criminal Procedural Code (Rättegångsbalken SFS 1942:740).
Swedish Penal Code (Brottsbalken SFS 1962:700).
International Legal Assistance in Criminal Matters Act (Lag om internationell rättslig hjälp i brottmål SFS 2000:562).
Act (2005:500) on Recognition and Execution of European Freezing Decisions (Lag om erkännande och verkställighet inom Europeiska unionen av frysningsbeslut).
Act (2008:369) on the Procedure on Confiscation of Proceeds of Crime in certain cases (Lag om förfarandet vid förverkande av utbyte av brottslig verksamhet i vissa fall).
Act (2009:62) on Measures against Money Laundering and Terrorist Financing (Lag om åtgärder mot penningtvätt och finansiering av terrorism).
Act (2011:423) on Recognition and Execution of Confiscation Orders within the European Union (Lag om erkännande och verkställighet av beslut om förverkande inom Europeiska unionen).

Ordinance (2011:578) on Recognition and Execution of Confiscation Orders within the European Union (Förordning om erkännande och verkställighet av beslut om förverkande inom Europeiska unionen).
Act (2014:307) on Penalties for Money Laundering Offences (Lag om straff för penningtvättsbrott).

GOVERNMENTAL BILLS

Bill 1968:79 Proposition till riksdagen med förslag till lag om ändring i brottsbalken.
Bill 1990/91:127 Regeringens proposition om Sveriges tillträde till FN:s narkotikabrottskonvention m.m.
Bill 2002/03:67 Regeringens proposition om Sveriges antagande av rambeslut om verkställighet i Europeiska unionen av beslut om frysning av egendom eller bevismaterial.
Bill 2004/05:55 Regeringens proposition om Sveriges antagande av rambeslut om tillämpning av principen om ömsesidigt erkännande på beslut om förverkande.
Bill 2004/05:115 Regeringens proposition om lag om erkännande och verkställighet inom Europeiska unionen av frysningsbeslut.
Bill 2004/05:135 Regeringens proposition om utökade möjligheter att förverka utbyte av och hjälpmedel vid brott m.m.
Bill 2007/08:68 Regeringens proposition om förverkande av utbyte av brottslig verksamhet.
Bill 2010/11:43 Regeringens proposition om erkännande och verkställighet av beslut om förverkande inom Europeiska Unionen.
Bill 2013/14:66 Regeringens proposition om erkännande och verkställighet av beslut om utvidgat förverkande inom Europeiska Unionen.
Bill 2013/14:121 Regeringens Proposition om en effektivare kriminalisering av penningtvätt.
Bill 2015/16:113 Regeringens Proposition om bättre straffrättsliga verktyg mot organiserad brottslighet.
Bill 2015/16:155 Regeringens Proposition om utökade möjligheter till förverkande.

COMMISSIONS OF INQUIRY

SOU 1999:147 Effektivare förverkandelagstiftning.
SOU 2012:12 Penningtvätt, Kriminalisering, förverkande och dispositionsförbud.
SOU 2015:67 För att brott inte ska löna sig, Betänkande av Utredningen om utvidgat förverkande, m.m.

DEPARTMENTAL REPORTS

Ds 2006:17 Utvidgat förverkande m.m.
Ds 2007:18 Verkställighet inom Europeiska Unionen av bötesstraff och beslut om förverkande.
Ds 2012:51 Erkännande och verkställighet av beslut om utvidgat förverkande inom Europeiska Unionen.

GOVERNMENTAL DIRECTIVES

DIR. 2013:14 Justitiedepartementet, Kommittédirektiv till Utredningen om utvidgat förverkande.

DIR. 2014:22 Tilläggsdirektiv till Utredningen om utvidgat förverkande.

REPORTS OR OFFICIAL DOCUMENTATION

Yttrande från Svea hovrätt, Utvidgat förverkande m.m. (Ds 2006:17), Dnr 561/06.

Yttrande över Departementspromemorian Utvidgat förverkande m.m. (Ds 2006:17), R-2006/0939.

BRÅ Rapport 2008:10, Tillgångsinriktad brottsbekämpning, Myndigheternas arbete med att spåra och återföra utbyte av brott.

Handbook on confiscation etc from the Prosecuting Office, Utvecklingscentrum Stockholm, 2010.

Riksrevisionen, Statens Insatser för att komma åt vinster från brottslig verksamhet, RIR 2010:26.

BRÅ Rapport 2011:20, Bekämpning av Organiserad Brottslighet, Utvärdering av den myndighetsgemensamma satsningen mot grov organiserad brottslighet.

Tillsynsrapport, Tillsyn – brottsutbytesfrågor, Utvecklingscentrum Stockholm, December 2011.

Rikspolisstyrelsen, Inspektion av polismyndigheternas handläggning av förverkande av utbyte av brott och brottslig verksamhet, Inspektionsrapport 2012:7, August 2012.

Ett nytt arbetssätt – utredning av förverkande m.m., Handledning, RättsPM 2012:10, Utvecklingscentrum Stockholm, December 2012.

Verksamhetsplan för 2013, Åklagarmyndigheten, 2013.

Tillsynsrapport 2014:8, Polismyndigheternas handläggning av förverkande av utbyte av brott och brottslig verksamhet, En uppföljande rapport, Rikspolisstyrelsen, 2014.

BRÅ Rapport 2014:10, Gå på pengarna, Antologi om tillgångsinriktad brottsbekämpning.

Pressmeddelande, Justitiedepartementet, 2 September 2014, Utökade möjligheter att beslagta brottsvinster.

Rapport, Myndighetssamverkan på brottsutbytesområdet, November 2014.

Rapport, En myndighetsöverskridande handlingsplan för brottsutbytesarbete i samverkan, Januari 2015.

Rapport Riksrevisionen; Riksrevisionens uppföljningsrapport, 2015.

Redovisning av resultatet av den särskilda satsningen mot den grova organiserade brottsligheten, Myndigheter i samverkan mot den organiserade brottsligheten 2014, Stockholm 2015.

Money Laundering, Legal Memorandum 2015:2 from the Prosecution Development Centre Stockholm and the Swedish Economic Crime Authority.

NORWEGIAN SOURCES

ACTS

Almindelig borgerlig Straffelov, Act of 22 May 1902, No. 10.
Straffeprosessloven, Act of 22 May 1981, No. 25.
Straffeloven, Act of 20 May 2005, No. 28.
Norwegian Penal Code, Act of 19 June 2015, No. 65.

GOVERNMENTAL BILLS AND OFFICIAL DOCUMENTATION

Ot.prp. Nr. 8 (1998–99), Om lov om endringer i straffeloven of straffeprosessloven mv (inndragning av utbytte).
Ot.prp. Nr. 90 (2003–2004), Om lov om straff (Straffeloven).
Regjeringens handlingsplan mot økonomisk kriminalitet, Justis- og Politidepartementet og Finansdepartementet, 2011.
Betenkning: Sivilrettslig inndragning rettet direkte mot formuesgoder, drafted by professor Jon Petter Rui, Bergen.

COMMISSIONS OF INQUIRY

NOU 1996:21 Mer effektiv indragning av vinning.
NOU 2002:4 Ny straffelov.

DANISH SOURCES

ACTS

Danmarks borgerliga Straffelov, 1930.
Act of 10 June 1997, No. 411.

GOVERNMENTAL BILLS AND OFFICIAL PUBLICATIONS

Forslag til Lov om ændring af straffeloven, retsplejeloven og våbenloven, Folketinget 1996–97, Lovforslag nr. L 98.
Samarbejdet om retlige og indre anliggender, En analyse af EU-lovgivning omfattet af retsforbeholdet, Regeringen Marts 2015.
Notat om tilvalg af konfiskationsdirektivet, 2015, see www.justitsministeriet.dk.

FINNISH SOURCES

ACTS

Strafflag, Act 39, 19.12.1889.
Legislative Act 875 of 26.10.2001.

GOVERNMENTAL BILLS AND OFFICIAL PUBLICATIONS

Regeringens proposition till Riksdagen med förslag till revidering av lagstiftningen om förverkandepåföljder, RP 80/2000.
Effektiviserat åtgärdsprogram för bekämpning av grå ekonomi och ekonomisk brottslighet 2012–2015, Statsrådet 19.1.2012.
Revidering av strafflagens allmänna bestämmelser om förverkandepåföljder, betänkande från konfiskationsarbetsgruppen 3/2015.
Pressmeddelande från Justitieministeriet, Arbetsgrupp vill öka möjligheterna att döma vinning av brott förverkad till staten, 20.1.2015.
Regeringens proposition till Riksdagen med förslag till lagar om ändring av 10 kap. i strafflagen och av 6 och 7 kap. i tvångsmedelslagen, RP 4/2016 rd.

INDEX

ABOUT THE AUTHOR

Dr Malin Thunberg Schunke is an Associate Professor in Criminal Law at the University of Uppsala. She holds an LLD in Criminal Law (Uppsala University) and an LLM in Criminology and Criminal Justice (King's College, London). Her research interests lie in national and international criminal law, particularly EU judicial cooperation in criminal matters and human rights. She has been an Apprentice Judge at Stockholm City Court and has been working for several years as an Assistant Prosecutor at the Prosecuting Office Stockholm.

www.ingramcontent.com/pod-product-compliance
Ingram Content Group UK Ltd.
Pitfield, Milton Keynes, MK11 3LW, UK
UKHW051926100926
8556IPUK00022B/1386

9 781780 684789